Augustine and Postmodernism

INDIANA SERIES IN THE PHILOSOPHY OF RELIGION
MEROLD WESTPHAL, GENERAL EDITOR

Augustine and Postmodernism

Confessions and Circumfession

Edited by John D. Caputo and Michael J. Scanlon

INDIANA UNIVERSITY PRESS
BLOOMINGTON AND INDIANAPOLIS

This book is a publication of

Indiana University Press
601 North Morton Street
Bloomington, IN 47404-3797 USA

http://iupress.indiana.edu

Telephone orders 800-842-6796
Fax orders   812-855-7931
Orders by e-mail iuporder@indiana.edu

Augustine and postmodernism : confessions and circumfession / edited by John D. Caputo and Michael J. Scanlon.
      p.   cm. — (Indiana series in the philosophy of religion)
   Includes index.
   ISBN 0-253-34507-3 (cloth : alk. paper) — ISBN 0-253-21731-8 (pbk. : alk. paper)
      1. Augustine, Saint, Bishop of Hippo. Confessiones.   2. Derrida, Jacques.
   3. Philosophy, European.   I. Caputo, John D.   II. Scanlon, Michael J.
   III. Series.
   BR65.A62A94   2005
   270.2'092—dc22

                                                              2004014357

1 2 3 4 5   10 09 08 07 06 05

To Dennis M. Cook, in memoriam; *to the Cook family; and to the three thousand victims of September 11 and their families*

Contents

ACKNOWLEDGMENTS

The editors wish to acknowledge the support of Villanova University in making possible the conference "Religion and Postmodernism 3: Confessions," on September 27–29, 2001, on which this volume is based. We thank in particular Rev. Edmund Dobbin, O.S.A., President of the University, for his continuing support and encouragement, Dr. John Johannes, Vice-President for Academic Affairs, Dr. Helen Lafferty, University Vice-President, and Rev. Kail Ellis, O.S.A., Dean of the College of Arts and Sciences, without whose generous financial assistance we would not have been able to organize this meeting.

We also thank Anna (Misticoni) Monserrate, the secretary to the David R. Cook Chair of Philosophy and the Josephine C. Connelly Chair of Theology, whose hard work and efficiency made this meeting such a success, and Terry Sousa, of the Villanova Connelly Center, who met with her usual dispatch and good humor the task of scheduling the meeting rooms and providing receptions and meals for so many visitors to our campus.

Finally, we thank Jacques Derrida for the generosity and grace with which he has participated in this and other conferences at Villanova University. He has been a great friend to Villanova over the years.

John D. Caputo, "Tears Beyond Being: Derrida's Experience of Prayer," previously appeared in *Théologie négative*, ed. Marco M. Olivetti (Padua: CEDAM, 2002), pp. 861–80, and is here reproduced with permission of CEDAM.

Augustine and Postmodernism

Introduction

The Postmodern Augustine

John D. Caputo and Michael J. Scanlon

September 11

We thought we had gathered to talk with Jacques Derrida about St. Augustine's
Confessions, and the "repetition" of Augustine's *Confessions* in Derrida's "Circumfession," in Heidegger, Lyotard, Ricoeur, and Arendt. And so we did. But none
of us could have foreseen that the third Religion and Postmodernism conference, whose papers we are here reproducing, would take place sixteen days after the events of September 11. Everything that transpired over the three days of
the conference—September 27–29, 2001—was reinscribed within the context
of that terrible shock and horror. Dennis M. Cook, 33, an employee of Cantor
Fitzgerald located on the 106th floor of the North Tower and the son of Judy and
David R. Cook, the generous benefactors who funded the endowed chair that
cosponsors the "Religion and Postmodernism" conferences, was lost that day. He
left behind his wife, a three-year-old daughter and a three-month-old daughter.
His mother, Judy Cook, had been planning to attend the conference. Derrida
himself was in China on September 11, and for a while we were not sure whether
he or the other distinguished visitors coming from Europe and from around the
country would be willing or even be able to fly to Philadelphia. But with the exception of Catherine Malabou, who was kept home by the illness of her son, all
of the invited speakers came, and we experienced only a minimal loss in atten-
dance. Nearly everyone in the room had nervously boarded a plane or made use
of public transportation to get there; most of us knew someone, the way we at
Villanova knew the Cook family, whose life had been lost or forever changed by
that tragic day.

We thus have dedicated this volume to Dennis M. Cook, to the Cook family,
and to the three thousand victims of September 11 and their families.

After the Event

We had come to talk about one event, the repetition of the *Confessions* in Derrida and contemporary Continental thought, but we could not do so without talking about another inescapable event that would be superimposed on our chosen topic, so that our conference was very much "after the event," literally, after this appalling incident, even as it was in search of, inquiring after, what Derrida means by the "event." That was obvious from the first words spoken by Derrida on the opening night.[1] While these remarks were made by way of a commentary on the paper of Geoffrey Bennington, which they certainly were, in part, they function so well as an introduction to the entire conference, and they speak so nicely to the general question of what Derrida was doing when he composed "Circumfession," that we have decided to place these remarks first and entitle them "Composing 'Circumfession,'" followed by the "Roundtable," which actually was the concluding session of the conference.

New York appears several times in "Circumfession." It is a part of the narrative, which is the story of this least and last of the Jews, as he calls himself. New York, Derrida told us, has always had a special meaning for him, above all at the time of Yom Kippur, when he is regularly in the city. It was in New York that he began to break off his observance of this most sacred of holy days and so to make the cut with Judaism. Was the cut final—or did his Judaism simply make an inner migration, so that he lived henceforth like a self-imposed Marrano? The events of September 11, an attack upon the symbol and the substance of New York, were not entirely unpredictable (and to that extent not an event in the rigorous Derridean sense). Above all, they call, first, last, and always, for infinite compassion for the thousands of innocent lives that were lost and for the many thousands more lives that were forever changed by the events of that day.

After infinite compassion, that tragic day requires repeated and diverse analyses of the causes and consequences of the attack from many points of view, for if it is without justification, it is not without explanation, and it is the task of the intellectual to explain and analyze. What more salient example of the place of religion in the postmodern world? What more bitter example of the ties between religion and violence? At the end of the conference, in the discussion from the floor at the Roundtable, Derrida returned to the topic again and worried aloud, and prophetically, that the political climate of intense public outrage would cloud reflection and make suspect anyone who investigated the reasons for it. He worried that the tragic events of that sad day would be put to "rhetorical abuse." Whoever dares to analyze this event, however much they condemn it, however much they are outraged by its violence, risks being declared a traitor to the country, a traitor to the dead, "soft on terrorism."

The Postmodern Augustine

In the last fifteen years or so of Continental philosophical reflection, God has been making a comeback among continental philosophers and, along with God (who, if the truth be told, was doing just fine without the philosophers), one of the West's most passionate and God-filled men, Augustine of Hippo—whence our slightly impish title "The Postmodern Augustine." Consider this remarkable constellation of facts. In 1989 Jacques Derrida wrote "Circumfession," a journal he kept as his mother lay dying in Nice, like Monica in Ostia, creating an odd and beautiful dialogue with Augustine that contained long grafts of Augustine's *Confessions* in Latin. Here Derrida confesses the secret that he is a man of prayers and tears, that he is interested in Augustine because of his love for writers who weep. By the same token, the last work on which Lyotard was working, incomplete at the time of his death in 1997, was his *The Confession of Augustine*, published a year later. In 1995 Heidegger's 1921 lecture course "Augustine and Neoplatonism" was published in the *Gesamtausgabe*. It has recently appeared in English translation, even as a translation of Hannah Arendt's doctoral dissertation on Augustine, begun in Heidelberg in 1929 and revised in New York in the late 1950s and early 1960s, was published a year later, in 1996. Paul Ricoeur, of course, had been interested in Augustine for years, and the *Confessions* played a central role in the writing of *On Narrative*. (It is not often recalled that Camus—the third French-speaking Algerian philosopher on this list—had written his dissertation on Neoplatonism, which included a chapter on St. Augustine.)

So what could be more appropriate than a conference that would examine this remarkable phenomenon, and what more appropriate than to do this at Villanova University, a Roman Catholic university founded and conducted by the Order of St. Augustine and dedicated to the spirit of St. Augustine and to his *caritas* tradition? And what could be more appropriate than to undertake this reflection in dialogue with Jacques Derrida, the guiding spirit of the Villanova conferences on religion and postmodernism, whose remarkable career, intersecting as it has over the years with so many currents in contemporary life, has in these later years intersected with St. Augustine? The topic for this conference was written in the stars (which is what we told the administration when we asked them for the money to fund it!).

Situated at a point still very early in the formation of the tradition of metaphysical theology and more than a millennium before the formation of modernist systems of onto-theologic, Augustine's search for God is at once philosophical and scriptural, Neoplatonic and personal, metaphysical and anchored deeply in the dynamics of pre-philosophical experience. Nowhere is this more evident than in the pages of the *Confessions*, which are astir with the passion of his search for God, or of God's search for him, so that his confessions are the records, the "acts" (*acta*), more of God's doings than his. It is little wonder that it is the *Confessions* that have drawn the attention of Heidegger, Derrida, and Lyotard. The enduring timeliness of Augustine is in no small part a function of his passionate phenomenology *avant la lettre* of the temporality of the heart's restless love of God. Citing Augustine's question, "What do I love when I love you, my God?" Derrida asks himself, What else can I do but make that question my own? What else has Derrida been doing all his life than asking himself that question, with the understanding that the constancy of the name of God in his life goes under many names, so that it is subject to an endless and unstoppable translatability?

In his opening remarks to the conference, Derrida gives us some insight as to what he was thinking as he undertook his wager with Geoffrey Bennington to write something that would not be captured by the Derrida program ("Derridabase") that was being written up above by "G." (G. stands for Geoffrey, but also for Georgette, the mother/matrix, and, in the English translation, serendipitously, for God). He contests G.'s reading by invoking secrets that G. — that none of us — could ever have guessed. Like the secret reference — he constitutes this as a secret by revealing that it is a secret — in his use of *sero te amavi* (too late have I loved you) in "A Silkworm of One's Own," a secret he says that he absolutely will not reveal.[2] That is the essential unreadability of this text that, far from bringing reading to a halt, provokes reading all the more. This is the same passage from the *Confessions* on which Lyotard focuses his reading of the essential belatedness of the instant in the *Confessions,* but for Derrida it has a fundamentally different, and secret, sense.

Derrida feels obliged to confess that his reading of Augustine is a kind of intentional misreading or mis-leading of Augustine, carrying Augustine down paths that Augustine himself will not travel, all this in the hope that an event would be produced. At first, he tells us, at the time he was writing "Circumfession," he thought that producing an event meant that his text would be a "performative," a carrying out in deed of a deconstruction, producing the event of a transgression that deforms and reforms the program being run overhead. But upon further consideration, he has since concluded that a conventional performative in fact neutralizes the event because it is bound by the conventions that constitute it. A performative can be carried out only in virtue of the standard conventions that make it possible, as when, given all the right conditions, saying "I do" really makes me married. I am making the truth by invoking the conventions. But a more radical event would both twist free of these conventional conditions and also not depend on any act performed by me, as if I could produce an event, as if events were subject to egological commands. The I is the subjected subject of the event, submitted to it; it is not its subject-author. This more radical event is what Derrida means by a "perver-formative." An event is unpredictable and comes over me, like a defenseless infant being handed over to the mohel who leaves a scar on his body. The event must be visited upon the subject, and only in so doing will it — not I — make the truth, *facere veritatem.* Thus, Derrida distinguishes a (relative) hospitality of invitation, when I invite a preselected group of guests from an (absolute) hospitality of visitation, when I am visited by the uninvited and unforeseen. That unforeseeable visitation is what is required if there is to be, in "Circumfession," not so much a confession of an event — which would be an intentional act on my part — as an event of confession, which would overtake me.

That means that to confess is the act, not of an autonomous author but of a subjected subject, an act, not of autonomy but of giving up this autonomy. For there is no less autonomy in assuming responsibility for a transgression, in confessing and saying that I will repent and improve and reconcile with the other, than there was in the original transgression. The more radical confession would repent of *all* this autonomy, in the repentance no less than in the transgression, constituting an incision, or circumcision of the decision, of the autonomy of the decision. The more radical confession is never "mine" but the decision of the other in me who comes over me—of you in me—just as in the *Confessions* it is God who turns Augustine around and Augustine who is answering. It is always the other who confesses in me. That is why, Derrida insists, it is the mother who is at the center of "Circumfession"—a point that stands in striking contrast with Heidegger's very virile reading of the *Confessions* in which Monica is never so much as mentioned! It is the mother who is always being confessed, always being mourned; for she is dying, is all but dead, and will in fact die soon after the French text is published. But at the time of writing "Circumfession," her impending death hovers over the text unpredictably, and he cannot know when it will come, when it will overtake him—or even, for that matter, whether he will not die first; it is not up to him. The unforeseeability of her death, of his, of death itself, in that order, make for the event. That is the eventiveness of the event of "Circumfession."

In the Roundtable, in his response to Philippe Capelle's question about the "I" in "*I* confess," Derrida says that any such "I" as is to be found in "Circumfession" is not the autonomous author of a confession but an effect, an I that has been constituted by the circumfession. Whoever says "*I* confess" with the full force of "I" cannot be confessing at all. One has already exonerated oneself from the crime by declaring that this crime is one thing but the I who confesses it is another. The only true confession could not be signed by anyone, by any "I." If I say, "I confess"—or "I give," or "I forgive," which obey the same law—that would be a perjury. When the confession is "true," in the sense neither of correspondence nor of *aletheia*, but of being true, ringing true, made truly, or making truth, *facere veritatem*, then this very "I" is confessed and given up.

The question of the "I" returns one more time in Hent de Vries's question about the indifference or formality of a structure like "messianicity" vis-à-vis the concrete historical confessions like Judaism and Christianity. In his response, Derrida says he can identify a certain "indifference" in the formal, empty exemplarity of the "I" of *The Post Card* and "Circumfession," where the "I" refers to everyone and so to no one in particular, for it is not restricted to the empirical or autobiographical (auto-bio-thanato-graphical) self of the author. It is a literary *I*. That is why he fears that we might be inclined to think he did not *really* steal those grapes from the Algerian landowner but was simply inscribing himself within a literary tradition, a point he brings up in response to Catherine Malabou. He himself, Jacques, Jackie, cannot be identified with what is said in "Circumfession"—or rather, what is said there cannot be identified with and reduced to him. He is speaking in the most concrete and intimate terms of his secret life in order to outdo G. But at the same time, this is not about him. He is making a larger point, an exemplary one, so that if "Circumfession" is to be a success, his own peculiar story will be cut, to use a splendid image of David Wood, at just such an angle as to reveal every life. So this "I" is at one and the same time an absolutely unique, idiomatic, and secret self who takes the Geo-program up above by surprise, and a universal self, a token of a universal type, an exemplary I. As he says in response to a question from the floor, as soon as he begins to speak, of however intimate or personal an affair, he is already in the sphere of ideality, of the universal, of a certain "indifference"—not in the sense of not loving or not caring, but in the sense of the generality of the trace, which inserts an irreducible distance into proximity. When two lovers speak in the night, whispering to each other the most intimate and private things, they have recourse to the universal. The whole dialogue could be put in the mouths of characters in a novel and would then take on universal significance. If "Circumfession," or any other confession made *in litteris*, is to be a success, we will all find our stories there. We are all (at some time or another) observing a death watch over our mother; we are all circum-cut from the faith of our childhood home; we have all stolen grapes or pears or something; and we all confess to rightly passing for an atheist, or a theist—at least, at best, rightly passing for something.

That brings us to Richard Kearney's question about why says he "rightly passes" (*je passe à juste titre*) for an atheist instead of just saying "I am" (*je suis, c'est moi*) an atheist. Once again, the question turns on the question that the *I* has become to itself. He does not say "I am" an atheist for the simple reason that he does not know. There is within each of us a believer and a nonbeliever, and the one does not give the other any rest. The only genuine belief would recognize to what extent belief is filled with unbelief—at times almost overcome by unbelief—so that one does not know whether at some point, under an absolute white light, one would find that one does not believe and one's life has been a ruse. By the same token, the only true unbelief, atheism, would acknowledge that it is invaded by belief, irresistibly drawn by God, haunted and hunted down by God, from whom one has been fleeing all one's life long. So the difficulty in the expression "I rightly pass for" is lodged, not so much in the "passing for," but in the I, for there is no I, at least not one I. Or if there is, the "I" is a kind of shorthand for a competition that goes on within me for the right to speak for the multiplicity, for the corporation that I am: I who "preside" over this corpus, as Husserl rather optimistically puts it.

In responding to Kearney, Derrida says that to say that God exists it is enough to say that religious faith in God exists, so that the name of God is always already in play. Given the omnipresence of religious practices and the name of God, the question is not so much *whether* God exists as it is what we love when we love our God, and what the God we love means, what is translates into, which means what we do. Something is intended when the name of God is invoked in so many different contexts and traditions. Perhaps it is a neurosis—William James opens *The Varieties of Religious Experience* with a similar hypothesis: it just may be that religious people are able to experience religious phenomena because they are a little neurotic. Perhaps that is a condition of religion. But then we must find what drives this neurosis. If God does not exist, how powerful He must be to produce such massive effects!

That is also why a confession is never made just once. Like the *oui, oui*, like an oath or a promise, the event of a confession is not a one-time event but a repetition; for the self, as Augustine shows so beautifully, is spread out in time and does not possess itself all at once. That is also why Derrida says, in answer to a question from the floor, "My confession is subject to endless revision, refinement. As time unfolds the meaning of the transgression, I find that I have more to confess or have to confess otherwise."

The Essays

The opening paper in the conference, "Time — for the Truth," a comparative discussion of Derrida and Lyotard on Augustine's *Confessions*, was, appropriately, delivered by Geoffrey Bennington, whose bet or contract with Derrida was the occasion for "Circumfession," which was itself the impetus for the conference. Bennington began with the confession that he finds "Circumfession" unreadable, which came as a relief to all of us who have had the same experience. If "G." himself, who occupied the theological position of God, omniscience, and the "program" on the upper page of the text, and who had translated the book into English, could still find it unreadable, then there was hope for the rest of us. Of course, unreadability is a precisely crafted concept in Derrida. Unreadability is the condition of the possibility of reading, the "truth of reading," since if something were completely and transparently readable, we would lose interest in it almost at once.

Indeed, to take G. by surprise, to produce an "event," something G. could not read or anticipate by means of "Derridabase," was the whole idea. Against G.'s position of producing a timeless, eventless statement of what Derrida was or must be doing at any given time, Derrida would try to produce the time of an event, the time of or for the happening of a confession that does or makes the truth but does not belong to the order of truth as *adequatio* or *aletheia*. Augustine is not confessing before God anything God does not know already, so information cannot be the point. Now it is tempting to schematize this text temporally by saying that this bet produced the event which launched the "later" Derrida, which exceeds Derridabase, which thus would have been formalizing only the "early" Derrida. But the "early" Derrida is as much an event to come as anything that comes later.

Lyotard, on the other hand, is also a philosopher of the event and the time of the event whose book on the *Confessions* follows Augustine's clue that time is something we know only by not knowing it thematically. Time has the structure of the prereflective now of a presentation that has always already escaped presentation if it is reflected upon in the present, so that it can only be presented indirectly. Time also has the structure of Freudian *Nachträglichkeit*, in which an original experience is not experienced originally but only later, *sero te amavi*; and hence there is a structural and constitutive gap (*differend*) between the original inarticulate temporary experience ("infancy") and any possible later articulation ("adulthood"). So too, God's "absolute" visitation of Augustine in the *Confessions* cannot be directly presented. While Augustine thinks that he is catching up with himself, gathering up his *distensio,* in making the event of this confession happen before God's absolute event, he is being duped. The cut is primal and the gap irreducible, even as for Derrida circumcision means that we are incised, cut off, from the truth. Lyotard and Derrida alike offer "cisional" confessions, confessions of the cut.

Hent de Vries addresses a similar point by raising the question of the "instant," which constitutes the temporality of the moment of confession or conversion in Augustine, Derrida's "Circumfession," and Lyotard's book on Augustine. Derrida's text is aimed at producing a singular nonsynchronizable "event," which takes the timeless theologic Geo-program up above by surprise, although Derrida oddly never thematizes Augustine's famous thematizing of the question of what time is. Such an event—his confession that he has lived in prayers and tears, his secret religion—happens like a miracle, without cause, an analysis that is also confirmed by a comparable analysis of the event in Jean-Luc Marion. The temporality of this event—a double temporality, that of the instant itself and that of its contact with something eternal or omnipresent—is best understood, on De Vries's reading, in terms of Pierre Hadot's account of the tradition of "spiritual exercises." Marcus Aurelius, for example, proposed a regime of daily practices to learn how to concentrate the whole of life in the infinite value of an instant. In Derrida, on the other hand, the event has the sense of the surprise, the unexpected, which experiences the omnipresence of God, albeit a God who is subject to endless chain of substitutions with other names.

Lyotard too wants to differentiate the instant as the living present from Augustine to Husserl, from another experience of the instant as the postponed moment, always already waited for, always pending. Augustine's *Confessions,* he holds, are, like Beckett, written under the sign of "waiting" for the future, but a waiting that goes back through the past. The instant thus is not only evanescent but also immutable, something that does not pass by, something atemporal and infinite, for it is always the living present in which I think the evanescent passage by which the future becomes past, which is an echo of eternity in time. It is just this atemporal present in Augustine that is disputed by Lyotard and Derrida. Rather than eternity, the instant of time for Lyotard is marked by a mystical hope. Life is *distentio,* procrastination; but it is a hope, not despair, not unlike the hope that Derrida expresses in the constancy of God, which is omnipresent to him in the event but which goes under many other names.

Conference coordinator John D. Caputo examines in more detail Derrida's revelation in "Circumfession" of the surprising secret that he is a man of prayer. Caputo is interested in how it can be that Derrida is a man of prayer while rightly passing for an atheist. Far from undermining the character of his prayer, Caputo maintains that this quasi-atheism in fact constitutes and intensifies it. Making use of a pivotal essay by Jean-Louis Chrétien on prayer as a "wounded word," "Circumfession" represents a salient case of a cut and wounded word. Being a little lost, Derrida's circumfession is like a postcard gone astray, beset by *destinerrance*, sent off only to arrive heaven knows where, addressed to the "secret," which is not to be identified with the *deus absconditus*, which is in fact a more assured destination and the stuff of a *docta ignorantia*. For the secret kept from him is that there is no Secret Truth, that we are circum-severed from the Truth, deprived of *verité* and *savoir absolue*, and so he does not know to whom to pray, his condition of nonknowing being more adrift, more radical, than the prayer of a negative theologian to the *deus absconditus*. Yet that is, by the very terms set by Chrétien, an even more intense prayer. Who is more in need in prayer, who prays more earnestly to be able to pray, who issues more wounded words, than one who does not know if there is anyone to hear his prayers? Who can say more earnestly, "Lord, hear our prayers"?

The topic turns to Heidegger when Catherine Malabou explores the ambiguity of the expression *facere veritatem* (an expression seized upon by both Derrida and Heidegger in their discussions of the *Confessions* X, 1). The expression means both to do/tell the truth by confessing and to make the truth by making/ writing a book of true confessions. Heidegger emphasizes that this *facere* is a factor of existential facticity, that only a thrown-factical being has anything to confess, as opposed to fabrication, which belongs to the metaphysics of production. Malabou has two questions: (1) Does Derrida's rumination on this phrase owe anything to Heidegger? and (2) What is the sense of "life" in this auto*bio*graphy, if it is not a matter of recounting information on the course of Augustine's (Derrida's) life? Her answer is that Heidegger and Derrida alike are not in interested simply in life, but in the Being of life. It must be noted, Malabou says, that Heidegger never mentions "avowal, fault, or asking for pardon," because confession for him is primarily a way of feeling one's factical thrownness, and what is confessed is less a guilty deed — it makes nothing known — than the being of facticity. Confession, making the truth, thus effects the very Being or form of the self, lacking which I am deformed (*deformis*), inauthentic. The "destruction" of the Augustinian analysis would turn on exposing the extent to which Augustine still operates within the primacy of the present and hence of *Vorhandensein*. From the standpoint of the *Beiträge*, confessing the self is making/machinating/producing it, forming the form of the I, and hence it belongs to the horizon of the *Machbarkeit* of Being and hence to the will-to-power. Derrida emphasizes that doing/ telling the truth is not a matter of conveying information, since God already knows what Augustine has on his mind, but of asking for pardon. For Malabou, this means that Derridean confession is watched over by the ontological difference, that confession for him does not confess anything ontical. Derrida does not ask for pardon for anything in particular because he is concerned with the very facticity of existence, with the Being of facticity, not with any ontico-factical fault. The play between facticity and fabrication is found in the play between the body, his own, his mother's, and the theological program that Geoff is running overhead. Above all, the two texts are gathered together by what Derrida calls "therapeutic harassment," the zeal of doctors to keep the terminally ill alive, which also goes under the name of undecidability—for who and how is one to decide whether someone should go on living, when death shall come? Are not circumcision and confession ways of harassing life in order to keep it alive? In Derrida, the form of the I is a fluid, the flow of blood and running sores of the other, not "I am," but "she is in me."

In Derrida's commentary on this paper, in which he expresses great admiration for Malabou's text, Derrida confesses that he did not know Heidegger's Augustine lectures and that he had still not read them, so that whatever connections Malabou has unearthed arise from a discovery of the internal rhythms of their thought, not from any actual influence. Derrida also puts a certain distance between himself and any ontologizing of his aims in "Circumfession." His distinction between telling the truth as giving information and confessing the truth as avowing one's faults is not a distinction between the ontico-factual and the ontological Being of confessing. On the contrary, "Circumfession" is through and through an ontical exercise, always directed at concrete episodes, like stealing the grapes from his Algerian neighbor's vineyard, which, as in Augustine and Rousseau, involved a youthful theft. Indeed, Derrida uses this occasion to go on at some length to explicate the difference between himself and Heidegger and to confess that he was always trying to write a text that would scandalize Heidegger, a text that Heidegger could not bear to read. To write about his circumcision—can you imagine Heidegger saying that?—about bedsores and running wounds and fellatio is removed by an abyss from *Seinsdenken*. Might it be that Derrida shows that one cannot transcend the "horizon of life"—above all, not if one also wants to talk about death? Might it be that Derrida's text is situated precisely where Heidegger's is not—with the woman and blood, with asking for pardon, and with life, none of which are matters for thought for Heidegger?

After carefully situating the Augustine lectures of 1921 in the context of the phenomenology of religion lectures of the preceding semester, Philippe Capelle identifies the core theme of the Augustine lectures: Heidegger is centrally interested in the question of the facticity of life, which Augustine has discovered but at the same allowed to drift out of view by the recourse Augustine has to Greek metaphysics. The difficulty of factical existence is blunted and attenuated by the doctrine of the *fruitio dei*; historical turmoil is brought to eternal rest in God. Moving away from the framework of the *Confessions*, therefore, Heidegger resolves in the "The Concept of Time," the 1924 lecture at Marburg, to think of time, not theologically from the standpoint of eternity, but in more rigorously phenomenological terms by understanding time in terms of time itself. But Capelle contends that Heidegger neither does justice to Augustine in this lecture nor concedes what he is borrowing from Augustine. Heidegger does not quite acknowledge the debt of his idea of "anticipation" (*Vorlaufen*) to Augustine's notion of *intentio*, by which Augustine means the positive temporalizing of the soul to those things that lie before it as it turns away from sin and toward God, an idea that is reinscribed in *Being and Time* as Dasein's *Vorlaufen* into death. So contrary to Heidegger's analysis, the Augustinian category of *memoria* is indeed a category of factical life, because even while its end and goal are an eternal life over and beyond factical time, eternity itself is never given; what is given is the stretching out to eternity in time, which is a lived experience of life in time. It is not that Augustine abandons facticity while Heidegger is faithful to it, but rather that Augustine and Heidegger have different views of what the anticipatory temporalizing of factical life is stretched out toward—God or death, neither of which is actually given. Finally, Capelle concludes, while there can be no doubt that Heidegger's path of thought carries him beyond or outside theology, there also can be no doubt that his path is forever marked by its theological provenance, and in particular by its original dialogue with Augustine.

The next two papers take up the readings of Augustine offered by Ricoeur and Arendt. Richard Kearney focuses on two of Ricoeur's texts on Augustine's *Confessions*: the opening chapter of volume one of *Time and Narrative*, entitled "The Aporias of the Experience of Time in Book 11 of the *Confessions*," and an article written in 1985 entitled "Evil: A Challenge to Philosophy and Theology." The first aporia that Ricoeur identifies in the *Confessions* is that of the *being and the non-being* of time. He spends significant time on Augustine's innovative thesis of the "threefold present." Replacing the old cosmological basis of time with a psychological basis (memory, attention, expectation), Augustine locates the nothingness of time in the *distentio animi*, an ever-present discordance in the concordance of the intentions of memory, attention, and expectation. Augustine's answer to the *distentio* is, of course, the *intentio animi* in the hope for eternity, an answer that is not merely a matter of Christian apologetics! The link between the Augustinian notions of time and evil is the experience in both of non-being. In a world understood as God's creation, evil must be a *privatio boni*—it cannot really "be" since all that is comes from God. Ricoeur commends Augustine's radically *moral* vision of evil—*omne malum aut peccatum est aut poena peccati*, even though it leads to many problems, especially that of unjust suffering. Augustine's answer to this problem is his doctrine of original sin, but that leads to the problem of determinism. Augustine's metaphysical and metaphorical (genetic inheritance) theodicy is experientially dissatisfying—as are all later theoretical theodicies. Ricoeur suggests that we look for a more ethical and practical response to this enigma. Kearney finds in Ricoeur three modes of response to the Augustinian aporias of time and evil: (1) practical understanding in terms of Aristotelian *phronēsis* joined with ethical narrativity; (2) working-through suffering through mourning and lamentation; and (3) the marvelous gratuitousness of pardon, where Ricoeur rejoins both Augustine and Jacques Derrida.

Conference coordinator Michael Scanlon takes up Hannah Arendt's dissertation, *Love and Saint Augustine*, which was published in English in 1996. Significant discussion on the extent of Augustine's influence on the life work of Arendt followed. Several commentators agreed that this influence was lifelong. Arendt is well known for her contention that Augustine was "the first philosopher of the will" after St. Paul's discovery of the will. Thus for Arendt, while the mind is the discovery of Athens, the will is found in the soil of Jerusalem. This paper offers a historical/theological corroboration of Arendt's position. Augustine's "What are we but wills?" summarizes the distinctive character of his Christian anthropology. In an early work, *De libero arbitrio*, he defends free will against the charge that God is in any way the cause of evil. The path to the moral self is the will's choice for God. This discussion of the will leads to the Augustinian notion of personhood, a notion discovered by the prophets of Israel in relation to their Personal God, and an understanding of the human self mediated through Augustine to the West. Augustine understands the empowering of the will, which is the core of personhood, through God's gift, the grace of the Holy Spirit. The effect of this grace is *libertas* or freedom, the power to do the good, a power beyond the ambivalence of *liberum arbitrium* or free will. Love becomes the "how" of this freedom, a love of God made real and concrete in love of neighbor. From Augustine Arendt developed her distinctive metaphor, "natality," the potential for new beginnings; for her this is the reason God created humanity. Arendt replaced the philosophical ultimate, Being, with the biblical Creator, the Source of that "neighborly love" which remains the basis for our hope in this abysmally troubled postmodern world as it was for Augustine in his time of the premodern "peace" of the Roman Empire. As Augustine's work provided "new beginnings" beyond pagan antiquity, Arendt always promoted the same hope for "natality" now.

Mark Vessey's essay brings to the table a considerable learning in Latin literature and an impressive familiarity with Jacques Derrida. Vessey notes that Derrida always speaks of St. Augustine, his fellow countryman, with respect and love. Thus, when he composes his quasi-autobiography, *Circumfession*, he incorporates his own deconstructive reading of Augustine's "autobiography," *The Confessions*. Vessey quotes Derrida's decision to make Augustine's language "his chosen one for a year," and then raises the question, Why Augustine? Why *Confessions*? admitting that "even with all the time and space of this world here below (cf. *Conf.* XII, 32, 43), we should not expect to get to the bottom of this question." Vessey finds it curious that, of the thirteen books of *Confessions*, the only one not represented by at least one quotation in *Circumfession* is Book VIII, in which Augustine famously recounts his "conversion" in the garden in Milan in 386. But Book VIII reveals the "theologic program" of Augustine's life as now narrated; it is the hinge on which the work turns. For Derrida, even if in some sense his conversion has already occurred, it is still to come in some future perfect tense rather than being textually enfolded in the manner of Augustine. Vessey detects a certain violence in Augustine's turn from the narrative of himself to the exegesis of Scripture at the beginning of Book XI and suggests that it may be because he was engaged in a correspondence that was assuming the character of a duel with Jerome, the self-creating master of the Latin Bible. For Vessey, Jerome is at the origin of that preoccupation with the Bible and the rise of Christian writing which influenced literary theory for centuries. And Vessey sees the signature of Jerome on many pages of the *Confessions*. Indeed, it may have been his reading of Jerome's *Famous Men* that enabled Augustine to discover a program of Christian literary activity in which he would inscribe his theory of an inner instruction by a divine *logos*, destined almost fifteen centuries later to catch the eye of an "angel reading" like Jacques Derrida.

The next two essays, by two internationally recognized Augustine scholars, quite remarkably—this was not planned but perhaps was the prospect of a deconstructive dialogue with Augustine—take up the question of what Augustine did *not* confess. James O'Donnell treats us to a hermeneutics of suspicion on Augustine's *Confessions* with a focus on their "truth." The very title of his essay testifies to the presence of Jacques Derrida, a current champion of many and many different readings of classical texts. Was the story about Alypius in *Confessions* III, 3, 6 based on fact? We will never know, but up till now no one registered a doubt. The only narrative that has evoked doubt is the garden scene in Milan. Yes, maybe Augustine is making his own kind of truth out of his past. O'Donnell warns us that the genre of biography itself powerfully compromises with the confessional style, so that it is quite difficult to see what Augustine is up to.

O'Donnell proposes multiple narratives to know the life of Augustine, all quite different from the story of the *Confessions*. He presents three versions of the same evidence and the same life, following Augustine's return to Africa from Milan. The first is the familiar one from the *Confessions*—how Augustine was forced to accept ordination against his wishes. The second has Augustine living the life of a country squire on his family property in Tagaste, carefully minimizing the expenses of that kind of citizenship, until his son dies, leaving him no heir; he then sells his property and slips away to Hippo to take up duties as a minor cleric, not from religious devotion but to evade the duties of citizenship. A third version has Augustine in a Platonic retirement from all kinds of worldly activities, but again, the death of his son led him to consider other possibilities when he visited Hippo, where, to his horror, he was ordained. He left Hippo and scandalously fled back to Tagaste, where bad conscience then brought him back to Hippo, resigned to his future. The last version seems most persuasive to O'Donnell, who proceeds to support it from the *Confessions* themselves. Augustine's great achievement was to see that confession could be self-constructive rather than self-repudiation.

Elizabeth Clark offers a "Derridean reading" of the *Confessions* to balance the tendency of scholars to overlook gaps, aporias, and exclusions in Augustine's great work in their search for "presence." The particular "gap and absence" on which she focuses is the mysterious erasure of the Donatists both from the *Confessions* and from his late-in-life reconsideration of that text in his *Retractions*. Augustine, the great philosopher of memory, had no theory of forgetting! It seems that the Donatists, the predominant form of Christianity in fourth century Africa, are absent from the *Confessions* because their theology was not "intellectual" enough to gain Augustine's respect. Another reason Clark suggests was the successful Romanization of North Africa, leading the greatest writer of Latin to dismiss Donatism as provincialism. In fact, it took Augustine some time to acquaint himself with Donatism in order to launch his polemics against it. Clark ends with a suggestion that Augustine's writings against the Pelagians from 412 to 430 might offer an appropriate matrix for consideration of "Derridabase" and "Circumfession." Here we find Augustine's central concerns—grace, free will, and predestination. Against Pelagius, Augustine insisted on the impotency of fallen free will and the sovereign efficacy of the grace of the predestining God. By embedding Bennington's "Derridabase" and Derrida's "Circumfession" in this different Augustinian context pertaining to freedom and predestination, an unexpected displacement occurs. Clark has Derrida becoming Pelagius, not Augustine, as he protests against Bennington's attempts to control him! Bennington becomes God; and Augustine, the opponent of Pelagius. To attack the omniscience of the divine Bennington, who has everything about Derrida predestined, Derrida-Pelagius can find his salvation through unpredictability or undecidability in the future tense.

We conclude with the essay by Jean Bethke Elshtain, who reminds us that Augustine's works are often "bold strokes on an expansive canvas." His work is at once theological, philosophical, historical, cultural, and rhetorical, with rich surface and vast depth. His work in political philosophy and theology has been characterized as "political realism." Avoiding his expansiveness, authors quote "bits and chunks" of *The City of God* ("Augustine Lite") to illustrate this pessimistic "realism." For Elshtain, however, Augustine's "expansiveness" is welcome—her chapter highlights key points in Augustine that are rich with implications for political theory beyond "political realism." In her section, "Augustine on the Self," Elshtain finds in Augustine's complex reflections on human selfhood anticipations of the postmodern efforts to de-throne the Cartesian subject even before that subject got erected. Augustine's "I doubt, therefore I exist" is already an indictment of the clarity of the Cartesian "I think." Augustine begins with beginnings, with infancy, where the lack of language creates the desire to communicate; he appreciates the role of embodiment as epistemologically significant; he accepts a humble skepticism wherein our beliefs are warranted by a love that reaches out to others and to God, its source. In the section "Augustine on Social Life," Elshtain elaborates further on her claim that human beings are social all the way down. The City of God is the community of Christian pilgrims anticipating the heavenly kingdom through *caritas* in struggle with *cupiditas*. Civic order is not just a remedy for sin; it is the task of Christians to minimize *cupiditas* and maximize *caritas* whenever and wherever possible. Elshtain ends her paper with "Augustine on War and Peace." Augustine's "political realism" admits the tragic necessity of war against aggression and to protect the innocent, but this common interpretation must not forget his insistence on the virtue of hope and the power of *caritas*.

NOTES

1. For an interesting convergence and helpful expansion of these remarks, see the interview conducted with Derrida by Giovanna Borradori that took place about a month later, on October 22, 2001, in New York City, in *Philosophy in a Time of Terror: Dialogues with Jürgen Habermas and Jacques Derrida*, ed. Giovanna Borradori (Chicago and London:

University of Chicago Press, 2003), pp. 85–136. This volume is quite helpful also in dispelling Derrida's much misunderstood relationship to the Enlightenment.

2. Augustine's text, in Latin, is the epigraph of chapter 1, and it is adverted to from the opening paragraph on, for example, when he says that he learned in childhood never to be late for prayers. See Hélène Cixous and Jacques Derrida, *Veils*, trans. Geoffrey Bennington (Stanford, Calif.: Stanford University Press, 2001), pp. 21, 67 passim.

PART I

After the Event

one
Composing "Circumfession"

Jacques Derrida

I want to say, first of all, that I am so pleased and honored to be back here at Villanova once more with so many friends. I am overwhelmed by your hospitality and all the more so under these tragic circumstances when I wanted to be, and I do feel, closer to you than ever, sharing, of course, all of your grief and mourning and compassion. I was in Shanghai on September the 11th, and then I went back to Europe—Paris and Frankfurt. Since then I have never stopped trying to realize the event, what happened to these places, especially to the Twin Towers, which beyond everything general which can be said about them, and has been said about them, are very dear to my heart. What happened on one hand was an unpredicted event, no doubt, as a singular event, but perhaps not so unpredictable. That means that through and despite our infinite and hopeless compassion for so many innocent victims, we should go on and analyze in a responsible, courageous, and endless fashion what made this terrifying and unpredicted—unprecedented—event possible, in all its dimensions, with all its premises, causes, and consequences all over the world. Except for the dead victims, I'm not sure that anyone in the world today could or should escape such a reflection, which in many cases could lead to some precise judgment and confession.

I have discovered Geoff's text just now, so I am not prepared. That was the contract—to respond. And not being prepared for the event is part of the problematic. An event is something you are not prepared to experience. What I realized, listening to this wonderful paper, is that everything has been said by Geoff

As explained in the Introduction, these remarks by Jacques Derrida were originally made at start of the conference, as a commentary on the paper of Geoffrey Bennington.—Editors.

before I wrote "Circumfession" and that was my problem, because he knows the temporality of these things, of this process. He had written "Derridabase" before I started writing "Circumfession," so everything was said in advance. And then, thanks to Jack Caputo, everything has been said after. So what is left?

The problem is the *event*, as Geoff just said. What I realized when I wrote "Circumfession" is something that became clearer to me *nachträglich*, years after the fact. Of course, what I wrote in "Circumfession" was that I was trying to write something that Geoff's text, or system, or formalized interpretation, could not predict precisely, could not foresee or could not account for. I wasn't sure I would succeed. I'm not sure I have succeeded in doing so. But that was the strategy. But in order to do so, I was relying on the fact that I was producing a text in my own idiom, a text as a singular signature that, as an event, not as a content or as a meaning, as a singular event, could not be part of, or integrated by, Geoff's text. But at the time I thought that this experience was, to oversimplify, of a performative genre, of a performative structure. Usually one thinks that a performative speech act consists in producing the event that it speaks about.

But since then I realized two things, again to oversimplify. First is the question of translation. Geoff's account was and remains impeccable in terms of the concepts, the logic of everything I have tried to say, I would try to say. But the problem and the test that he in fact had to experience was not while he was writing "Derridabase," but the day he would try to translate "Circumfession" into English. Again, he has done an impeccable translation, a wonderful translation. But today I took a look at it again and I said, "Well, he could not translate some things," such as, if you look just at the beginning, the word "*cru.*"[1] He has done a wonderful job translating *cru*, "crude." I don't remember, I don't want to impose a close reading. But *cru* in French means at the same time crude, raw, and sometimes it is translated as vintage, but also "believed"—from *croire*. These pronunciations of the single word, a three-letter word, *cru*, remain untranslatable. This is the kind of thing, as an event within the language—not an event of my life— an event within the language, which is not translatable. This untranslatability, that is, its uniqueness, is the kind of presentation of the present which cannot be presented. That's the first species of limit in the formalization, in readability. *Cru* is unreadable. Even for me, it's unreadable.

Now, the second limit had to do with the death of my mother and performativity. As I said a moment ago, I assumed for a long time, despite a number of reservations I had about Austin's theory of constative and performative speech acts, that the performative speech act was a way of producing an event. I now think that the performative is in fact a subtle way of neutralizing the event. As long as I am to speak performatively, I have to do this under certain conditions, conventions, conventional conditions. I have the ability to do this and to produce the event by speaking. That is, I can or I may master the situation by taking into account these conventions. I may open the session, for instance. I may say "yes" when I get married, and so on. But because I have the mastery of this situation, my very mastery is a limitation of the eventness of the event. I neutralize the eventness of the event precisely because of the performativity.

So, coming back to "Circumfession," I was not only trying performatively to challenge Geoff's powerful account of what I had been doing or what I could do. I was not only doing that. I was waiting without waiting for the death of my mother. That is, the event was unpredictable to me. I did not know when my mother would interrupt my sentence, in the middle of a sentence. This event could not be produced by a speech act. What characterizes an event is precisely that it defeats any performativity, that it happens, precisely, beyond any performative power. So what couldn't be accounted for in "Circumfession" is not something that I would have organized in order to challenge or to defeat Geoff's "Derridabase." It was something which would happen to me without any possibility for me to anticipate, to predict, to foresee, or to perform. It is this limit of the performativity that in fact draws the line we are now analyzing. The interest we are taking in speech act theory in the academy perhaps has to do with the illusion that, by using performative utterances, we produce events, that we are mastering history. The event is absolutely unpredictable, that is, beyond any performativity. That's where a signature occurs. If I so much insist on circumcision in this text, it is because circumcision is precisely something which happens to a powerless child before he can speak, before he can sign, before he has a name. It is by this mark that he is inscribed in a community, whether he wants it or not. This happened to him and leaves a mark, a scar, a signature on his body. This happened before him, so to speak. It's a heritage that he cannot deny, whatever he does or he doesn't do.

Today, preparing this session without being able to prepare it, because I didn't know Geoff's text, I was looking at this book [*Jacques Derrida*]. I arrived yesterday in New York from Paris, also having been in Frankfurt, and first in China. Today, for some of you at least, it is Yom Kippur, the Day for Forgiveness. That's the way one translates it, although it is more complicated than that. The Day for Asking for Forgiveness. In "Circumfession," I again and again recall the number of times I arrived in New York for Yom Kippur. If you will allow me, I quote two such references:[2]

> . . . *but why the desire to name New York, where 21 years ago, on notebooks lost in Algeria in '62 unless they're hidden here, I had begun again, at the Hotel Martinique. . . .*

The Hotel Martinique was my first hotel in the United States. Now it has been destroyed, two years ago. I think now it's a Holiday Inn. Hotel Martinique, that's where I was with my wife the first time I landed in New York in '55, and we had a fabulous time.

> . . . *at the hotel Martinique, to write 'for myself'—follow the New York thread, from trip to trip, up to this one, the Kippours of N.Y., the cut with Kippour, the noncircumcision of the sons—up to that year when, coming out of a restaurant near the MOMA, I enter a 'reformed' synagogue. . . .*

The cut with Kippur. That is the time when I started not to observe Yom Kippur, and this has to do with New York. The second occurrence of Kippur:[3]

> *the day of the Great Pardon, presence of white, my immaculate taleth, the only virgin taleth in the family, like the feathers of the cocks and hens that Haïm Aimé. . . .*

My father.

> *. . . wants to be white for the sacrifice before Kippur, the Rabbi cuts their throats in the garden after feeling under their wings, holding the knife between his teeth . . .*

The *"cut with Kippur"* and *"the uncircumcised sons"* means that at some point I stopped observing, fasting, on the day of Kippur. My question is always, when I did so, did I leave, did I abandon Judaism, or Jewishness, and Kippur? Or did I become, let's say, a Jew of the interior, that is, Christian or Protestant, that is, interiorizing the physical, literal, gesture of the ritual itself?

Speaking of forgiveness—of course, I have to say something since the topic of this conference is St. Augustine's *Confessions*—I should try and say something in the wake of what Geoff has just said about the relation to Augustine in this text, which is a very strange one, as you probably know. On the one hand, I try to address in my own way the question of belatedness, the question of temporality. When I read Lyotard's book—after he died, of course—I was struck by the fact that he quotes exactly the same sentence by Augustine that, as Geoff mentioned earlier, I used as an excerpt to another text called *"Un ver à soie,"* "A Silkworm of One's Own"[4]—*sero te amavi,* "Too late have I loved you." It was too late when I loved you. Late is always too late. "Too late" doesn't mean anything. Late is too late. When you say late, it's already too late. But what cannot be read, speaking of readability, is precisely what I do in this text *"Un ver à soie,"* when I write, as an excerpt, *sero te amavi.* I swear it's unreadable, because there is a secret in these words, in my own way of signing these words, Augustine's words. I'm sure that the secret cannot be Lyotard's or anyone else's. I won't tell you what the secret is, of course. But I can tell you, I can bear witness to something. I am quoting something that Geoff has said about the "impossibility of bearing witness." That's what Blanchot also said somewhere. Blanchot speaks of something like that, attesting to the fact that one cannot attest to, bearing witness about the impossibility of bearing witness. You do something when you bear witness to the fact that you cannot bear witness. You don't do nothing. When I tell you there is a secret here, that *sero te amavi* is a secret, you should know that there is a secret. You don't know what the secret is, but there is a secret here, and that is reading the unreadable. It is readable. *Sero te amavi* is readable. You can read, you can understand, you can even write volumes and volumes, and that's been done, on Augustine's *sero te amavi.* In fact, he's addressing the beauty of God. It's the beauty of God that he loves too late. But the way I use these words in *"Un ver à soie,"* it means what Augustine means but it means something else, which remained and will remain secret as long as I want. There are a lot of such things in this text—not only in my text, but in every text—a lot of such things that bear witness to something for which one cannot bear witness.

Now that's the reason why I try to borrow from Augustine. I've a great admiration for Augustine, of course, and the feeling that I don't know him enough; I will never know him enough. That's one more reason to ask for forgiveness of him. But on the other hand, I try, not to pervert him, but to "mis-lead" him, so to speak, into places where he couldn't and wouldn't go. For instance, when one asks for forgiveness, when one confesses—and Geoff powerfully analyzed the structure of this thing—it's not a question of truth, at least not a question of the constative truth. When I ask, when I confess, I'm not reporting a fact. I can kill someone. I can hijack a plane and then report; it's not a confession. It becomes a confession only when I ask for forgiveness and, according to the tradition, when I promise to repent, that is, to improve, to love, to transform my hatred into love, to transform myself, and to do so out of love. It's not a matter of knowledge. It's not a matter of making the other know what happened, but a matter of changing oneself, of transforming oneself. That's what perhaps Augustine calls "to make the truth." Not to *tell* the truth, not to inform—God knows everything—but to *make* the truth, to produce the truth.

What does it mean to "make" the truth? If you make the truth in the performative sense that I mentioned earlier, it is not an event. For the truth to be "made" as an event, then the truth must fall on me—not be produced by me, but fall on me, or visit me. That's "visitation." Usually when I refer to hospitality (using and not using Levinas's concept of visitation), I distinguish between hospitality of "invitation" and hospitality of "visitation." When I invite someone, I remain the master of the house: "Come, come to me, feel at home," and so on, "but you should respect my house, my language, my rules, the rules of my nation" and so on. "You are welcome, but under some conditions." But "visitation" is something else: absolute hospitality implies that the unexpected visitor can come, may come and be received without conditions. It falls upon; it comes; it is an intrusion, an eruption—and that's the condition of the event. Sometimes the event happens against the background of a horizon. I see the other coming; I see the event arriving; I foresee it; there is a horizon. That is a very indispensable axiom of phenomenology, ontology, hermeneutics—the horizon, horizon of expectation. Whenever there is such a horizon of expectation, nothing "happens" in this strict and pure meaning of the "event." For something to happen, it must remain unpredictable, that is, must not come from the horizon. I should not see him or it coming in front of me, but it must fall on me—either from above, so that I cannot see it coming, like a bomb or an airplane or God, or behind or beneath, but not in front of me.

There is no horizon for an event, no temporal horizon. The event is the limit of the limit—because *horizon* means in Greek "the limit"—the limit of the horizontal limit, that is, of what comes to me, in front of me. This limit is precisely the condition of the event, that it comes from above, behind, through the unconscious, or underneath. That's the condition of the event. Now given these structures, which disrupt precisely what one calls in Western philosophy "temporality," the linear or nonlinear succession of "nows," where we have a horizon of the future, the coming, the next now, the coming now, what has confession to do with the interruption of this temporal horizon? I am trying to say something that I didn't say in "Circumfession." I'm just precisely improvising. I'm just letting things happen unpredictably, having almost no notes, having not read Geoff's text in advance.

When one asks for forgiveness, when one confesses, one doesn't know for what and to whom. According to the tradition, if I knew what to confess and to whom, who confesses what and to whom, then there would be no event. Geoff distinguished between the event confessed by the confession and the event of the confessing itself, of the confessing experience itself. The event confessed, the confessing event. Now, if such an event, one of the two, has already a "what" or a "who" that is an identifiable object and subject, then nothing happens. No confession and no asked for forgiveness happens. The confession happens when I don't even know who confesses and who asks for forgiveness for what. Again and again, not only in "Circumfession" but in other texts, as in *The Postcard* and others, I insisted on the fact that as soon as I write, or as soon as I leave a trace, I'm already asking for forgiveness, not knowing to whom precisely, "God" being the name of no one, of God knows whom. Why is this so? Because when I leave a trace, I already know without knowing that this trace — even if I try to distill it, to refer it to someone, if I send it to some singular, irreplaceable, unique one — as a trace, it could be lost and read by anyone. Take the example of a love letter, for instance. I send a love letter to someone and say, "That's for you, only you, and you are the only one who can decipher this letter. It's a secret." As soon as I write this, as I sign it and leave a trace, it becomes available for everyone, if not for everyone, at least for others. And I'm already in a position to confess that I sinned, because I was guilty of leaving a trace, which is not distinct or accessible only to the unique one, be it to God or anyone, a person, a man or a woman, even any living being, even what one calls an animal.

As soon as I leave a trace, I have to ask for forgiveness, because I imply, I assume, that it is interesting. When I write or I leave a trace or I publish it, even if I say, "Well, it's just nothing, it's just improvised," nevertheless, I present it, implying that it is interesting. Even now, I say I have nothing interesting to say, that I'm just improvising, that I did not prepare. Nevertheless, the fact that I present myself and take your time implies that I think it might be interesting. And then, of course, there is guilt and I'm ashamed and I ask for forgiveness. That's the first layer of guilt. The second layer is, as I just mentioned, the fact that I don't know whom I'm addressing now. Of course, my first addressees could be or should be Geoff, or Jack, because I know that they know this, that they know that I say this. But I try to speak as if they were not here, because if it were the three of us, we wouldn't address this question; we would just keep silent on this subject.

Let me go back to some of Geoff's statements. He spoke at some point of *my* confession, at the beginning when he confessed, "My confession, though there is something odd about that possessive adjective, something unsettling already about claiming a confession as mine, also has to do with reading." That's exactly what I tried to say, in a very awkward way, a moment ago. If I am certain that this confession is mine, that I am the one who not only did this but is responsible for this, and who is now responsible for repenting and improving, than there is nothing. It's over; that's the end. What is terrible in confession is that I'm not sure that I am the one who can claim the mastery of or the responsibility for what has been done, and I am not the one who can claim to be improving and to be good enough to repent. That's why I say in "Circumfession" again and again that when one confesses—I don't know if it is English, but it is French—when one confesses, one always confesses the other. One confesses the other. Even if I confess myself, if I confess having done this and that, I am confessing another one. That's the structure of confession. I cannot confess myself. If I confess that I did so and so, that is the other. That is already the other I'm confessing. I make the other confess the crime; otherwise, I couldn't confess. There is this division, this divisibility of the confession which structures the confession, so that I never confess myself. A confession is never mine. If it were mine, it wouldn't be a confession. It is always the other in me who confesses. This is consistent with something I tried, after having written "Circumfession," again and again to reaffirm, namely that a decision is always passive and a decision of the other. This is something no philosopher as such can legitimate, can accept, that a decision is passive. That is a scandal in philosophy, a passive decision, but decision is passive. It's the other who decides in me. It is always the other who makes the decision, who cuts—a decision means cutting. That is the etymology; to decide means to cut. It is to interrupt the continuity of time and the course of history, to cut. For such a cut to occur, someone must interrupt in me my own continuity. If I decide what I can decide, I don't decide. For me to decide, I must have in myself someone else who cuts, who interrupts the possibility. If I do only what I can do, what is possible for me, I do nothing. The decision is the other's decision in me.

This is also true for the confession. The confession is the other's confession in me, which deprives the confession of any common sense. It is meaningless. A confession must remain meaningless. If a confession is meaningful, it's nothing. It means that it's a confession in order to reconcile, to reach some reconciliation, some redemption, to improve myself, to change myself, so there's a teleology of confession. If confession is guided by a teleology, it is not confession. It's just an economy, it's a therapy, it's whatever you want. Confession must remain meaningless, as well as forgiveness. If you forgive in order to reconcile with the other, or to make life in society easier, or to heal away, then it's not forgiveness. Forgiveness as well as confession must remain meaningless. It is always the other in me or the other *as* me who decides and who confesses, which doesn't exonerate me from my responsibility. I'm responsible for the other. I remain responsible, despite the fact it's the other who confesses, whom I confess or who confesses in me, and who decides in me.

That's why, again and again, it seems that the mother is at the center of "Circumfession." I always say I'm confessing my mother; that is, I refer to some possible sin of my mother, and I am already mourning her while she is not dead yet. I am confessing her. So "I confess" means "I confess my mother." That's one of the differences—among so many others—among all these different confessions. Augustine writes *Confessions* after his mother's death. Lyotard publishes posthumously his *The Confession of Augustine*. I wrote "Circumfession" while my mother was alive but not able to identify me, to recognize me, to name me, to call me. Again, between the French publication in the original idiom of "Circonfession" and the English translation, my mother died. That's why Geoff had to add at the end of the English version of the book that Georgette Derrida, my mother, died. That was a few months after "Circumfession" was published in French. The unreadability that Geoff referred to again and again had to do with precisely this structure of the event, which must remain meaningless, unpredictable, with no horizon of expectation. We have as our responsibility to read the unreadability as such, to take into account with some expertise what remains unreadable.

Coming back to the 11th of September—on one hand, it was a unique event, absolutely unique, as unique as were the victims, the thousands of people who died. Unique, irreplaceable victims and an irreplaceable, unique event. We mourn this unique event, but at the same time we have to do our best, responsibly, to account for what happened as unpredictable here, as unpredicted here. That is because we can analyze a number of things that, up to a certain point, without reducing the uniqueness of the event, could account for what happened this day; we can undertake a number of analyses on many levels: political, economic, ethnic, and religious—religious perhaps more than any other.

When Geoff said that I radicalized this question of truth up to the point of claiming that confession has nothing to do with truth, I think he is right. But at the same time, since I do not want simply to get rid of the truth value, I would prefer to say that even if one agrees that confession has nothing to do with truth in the theoretical constative mode, nor perhaps with truth in some performative mode, there is something true with the event. That's why Paul de Man speaks of *die Wahre* not *die Wahrheit*, the true not the truth. The event as something to do with the true, if not the truth. We have to elaborate another truth of the true, another way of experiencing the truth, if one wants to avoid giving up in the face of this terrible problem. There are requirements. There is something demanding about thinking this event, something demanding beyond the theoretical value of the truth. There is something demanding which I would perhaps call "true" in a different way.

Geoff mentioned perjury in passing. For a long time—more and more after "Circumfession," although I speak of perjury in "Circumfession"—I tried to formalize the concept of perjury, not only as a crime, a guilt, or sin, or lie (perjury is a kind of lie), but as a structural necessity. Perjury cannot be eradicated because it is part of a true or truthful promise of telling the truth. One way of doing this (there are many ways, I cannot mention all of them here) has to do with Levinas's concept of the third. The third one, perhaps, could be compared to what I said a moment ago about *destinerrance*, the fact that I could not intend, I could not send a trace or reserve a trace, for a unique person. The relation to the face is the relation to the other, for Levinas, in a dual face to face, in a dual relationship. But already in this dual relationship there is a third one, a third party. That's what he calls justice. Justice starts when you have to compare. You have to take into account that we are more than two when the institution, the state, enters the scene. As soon as I refer to the other, I speak to the other, I'm engaged in a face-to-face relationship; there is a third party involved. My promise to the other, to the unique other, is already betrayed by the witness, by the fact that it is already mediated in a language which is a general language, which is not a unique signature. The very promise, the most sincere and truthful promise, is already corrupted by a perjury. In justice, the perjury is constitutive of justice, constitutive of the most authentic relation to the other. This perjury cannot be erased, cannot be eradicated. As soon as I relate to the other, there is something to be forgiven, some forgiveness to be asked for.

Thank you.

NOTES

1. "Circonfession: cinquante-neuf périodes et périphrases," in Geoffrey Bennington and Jacques Derrida, *Jacques Derrida* (Paris: Éditions du Seuil, 1991), pp. 7–11; "Circumfession: Fifty-nine Periods and Periphrases," in Geoffrey Bennington and Jacques Derrida, *Jacques Derrida* (Chicago: University of Chicago Press, 1993), pp. 3–8.

2. "Circonfession," p. 188; "Circumfession," pp. 201–202.

3. "Circonfession," pp. 27–28; "Circumfession," pp. 245– 46.

4. Jacques Derrida, "Un Ver à soie," in Hélène Cixous and Jacques Derrida, *Voiles* (Paris: Galilée, 1998); "A Silkworm of One's Own," in Hélène Cixous and Jacques Derrida, *Veils*, trans. Geoffrey Bennington (Stanford, Calif.: Stanford University Press, 2001).

Confessions and "Circumfession"

A Roundtable Discussion with Jacques Derrida

Moderated by Richard Kearney

Richard Kearney: You are all very welcome to this final session of this third conference on Religion and Postmodernism. I propose that we might usefully proceed, as we have done in previous years, by starting off with each of the participants putting a question or a comment to Jacques Derrida and then inviting Jacques to reply. When everybody has had their turn, we will open the floor to discussion.

We are, as you know, discussing two main texts here at this conference, two confessions of different kinds: Augustine's *Confessions* and Derrida's "Circumfession." I would hope that in our final session we will in some way build bridges between those two texts and learn to traverse between them, as we have been trying to do over the last two days.

I just want to preface the questions with a brief quotation, which echoes in a way Jack Caputo's opening quotation in his remarks of the conference on Friday, namely the conclusion to our last roundtable discussion. As we were winding up, I heard a rumor that there might be a third conference, and if Jacques Derrida did return to Villanova he should be wary, because there was a known legend that if somebody visited an Augustinian institution or monastery a third time he almost automatically became a novice. The question was then raised as to whether, if Jacques Derrida returned, he would become a novice, or this Augustinian institution, Villanova, would be deconstructed. Well, that was the question; it was a rumor that as you know transpired to be true. At least the first part, that the conference took place. As to the outcome of the conference, that remains to be seen, in terms of who deconstructs whom. But there was a brief response by Jacques on that occasion, which he may have forgotten, but it went as follows (and it may be appropriate to quote it now in the final remarks of the last roundtable discussion):

I wanted to add an anecdote to what Richard has just said. Before giving a seminar in forgiveness and perjury, I gave a three-year seminar on hospitality, in which I often referred, not just to Christianity or to Judaism, but also to pre-Islamic culture. The hospitality which was required among nomadic communities was such that when someone lost his way in the desert, the nomadic community should receive him, should offer him hospitality for three days. For three days they had the obligation to feed him and look after him, but after three days they could kill him.[1]

So, I will be Jacques Derrida's bodyguard here tonight, on the occasion of this third conference!

Mark Vessey: I want to take up the issue of the literary genre of confession, from the point of view of the genre of composition—or indeed of de-composition—from the point of view of the genre of citation, in view of excitation. I'm going to read a section of Periphrase 45, add a comment, and then I hope put a question. It's toward the end of that period:

> . . . above all, do not believe that I'm am quoting [this is just after a quotation] any more than G., no, I'm tearing off my skin, like I always do, I unmask and *de-skin* myself while sagely reading others like an angel, I dig down in myself to the blood, but in them, so as not to scare you, so as to indebt you toward them, not me.

I will omit, cut out, a quotation from the notebooks and pick up Derrida's text a moment later:[2]

> I do not know SA, less than ever, I like to read right on the skin of his language, my chosen one for a year, and like an angel but unlike angels, is this possible, I read only the time of his syllables—"Whereas they read [Augustine is quoted here in the Latin[3]] without syllables of time or other times (plural). They read what Thy eternal will wills. They read, they choose, they love. They always read, they read forever, and what they read never passes away, their book is not closed.

Henri Marrou, a very eminent French scholar of Augustine of the last century famously declared on one occasion, "*Saint Augustin compose mal*," "Augustine writes badly"—as a stylist, and then cited a number of instances where the syntactic structure of a sentence in Augustine really did not conform to anything like classical Ciceronian models. Whatever else you can say about Augustine, according to Marrou, he wasn't much of a Latin stylist. Ten years or more later, Marrou came back to that youthful judgment of his and retracted it; he said that was the judgment (he now realized) of a young barbarian.[4] He simply had not grasped the principle, the mastery, of Augustine's particular way of composing, which indeed was not quite classical or Ciceronian, but was nonetheless—he now conceded—a perfectly good way to compose. An extraordinary way, though never more extraordinary than in the *Confessions*, which I think must have struck all readers at the time as really very oddly composed from the very first sentence onward—wherever you think the first sentence ends. It is one of the distinguishing stylistic features of the *Confessions* that it runs on in an almost seamless set of periphrases, which catch up in their course pieces of text from all sorts of places (especially, of course, pieces of Scripture), usually not to cite, but simply to consume, to assimilate, though occasionally to cite. One could say of this passage in Periphrase 45 of "Circumfession," about the way in which Derrida reads like an angel, yet not like those angels of whom Augustine speaks, reading beyond time, I suppose, that according to ordinary canons of literary or philosophical or academic writing that the author of "Circumfession" composes badly, that Derrida *compose mal*. I, as the young barbarian that I still am in my own mind anyway, might even assert as much in order later to be able to retract the opinion. I wonder about the motives for your choice of Augustine that year, the year when you would be reading him like an angel, though not one of his. Here's my question: How far was that choice influenced by a sense of the possibilities, for you, of Augustine's odd style of composition, his own way of cutting and consuming texts, by citation and other means, and always for the sake of excitation, since, as he says, he writes the *Confessions* to excite his own affection, and the love of others, for his God?

Jacques Derrida: Thank you. This is much more than a question. Thank you for everything that you said. Really—I'm not lying now—I do not remember why, at the beginning, when I started writing this ["Circumfession"], after having read Geoff's text, I had chosen St. Augustine. I do not remember why. I swear. The fact is that I have always been interested in St. Augustine, at least superficially and in a discontinuous fashion. In the seminars I had been giving during the years before 1990, St. Augustine came back again and again, on subjects such as "eating the other," cannibalism, the rhetoric of cannibalism, the relation to the mother, the theme of the milk. I came back to St. Augustine many, many times in my life, but why I have chosen St. Augustine at that time, I do not remember. Once I started, then everything followed.

Now, speaking of citation and excitation, just a week ago I was in Germany, quoting a text by Adorno quoting Benjamin on quoting, on citations.[5] Benjamin says that when one cites, when one makes a quotation, it is not simply an academic exercise. We act, then, or I act then, as a *Räuber am Weg*, as someone who is a "highway robber," a *brigand de grand chemin*. Quoting is not an innocent operation; it is really violent, a violent appropriation. In the passage you quoted, when I say that I am just quoting in order to be less pathetic, to spare you, so as not to scare you, I quote the others just to avoid the pain. But at the same time, of course, that's the exercise. At the same time, of course, I de-skin myself. It's a very violent operation on myself. The fact is that, speaking of literary genre (this was your starting point), I've always been interested in the series of confessions in which it is as if writing for the first time, as the only one exhibiting oneself, as Rousseau did, they were just quoting one another. I realized that, in fact, Rousseau—there is a text just to be published now in France where I analyze these things—at the age of sixteen, like Augustine at the age of sixteen, had to confess that he has been stealing something, pears or something, for no reason, something that was totally useless. Both [Rousseau and Augustine] at the same age steal pears or apples, and this act of stealing something was the beginning of their experience. So I was wondering: did Rousseau really steal these things, or is he simply, as an exercise, trying to inscribe himself in this great tradition of confession? The fact is, I myself, in "Circumfession"—and I was not lying—confess to having been caught by a landowner in Algeria for having stolen grapes.[6] It happened to me! This remains for me a wound! It meant something, which counts in my life! The fact is that it *did* happen, but it looks like an exercise, a quotation in a genealogy of literary genres. That's why it is at the same time sincere, brutal, and at the same time a literary experiment. My suspicion is that St. Augustine opened the history of this genre, and I was interested in this origin, too.

Now, of course, if I try to remember something that I do not remember, the reason why I've chosen this text [Augustine's *Confessions*] is probably because in this seminar I was referring not only to milk but to tears. I was impressed by the number of times in which Augustine refers to his tears, and I say in "Circumfession" that I'm interested only in writers who cry or weep, which excludes a number of people—of men, I mean. Of course, in this seminar I refer to Monica, to the death of Augustine's mother. I was writing this when my mother was dying. That is probably the starting point. This morning I forgot to say to Jack Caputo that I agreed with him that Heidegger never mentioned Monica, nor anything feminine in this story. This has to be taken into account.

Elizabeth Clark: My question is more pedestrian than Mark's. I wish to move to a different disciplinary framework, namely, that of history. In America, the historical profession, at least until recent years, has been dominated by social historians who often scorn intellectual history and who claim that they work on "documents," not on "texts"—perhaps hoping to sidestep issues raised by literary-philosophical theory. Of course, there are some historians here (such as Joan Wallach Scott) as well as in France (the late Michel de Certeau, and Roger Chartier) who have attempted to erase that divide between social history and intellectual history. What aspects of your work do you consider the most interesting, or useful, for historians?

Jacques Derrida: I think that historians have to [be] or should be interested in theory, in the status of the documents, of the texts, that they are analyzing and interpreting, and not all of them do that. But in my own small case, on the one hand, I'm a very bad historian, but I dream of being a historian. Really, I dream this. In fact, I think I said this somewhere, the only thing I'm interested in is history. But I'm not doing what I should do. Nevertheless, I try each time to sketch or to indicate the necessity of starting with the history of what I'm trying to explore, to go back simply to these texts I start with. I did my homework—not enough—but to read historians on the history of confession and the history of this literary genre. I'm constantly trying to take into account the work of historians that

I don't do myself but that I think it is absolutely necessary. That's why I consider very unfair to me the judgments that say that what I'm doing is totally ahistorical. From the very beginning, in *On Grammatology*, I was just doing history, in my own way, and of course I was also questioning the concept of history, which is assumed by historians and even by philosophers and philosophers of history. Sometimes the concept of history—say, as theological—has to be questioned and deconstructed. There should be a deconstruction of the main assumptions of historians, of historiography, even of the philosophy of history, not in the name of the eternal, of something ahistorical, but in the name of some other concept of history. I am sure that the historians who are interested in strange texts, in texts which are not the usual corpus, are doing something indispensable. I should add, just as an example, the historical work that is required, at least implicitly, in "Circumfession" has nothing to do with confession, the history of confession, but with the history of circumcision (not only in Judaism but in other cultures) and the link between circumcision and excision. The difference is not only the past of this anthropological history but what's going on today with circumcision and excision, which is to me a very dramatic and demanding question—especially excision.

Philippe Capelle: My question will be connected with this question of history, and it will be very short. It is about the status of *memoria* in your thought. I come back to the wonderful commentary that Geoffrey Bennington gave us the first day, and I remember the answer given by Jacques Derrida about the relationship between the truth and the event. If the event has to do with the truth, as Derrida said, and we can understand that in "Circumfession," what about *memoria*, the memory of the event? Augustine's *Confessions* constitute an event, but when Augustine says "*I confess*," the memory of the events is present in that "*I confess*." How is it that the memory as such, not elements of the memory but the memory as such, is present when you say "*I confess*" in "Circumfession"? What is the semantic part of this concept?

Jacques Derrida: That is a very difficult question. You see my difficulty, to answer huge questions quickly, because we do not have time. The "I" of the "I confess" is the problem in this text. That is why at the very end of "Circumfession" I ask the question of signature. How could I sign, being this and the opposite? I cannot sign this circumfession, which means that the "I" is not constituted prior to the confession. The confession, or the circumfession, which is not a Christian confession, this strange thing that I call circumfession, this hybrid of Judaism, already a strange sort of Judaism and Christianity, is a monstrosity. But what this monstrosity is about is not the confession of a prior "I" (an "I" that would be prior to the confession), but the circumfession trying to constitute an "I," as if it were possible. I would never say "*I confess*." I probably wrote this, but if someone says "*I confess*," I would say "you are lying." Why? Because if I say "*I confess*," it means that I am what I am, who I am, identical with myself. I confess something, a crime, and my confessing a crime means that I am not one with my crime, so I exonerate myself from the crime when I confess. I am who I am, so if I'm able to confess, that means that first I'm different from—here is the question of memory—the one who committed the crime. So "I" don't confess. If I am able to confess, I don't confess. That's why the question of the "I" is essential. Perhaps there is confession, but if there is confession, no one would be entitled to sign the confession. If I sign the confession, that would be perhaps useful for the police or for God, but I wouldn't call this a confession. The confession crosses me if it happens. If it happens, circumfession crosses me, marks me, or wounds me, but I wouldn't say "*I* confess," although I wrote this. The whole text, which cannot be summarized in one sentence, challenges the possibility of saying "I confess," as well as saying "I give" or "I forgive" or "I decide." In all these cases, the "I" is in contradiction with what it is supposed to do or to say. The question of the "I"—"the form of an I," as Catherine Malabou wrote—is the question. I'm not relying on any reliable ego in this. Of course, that's why autobiography is not here a genre; rather, it is a question of the possibility of what *they* call autobiography, the *autos* in life. So that is the series of questions. When I challenge the truth as theoretical, or as determinate judgment, or as constative or even performative,[7] when I say that to "make the truth" does not mean to me a constative or performative, that is a way of trying to think another truth. I don't want to give up the idea of truth, the idea of the true. It's a way of trying to think, that is, to remember that the event is true. I would not distinguish between thinking and memory. That's very classical. Heidegger would say the same thing. The event is something that is true, the true being—not the truth—of which cannot be denied. It happens beyond any performativity, beyond any theory. It happens, and that is true—it's "being true," which doesn't belong to the truth in terms of *aletheia, homoiosis, adequatio,* and so on, but true. It happens. If it happens, this is the way it happens. In this being true, it is difficult to distinguish the undeniability of the true and the fiction, the phantasm, and the spectrality. That's why I am so much interested in phantasm. Phantasm is an event. All these conceptual oppositions are challenged by this question.

Richard Kearney: So Jacques, you said it's possible to distinguish between the true and the spectral, or it's not possible?

Jacques Derrida: It's not possible.

Richard Kearney: It's not possible?

Jacques Derrida: It's not possible, no. The spectral is true in this sense, though. Phantasm is true as an event. It's true in a certain way. In a certain way, of course, that is so with religion, too, the question of God. You can say God is phantasm, but it [this phantasm] happens. We have to account for this, which is not easy.

Richard Kearney: Unanswered questions zone, as in this conference. Philippe, maybe you might like to come back on that later, but I'm going to pass on to Geoffrey.

Jacques Derrida: I apologize for being so brutally quick.

Geoffrey Bennington: Thank you. I was planning to try to raise again—and I think I won't immediately, as there's some movement of hesitation—to raise again the question of the sexual, the libidinal. But, in fact, I'm more inclined, given what you just said, to ask you a question about God, to ask you whether you think that, across your work, the name "God," or the concept of God, or the treatment of that concept, has changed. I'm thinking for example of a very striking text and foot-note in *Speech and Phenomenon* where you are analyzing the statement I am, *je suis*, which is obviously germane to the kind of declaration that confession often might seem to be making.[8] Here you say two very trenchant things. First, in the text, you say that the statement "I am that I am" is the confession of a mortal (*"Je suis celui que je suis l'aveu d'un mortel"*). It had a reference to God, to a confession or avowal, and to mortality. Then, I think this is in the footnote, in a very striking formulation, you say that the falsity of the claim "I am immortal" is the truth of the classical concept of truth. That's the first moment where God appears in a particular way. I think I'm only going to give three instances. I'm sure there are many more. Toward the beginning of the text "How To Avoid Speaking," you refer quite rapidly to the situation of always already finding oneself in language.[9] One is always already in language, and in a very breezy parenthesis you say, this is what theology calls God. The third instance is much more recent, much more what we've been talking about in and around *Circonfession*, and this would be a way in which God is more positioned as a figure of a position, of an addressee of indeterminate status, or some way of thinking about an address before the specification of an addressee. Now, seen superficially, these seem like three rather different characterizations of God. I'm interested in what your thoughts are about that, or whether in fact there is some continuity across those three moments that isn't immediately evident.

Jacques Derrida: This is not "superficially"; you've done good work. You say more than I could say. You are providing me with the matrix of a long discourse. I didn't remember, for instance, "This is what theology calls God." I totally forgot that, and so we'll have to reconstitute the context. Now, of course, it's irresponsible for me to try to answer such a question, but let me say a few words nevertheless. You remember in "Circumfession," there is a moment where the I, this fictional signatory of the text, says "I just remembered the word *God*."[10] I try to remember when the word appeared in my life. When was the first time, in my family, when the word occurred to me? I had forgotten—as if the word, the name God, was something that could be forgotten, like the name of someone you meet just once in the street and you forget. No doubt there are a number of different contexts and different uses, different references, of the word *God* in all these texts. But there is, I will argue, some continuity in the obsession with the name, with the names, of God. Of course, there are texts, more scholarly texts, in which I address the question of the names of God, say in "How to Avoid Speaking," but I won't recall this. "I am that I am," as you know, is the vulgar translation of a very complex Hebrew sentence in which the question of time is very difficult. There's a future involved and a past. It's not simply a present. In Hebrew, it doesn't mean "I am who I am." It's more complex. But when I say it is the confession of a mortal, in a demonstration that I cannot reconstitute here, it means that it's not necessary for us to think of God as immortal. As Christians know, God is mortal, and the death of God is a Christian theme. Hegel reorganized, dialecticized, the possibility of God's death and of the infinity of God becoming finite in order for it to come back to itself through death. So death, Jesus' death, is in an essential moment in the essence of God. But I say that language is what has to be constantly presupposed, and this is what theology calls God. Wherever in logic there is an absolute presupposition, we can always call this God. God may be the name for any *x* being presupposed in language. This would be the link with what was probably, in my own life, the most constant reference to what may be called God. From my childhood home, this could be named God without any possibility of knowing what it is, or possibility of determining any content to this name—I won't say "concept" but "name"—of God. It is the question of the addressee, that is, the other. The addressee—precisely because of the structure of the trace, when a trace is addressed and left without any firm and assured destination—[is indeterminate]; we don't know whom we are addressing. Even if I know now that I'm addressing you, I know that because my language is intelligible, to some extent, it can be addressed to others. The indeterminacy of the addressee is part of the structure of the trace. God would be this one to whom I am supposed to speak, the other unknown and undetermined, which is presupposed not only by my speech but by any trace. Of course, the best example of this trace of what I call *destinerrance*, wandering destination, destinerring, which could not be a theoretical one, a theoretical speech act, but something pre-theoretical, would be prayer. Not when I pray by asking for a favor of God, not when I am kneeling, but simply when I address the other, when I leave a mark, a trace, destined to I don't know whom because it can always be lost. I'm asking for something. I address you, "Please answer me." And even if you don't answer me, I promise I'm speaking to you. I'm addressing you. I'm leaving a trace [directed] to you. God would be the name of this absolutely unknown indeterminate addressee. The possibility of the address is implied not only in any speech act, but implied in any left trace, left not only by human beings but by any living being. When someone leaves a trace—an animal leaves a trace—not mastering the destination of the trace, then these unknown addressees might be called God. That's the original religion, so to speak, which does not mean that this genesis of religion reduces religion to nothing, but that's the condition for a relation to what I call God, in all these contexts. I have to stop. I promise what I write on this subject is less weak than what I say now, but I cannot, of course, improvise.

Richard Kearney: I am sure we'll come back to it when we open the floor for questions.

Hent De Vries: I would like to ask a question which I hope follows up on the things that were just said. I would like to return briefly two motifs, or three perhaps, that were broached today, namely that of the phenomenological *epoché*, that of formal indication, and perhaps of a certain indifference. You said today during the discussion, and it was reiterated throughout the conference, that "Circumfession" is a unique text, speaks of a unique event, in that it speaks of circumcision, not as an abstract or an historical category, but of *my* circumcision. Yet at the same time, there is a structure of exemplarity so that one can generalize, universalize, or in a more complex sense speak of this as something that is the example of much more than the story of my life. My question relates to another important motif in "Circumfession" that I would like to ask you to comment on a little bit more, namely, the formulation "I am the last of the Jews," "I am the last of the eschatologists."[11] We could also perhaps extend this to "I am the last of the confessors." My question is this: to what extent does that formulation, *je suis le dernier*, entail a certain privilege of indifference—let me keep that word, which has everything to do with formal indication, or phenomenological *epoché*, and everything that they entail? I think once you understand the phrase "I'm the last of," as you have elaborated powerfully, this implies the possibility not anticipated by any orthodoxy or heresy, of being at once infinitely close to, and at a infinite remove from, the tradition that one happens to find oneself in, and one does that by both affirming and negating it. Now my question is, when you articulate that possibility of relating to religion, for example, by being at once close to, and then at an infinite remove from, that tradition, what does that entail? Could we distinguish between what I could call a concrete alliance and a certain articulation of a more formal structure? It is clear in the text of "Circumfession," but also in other texts, in *Adieu: Emmanuel Levinas*[12] for example, that when you speak of God as the best example, or of what we call God, you use the figure of God as something that is almost like a stand-in but that could be called by other names as well. One day we may not want to use the name at all, or we may not be able to use the name. Similarly, you are interested in a structure of responsibility in Levinas and the texts of Levinas that Levinas himself says manifests itself, reveals itself, even before the word *God* is pronounced. Now, my question is this: Does this not imply a relative indifference with respect to tradition? How does one nonetheless select one's discourse, one's idiom? Why speak, for example, of messianicity without messianism, but not of Christianicity without Christendom? What is the necessity, or the obligation, or the strategic choice that makes one inhabit a certain idiom? The answer probably cannot be history or biography or any other psychological motif, because we are here working after the *epoché*, having gone through the formal indication. If that distinction can be made, as you said today when you commented on Heidegger, to what extent can one distance oneself from what you have called an aporia, the logic of presupposition? In other words, is the way in which Judaism, Christianity, and other traditions appear in these texts on religion not somehow caught in a dilemma between what I would call, indeed citing your own text *Aporias*,[13] the logic of presupposition, which runs also the risk of a certain metaphysical possibilism, being interested in the possible without inevitably losing sight of this or that concrete possibility, and, on the other hand, the other horn of the dilemma, becoming too concrete, too pragmatic? Of course, you have coined the term, in "Toward an Ethic of Discussion," the Afterword to *Limited, Inc.*,[14] "praggrammatology," which would be situated at the intersection precisely of the structural aspect of any possible tradition and its concrete names or instantiations. But isn't there, and shouldn't there be, a certain privilege of what I called at the out- set a certain indifference, which I don't mean in any pejorative sense, but as pre- cisely indeed the possibility of any concrete tradition?

Jacques Derrida: Thank you. That's a beehive of very difficult questions. No doubt there is a mixture, which is not only mixture but an alliance in me, and probably not only in me, of interest, concern, and indifference—a certain indif- ference being the condition for thinking. In what sense indifference? When I speak of exemplarity, it implies some indifference—whether it is this or that is indiffer- ent. For example, we're addressing the question of the "I." Nothing is more unique and more exemplary—that is, non-unique—than the "I." Everyone says "I." Each time, the "I" is absolutely irreplaceable. No one can substitute for myself, espe- cially when I have to take responsibility; it's absolutely unique. At the same time, Hegel has taught us that the "I" is the most universal substitutable word. So you have in the "I" at the same time the unique involvement of an irreplaceable be- ing and an empty, indifferent reference to something, to any example. Remem- ber Hegel also said, "God cannot be an example," not a *Beispiel*. The name of God cannot be taken precisely as an example, but I would challenge that. I spoke of this in answering Geoff's question. "God" is an English name; there are a num- ber of names, and the Jewish tradition is precisely interested in the namelessness of God or the multiplicity of names for God. The question of the name—the ques- tion of God is the question of the name. As soon as you take into account the struc- ture of exemplarity, you have this alliance of interest and indifference, of substi- tution. I've always been interested in this terrible logic of substitution. Of course, Levinas has too, but I discovered when I was giving a seminar on hospitality that the concept and the logic of substitution was not only the one that Levinas has put to work, but it is also a Christian notion. Louis Massignon refers to the sub- stitution of Jesus Christ, in which the substitution is not simply the replacement of the replaceable, but the replacement of the irreplaceable and the substitution of the unique. The logic of the substitution is terribly threatening and unavoid- able. I'm caught up in this aporia of substitution. If, for instance, when I say "Here I am," I am myself, this one, ready to respond or to take a responsibility at that very moment, I assume or imply that in my place anyone should do the same. It's at the same time a unique, irreplaceable place and a call for a universal replace- ment and substitution.

Now, when I say "I am the last of—," on the one hand, it's a description of some idiosyncrasy. I say somewhere that I am eschatological through and through. I say somewhere that I have a terrible taste for eschatology, for the last. I'm ob- sessed by it. That's mortality. So I am eschatological. When I say, "I'm the last of the Jews," it means, as you know, that there will be no Judaism after me; so I'm the best one, and I'm the exemplary Jew. At the same time, [I am] the worst, the last one, really. Both. That's exactly what I think. I'm being as non-Jewish as pos- sible, as atheistic as possible, so everything I say can be interpreted as the best tra- dition of Judaism and at the same time an absolute betrayal. I must confess, that's exactly the way I feel. That is, I'm constantly in this existential aporia. I feel both ways, and then I try as much as possible to interpret this idiosyncratic situation as exemplary. Then I say, well, to be torn apart by this contradiction is the condition for responsibility, the condition for a decision, the condition for addressing the other. If I were not caught up in this contradiction, if I knew what to do, there would be no responsibility. So, I have to experience this terrible contradiction, which is not dialectical, in order to say "I," to take the responsibility, to address the other as such. I try to take my own idiosyncrasy as a resource for something universal. That's the logic I try to exemplify in *The Monolingualism of the Other*. I remember in *The Post Card*, in the "*Envois,*" one more link with the question of literature and fiction, that when I say "I" nobody will be able to charge me with this or that, because I may be quoting.[15] What is "I"? The "I" is doing that. It's not me; the "I" is not me; it's literature. Even before literature, when I say "I," I may imply some quotation marks around the I because of its structure, which is unique and universal. The "I" is not mine. That's indifference *as* the condition of responsibility, some indifference. I realize what I'm saying here is inconsistent in a certain way, but this is a kind of inconsistency that I take seriously. That is the question of seriousness again. Literature. Is literature serious? Am I serious? Was I serious when I wrote "Circumfession"? I couldn't tell. It depends on you. That's the structure of *The Post Card*. What I say in *The Post Card*, what I write, is to be signed by the other. It's the other's decision to decide. It's up to the other to decide whether I'm serious or not. If you take me seriously, or if you don't—

Richard Kearney: Thank you, Jacques. Before moving on to the next stage of the discussion, I just want to ask you a question on behalf of Jack Caputo, who probably should be sitting up here at the empty place, but in his modesty as co-director of the colloquium absented himself. Two very quick questions: firstly, the phrase which Jack and I have often been puzzled by, but now we have a chance to put it to you, "I rightly pass for an atheist,"[16] why don't you simply say "I am an atheist?" Secondly, when you speak about God in "Circumfession" and elsewhere, are you "mentioning" or "using" God? But, the first question first.

Jacques Derrida: It's the same question. If I knew, I would say that I'm an atheist or I'm not, but I don't know. I don't know for the reasons that I've been trying to explore for years and years. It depends on what the name God names. It depends on a number of questions we are addressing now. You remember in this passage it is my mother who asks me, "Do you believe in God?" and she was frightened by the idea that I would be an atheist. She couldn't understand that. But am I anything else than I'm supposed to be? *Je passe pour athée*. In some circles, it depends on the context. There are community contexts in which that I'm considered an atheist, others in which I am not, and I don't know myself. I would answer these questions with an endless number of protocols, and that's what my life is made of. That's why, from the very beginning of my debate with Searle, and in *The Post Card*, I challenged the possibility of having a rigorous criterion to distinguish between mentioning and using. When I say "God," when I say "I," of course, in everyday life, no doubt, you can distinguish. When I say "I have a train to catch," I'm not quoting, I'm not mentioning, I'm using the word "I." But in the structure of the statement you don't have rigorous criteria to distinguish between mentioning and using. I think that, in the case of God, it's more than ever the case that it's impossible to distinguish between mentioning and using. If you are a radical atheist, and you just mention the word *God*, that means that you are supposed to understand what that word means, that you inherit the word in a culture that you are raised in, a culture in which the word *God* means something. For me, even if I say God doesn't exist, I would immediately say the opposite. God exists to the extent that people believe in God. There has been a history, and there are religions. For me, religions are the proof that God exists, even if God doesn't exist. That's the question. Even if I were able to demonstrate, against all the canonical proofs of the existence of God, that God doesn't exist, it wouldn't demonstrate that God doesn't exist, because religions exist, because people believe in God. They behave and organize their lives according to this belief. There have been not only some events attesting to the fact that people believe in God, but everything in humanity is organized according to this belief. So that's enough. That's God's existence to me. Not simply Christian God, Jewish God, the Islamic God—*something* exists which is named God differently, with different meanings, with different images, with different rights, rituals. But something happened, even if you follow Freud, as a neurosis. Perhaps it's a human neurosis, but human neuroses attest to the fact that something has produced this neurosis. That's God. God is the name of this pathogenic power that produces neurosis, psychosis, paranoia, wars, peace, love, and so on and so forth. Isn't that enough? God exists even if, and especially if, he doesn't exist, because how powerful this nonexistence should be to produce such extraordinary phenomena in what is called man. I never said this publicly up to now.[17]

Richard Kearney: Well, we won't tell anyone.

Jacques Derrida: Please don't.

Richard Kearney: No, no, it's between us. Now I would like to suggest that, with the indulgence of the roundtable participants, we open the discussion immediately to the floor.

Question (Unidentified): I want to speak in relation to the notion of an "I" that confesses. Can the assuming of an "I" also be understood as the assuming of a "we?" In connection with this I wanted to get to the issue of the distinction between a "difference in kind" and "difference in degree." Both the case of the "I" and the "we" depend on a notion of unity, of an "in common."

Jacques Derrida: The difference between "I" and "we" is not a difference in degree. It's a very serious question, the question whether confession can have "we" for a subject. It's a very difficult question. Can we say "we confess?" Today I pay a lot of attention to this phenomenon. There are a number of situations in which nations, communities, head of states, speaking as "we," ask for forgiveness for crimes against humanity, and not only in European cultures, but also in Japanese and

Chinese cultures. The question is, when a Japanese prime minister apologizes for what has been done against the Chinese, is he speaking within a Japanese culture or is he already importing, or inscribing what he says within a European model of international law? That would be one of the directions I would try, if we had time, to answer this question.

Question: My name is Gad Horowitz (University of Toronto), Gad, the son of Aaron the Levite. I too am the last of the Jews. I don't think it's a simple matter, and I'm sure you won't disagree, to be infinitely close to and infinitely distant from a tradition such as Judaism, or any other tradition. One of the first things you mentioned, on our first day, was Yom Kippur, the Day of Atonement. You've just been talking about the difficulty of confessing as a "we." In the service of the Day of Atonement, the whole congregation, together but separately—because everyone is talking at his own speed—is saying all at once "We have done this, We have done that." They've gone through every possible sin. Everyone as an individual confesses to every possible sin whether they've actually done it or not, because, among other reasons, they don't know. So the relationship between the "I" and the "we" is constructed in Judaism in a very interesting way, which is simultaneously extremely individual and extremely collective. I don't think there's anything like this in any other religion, but what do I know about other religions? Another thing is the *kol nidre*,[18] which is the most important prayer that begins the Yom Kippur service, as you may or may not know—

Jacques Derrida: I know.

Questioner: Well, okay. But how many people know that *kol nidre* is recited three times to make sure nobody misses it? Everyone in the Jewish tradition tries to ignore the obscurity of this prayer and not to think about it. It's not even a prayer. It's a declaration in and through which God cancels all the vows, promises, etc, not that have been made, but are to be made in the coming year. They will have been cancelled in advance. What could this mean?[19] Gibbs, in his book *Why Ethics?*[20] says that it's a very obscure prayer and that's the first and only thing he says about it. I suppose that I would like to give you an opportunity to say a little bit more about is the complexity of your relationship to Judaism at this time and in this place, since one of the things that one continues to miss here is a certain ecumenical spirit. There is a kind of dialogue here, which of course makes sense, between Derrida and Augustine; it makes total sense. But at the same time where are Judaism, Buddhism, Hinduism, and Islam? Islam is more important than ever before. Given the events of September 11, Islam brings itself forcefully to our attention. How long will we ignore it?

Jacques Derrida: Thank you. To respond to your question would take a long time. But on the *kol nidre* I would urge you to read a text by a psychoanalyst named Theodor Reich. That's just in parentheses. Now, of course, as are you and probably as is everyone here, I'm amazed by what's happening here between Christians, Catholics, Augustinians, and me. You can trust me. I am not totally unaware of the strange situation, and that is what has to be analyzed—what's happening between deconstruction and the United States. Because this couldn't happen with French Augustinians. There are a number of threads that could be followed to try to understand what's going on now, and I'm as attentive to it as possible. If I may, because we don't have time, I refer you to a text I wrote long before the current events entitled "Faith and Knowledge" in which I try to approach the question of Islam today. I cannot say more now.

Question (David Crownfield, University of Northern Iowa): Yes, again on the question of God. First, I recall that Gabriel Vahanian, in an exchange with Jean-Luc Nancy a number of years ago, responded to a question about whether God exists by saying, "But of course God exists; God exists in the texts." That relates to some remarks you made a little earlier, but also it leads to my question with respect to God and texts. Erich Auerbach in *Mimesis*[21] comments with respect to the gospel of Mark that it is an innovation in classical literature in its treating with dignity and seriousness and respect the lives of ordinary fishermen and carpenters and serving maids and so on. Clearly, that is a function of a text in interplay with the role of the question of God. I use this as prologue to question back in Augustine's *Confessions* where he says, early on as we all remember, "You have made us for yourself, O Lord, and our hearts are restless until they rest in you." This counter-point of rest and restlessness is the thing that intrigues me at the moment. How is it that the figure of God can function—in all its eternity in Augustine's perspective—so powerfully within the text as to sustain the candor and thoroughness of the account of the restlessness, the self-inconsistencies, the confession, the finite, temporal, equivocal confession, which is enabled by the textual figure of the eternal God? How is this literary move accomplished? Obviously, I'm looking beyond the merely literary, but I want to frame it in that context.

Jacques Derrida: You know I'm often charged with using a notion of text that is so wide that everything becomes a text. When I say what attests to the existence of God, even if he doesn't exist, is in the text, I mean not in the written text, not on paper, but in the world as a text. That's what I called the text. I won't repeat that again, but I have elaborated this concept of the text. Now, when you say "powerfully"—God so powerfully does this or that. That is the question of power, the question of the sovereignty of God. We usually identify God with the almighty, that is, with absolute power. I'm trying now in seminars and in texts, by following a political thread, to deconstruct, so to speak, the onto-theological politics of sovereignty. God is supposed to be absolutely powerful in our tradition. I don't know if it is Christian or not. I'm trying to think of some unconditionality that would not be sovereign, that is, to deconstruct the theological heritage of the political concept of sovereignty, without abandoning the unconditionality of gifts, of hospitality, and so on. That means that some unconditionality might be associated, not with power, but with weakness, with powerlessness. Now some would say this is still Christian. There is in Jesus Christ some weakness, some vulnerability, some powerlessness, but there you see that the powerlessness, of course, is also a sign of the almighty. I'm trying to think of some divinity dissociated from power, if it is possible. This would have heavy ethical and political consequences, but it would deserve a long, much longer answer.

Question (*George Heffernan, Merrimack College*): My question is about the motto under the coat of arms of Villanova University, under the aegis of which the conference is taking place. I'm not here to suggest that the motto be changed — that would be ludicrous — but I do want to point out that the way priorities are set in the motto is not unproblematic for the purposes of discussion about post-modernity and philosophy of religion. The motto doesn't say "*veritas, diversitas, caritas.*" It says "*veritas, unitas, caritas.*" I don't need to say once more what so many have said, namely, that there's a sense in which every text that has been spo-ken, or said, or read, or heard at this conference has had as its subtext or context the events of September 11th. It seems to me that whatever else we do say about those events, and however we interpret them, it might perhaps be safe to say that those events are reflective of a profound axiological heterophobia that is wide-spread in our world, if it does not actually pervade it. I was wondering about what we do in the Augustinian tradition, in the philosophy of religion, and even in post-modernity that is inspired by Augustine, because it again seems that there's ten-sion, an ineluctable or inevitable tension, between the quest for *veritas* if the mode in which we do it is supposed to be *unitas,* and the means by which we do it is supposed to be *caritas.* Classic resolutions or pseudo-resolutions of the dilemma aren't going to help. You can't say any longer, well, I love the Pelagian but hate Pelagianism, I love the Manichean but I hate Manichaeism, I love the Donatist but I hate Donatism. No more than we can say today that we love the terrorist but we hate the terrorism. Facile solutions won't work. I'm wondering what a panel of philosophers of religion would say from a postmodern perspective, but also I think from an Augustinian perspective, about how to resolve the obvious tension between *unitas* and *caritas.* It seems like if we can't love all, we can't have all as one, then there's going to be some irreducible other when it comes to the values that we have. What do we do about that?

Jacques Derrida: I'm not sure I got everything.

Richard Kearney: This is your chance to deconstruct Augustinianism.

Jacques Derrida: If I missed, and I probably missed a number of things in your intervention, if I missed something essential please forgive me. First, I would protest against the word postmodernity. I never used this word. I'm not responsi-ble for the use of this word here or anywhere else, nor am I responsible for this.

George Heffernan: I wasn't accusing you of anything.

Jacques Derrida: I have just landed here. I would be sorry if we started to use the events of September 11th as a weapon, as one more weapon. That would be terrorism. I'm afraid that's what is coming, that people will refer to this terrible event in ways which have to be analyzed coldly and not to be abused. Of course, like you and everyone, I'm against terrorism, if it's useful to emphasize this. I don't say I'm against terrorism and I love the terrorist. I never said that.

Richard Kearney: I think his point was about the old solution that you love

Augustine but you don't associate Augustine with the sins of Augustinianism, you can love the terrorist, the sinner, but not the sin—

Jacques Derrida: No. There's a difference here between the question of Augustine and Augustinians and the question of terrorist and terrorism. I can love Augustine, even though my relation to Augustine himself is very ambiguous. Now, my relation to terrorists is very simple. I'm against terrorists and terrorism, so please don't use this argument. I have been in this country for three or four days, and I feel something that I don't like in the pathos of the reaction to this terrible event, the rhetorical abuse of the reference to this terrible event. We have to analyze what happened coldly and responsibly. Now what was the point?

George Heffernan: I thought the question was pretty clear, that it was not an accusation at anyone in any sense of the term. It simply was an invitation, even an exhortation, for us to think about our priorities when it comes to excluding others who have values different from us. The line of questioning is anything but an accusation. It is anything but an insinuation that anyone is for terrorism, Professor Derrida, and I think that the question speaks for itself.

Jacques Derrida: I think that everything that was said, not only by myself but by a number of us here, about the other, about the attention that has to be paid to the other as irreducibly other—and you can put any example under the word "other," any other—and what I said about the addressee, or the originality of our relation to the other before me, all this was already a response to your question, if I understand you.

Question (Leon Redler, London): I come to this discussion from a different place than most of the people here. I'm not a philosopher. I'm not a theologian, but a physician and a psychotherapist, having expatriated myself from New York about thirty-five years ago to work with R. D. Laing and his existential phenomenological approach. I and some colleagues have been trying to extend Laing's work and we are benefiting very much from the deconstructive work of Jacques Derrida and the ethics of Emmanuel Levinas. I'm here today really through the gift of having read Jack Caputo's *Prayers and Tears of Jacques Derrida*,[22] which moved me to tears. I'd like to pick up on a few points from different talks this morning, just very briefly. One, the term "therapeutic harassment," and the other from Hent De Vries's comments after the talk, the expression "mental spiritual exercises." The third thing is the matter of circles, because there's a lot about circles and returns here today. Finally, there's the matter of Jacques Derrida saying he's not consistent. Whether or not God exists, thank God for his inconsistencies. I think Derrida has helped to open the way to spiritual understanding and meaning for many, and certainly for me, and I see his work as a kind of a positive therapeutic harassment in terms of interrupting, disrupting, breaking open a circle. I wanted to say that it seems to me maybe we can emphasize, rather than circles and circumference and even circumcision, rather than that 360 degree move, a 180 degree move of turning around, like we see in chapter 1 of Isaiah, where Isaiah tells the Hebrews that they are turned around backwards, sick from head to feet. Referring also to Corinthians 13, where now I see in a mirror which distorts, but I will come to see face to face, which again is a kind of a turning around. It seems to me we have to give attention to something much greater than a mental spiritual exercise, because a turning around means turning around with one's whole heart and body and soul, as in the Hebrew prayer, you should love the Lord with all thy heart, with all thy soul, with all thy mind, and be mindful of these matters when one's sitting down, standing up, or walking along the way. It's really a plea for taking into account that spiritual exercises have to be wholehearted and with everything we've got.

Jacques Derrida: Just two words about turning around. In the *circum* of circumcision, circumfession, it's not a full circle, but a wound. There's a scar, something that remains open, not a full circle. Then, speaking of therapy, I have nothing against therapy, of course. We need it, not only individually but socially and historically. But I would argue that an experience of forgiveness, or confession, or anything of that sort, which had simply a therapeutic aim would fail, would not be worthy of the name. If I forgive only in order to reach a reconciliation, a reconstitution of the social body, of the social relation, if I forgive or give or confess with a therapeutic strategy, that is, a teleology, to redeem, or to "heal away," as they say in South Africa, then it wouldn't be pure confession or pure forgiveness.[23] At some point we have to give up the therapeutic, which doesn't mean that I'm opposed to therapy, but I would not reduce these things to therapy.

Question (Holly Johnson): I do have a very short question. I would like to know: can a confession be revised? And if so, who does it, and what are the implications?

Jacques Derrida: On the one hand, to be brief—it's an enormous question—an act of confession should take place just once and for all; so there is no revision, in principle. On the other hand, of course, the confession has to be not only revised but renewed and re-confirmed. If I ask for forgiveness, if I confess something just now, if I say "I confess that I've done so," and then forget it, it's not a confession. A confession has to be confirmed like an oath or like a promise. It has to be confirmed, that is, repeated and renewed tomorrow and the day after tomorrow. One of the difficulties is to know what I am confessing. Do I know what I have to confess and who has to be forgiven? Usually, we associate confession with forgiveness, with asking for forgiveness, but should I ask to be forgiven *myself*? Please forgive *me*? or Forgive me *my crime*? Forgive me what? That's the difference between the who and the what. Should forgiveness forgive someone? Or forgive someone for something? The process of determining the who and the what of the sin, or the crime, is a process. It has to be refined. Perhaps my confession today was not refined enough, and I have to revise it. In fact, my crime was more serious than I thought, or I find that I have killed more than one person. That's revision. But at the same time, it must be unique and once and for all. This is an inconsistent answer once more.

Question (Noel Vahanian): I am coming to be and I am ceasing to be, and therefore I forfeit my credibility. I affirm my instability. I inscribe my invisibility. I remember that I'm not remembered, never remembered, as the alterity within me, which is not me. But I write, I speak, I am recorded. At what point am I granted, not the gift to do so, but the temporal place to do so? I am coming to be and I'm ceasing to be. I'm rebelling against admitting otherwise, be it through history or literature. At what point am I allowed to speak *hors-texte*, if that's even possible?

Jacques Derrida: It depends on the way you determine the concept of text. If it's the usual concept of text, that is, the page, the book, or the finite context, then I may be out of the text, I may be excluded from the text, and then the question you raise is necessary. You are someone excluded from the text or the context or the ensemble, and then the ethical, political questions are unavoidable. But if you, on the contrary, enlarge the concepts of text, then no one is out of or excluded. It depends on the way you determine the text and the context.

Question (Valerie Dixon): I'm an assistant professor of Christian ethics at the United Theological Seminary in Dayton, Ohio. My question is for Professor Derrida and Richard Kearney. For Professor Derrida, you spoke earlier about the alliance between interest and indifference. Richard, in your presentation, you spoke about a response to evil as protest and forgiveness. Now, Jesus said to love your enemies, so my question is, what would happen if we substitute love for interest? And what would happen if we go beyond forgiveness to love?

Jacques Derrida: Indifference and non-indifference—I have no measure, no rule, no general criteria, to define this relationship. The only thing I know is that I could not survive, no one could survive, either a total indifference or a total non-indifference. As soon as I speak, for instance, even before I speak, I have to be indifferent, that is, to use general words for concepts in which some indifference is implied. I cannot speak to you, address you, without some indifference, some generality, some distance, some trace, which is a way of erasing the presence, the proximity, and the continuity. Some indifference is necessary even for the most authentic relationship to the other. I would prefer, in that case, to speak of interruption. The interruption is needed for any relationship with the other, as such. That is, my relation to the other, my rapport with the other, implies a break. Without a break, there would be no respect for the other, no relation to the other as such. This interruption is at the same time an interest in the other and a space, a distance, an indifference. This mixture of indifference and non-indifference is the structure of our experience. I used the example of language, but even before, even in a pre-linguistic experience, I have to be at the same time indifferent and non-indifferent. In each situation, of course, there are different modalities of this mixture.

Richard Kearney: I'll just say a brief word, and because I'm aware that there are two questions to come in just a few moments. Protest and forgiveness. Protest, I think, is not only possible but absolutely necessary. Forgiveness, as I said at the end of my talk, is impossible but also absolutely necessary. You cite "Love your enemies." There are situations in all of our minds where that is impossible, and yet it has to be made possible. So who makes it possible? It seems to us that we can't, so if it really is impossible in the way we discussed it in various talks, in the way that Jacques Derrida has discussed it in his writings on the gift and on justice and on forgiveness, can we make the impossible possible? Or if we can't, who can? And is that other in us or other than us that might be able to make the impossible possible God, or what we call God? It seems to me that if we don't make the impossibility of forgiveness possible, then there is no way out of the cycle of vengeance and revenge and the empires of good and evil turning on each other that we simply cannot put up with for much longer. That would be my quick response, but maybe we can talk about it more afterward.

Question (Scott Gotbreck): From the University of North Texas. My question pertains to a question that Geoffrey Bennington didn't get to in asking about the libidinal with respect to St. Augustine's *Confessions.* My question centers on the moments leading up to the confession. Augustine makes reference to his desire for a "now," for a now that never seems to come, a now which is always procrastinated. In Geoffrey Bennington's discussion of the libidinal, ontological, internal time consciousness is quite interesting to me. I was wondering if I could inspire a comment on, not the temporal mode of the confession, but rather the temporal mode of the conversion that moves that procrastinated "now," the now which can never quite seem to be achieved at the moment of conversion, into a temporal shift, one that Lyotard actually addresses and refers to as a turning inside out. Could I inspire a comment on the moment of conversion, as opposed to the temporal mode of confession?

Jacques Derrida: The concept of conversion is very enigmatic. Of course, we think we understand what it means in Augustine's case, in some Christian cases. But the notion of conversion is not necessarily determined by a Christian logic. What is conversion? The moment when there is an absolute break in history, in the course of time and history, when suddenly everything in one's own existence, not only body and soul but in one's own time and history, turns and is totally reversed. This not only may happen, but should happen, beyond any Christian determination. Now each time I, in a non-Christian culture, address the other in order to confess — but we need another word, to change, to make a decision to change — there is a moment of conversion. Every responsibility is a conversion. Out of this very general concept of conversion, how do we determine the history of what one calls Christian conversion, a conversion to Jesus, to a Christian God? That's something else. Obviously, in St. Augustine, the writing of the *Confessions* followed the conversion and told the history of the conversion, but was it the same with Rousseau? Is it the same with people who today would write an autobiography or modern confessions? I don't know, but this would demand a history of what one calls conversion.

Question (Dana Hollander): I'm teaching philosophy this year at Michigan State University. Professor Derrida, you said just now that you are troubled by the rhetorical abuse of the events of September 11th. I was wondering if you could say something more about what gave rise to that observation.

Jacques Derrida: I think the temptation might be to charge everyone who would try—beyond the moment of compassion, of indignation, and of condemnation—to analyze what's happened, why and to whom, to charge this one with being indulgent, "soft on terrorism," as if we had to give up our responsibility as philosophers and as intellectuals. We have to analyze this event in all its dimensions. Of course, the event was terrible. No one in the world, almost no one in the world, could challenge this. It's terrible. It's a trauma. It's in some way unique and unprecedented—although this could be also perhaps discussed.[24] But however legitimate this condemnation may be, this doesn't dispense us from a call to an endless analysis, a political, economic, historical, philosophical analysis. My guess is that for some it would be difficult to publicly address these questions, and not only in this country. That's what concerns me, and as you can see I'm ready to say this publicly. This doesn't mean, of course, that I was less moved or less outraged by these things.

Richard Kearney: On that sober and very timely note I reluctantly bring these proceedings to a close. I thank you all for coming, the participants for the papers they have given over these last two days and for joining us in the discussion this afternoon, and of course Jacques Derrida himself, who once again and for the third time has been the presiding spirit in our deliberations. Lastly, we thank the three graces, Jack Caputo, Michael Scanlon, and Anna Misticoni, who have organized this event once again for us, which, I think you all agree, was a tremendous success. I would like now to call on Jack Caputo to say a few final words.

Jack Caputo: I just want to say *adieu*, which is a word that Emmanuel Levinas and Jacques Derrida have both taught us to use. I trust that all of you will agree with me that this dialogue between Jacques Derrida and St. Augustine is an important one. Speaking for myself, I have learned to read Augustine better than ever, I think, as a result of "Circumfession." I must say that my favorite passage is "I rightly pass for an atheist." I think that's a marvelous formula for all of us, for whatever we rightly pass as, including believers. The most believers can say for themselves is that they "rightly pass" for a believer, like Johannes Climacus, who would never claim to *be* a Christian. There's a believer in me, and there's a nonbeliever in me, and neither one of them will give the other any peace; and that aporia, that impossibility, as Jacques has taught us, is the condition of the possibility of believing. At the very end of "Circumfession," in Periphrase 59, Jacques speaks of being "severed from the truth" (*sevrée de la verité*).[25] In the end, the cut in "Circumfession" is to be cut off from any kind of absolute truth, cut off from the Absolute Secret, which is why we must believe, believe profoundly, even unto death, even to be willing to die for what we believe. But because we're cut off from the absolute truth, we are not willing to kill for what we believe, which is one the lessons of September 11. We do the best we can, and the best we can do is to rightly pass for this or for that. I think that Jacques Derrida scrambles the distinction between atheism and theism. On a deeper level, I don't know what it means, given what I understand by God, to say that Jacques Derrida is an atheist—but then again, he did not say "is" but "rightly passes." Jacques Derrida teaches those of us who have a religious tradition what it means to be religious. I won't say Jacques is my favorite "theologian," because he is already unhappy about my using the word "postmodernism," and I do not want to make him more unhappy. But I will say that we who have a religious tradition are profoundly instructed by his journey.

God be with you, Jacques, and God be with all of you. *Adieu* to all of you.

NOTES

1. Jacques Derrida, "On Forgiveness: A Roundtable Discussion with Jacques Derrida," in *Questioning God*, co-edited with Mark Dooley and Michael Scanlon (Bloomington: Indiana University Press, 2001), p. 71.

2. Jacques Derrida, "Circumfession," in Geoffrey Bennington and Jacques Derrida, *Jacques Derrida*, trans. Geoffrey Bennington (Chicago: University of Chicago Press, 1993), pp. 240–41.

3. *"et ibi legunt sine syllabis temporum, quid uelit aeterna uoluntas tua, legunt, eligunt et diligeunt; semper legunt et numquam praeterit quod legunt [—] non clauditur codex eorum—"* Augustine, *Confessiones*, XIII, xv, 18. Vessey is using his own translation. See "Circumfession," pp. 241–42.

4. Henri-Irénée Marrou, *Saint Augustin et la fin de la culture antique* (Paris: E. de Boccard, 1938), p. 61: "Saint Augustin compose mal. . . ." Cf. his "Retractatio," appended to the second (1949) and subsequent editions: ". . . jugement d'un jeune barbare ignorant et présomptueux" (p. 665).

5. See Jacques Derrida, *Fichus: Discours de Francfort* (Paris: Galilée, 2002), which is the text of the lecture Derrida gave in Frankfurt upon being awarded the Adorno Prize on September 22, 2001, the week before the Villanova conference. This award is given in recognition for outstanding work, in the arts or in any of several disciplines, in the spirit of the Frankfurt school.

6. "Circumfession," pp. 159–60.

7. "Even performatives"—because while performatives are closer to the "event," they depend upon community-wide conventions that preclude the possibility of the singularity of the event. See Derrida's "Composing 'Circumfession'" in this volume; and Jacques Derrida, *Voyous* (Paris: Galilée, 2003), p. 123.

8. Jacques Derrida, *La Voix et le phénomène* (Paris: PUF, 1967), p. 61 n. 1; English: *Speech and Phenomena and Other Essays on Husserl's Theory of Signs*, trans. David Allison (Evanston, Ill.: Northwestern University Press, 1973), p. 54 n. 4.

9. Jacques Derrida, "How to Avoid Speaking: Denials," trans. Ken Friedan, in *Derrida and Negative Theology*, ed. Harold Coward and Toby Foshay (Albany: SUNY Press, 1989), p. 98.

10. Derrida, "Circumfession," p. 117: "Well, I'm remembering God this morning, the name, a quotation, something my mother said . . ."

11. Derrida, "Circumfession," pp. 75, 154, 190.

12. *Adieu: To Emmanuel Levinas*, trans. Pascale-Anne Brault and Michael Naas (Stanford, Calif.: Stanford University Press, 1999).

13. *Aporias*, trans. Thomas Dutoit (Stanford, Calif.: Stanford University Press, 1993).

14. *Limited, Inc.*, trans. Samuel Weber and Jeffrey Mehlman (Evanston, Ill.: Northwestern University Press, 1988).

15. *The Post Card: From Socrates to Freud and Beyond*, trans. Alan Bass (Chicago: University of Chicago Press, 1987).

16. "Circumfession," p. 155; see "Circonfession: cinquante-neuf périodes et périphrases" in Geoffrey Bennington and Jacques Derrida, *Jacques Derrida* (Paris: Éditions du Seuil, 1991), p. 146: "je passe à juste titre pour athée."

17. See "The Becoming Possible of the Impossible: An Interview with Jacques Derrida," in *A Passion for the Impossible: John D. Caputo in Focus*, ed. Mark Dooley (Albany: SUNY Press, 2003), pp. 29–30, and John D. Caputo, "A Game of Jacks," ibid., pp. 41–43.

18. "The Kol Nidre is a declaration rather than a supplicating prayer, as such, which states that all vows made by us to God, made unwittingly or rashly during the year (and unfulfilled) shall be considered null and void. This declaration is made because we take vows so seriously that we consider ourselves bound, even if we make the vows under duress or in times of stress when we are not in full control. This formula gave comfort to those who were converted to Christianity by torture in various inquisitions, yet felt unable to break their vow to follow Christianity." "Holidays and Holy Days—Days of Awe," http://members.aol.com/porchfour/holidays/dayofawe.htm.

19. For a more detailed discussion of this point, see Gad Horowitz, "Global Pardon: Pax Romana, Pax American, Kol Nidre," *Bad Subjects*, No. 58 (December 2001), www.eserver.org/bs/58/horowitz.html.

20. Robert Gibbs, *Why Ethics? Signs of Responsibilities* (Princeton, N.J.: Princeton University Press, 2000), p. 199.

21. Erich Auerbach, *Mimesis*, trans. Willard R. Trask (Princeton, N.J.: Princeton University Press, 1968).

22. John D. Caputo, *Prayers and Tears of Jacques Derrida: Religion Without Religion* (Bloomington: Indiana University Press, 1997).

23. See Derrida's discussion of this point in connection with the South African example in "On Forgiveness," in *Questioning God*, pp. 58–60.

24. Inasmuch as it was preceded by a previous attack on the Twin Towers, it was not completely unpredictable. In that sense, it does not meet the conditions of a singular "event." See Derrida's "Composing 'Circumfession'" in this volume; for a further analysis of September 11, see "Autoimmunity: Real and Symbolic Suicides: A Dialogue with Jacques Derrida," in *Philosophy in a Time of Terror: Dialogues with Jürgen Habermas and Jacques Derrida*, ed. with commentary by Giovanna Borradori (Chicago: University of Chicago Press, 2003), pp. 85–136. This conversation was held just days after the Villanova Roundtable.

25. "Circumfession," p. 314.

PART II

Confessions and Circumfession

three
Time—for the Truth

Geoffrey Bennington

Time for the truth. Of course I have a confession to make to you all. Or rather, two confessions at least, one of which is perhaps more external to the paper I shall be reading tonight, the second perhaps more internal. In each case, though—and here both confessions are absolutely germane to my theme and topic—the confession has to do with *events*. The more external confession is simple: when I accepted John Caputo's invitation to participate in this conference, I did not know that a certain sequence of events would bring me here after a recent period in which I have been packing up my academic and personal life in England and moving to Atlanta to begin a new job there. And still less did I know, of course, that just a few days after my arrival, what we might just call "the event" of September 11 would, literally, befall us. I imagine that this event will more or less explicitly be dictating everything that happens here in the next two days, and my first confession, then, is simply that the paper I shall read is affected by that event in the relatively "external" sense of being relatively unfinished, unpolished, and disorganized.[1]

My second, more "internal" confession is both infinitely more trivial and, for me, simultaneously more troublesome. Like all confessions, perhaps, this one gathers to it issues of truth and untruth (or at least of veracity and mendaciousness), of true and false witness, of exposure and concealment, of innocence and guilt, of self-aggrandizement and self-abasement. My confession (though there's something odd about that possessive adjective, something unsettling already about claiming a confession as "mine") also has to do with *reading*. Perhaps confession as such, in the obscurity of its concept, always has to do with reading (we know, for example, what role reading, the confession of reading, plays in two of our tradition's founding *Confessions*, those of Augustine and of Rousseau), in which case this confession will be still less "mine" or mine alone.

My confession is this: I am, I fear, unable to read the texts I am to discuss to-day. Jacques Derrida's "Circonfession" and Jean-François Lyotard's *La Confession d'Augustin* remain for me unreadable. Something in these two texts, two such different texts, two such different events, frustrates and outdoes my supposed professional competence as a reader (a supposedly competent reader of these two authors at least), opens for me a fearful zone in which accurate gloss and pedagogical clarity appear inaccessible—and perhaps even undesirable. I confess, then, that both of these texts exceed or overwhelm my perceived ability to read, and that they do so, not so much *in continuity with* my professional reading competence, not just by extending and stretching that competence to its farthest reaches and then carrying on beyond into some darker beyond that I could still hope to penetrate and illuminate by dint of prolonging my efforts along familiar lines—not so much that as by striking and breaking that competence from the start, taking it by surprise as soon as these texts are opened, visiting it violently like an infraction I can neither prevent nor exactly welcome. The event of that discomfiting visitation or infraction, however, brings with it something like a truth of reading itself: we read because we do not know how to read, as Lyotard has Augustine say, and we might be inclined to argue that reading as such only ever takes place in an experience of unreadability, an unreadability to which reading would therefore, constitutively, confess.[2]

These two texts are very different, of course, in tone and manner, in discursive status and pragmatic position, as different as their authors themselves in their complex history and friendship. And if they both exceed my ability to read, they do so differently. "Circonfession" is openly and explicitly written *against* my ability to read: not just against my ability to read insofar as I might be the figure of any reader or aspirant reader of Jacques Derrida, but against *my* ability to read, addressed explicitly to me *as* unreadable. "Circonfession," let us say, puts my reading of Derrida, as proposed in the "Derridabase" running more or less smoothly and confidently in the light upper part of the page—puts my reading to the test, and thereby to some extent puts it to shame, even as it offers itself to me as a gift ("This is a present for him alone," says the penultimate period, a present I have perhaps—like all good presents perhaps—so far failed quite to receive—I think it is no accident that Derrida here uses the slightly less common French *présent*, rather than *don*, for "gift" or present, if only because, as the next and final period has it, "it's enough to recount the 'present' to throw G's theologic program off course, by the very present you are making him . . ."). This structure, called for by the explicit contract that Jacques Derrida and I came to when planning the construction of a coauthored book about him, as stated in the preliminary note to the book, the only genuinely cosigned page, this "friendly bet" called up two challenges: the first, that I produce something approaching a general systematization of Derrida's thought; the second, that Derrida immediately prove that systematization to be inadequate by writing something that it did not, and perhaps could not, account for, however carefully or even desperately the systematic account tried (especially in its final *envoi*) to announce its own preparedness for that counter-move (I knew what was coming, but I never expected *this*). And this is thematized almost immediately in "Circonfession" itself, in its third "period" or "periphrasis," which I will quote in my translation (which is not straightforwardly a reading, of course: I may have translated "Circonfession," but that does not mean I was able to read it, for translation stands in an odd, discontinuous relationship with reading to the extent that I am tempted to say that in order to translate I must *not* read):

> If I let myself be loved by the lucky vein of this word [this word *veine* also *meaning* "luck" in colloquial French], this is not for the *alea* or the mine it's enough to exploit by hacking out writing on the machine, nor for the blood, but for everything that all along this word "vein" [the length of this word "vein"] lets or makes come the chance of events on which no program, no logical or textual machine will ever close, [for everything that] since always in truth has operated only by not overcoming the flow of raw happenings, not even the theologic program elaborated by Geoff who remains very close to God, for he knows everything about the "logic" of what I might have written in the past but also of what I might think or write in the future, on any subject at all, so that he can rightly do without quoting any singular sentences that may have come to me and which that "logic" or "alogic" would suffice to account for, transcendental deduction of me, so that I should have nothing left to say that might surprise him still and bring something about for him, who you would be tempted to compare to Augustine's God when he asks whether there is any sense in confessing anything to him when He knows everything in advance, which did not stop my compatriot from going beyond this *Cur confitemur Deo scienti*, not towards a verity, a severity of avowal which never amounts merely to speaking the truth, to making anything known or to presenting oneself naked in one's truth, as though Augustine still wanted, by force of love, to bring it about that in *arriving* at God, something should happen to God, [*qu'en arrivant à Dieu, quelque chose à Dieu arrive*] and *someone* happen to him who would transform the science of God into a learned ignorance, he says he has to do so in *writing*, precisely, after the death of his mother . . . (Circ. 18–19 [15–18])

Derrida's conceptual move in this context (for of course there are still conceptual moves throughout "Circonfession," even as its point—as always in Derrida—is to disrupt, *at some points*, the order of conceptuality) is to disengage confession or avowal from the control of the concept of truth and follow it toward a thought of the event: in confession, already in Augustine, says Derrida, something *arrive à Dieu*, something arrives at God, and in that arrival, something happens to God, so that God (whoever or whatever is in the position of God thus addressed), knowing everything already, did not quite know *this*, or perhaps, knowing this all along, is still surprised by this arrival or event which as such shakes the hold or dominion of truth. And this *happening* in the event of confession or avowal, which makes it always more than just a statement or constatation of truth, is regularly thematized and enacted throughout the text. Already the second "period" refers to an "aveu sans vérité . . . sans hymne . . . sans vertu" (16 [14]), and Derrida rapidly and characteristically radicalizes this to the point where he can claim that confession has *nothing to do* with truth.

"Time—for the truth," I said. You will have already no doubt had a premonition of a double possibility in that title. On the one hand, the more obvious reading is something like "the time has come for the truth (to be told)," the classical Pauline eschatological reconciliation of time and truth assigning a time *to* and *for* the truth, the appointed or appropriate time, *kairos idiois*, or the fullness of time, *pleroma tou chronou*, the time announced when time and truth will coincide and time will, in truth, end. But you will also have heard a more threatening possibility, perhaps, according to which the time would be up, truth's time having come, not in the sense of a fulfillment or resolution, but in the sense that truth would be the next casualty of time, truth itself, after so many other concepts, finding itself now up against its time, time having come to truth, not to find and say its truth, but precisely to make something happen to truth, to produce an event or strike a blow unrecoverable by any teleological economy of truth. Our problem would then be to understand something about the time of such a time or such an event.

Derrida first relates this question to the future. Something intolerable about the *théologiciel* put forward in "Derridabase" would be its claim to know and reduce the future itself. Producing a "logic" or "grammar" of Derrida in the absence of all real citation, I would have implicitly removed all events, all sentences (a memory here, perhaps, in period 5, of Lyotard's forceful alignment of sentence and event in *Le différend*) from all time, produced something like an eventless eternity:

> . . . he cuts out and circumscribes words and even concepts but words or concepts do not make sentences and therefore events, and therefore proper names, supposing that sentences are proper names, let's say that they lay claim to be proper names, which words are never supposed to do, and he has decided, by this rigorous circumcision, to do without my body, the body of my writings to produce, basically, the "logic" or the "grammar," the law of production of every past, present, and why not future statement that I might have signed, now future is the problem since if G., as I believe he was right to do and has done impeccably, has made this theologic program capable of the absolute knowledge of a nonfinite series of events properly, not only the enunciation of this law can ultimately do without me, without what I wrote in the past, or even what I seem to be writing here, but do without, foreseeing or predicting what I could well write in the future, so that here I am deprived of a future, no more event to come from me, at least insofar as I speak or write, unless I write here, every man for himself, no longer under his law, improbable things which destabilise, disconcert, surprise in their turn G.'s program, things that in short he, G., any more than my mother or the grammar of his geologic program, will not have been able to recognise, name, foresee, produce, predict, *unpredictable things* to survive him, and if something should yet happen, nothing is less certain, it must be *unpredictable*, the salvation of a backfire. (Circ. 29–32 [28–31])

But this dimension of futurity cannot itself simply contain the eventhood of the event, salvo as much as salvation that the event, as constitutively unpredictable, might here promise. The obvious and tempting temporal construal of these relations would be to write off the past as having indeed been more or less adequately processed and captured by the pseudo-program called "Derridabase," to concede that it might, at least in principle if not always in fact, have managed to formalize the system of something that then might be called "early Derrida," and to place the time of the event that "Circonfession" itself and subsequent texts would have produced as futural with respect to "Derridabase," which could then (and how could I not confess to this as a tempting reading, an "appeasement," to use a word Derrida underscores in the opening period of "Circonfession"?) draw comfort and credit for having successfully produced the truth of that "early Derrida," withdrawn its temporality by locating it and dating it in time and truth, *and* draw credit for having provoked the very event that would exceed it, for having called or conjured it up, and thereby launched "later Derrida" on his way. But this tempting reading, this insufferably tempting reading, could support itself only by ignoring the complexities of time, truth, and event that "Derridabase" itself already claims to understand, and this is why in period 6 Derrida himself immediately qualifies the appeal to the future that we have just been reading:

> . . . fighting with him over the right to deprive me of my events, i.e., to embrace the generative grammar of me and behave as though it was capable, by exhibiting it, or appropriating the law which presides over everything that can happen to me through writing, what I can write, what I have written or ever could write, for it is true that if I succeed in surprising him and surprising his reader, this success, success itself, will be valid not only for the future but also for the past for by showing that every writing to come cannot be engendered, anticipated, preconstructed from this matrix, I would signify to him in return that something in the past might have been withdrawn, if not in its content at least in the sap of the idiom, from the effusion of the signature, what I was calling a moment ago by the name and that I would be trying, against him . . . to reinscribe, reinvent . . . (Circ. 33–34 [32–33])

My hypothesis today is that this temporality of the event (of the event of an avowal or confession not finally ruled by the value of truth—whence perhaps the early appearance a little later in this same period of the subsequently crucial concept of *perjury*) provides at the very least a point of contact with Jean-François Lyotard's posthumous—and unfinished—*La Confession d'Augustin*. Derrida pushes this dissociation of confession and truth to the point of paradox in period 9, commenting on the Augustinian figure of *making* or *doing* the truth:

> Making *truth* has no doubt nothing to do with what you call truth, for in order to confess, it is not enough to *bring to knowledge*, to make *known what is*, for example to *inform* you that I have done to death, betrayed, blasphemed, perjured, it is not enough that I *present myself* to God or you, the presentation of what is or what I am, either by revelation or by adequate judgement, "truth" then, having never given rise to avowal, to true avowal, the *essential* truth of avowal having therefore nothing to do with truth, but consisting . . . in asked-for pardon. (pp. 49/48)

Lyotard too, in an idiom both very similar and very different from that of Derrida, is concerned to think about the *event* of confession, and thereby its temporality, in a way which, implicitly at least, also suggests an economy of confession, as writing and signature, more powerful than the economy of truth within which it would traditionally be held. His enigmatic posthumous text *La Confession d'Augustin* suggests that, "under" the phenomenology of internal time-consciousness that Husserl reads in Book XI of the *Confessions*, Augustine "sketches . . . a libidinal-ontological constitution of temporality" (pp. 37–38). This suggestion and its further elaboration in the book implicitly invite the reader of Lyotard's work to reconsider all his previous writing in an effort to bring together its apparently disparate periods and concerns: here, it would appear, is an opening to the thought that the early "phenomenological" Lyotard and the mid-period "libidinal economy" might be read together again, belatedly, posthumously, after the "linguistic turn" of the 1980s, in the late "childhood" writings of the 1990s. Such a reconsideration, the broad lines of which I can do no more than sketch out here, will to some extent confirm my own earlier contention that Lyotard's thinking can be centered around the motif of the *event*,[3] but will question the confidence which that earlier presentation showed in the power of the sentence-based philosophy of *Le différend* (1983) to produce an adequate analysis of, among other questions, time.

Augustine's famous comment, which analyses of time seem always destined to quote, "Si nemo a me quaerat, scio; si quaerenti explicare velim, nescio" ("If no one asks me, I know; but if I am asked and want to explain it, I do not know"; *Confessions* XI, 14) should perhaps be taken less as a preliminary gesture, recognizing a difficulty that philosophy will then confront and resolve (so that the natural *telos* of any philosophical explanation of time is to overcome that not-knowing and replace it with clear and explicit knowledge), and more as a positive claim: perhaps time is such that my knowledge of it can only ever be of the order of non-knowledge, or a "knowledge" that disappears when questioned or called to present itself in the form of a theory or a thesis. If time is such that I "know" what it is only when not called upon to thematize or explain it and see that "knowledge" dissolve or disappear when I attempt to articulate it, then it would bear some resemblance to the problem of lateral vision as discussed by Lyotard in *Discours, figure:* the attempt to bring lateral vision into focus immediately loses the object we were trying to investigate just by transforming it into the focal vision that by definition it is not.[4] This analogy suggests that time may be of a similar order, simply lost (or at least distorted back into shape) in any thematic or thetic presentation, and therefore calling for modes of indirection in writing that philosophy traditionally finds difficult to admit. On this view, the problem of time would require philosophy to accept and even affirm the unknowledgeable knowledge suggested by Augustine, not in a gesture of renunciation (simply giving up the question as beyond the reach of philosophy, to be left to the implicit knowledge Augustine suggests), but in an effort of writing (not necessarily of a recognizably "literary" nature, nor simply giving up traditional philosophical demands for consistency and rigor) that would attempt to engage otherwise with this essential obliquity of time, to respect the "knowledge" I have of it when no one asks me, without forcing it into the non-knowledge that emerges when I am called upon to give a philosophical account.[5]

The analyses of time as "presentation" in *Le Différend* are in this respect helpful, not so much in that they would provide a definitive philosophical account of time, but in that they show up the formal impossibility of any such account and to that extent already call for the more allusive and oblique treatment produced by Lyotard in the texts of the 1990s, culminating in the *Confession d'Augustin* itself. *Le Différend* and other associated texts in the 1980s suggest that a sentence "presents" a "universe" *now*, absolutely now, in an event of presentation that constitutively escapes presentation in the universe thus presented. Time can be presented in the form of various temporal markers and relations (deictics and/or date and time-names) in the universe presented, but the event of presentation itself can only ever be presented in a subsequent sentence that takes as its referent the event of presentation of the "first" sentence. But that subsequent sentence itself always again involves a presentation that it cannot itself present, and so on.

This structure is not offered as a definitive account of time but as an account of how time must in part escape any definitive account, the event or occurrence of presentation "as such" being rigorously unpresentable (having no "as such"). This is why, in *Le Différend*, Lyotard can reasonably claim that his insistence on "now" ("absolute" now, not yet bound and situated) as the time of the event does not amount to a revival of the "metaphysics of presence,"[6] and why he can confidently assign as a paradoxical task, to philosophers and others, "to present that there is some unpresentable,"[7] the unpresentability of presentation "itself" giving the resource for inevitably failing attempts to present it in its unpresentability, or as more positively put, to "bear witness" to that unpresentability, such "bearing witness" then being the task (in a quasi-Kantian sense) of philosophers as well as writers and artists.[8]

Once time is thought of on the basis of unpresentable presentation and the "absolute now" that any act of temporalization or thematization presupposes, binds, and thereby forgets (transforming "now" into "the now"), then the pre-synthetic rhythm of presentation becomes the non-subjective "ground" for all (even "passive") syntheses, explaining a claim from a 1987 text called "Time Today" about the self being "essentially passible to a recurrent alterity." This allows Lyotard to analyze the Cartesian *cogito*, for example, as non-foundational in that it relies on the synthesis of two distinct occurrences of the pronoun "I" (in "I think" and "I am") across two distinct sentence-events, that synthesis requiring a third sentence to be carried out (*Le Différend*, §72).

Although the description given in *Le Différend* and other texts from the 1980s is "formal," and to that extent disallows any particular content being ascribed to the event of presentation, it is striking that Lyotard (here, as is often the case, quite close to Derrida), both before and after (but not during) *Le Différend*, seeks help from psychoanalysis to complicate the phenomenological picture with which he begins.[9] In *La voix et le phénomène* in 1967, Derrida had briefly invoked Freud in the context of his own reading of Husserl's *Lectures*, and more specifically suggested that the temporal configuration named by Freud as *Nachträglichkeit* would exceed the descriptive possibilities of Husserl's account (a little earlier, in 1966, Derrida had suggested that *Nachträglichkeit* was Freud's "true discovery," and stressed the rhythmic discontinuity of the temporality implied by Freud's "Mystic Writing Pad"[10]) by introducing into the flow of Husserlian time a radical discontinuity unaccountable in terms of the Husserlian concepts of retention and protention, representation and imagination.[11] And Lyotard himself comes to make massive use of this Freudian figure in his late work, often centered on the motif of *infancy*.[12]

Nachträglichkeit can itself be given a formal description in the sense that in it the Husserlian flow of instants is interrupted by a time which jumps discontinuously from a past with which the present has no conscious retentional or re-memorative link. According to Freud, as early as the *Project for a Scientific Psychology* (1895), a traumatic childhood "experience" is repeated in later life with an experience of uncontrollable and incomprehensible affect: the temporality here is one in which the original "experience" was not really experienced as such at the time of its occurrence and is in a sense *experienced for the first time in its repetition* long after the event: but this second experience, with the affective charge carried from its "first time," appears as a disruption of ability of the later time-consciousness's ability to process it, and is certainly not simply a "memory" of the first event.

The claim, as in Derrida, is that this configuration escapes in principle the type of account of temporality that Husserl is able to provide and generates paradoxes for phenomenological description in that the affect (and even the event) involved cannot confidently be situated as anywhere simply "present."

Lyotard's favorite example is the first that Freud gives in the *Project for a Scientific Psychology*, and indeed, he provides a detailed reading of that case in a text entitled "Emma," taking its title from the name Freud gives his patient.[13] In *Heidegger and "the jews,"* its structure is summarized as follows:

> A first blow, the first excitation, shakes up the apparatus so excessively that it is not registered. A whistle at a frequency inaudible to the human ear (but the dog can hear it), an infra-red or ultra-violet colour. In terms of general mechanics, the force of the excitation cannot be "bound," composed, neutralised or fixed by other forces "within" the apparatus, and as such does not give rise to representation. This force is not put to work in the mind's machine. It is deposited there . . .
>
> The first blow, then, strikes the apparatus with no perceptible internal effect, without affecting it. A shock without affect. At the second blow there takes place an affect without shock: I am buying linen in the shop, anxiety overcomes me, I flee, and yet nothing had happened . . . And it is this flight, and the sentiment that accompanies it, that teaches consciousness *that* there is something there, without its being able to know *what* it is. Informed of the *quod*, but not

of the *quid*. This is the essence of the event, that *there is* "before" *what* there is. (pp. 34–35)

It looks, then, as though Lyotard is here appealing to a specific Freudian example to support his general, "formal" descriptions in *Le différend*. What Freud presents as a specific, and indeed explicitly "abnormal" temporal configuration (that of neurosis), is taken up and generalized to the structure of time "itself," in which events of presentation essentially occur pre-ontologically (the "that" of the event before its "what," the *quod* prior to the *quid*) and are taken up and presented *as* events only after the fact in a subsequent presentation.

But Lyotard is taking more from Freud than some incidental confirmation of the formal structures we have laid out. Freud, from his earliest descriptions of this configuration in the *Project for a Scientific Psychology*, grounds it in what he refers to as "the sexual prematuration of human beings." In other words, the kind of temporal structure referred to as *Nachträglichkeit* is, *in fact*, not just formal, but *essentially* bound up with questions of what Lyotard often calls just "the sexual," and more especially with the issue of sexual difference, as marked in the psychoanalytical account of castration.

It is extraordinarily difficult to come to a satisfactory description of the relation between what I was calling above a "formal" account of time, and the "content" given to that description once this psychoanalytical material is introduced. This "extraordinary difficulty," which Lyotard can hardly be said to have solved, may indeed itself be of the same order as that we began with from Augustine, where the specific "non-knowledge" of time might, I suggested, be taken less as a provisional statement of a confusion later to be triumphantly cleared up by philosophical reflection, and more as a "positive" characterization of the problem of time itself. Lyotard himself regularly suggests that the question of "the sexual" results from an unmasterable "violence," for example in one of the key texts around the notion of infancy, referring to "the event of sexed reproduction in the history of living beings. And in individual ontogenesis, the echo of sexual difference, which is the event whose savagery the entire life of the individual is taken up with 'sorting out [*régler*].'"[14]

On this apparently de-transcendentalized account, then, philosophy itself (for example, in its attempts to come to terms with the question of temporality), would be part of that attempted "working out," and this would perhaps give us the means to return, in conclusion, to the claim in the *Confession d'Augustin*, that Augustine might be said to be elaborating a "libidinal-ontological" account of time. For where *Heidegger and "the jews"* claims that the temporality implied by *Nachträglichkeit* "has nothing to do with the temporality that can be thematized by the phenomenology of consciousness (even that of Augustine)" (p. 33), the posthumous book, as we have seen, seems to ascribe to Augustine himself, "under" the phenomenological description, just the kind of "libidinal-ontological constitution of temporality" we have been brought to via Freud.

The problem Lyotard has here is one that has been haunting all the "infancy" texts through the 1990s and concerns the status to be accorded to the specific detail of the psychoanalytical material that appears essential here: broadly speaking, we can formulate the problem as concerning the relationship between what one of the earliest "Supplément au différend" texts[15] refers to as "the transcendental status of *infantia*" (p. 54), and the apparently more anthropological issue of "the event of sexual difference." The temptation, which Lyotard appears both to recognize and to resist, would be to refer the description of time "itself," and the positive non-knowledge that seems to characterize it, to a specific moment in the Freudian description: the recognition of the symbolic structure of castration as constitutive of humanity as divided into male and female. On this reading, the structure of the event itself, the dislocation of presentation from itself as the "formal" basis of time, the priority of *quod* over *quid,* would find a foundational moment that it would always in a sense be repeating within the structure of *Nachträglichkeit* itself, and that event would be simultaneously the birth of temporality and of sexual difference.

But in fact, this is not the case. Lyotard's effort in these late texts is not, in spite of some tempting appearances, to ground the account of time as originary dislocation or dispossession in an originary *différend* between the sexes, but in a *différend* between "adulthood" and "infancy" (articulacy and the inarticulate) that certainly involves "the sexual" but does not accord foundational status to castration and sexual difference.[16] The "primary" *différend,* which seems, anthropologically speaking, always to pass, in fact, through that of sexual difference, remains "transcendental" in that it takes place, not between two distinct and incompatible ways of articulating time ("male" and "female"), but between articulation itself and the non-negative inarticulateness that Lyotard calls "infancy" or pure affectivity, the infancy that also figures so insistently in confessional texts from Augustine to Derrida.

Lyotard's point here is not to celebrate childhood or infancy "itself" in some nostalgic or idealizing spirit, or even simply to regret the imposition of adult articulation on childhood affectivity or so-called polymorphous perversity. Nor, as is perhaps the case in *Economie libidinale,* to extol the virtues of some undifferentiated libidinal "energy" or "force" prior to its various bindings and articulations. As its name implies, a *différend* entails difference and polemical encounter, and nothing of the order of pure presence. Just as the formal account of presentation suggested a fundamental non-coincidence or dislocation as the "origin" of time, and just as the passage through *Nachträglichkeit* radicalized that dislocation beyond the grasp of concepts such as retention and even *ek-stasis,* so the Augustine book, to which we can finally return in conclusion, will stress an irreducible belatedness in the experience of the event as the very object of confession.[17]

This motif of belatedness, however, can be misleading if it ever implies an eventual *catching up* with an earlier event. Just as in the analyses we summarized from *Le Différend,* where the apparent ability of a second sentence to present the event of presentation of a first sentence does not mean that any sentence ever catches up with presentation "itself," but through its own occurrence confirms the non-presence in general of presentation, so the "absolute event" of God's visitation in Augustine cannot ever become the object of a *successful* (however belated and confessional) presentation. The absolute character of God's visitation is absolute just to the extent that it disrupts temporal linearity: "How would the soul know if the syncope happens once or if it is repeated, when the syncope deprives it of the power to gather the diversity of instants into a single duration? Where to situate or place in relation, in a biography, an absolute visit? Relate it?" (p. 22); or, more radically, "The delay that brings despair to the confessant is not due to a failing of his chronology; *chronos* immediately and as a whole delays. From the fact that even the overpowering visit of the Other, even the incarnation of grace, if ever it truly arrives, subverts the space-time of the creature, it does not at all follow that it withdraws that creature from the . . . ordinary concerns of life" (pp. 35–36).

It is at this point that Lyotard makes the remark, from which we began, about the "libidinal-ontological constitution of temporality." The point here seems to be that "the sexual" shares its (a)temporal structure, as developed through the reading of *Nachträglichkeit*, with divine visitation to the extent that they are potentially indiscernible or at least of equal force: Augustine struggles to distinguish lascivious dreams from those sent by God (p. 39), lacking any sure sign that would separate them out or clarify them in the order of desire:

> Two attractions, two appetites, of almost equal force: what is lacking for one of them to win out over the other? A nuance, an accent, a child humming a tune? Who's talking transcendence here when divine grace is placed on the same level as a lure? Evil is perhaps not substantial, as the Manicheans think, just a matter of will, affirms the repentant, that is, of desire. But the trouble [*le mal*] is that one desires the good like one desires evil [*le mal*]. (p. 41)

And this infiltration of the possibility of evil, via desire, into temporality, would be confirmed in the discussion of memory: through memory, the I can indeed try to gather up the constitutive distension of time in order to gather itself up as "I," but in so doing it merely confirms the temporal disorder it is trying to overcome:

> The contents of memory . . . quiver with a chaotic dynamic that condenses, displaces, tips their images over into each other, endlessly disfigures them. Behind the guardian of time, supposed to keep watch over its order, under its cover, the work of the drives obstinately insists on making the grasp of events languish. The clear phenomenology of internal temporality hides a strange mechanism, the grammar of ways in which concupiscence conjugates the essential deception. (p. 51)

And this would be why Augustine is able to figure God's visit in the very erotic terms that characterize the deceptive concupiscence that that visit is so radically to overcome.[18] (And perhaps too why the motif of circumcision in Derrida, which arguably plays a structural role similar to divine visitation in Lyotard's version of Augustine, is also ambivalently and complexly sexualized at various points in "Circumfession.") The "phenomenological" account of time is inscribed into this more pervasive "libidinal" time, and to that extent itself becomes part of the confessional structure of Augustine's writing, something to be confessed (rather than just professed as a philosophical doctrine), and that structure itself draws out, in the very fact of writing itself, a temporality of desire and concupiscence, essentially complicit with guilty belatedness.[19] (The more Augustine confesses, on this reading, the more he has to confess, according to a logic that appears identical to the one laid out by Paul de Man in his reading of Rousseau's *Confessions*, according to which guilt is produced precisely *by* its confession.) On this reading, then, Augustine already "anticipates" the Freudian structures we saw Lyotard earlier setting against the Husserlian analyses of time. No doubt this mode of "anticipation" would *itself* have to be analyzed in terms of the *Nachträglichkeit* it also thematizes, and it would to that extent escape from any standard account of philosophical history and demand a re-thinking of the temporality and historicity of reading itself, as caught up in structures of belatedness and confession before it reads any particular content.[20] Just this structure, revealed by the confessional complicity of temporality itself and the order of "the sexual," dominates and undermines the phenomenology of temporality under the name of God himself: the experience of God's visitation or revelation is itself of the order of an event that disrupts all temporal grasp and management, including that of the confessional mode itself, which is caught up in the libidinal lure of concupiscence under the pretext of restoring and celebrating the "absolute event" of God: what Lyotard calls "the sexual" tricks and denounces the appearance of phenomenological or more general philosophical mastery, but itself gives rise to no more reliable knowledge claim, so that replacing the word "God" in Augustine with "the sexual" does not, of course, finally provide the true knowledge about time we thought we were seeking:

> *Dissidio, dissensio, dissipatio, distentio,* in spite of the fact that it wants to say everything, the I infatuated with re-membering its life remains split, separated from it. The subject of the confessional work, the first-person author forgets that he is the work of writing. He is the work of time: he waits on himself, believes he is acting himself and catching up with himself, but he is duped by the repeated disappointment that the sexual plots, right in writing, by putting off the instant of presence in all times and tenses.
>
> Thou, the Other, pure Verb in act, life without remainder, are silent. If it encounters you, the I explodes, and time too, without trace. He calls it god because that's the custom, for theology too is the work of consuetude. And here the *différend* is such, between your vertiginous visitation and thought, that it would be as foolish as theology, as false and deceptive to explain that, not the name "god," but the thing itself, *id ipsum*, above and beyond I, mad joy, proceeds from the sexual. For who can take the common measure of what is incommensurable? A knowledge that claims to do so, by stepping over the abyss, forgets it and re-offends. The cut is primal. (pp. 56–57)

The complex passage from the "formal" analyses of the *différend*, via the explicitly Freudian formulations around *Nachträglichkeit*, to Augustine, do not, then, simply represent an attempt to reduce the "transcendental" structure of time to the "anthropological" concerns of human sexuality. Paradoxically, pulling the formal description of essentially unpresentable presentation back through psychoanalysis appears here to give rise to a kind of ultra- (or perhaps radically infra-) transcendental claim ("the cut is primal"), which is scarcely even of the order of a claim, "bearing witness," rather, to the unavailability of what is here brought out to the order of philosophical clarity. This "primal cut," referred by Augustine to the absolute visitation of the absolutely other, does not propose any positive knowledge about time at all, and to that extent it paradoxically confirms our "positive" reading of Augustine's own preliminary profession of non-knowledge about time. To that extent it both confirms the "formal" analysis we took from *Le Différend* and performatively suggests the necessity of that formality's repeated collapse, time after time, into the contingency of events, which is all the time we have left.

In both Derrida and Lyotard, then, the *event* of confession (as writing and as reading) makes something happen to the extent that it disrupts just the kind of positive infinity that we often call "God." The event of the "present," the presenting or presentation of the present, both produces "God" as promised author and/or addressee of that event and outplays God, makes something happen to him, just insofar as the structure of presenting defies any gathering into a presence. This temporal structure is not teleological (though it cannot fail to produce the fantasy of teleological resolution). If "the primal cut" that Derrida and Lyotard bring in their different ways to their understanding and performance of confession is originary, it is also terminal and therefore interminable.

NOTES

1. The second part of this paper, on Lyotard, is in fact a condensed version of a longer discussion published just after the conference: "Time after Time," *Journal of the British Society of Phenomenology* 32, no. 3 (October 2001): 300–311.

2. The general relation between reading and unreadability is the object of a book in preparation.

3. See my *Lyotard: Writing the Event* (Manchester: Manchester University Press, 1988).

4. *Discours, figure* (Paris: Klincksieck, 1971), p. 159; see *Lyotard: Writing the Event*, pp. 73–74.

5. Although rarely thematized in Lyotard, it seems clear that this "effort of writing" also entails an inventive "effort of reading," as we shall see.

6. See *Le Différend* (Paris: Minuit, 1983), p. 114. The remark occurs in the course of a dense "Notice Aristote" inserted into the chapter on "Presentation" that I have been summarizing. In the same "Notice," Lyotard distinguishes his thinking about time from the later Heidegger of the *Ereignis* on the grounds that the latter still thinks of time in terms of gift and destination, i.e., in terms of instances situated within a *presented* phrase-universe, rather than as the bare "occurrence" of the event of presentation of that universe: "[Heidegger] persists in making of 'man' the addressee of the donation that gives and gives

itself in reserving itself in the *Ereignis,* and in particular he persists in seeing the one who accepts this donation as man fulfilling his human destination by hearing the authenticity of time. Destination, addressee, addressor [*destination, destinataire, destinateur*], man, are here instances or relations in universes presented by sentences, they are situated, *to logo.* The *There is* takes place, it is an occurrence (*Ereignis*), but it does not present anything to anybody, it does not present itself, and is not the present or presence. Insofar as a presentation is phrasable (thinkable) it is missed as an occurrence" (p. 115).

   7. This almost ungrammatical slogan first appeared in the polemical article "Réponse à la question: Qu'est-ce que le postmoderne?" (*Critique* 419 [1982]: 357–67, p. 364; reprinted with slight modifications in *Le postmoderne expliqué aux enfants* [Paris: Galilée, 1986], 13–34, p. 27), where it is in fact used to characterize "modern," rather than "postmodern" art. But Lyotard goes on say that "the postmodern would be that in the modern that alleges the unpresentable in presentation itself" (p. 366 [32]).

   8. I cannot here discuss Lyotard's extensive art-writing: in this context, see especially *Sur la Constitution du temps par la couleur dans les œuvres récentes d'Albert Ayme* (Paris: Edition Traversière, 1980); and *Que Peindre? Adami, Arakawa, Buren* (Paris: Editions de la Différence, 1987).

   9. As confirmed in Dolorès Lyotard's *Avant-propos* to the posthumous collection *Misère de la philosophie* (Paris: Galilée, 2000), Lyotard always envisaged writing a "Supplément au Différend" that would extend its analyses. Lyotard himself says as much in "Emma": "But what is lacking in [*Le différend*] is precisely what matters to us here and that I am seeking (as a philosopher) to supply: *quid* of the unconscious in terms of sentences?" (ibid., 57–95).

   10. "Freud et la scène de l'écriture," in *L'écriture et la différence* (Paris: Seuil, 1967), p. 337.

   11. *La voix et le phénomène* (Paris: PUF, 1967), pp. 70–71, also quoting the 9th supplement to Husserl's *Lectures* on the "absurdity" of a belated "becoming conscious of an 'unconscious' content."

   12. I give a fuller account of this motif of infancy in "Before," in *Afterwards: Essays in Memory of Jean-François Lyotard,* ed. Robert Harvey, Occasional Papers of the Humanities Institute at Stony Brook, no. 1 (Stony Brook, N.Y., 2000), pp. 3–28.

   13. This 1989 text is reprinted in *Misère de la philosophie,* pp. 57–95. It begins with some general reflections on the relationship between philosophy and psychoanalysis, and suggests a way of thinking about the not necessarily literary "effort of writing" mentioned above: "I attempt here to maintain the philosophical ambition [*prétention*]: to articulate in intelligible fashion on the subject of something beneath articulation [*l'en-deçà de l'articulable*], that is, a *Nihil,* which is also what excites this very ambition" (p. 60). This is evidently to be read as a version of the earlier "présenter qu'il y a de l'imprésentable" in its specifically philosophical inflection.

   14. *Lectures d'enfance* (Paris: Galilée, 1991), p. 64.

   15. This 1990 text, originally entitled "L'inarticulé ou le différend même," is reprinted in *Misère de la philosophie,* pp. 45–54, as "La phrase-affect (D'un supplément au *Différend*)." I have discussed this text in some detail in "The Same, Even, Itself . . . ," *Parallax* 6, no. 4 (2000): 88–98.

   16. "Emma" ends as follows: "In the perspective traced out here, the difference between the sexes is shocking, has an effect [*fait coup*] only secondarily to the *différend* between child-affect and adult affect. The classical thesis is that it is constitutive of the disorder of adult affectivity. There is, of course, an aporia intrinsic to sexual difference, as it

is articulated as an adult sentence: the feminine is an object quite different from the masculine, and conversely; and yet, their alterity is supposed to orient their affective destination. Their respective objectivity is supposed to direct their reciprocal objectality. It emerges from what I have suggested that the aporia does not reside in this contradiction of an alterity devoted to complementarity. It resides in the untranslatability of infant possibility into adult articulation. Moreover, if the difference between the sexes can be overcome, or thinks itself overcome, this is only to the extent that one or other of the two parties, or both, has recourse to this undifferentiated possibility. There is love only to the extent that adults accept themselves as children" (pp. 94–5).

17. Cf. *La Confession d'Augustin*, p. 17. Again, this motif would mark a point of articulation with Derrida's apparently very different reading of the *Confessions*, for example in "Un ver à soie," in H. Cixous and J. Derrida, *Voiles* (Paris: Galilée, 1998), trans. G. Bennington, in *The Oxford Literary Review* 18 (1996): 3–65.

18. The first part of *La confession d'Augustin* (which Dolorès Lyotard's note describes as the beginning of what would have been the definitive version of the text) opens with this scene of divine violation. I discuss this motif—and especially its insistence on the figure of *a tergo* penetration—in more detail in relation to this and other late Lyotard texts in "Before" (see note 14 above), especially pp. 18–23. The second part (an earlier draft which uses some of the same material) is here clearer as to the articulations I am bringing out (see pp. 75–77), at risk, perhaps, of losing some of the "performative" effects of disruption that Lyotard's "effort of writing" is attempting to produce.

19. "The confession is written posthumously in search of the anthumous, in *distentio*, then. . . . And *distentio* repeats its offence at the heart of confessional writing. It cannot catch up on the delay that it tries to fill, to make up by running after you, after the act. . . . The confession aggravates the delaying of the time it takes to write to proclaim the instant of your actuality, the time spent making up the delay . . . this time wasted gaining time on time" (p. 48).

20. In "Emma," Lyotard has some allusive remarks about a "philosophy of philosophical "reading." Although the context here is one of an apparently polemical stance against a generalized concept of "text," Lyotard is again clearly close to a deconstructive understanding of a textual temporality that is disruptive of any "history of thought" model. I have attempted to elaborate something of a "philosophy of philosophical reading" in the section "Le fil conducteur (de la lecture philosphique)" of my *Frontières kantiennes* (Paris: Galilée, 2000), pp. 109–30. See too, Michel Lisse, *L'expérience de la lecture, I: La soumission* (Paris: Galilée, 1998). It is striking that the second part of *La Confession d'Augustin* (see previous note) opens precisely on the question of reading. In this context, it would also be necessary to analyze Lyotard's writing itself in the book and notably the abundant (and all but untranslatable) use of post-poned syntactic resolution.

Instances

Temporal Modes from Augustine to Derrida and Lyotard

Hent de Vries

la conversion ne se dit que de l'instant [*conversion takes place only in the instant*][1]

Here, I would like to articulate a simple question. What happens if we add the reflections on time in Augustine's *Confessions* to the historical dossier from which Derrida's interrogations of the topos of temporality—from "Ousia and grammè" to *Shibboleth*—take their lead? How would the *Confessions* register among the classical sources—Aristotle's *Physics*, Hegel's *Enzyklopädie der philosophischen Wissenschaften* (*Encyclopaedia*), Husserl's *Vorlesungen zur Phänomenologie des inneren Zeitbewusstsein* (*The Phenomenology of Inner Time Consciousness*), Heidegger's *Sein und Zeit* (*Being and Time*)—that form the horizon for the figures of temporality (the temporal *modes*, not so much the existence or in-existence of time) that Derrida has indefatigably explored? What if "Circonfession" ("Circumfession," in English), together with texts such as "Sauf le nom" and *Mémoires d'aveugle* (*Memoirs of the Blind*), performs the singular task of *reinscribing* Augustine into the philosophical drama acted out between Aristotle and Hegel, Husserl and Heidegger (*reinscribing*, because for most of these authors, including Derrida, the *Confessions* was a reference all along)? To propose this would mean to raise the question of temporality— *quid enim est tempus*, what, then, is time?—only obliquely, given that in "Circumfession" it is never addressed directly, discursively, as such and in these terms, but is instead addressed poetically, rhetorically, in an indirect and testimonial vein—in other words, confessionally and, in a sense to be determined, *circumfessionally*.

In suggesting this, I am not implying that the turn to Augustine should be ascribed to some biographical or autobiographical peculiarity on Derrida's part. He is not the only contemporary thinker to have rediscovered Augustine—especially the meditations on time in the *Confessions*—with a certain delay and belatedness, in retrospection, and to have reinscribed him into a text that, given its confessional mode, is replete with *retractationes*. Indeed, "Circumfession" is not the only text to be punctuated with reconsiderations that redirect our attention to singular motifs, all of them announced but not all of them addressed—or confessed—before.

As I will indicate (without being able to reconstitute the relevant context in its entirety), Jean-François Lyotard has testified to a similar *confessio, conversio, retractatio*, and, as we shall see, spiritual exercise, all circling around the motif of a circumcision of the heart with "an incision," as he puts it, "from within."[2] In his latest writings, notably *La Confession d'Augustine* (*The Confession of Augustine*) and *Misère de la philosophie* (*Destitution of Philosophy*), we find a parallel turning to these theological archives, whose rhetorical and argumentative, figurative and semantic potential had so long seemed inaccessible to, and irrelevant for, philosophical reflection and the "honor of thinking."

In passing, let me note that, mutatis mutandis, the same could be said of Jean-Luc Nancy, who in a recent project entitled "La Déconstruction du christianisme" ("The Deconstruction of Christianity") covers, albeit indirectly, much of the same ground.[3] In fact, some instances of the temporal modes I discuss are most clearly expressed in Derrida's ongoing philosophical conversation with Nancy, especially in the central chapters of *Le toucher, Jean-Luc Nancy* (*Touching, Jean-Luc Nancy*). But let me concentrate here on the texts I mentioned at the outset and raise my simple question: What does it mean when Lyotard thinks of confession—here, "conversion"—in light of a peculiar temporal mode and asserts that "conversion only takes place in the instant," that is to say, can only be spoken of in terms of an instant (*la conversion ne se dit que de l'instant*), instantaneously, as it were?[4] I would like to trace this motif in some detail, not least because here we touch upon a topos central both to Derrida and to a whole tradition of spiritual exercises.

I will proceed in three steps. First, I will distill some elements from Derrida's "Circumfession" that set the stage and will sketch out some premises of my argument. Derrida's version of "conversion," I believe, entails a similar "instant."[5] Second, I will dwell for a moment on the work of Pierre Hadot, whose interpretation of the tradition of spiritual exercises will present a foil against which I want to situate the alternative logic of the instant in Derrida and Lyotard. And third, I will give a summary reading of Lyotard's *The Confession of Augustine*.

Derrida's "Circumfession"

Just as the citation in the opening lines of "Circumfession"—*cur confitemur Deo scienti*, "why we confess to God, when he knows (everything about us)"—forms part of the historical dossier, but not the literal text, of *Confessions* Book XI[6] (it is the title, Derrida reminds us, given to its first chapter by the seventeenth- century translator Robert Arnauld d'Andilly), the *Confessions'* literal question *Quid enim est tempus?* (What, then, is time?), although not explicitly mentioned in Derrida's text, seems omnipresent there. And yet, for the "duration of these few pages [*pendant le temps de ces quelques pages*]," Derrida writes, "Circumfession" follows a different "rule" (32/34). That rule can be rephrased as follows. Instead of addressing the concerns of the *Confessions* (or its question of time) head on, these pages aim to investigate—to circumnavigate and produce (or create, ex nihilo, miraculously and testimonially, as it were)—the very *possibility* of the future, past, and present "event."[7] The text—literally, the subtext—of "Circumfession" is oriented toward the invention of *"unpredictable things"* (31/32, a phrase given in English in the French text).

This does not mean that no further reference to *Confessions* Book XI is given, let alone that the question *Quid enim est tempus?* (What, then, is time?) is simply absent. On the contrary, there is, for example, the passage in which the confessor implores: "And speaking before you, confiding in you *at present* [my italics] what in another period I called my synchrony, telling you the story of my stories, I ask *numquid . . . cum tua sit aeternitas, ignoras, quae tibi dico* [since eternity is Thine, O Lord, dost Thou not know what I am saying to Thee? (XI, i, 1)], why it takes me the time that you give me, and *cur ergo tibi tot rerum narrationes digero* [Why, then, do I tell Thee the detailed story of so many things? (ibid.)], not for the truth, of course, nor the knowledge of it, *non utique ut per me noueris ea, sed affectum meum excito in te et eorum, qui haec legunt* [certainly, not for Thee to learn them through me, but to arouse my feeling of love toward Thee, and that of those who read these pages (ibid.)]" (75–76/74–75). But somewhat surprisingly, the implied temporal mode of these isolated motifs, taken directly from Book XI—Augustine's meditation on time—never becomes thematic as such.

The *"unpredictable things"* that "Circumfession" elicits and puts to work consist, first of all, in singular motifs (rather than motifs of some general category called "singularity"), which escape the formalization—beyond all idiom and independent of any citation—so aptly aimed at by the dates (the datability and, as it were, *already* being dated, indeed, outdated, too late) of Bennington's "Derridabase." The text at the top of the page with the God's eye point of view "presupposes a contract" and "a number of rules of composition"; it attempts to "describe," according to "pedagogical and logical norms . . . , if not the totality of J. D.'s thought, then at least the general system of that thought . . . by turning it into an interactive program which . . . would in principle be accessible to any user" (1/3).

In the text at the bottom of the page, by contrast, Derrida—in "fifty-nine periods and periphrases written in a sort of internal margin between Geoffrey Bennington's book and work in preparation (January 1989–April 1990)" (vii)—agreed to "show how any such system must remain essentially open." The shared "interest" of the two authors resides in the "test" and the "proof"—a *spiritual contest* of sorts—of this very "failure" (1/3). Derrida, so the arrangement went, would thus "write something escaping the proposed systematization, surprising it" (ibid.). This and nothing else, Derrida writes, is the "exercise [*exercice*] with and in which G.

and I are indulging," its "rightful dimension" being "a whispering, the *aparté* of a confessional where we are in for nobody, changing skin every minute [*à chaque instant*] to *make* truth, each his own, to confess without anyone knowing, why one would wish to know or to make that known, like a gift confession must be from the unconscious, I know no other definition of the unconscious" (233/216–17).

This reference to the unconscious explains why the confession revolves not only around an *always still to come* but equally around the vacant spot of an *always already having taken place and passed away*. The confession, the circumfession, is a response, a "postscriptum," as Derrida writes in "Sauf le nom." (In the libidinal parlance of Lyotard's *Confession of Augustine*, it is the aftereffect of an "advance blow"; we will come to that.) It is, Derrida says of Augustine,

> as if the act of confession and of conversion having *already* taken place between God and him, being as it were written (it is an *act* in the sense of archive or memory), it was necessary to add a *post-scriptum*—the *Confessions*, nothing less)—addressed to brothers, to those who are called to recognize themselves as the sons of God and brothers among themselves. . . . But the address to God itself already implies the possibility and the necessity of this *post-scriptum* that is originarily essential to it. Its irreducibility is interpreted finally, but we won't elaborate on that here, in accord with the Augustinian thought of revelation, memory, and time.[8]

"Circumfession" makes good upon that claim. Or so it seems, for the departure from Augustine's thought is no less obvious.

Drawing on the resources of the *Confessions*, Derrida undermines a format— that of formalization—which he does not hesitate to call an outright "theologic program [*théologiciel*]" (30/30). (It is also a cosmo-"geologic" program. We will come to this in a moment, not forgetting that "Geo" is the nickname given to his mother, "Georgette" [261/242], and that the earth, "the origin of the earth" [266– 67/247], plays an important role throughout Derrida's text.) Formalization is a "theologic program" because, like God, it pretends to see and oversee all there is (to say, to write, to confess). Thus, in "Circumfession" as in *Glas*, one version of Absolute Knowledge, of *Savoir absolu*, SA—here with the help of *Saint Augustine*— is played out against (or substituted for) another—another knowledge, another *savoir*, another having self, another having, relating to, oneself, *s'avoir*. This time the encounter happens in the space of a sublinear text (as in "Survivre" ["Living On"], in *Parages*), rather than in between two columns (as in *Glas*). The difference matters little. The format could just as well have been that of a polylogue (as in *Voiles* [*Veils*], in which "Un ver à soi" ["A Silkworm of One's Own"] speaks to Cixous's text "Savoir" in yet a different vein) or another—equally unpredictable— format still to be invented among so many inventions of the other (one recalls that *Inventions de l'autre* ["Inventions of the Other"] is the subtitle of *Psyché*).

Derrida does not simply deny some "presence" of an Absolute Referent—or addressor, address, and addressee. But this "presence" is affirmed only paradoxically, aporetically, in a virtually hypothetical and indeed confessional, *circumfessional*

mode, whose specific temporal mode—but also experience, trial, experiment—
should give us pause. In it, interestingly, the modern phenomenological procedure
of *epochè* and the destruction of the natural (or naturalist) attitude toward the
world—in Husserl's view a "conversion" in its own right—seems intertwined with
the ancient tradition of spiritual exercises. Derrida writes:

> I am trying to disinterest myself from myself to withdraw from death by mak-
> ing the "I," to whom death is supposed to happen, gradually go away, no, be de-
> stroyed before death come to meet it, so that at the end already there should be
> no one left to be scared of losing the world in losing himself in it, and the last
> of the Jews that I still am is doing nothing here other than destroying the world
> on the pretext of making truth, but just as well the intense relation to survival
> that writing is, is not driven by the desire that something remain after me, since
> I shall not be *there* to enjoy it in a word, *there* where the point is, rather, in pro-
> ducing these remains and therefore the witnesses of my radical absence, to live
> today, here and now, this death of me, for example, the very counterexample
> which finally reveals the truth of the world such as it is, itself, i.e., without me,
> and all the more intensely to enjoy this light I am producing through the present
> experimentation of my possible survival, i.e., of absolute death, I tell myself this
> every time that I am walking in the streets of a city I love, in which I love, on
> whose walls I weep myself. (190–92/178–79)

Less than a series of unforeseen motifs—for example, tears, blood, a brother,
another (hidden, given, unwritten, secret) name (83–84/81–82), a "white" and
"immaculate" or "virgin taleth," etc. (84/82, 245– 46/227–28)—the *unpredictable
things*" at which "Circumfession" aims concern, first of all, a "possibility," not least
the possibility (or possible actuality) of calling this "possibility" many limitless
names (that is to say, infinitely and with infinite respect, but also necessarily improper ones, as if *euphemy*—the discourse of apophatic and kataphatic speech—
and *blasphemy* were just two sides of the same coin, tossed up in the chance game
of a deprogrammed writing).

Not an abstract temporal structure, but a nonformalizable, nonsystematiz-
able, and nonsynchronizable—and in that sense, each time singular—instance
is at issue here, one that is testified to (and thus instantiated) in multiple ways.
Unlike the "Being" that, according to Aristotle (and with him Heidegger),
"says"—or, in Heideggerian parlance, "gives"—itself in manifold ways, instances
do not let themselves be gathered under one heading ("Being," "Truth," "Time")
whose meaning (*Sinn*) could be spelled out by metaphysics, ontology, or even
"thought." Nor are the motifs in question mere empirical occurrences (events, actions, words, or gestures), of which ontic or historical discourse could determine
the cause, the effect, and the referent (the sense or *Bedeutung*). The ontological,
like time, is multiplied, disseminated, and singularized beyond recognition—is
counterexemplary. Derrida writes:

> "*only write here what is impossible, that* ought *to be the impossible-rule*" (10–
> 11–77), of everything G. can be expecting of me, a supposedly idiomatic, un-
> broachable, unreadable, uncircumcised piece of writing, held not to the assis-

tance of its father, as Socrates would say, but to my assistance at the death of a mother about whom I ask *to ti en einai* before witnesses, for if G. contests me, it is in the sense of the witness who, through countersigning attestation, confirms the logic of the counterexample, by daring to kill the quotation marks, without quoting me, calling me back to the moment when, like twelve years ago, I did not yet know what circumcision means, *"is there* one? *for the moment it is just a word with which I want, in a more or less continuous way, but why, to do things, to tell stories."* (194–96/181–82)

What is evoked is thus the "possibility" of an event—past, present, or future—deemed to escape "absolute knowledge" no less than all its functional equivalents (archives, programs, databases, Derridabases, and the like). Not this or that event is at stake here—not even the singular instances mentioned earlier (tears, secret names, and the like)—but, if one can say so, the *eventhood*, even the *eventuality* of the event. As with the uniqueness of the event of absoluteness—which is also the absolution of experience or, at least, of the conditions and limitations of its possibility—analyzed by Jean-Luc Marion in *Étant donné: Essai d'une phénoménologie de la donation* (*Being Given: Toward a Phenomenology of the Gift*), the event in question entails the "possibility" (not the reality or "effectivity"!) of a revelation whose paradoxical form of donation *resembles* the irruption, ex nihilo, of the miracle. Not that the event is a miracle, but what we have come to term—for good and for ill—a miracle is the best (most adequate or most articulate) figure for it. Indeed, like the miracle, the general structure of the event remains "undecidable" with respect to the situation—and situatedness—of its occurrence and thus, as it were, "without an adequate cause"[9] of any kind.

In suggesting this, Marion comes close to Alain Badiou's analysis of the singularity of the event, forcefully presented with reference to "religion" in his *Saint Paul: La Fondation de l'universalisme* (*Saint Paul: The Foundation of Universalism*). As we shall see, his position also resembles that of Lyotard, for whom pure obligation cannot cause or regulate the actions it prescribes. In the section entitled "Ethical time," which concludes the chapter "Obligation" in *Le Différend*, Lyotard writes: "Causality through freedom is immediate, that is, without mediation, but also without recurrence. Its efficiency is *instantaneous* [my italics], pure will obligates and that's all. It is but 'beginning' . . . come what may."[10] That it comes to pass at all—or happens and is testified to—is nothing less than a miracle. Derrida says as much when he writes, in "Demeure," his reading of Blanchot's *L'Instant de ma mort* (*The Instant of My Death*):

any testimony testifies in essence to the miraculous and the extraordinary from the moment it must, by definition, appeal to an act of faith beyond any proof. When one testifies, even on the subject of the most ordinary and the most "normal" event, one asks the other to believe one at one's word as if it were a matter of a miracle. Where it shares its condition with literary fiction, testimoniality belongs *a priori* to the order of the miraculous. This is why reflection on testimony has always historically privileged the example of miracles. The miracle is the essential line of union between testimony and fiction.[11]

Consequently, one must associate the miraculous with "the fantastic, the phantasmatic, the spectral, vision, apparition, the touch of the untouchable, the experience of the extraordinary, history without nature, the anomalous."[12] Derrida does so consistently, pointing to monstrosity, the possibility of the worst, which remains forever the condition of the best.

This possibility, we said, has an irreducibly temporal dimension. "Circumfession," albeit indirectly, explains in what sense. Not only does Derrida state that "one date is enough to leave the geologic program behind [*sur place*]" (250/230), but the possibility of the event has, he writes, everything to do with "a sort of compulsion to overtake [*doubler*] each second . . . , doubling [*dédoubler*] it rather, overprinting it with the negative of a photograph already taken with a 'delay' mechanism," more precisely, "the memory of what survived me to be present at my disappearance, interprets or runs the film again, and already I catch them out seeing me lying on my back, in the depth of my earth, I mean, they understand everything, like the geologic program, except that I have lived in prayer, tears and the imminence at every moment [*à chaque instant*] of their survival, terminable survival from which 'I see myself live' translates 'I see myself die.'" (39–40/40–41).

We find this figure of a "doubling" of each second—a temporal procedure that in biblical exegetical parlance might find its counterpart in *allegory*[13]—in Lyotard as well, and I will return to it later. For now, suffice it to note that what escapes the cosmo-geo-onto-theo-logic program is, in the wording of "Circumfession," nothing "except that I have lived in prayer, tears and the imminence at every moment [*à chaque instant*]," etc. To be more precise, to have lived on in prayer and tears is to have lived in an "imminence at every instant"—speaking, like Augustine, with the mother "in the imminence of her death" (193/180)—in a "terminable survival" that converts the gift of life into a gift of death, a giving oneself death, or at least a seeing oneself, while alive, *as* dead and vice versa. Again, it is a topos Lyotard will repeat in *The Confession of Augustine*: "What was taken for life dies in it, and from out of this death there shines forth true life. . . . This classic inversion of the dead and the living weaves its motif through the whole of the *Confessions*, as is the case in the writing of the revelation, in the Psalms, Exodus, Genesis, in John and Paul" (8/25).

But then the cosmo-geo-onto-theo-logic program is also de- and reprogrammed on the screen (the skin, the sky) of an alternative personal computer and propelled—projected—far ahead of itself. In Derrida's words: "I write to death on a skin bigger than I . . . caelum *enim* plicabitur ut liber *et nunc sicut pellis extenditur super nos* . . . sicut pellem *extendisti firmamentum libri tui* [for "the heavens shall be folded together as a book," and now it is stretched over us like a skin. . . . Thou hast stretched out the firmament of Thy Book like a skin (XIII, xv, 16)]" (229–31/213–15). This works also in the opposite direction, since there is a no less permanent "violence of the void through which God goes to earth to death [*se terre à mort*] in me, the geologic program" (272/252). Indeed, from early on, Derrida continues, "the unforgettable power of my discourses hangs on the fact that they grind up everything including the mute ash whose name alone one then retains, scarcely mine, all that turning around nothing, a Nothing in which God reminds me of him, that's my only memory, the condition of all my fidelities" (273/252–53).

Plunged into the "history of penitence, from repentance to regret and contrition, from public avowal with expiation to private avowal and confession" (86/ 84)—a history he may have learned in part from historical studies such as Jean Delumeau's *L'Aveu et le pardon: Les Difficultés de la confession XIIIe-XVIIIe siè-cle* (*Confession and Pardon: Difficulties of Confession from the Thirteenth to Eighteenth Centuries*)[14]—but confronted especially with Augustine's work at "the delivery of literary confessions, i.e., at a form of theology as autobiography" (86–87/ 85), the author of "Circumfession" from here on raises a simple dilemma. Confessing the sin or the guilt of "letting my mother go or letting her down, already burying her under the word and weeping her in literature" (262/243), he wonders whether—in the presence of agony and scars (and hence *possible* death)— one can still be interested in "writing or literature, art, philosophy, science, religion or politics" (87/85). He wonders whether one's sole concern should not rather be the "memory and heart, not even the history of the presence of the present" (ibid.), philosophy's or ontology's sole concern from Aristotle through Hegel, up to Husserl and Heidegger. And then: "I wonder what I am looking for with this machine avowal, beyond institutions, including psychoanalysis, beyond knowledge and truth, which has nothing to do with it here" (87/85); "machine avowal," unlike Augustine (or so it would seem at first glance), for "since the computer I have my memory like a sky in front of me, all the succor, all the threats of a sky, the pelliculated simulacrum of another absolute subjectivity, a transcendence" (228/212).

In other words, the *"anamnesis"* (72/72) of "Circumfession," even where it recalls specific dates—and they are numerous!—circles around "the impassibility of a time out of time" (80/78). That might be said to figure an "immortal mortal," an all too "human inhuman, the dumb god the beast" (80/78), in short: a "contretemps" (65/65), a "no-time lapse" or "absolute lapsus," whose specific *mode*—to avoid the terms "modality" and "structure" here—is, again, far from obvious.

This would seem to be the task that "Circumcision" sets out to fulfill in its attempt to invoke "my religion about which nobody understands anything" (154/ 146): namely, to *"open again the wound of circumcision, analyze that form of secret, the 'my life' which is neither a content to be hidden nor an inside of the solitary self but hangs on the partition between two absolute subjectivities, two whole worlds in which everything can be said and put in play without reserve, with the exception not of this fact but of the bottomless stake of the other world, I write by reconstituting the partitioned and transcendent structure of religion, of several religions, in the internal circumcision of 'my life'"* (228–29/212–13). Such writing, even where it digs itself "to the blood" by reading others, is singular and idiomatic, not to say indexical and idiosyncratic. As it engages "several religions," it nowhere becomes irenic or ecumenical, let alone syncretistic. Indeed, we read: "You never write like SA, the father of Adeodat whose mother is nameless, nor like Spinoza, they are too *marranes*, too 'Catholic'" (250/231).

But it can engage "several religions" only because it belongs to—at least—two "times" at once. Both temporal and historical, the movement of faith—conversion, confession—"is" at the same time not of this world, eternal, the annulment of time, and the transformation of its ordinary concept. Faith marks the instant in which time, after having gone through a painful preparation, touches upon eternity, "consecrates time," and "begins a new time."[15] Derrida says as much when he speaks, in *Donner la mort* (*The Gift of Death*), of a temporality of the "instant," which, paradoxically, belongs to an "atemporal temporality," to an ungraspable "*durée*" that is incomprehensible and can only be affirmed.[16]

Spiritual Exercises?

To better situate this motif—or rather, to comprehend its incomprehensibility, *the reasons for its unintelligibility*—we should briefly contrast "Circumfession" with the tradition of spiritual exercises that runs from Greek, Hellenistic, and Roman antiquity through Augustine, Ignatius of Loyola, Descartes, and Pascal up to the early Wittgenstein and, perhaps, the later Foucault. What are spiritual exercises, and what concept of time—what *temporal mode*—do they imply?

As Pierre Hadot argues in his *Exercises spirituels et philosophie antique* (translated under the all-too-vague title *Philosophy as a Way of Life*, a title that has now also made its way back into French with the recent publication of a series of interviews with Hadot under the title *La Philosophie comme manière de vivre*[17]), the tradition of spiritual exercises is intimately linked with the attempt to establish—and live—"the value of the present instant."[18] As Hadot recalls, the spiritual exercises sought to realize a "state of attention" through a variety of techniques, all revolving around "intense meditation on fundamental dogmas, the ever-renewed awareness of the finitude of life, examination of one's conscience, and, above all, a specific attitude toward time."[19] They consisted in "practices that could be of a physical nature, such as regimes of alimentation, discursive practices, as in dialogue and meditation, or intuitive ones, as in contemplation, but that were all destined to operate a modification and transformation in the subject that practiced them."[20]

In the spiritual exercises "attention and vigilance presuppose continuous concentration on the present moment, which must be lived as if it were, simultaneously, the first and last moment of life."[21] As Marcus Aurelius writes in his *Meditations:* "Let your every deed and word and thought be those of one who might depart from this life this very moment."[22]

In spite of variations in historiographical and terminological detail, Hadot seems convinced of the relative unity of these spiritual exercises in method and aim over time. What interests him most is the expression and renewed study of "the existential attitudes underlying the dogmatic edifices"[23] encountered in antiquity. The tradition of spiritual exercises expresses the need for the self to turn away from everydayness. Such exercises insist on a gesture—a "conversion" or "*metastrophè*," that is to say, a "meditation," "dialogue with oneself," and "act of faith"[24]—to be renewed *at every instance*. (With a broad stroke, Hadot does not hesitate to compare it to Heidegger's concern, in *Being and Time*, with the more than simply conceptual distinction between so-called authentic and inauthentic existence.[25])

Here the differences between Derrida's "Circumfession" and the manuals and meditations of the spiritual exercises begin to emerge. Hadot writes: "Both the Stoics and the Epicureans advised us to live *in the present*, letting ourselves be neither troubled by the past, nor worried by the uncertainty of the future. For both of these schools of thought the present sufficed for happiness. Stoics and Epicureans agreed in recognizing the infinite value of each instant: for them, wisdom is just as perfect and complete in one instant as throughout an eternity. In particular, for the Stoic sage, the totality of the cosmos is contained and implied in each instant. Moreover, we not only *can* but we *must* be happy *right now*. The matter is urgent, for the future in uncertain and death is a constant threat."[26] But how is this *possible* if, as the confessor of "Circumfession" has it, we must live in prayer and tears, that is to say, in an "imminence at every instance" that converts the miracle of life into the disaster of death? For Hadot, the traditional (and perhaps his own) answer is clear: "Philosophy in antiquity was an exercise practiced at each instant. It invites us to concentrate on each instant of life, to become aware of the infinite value of each present moment, *once we have replaced it within the perspective of the cosmos*."[27]

Only this *cosmo-geo-onto-theo-logic* spirituality—accessible, of course, only in privileged moments—went hand in hand with peace of mind, inner freedom, and cosmic consciousness. By this, Hadot writes, "we mean the consciousness that we are part of the cosmos, and the consequent dilation of our self throughout the infinity of universal nature."[28] The motif of the present thus would go hand in hand with the "spiritual exercise of the vision of totality" that can be found, once again, in the *Meditations* of Marcus Aurelius: "Don't limit yourself to breathing along with the air that surrounds you; from now on, think along with the Thought which embraces all things. . . . you will make a large room for yourself by embracing in your thought the whole Universe, and *grasping ever-continuing Time* [*tòn aídion aiôna perinoein*, time everlasting]."[29]

But this cosmic consciousness, "the consequent dilation of our self throughout the infinity of universal nature," and the "vision of totality"—here, of life— could take different forms. Thus, Hadot notes: "For the Epicurean the thought of *death* is the same as the consciousness of the *finite* nature of existence, and it is *this* which gives an infinite value to each instant. Each of life's moments surges forth laden with incommensurable value: 'Believe that each day that has dawned will be your last, then you will receive each unexpected hour with gratitude.'"[30] Whether starting out from a meditation that expands on "life" or that starts out from "death," the intended result would be the same: locating infinite value in each singular instant.

Before spelling out what this means, I should point out that the central motif of a "vision of totality," the sense of *"fusion* with the Whole [fusion *avec le Tout*]"[31] that Hadot identifies with the mystic-cosmic experience, cannot be found in either Derrida or Lyotard—nor can it be found in the Greek and early Christian authors who began the tradition of spiritual exercises. In several contexts Hadot acknowledges having found it in Romain Rolland, whose invocation of the *sentiment océanique* also made its way into the opening pages of Freud's *Das Unbehagen in der Kultur (Civilization and Its Discontents)*.

But what exactly "is" the instant? Elsewhere, in *Qu'est-ce que la philosophie antique? (What Is Ancient Philosophy?)*, the tradition of spiritual exercises is said to differentiate between two ways of defining the instant, that is to say, the present. Thus, for example, the Stoics put forward, on the one hand, an "abstract" and "mathematical" understanding of the present in terms of a mere or virtual "limit between the past and the future." According to this interpretation—familiar also from the skeptical argument found in Book XI of the *Confessions*—there could be no present time, since time is "infinitely divisible" and thus reducible to an "infinitesimal instant."

Following a second definition, on the other hand, the present would be conceived "in relation to human conscience: it would thus represent a certain weight, duration, in correspondence with the attention of the lived conscience [*la conscience vécue*]."[32] This distinction corresponds to the opposition that Bergson, in *La Pensée et le mouvant (The Creative Mind)*, sees between "the present as a mathematical instant that is nothing but an abstraction and the present that has a certain weight [*épaisseur*], a certain duration [*durée*] that more or less defines and delimits my concentration [*attention*]."[33]

Only the second version of the "living present [*présent vécue*]," Hadot claims, could constitute the horizon of the concentration on the here and now aimed at by the spiritual exercise. The two interpretations would thus emphasize the *distentio* and the *intentio animi*, respectively. On Hadot's reading, the tradition of spiritual exercises privileges the latter.

At this point, one can easily see how Derrida's motif of the instant would necessarily point *elsewhere* and do so—for all its meditative quality, technique, and (I dare say) spirituality—in quite a different way. If the platonic philosophical theme expressed in Montaigne's "Philosophizing Is Learning How to Die"—and this source (not some communitarian virtue ethics in the sense of Alisdair McIntyre, Charles Taylor, or Martha Nussbaum) forms for Hadot the "indirect"[34] contact with ancient philosophy—is, as he asserts, "connected with that of the infinite value of the present moment, which we must live as if it were, simultaneously, the first moment and the last,"[35] then this concern seems also that of "Circumfession." But the differences between the two exercises (as well as that of Lyotard) should not be neglected. To live the present instant "as if it were the first or the last"[36] is not quite the same as linking onto "phrases" (Lyotard) or "singular dates" (Derrida) whose occurrence is neither first nor last. What is more, there is no parallel in Derrida or in Lyotard for the "naïveté" that Hadot takes from a famous dictum of Bergson's ("Philosophy is not the construction of a system but the resolution, taken once and for all, to look naively into oneself and around oneself"[37]). On the contrary, at least two different conceptions of "mode of life"[38]—and, consequently, two different views of its temporal mode and its "formative effect"[39]—are at stake here.

The question why this is so brings us back to that of the "instant," the now, the punctual, the point, the moment, the present *hic et nunc*, whose presentness, indivisibility, linear succession, and, as it were, topicality—as one of the tradition's most important philosophemes—Derrida has incessantly queried. From his earliest writings onward, the motif of the instant is not analyzed as that of the "instance of discourse"—to be distinguished from the "entire theory on the sign and on the differential relations between signs"—and the "sentence," the "moment" at which, as Benveniste has argued, "language is poured back into the universe [*reversé à l'univers*]."[40] Nor is the instant confounded with the "muscular time, with beginnings, breaks, and completions"[41] that Gaston Bachelard evokes in his *L'Intuition de l'instant* (the first chapter of which was translated as "The Instant" in an interesting collection *Time and the Instant: Essays in the Physics and Philosophy of Time*).[42] When the instant is said to have no "duration," let alone "temporal flow," its being "fragmented" or "structured" is neither a "failing" nor due to its "contamination" by "action" and "space" (as Bergson seems to have thought).[43] From the purported essentiality of the *punctum* (analyzed in *Psyché*, in the essay on Roland Barthes), not to mention the *nunc stans* or the "living present," to the "artifactuality" and "actuvirtuality" characterized by a singular temporality, a "deconstructed actuality," of sorts,[44] the motif of the instant is, on the contrary, incessantly displaced. The distance traversed runs from the instant that is the supposedly basic—and indivisible—unit of the linear time of sequenced and synthesized presences, to the instant that is not so much "infinitely divisible," reducible to the mathematical notion of an "infinitesimal instant," but—even more paradoxically and aporetically—*toujours en instance*, "always in abeyance," or better, "always pending," as "Demeure," citing Blanchot, reminds us.

But what would "always" mean here if not an altered—generalized—singularity (or singularism) of sorts: a *nunc stans* in a new guise, the *unexpected*, unpredicted, coincidence (if we can still say so) of heterology and tautology, of repetition and of repetition of the same? For one thing, it would mean that "the constancy of God" in life is, in "Circumfession" and elsewhere, omnipresent but "called by other names," so that the confessor could just as well "pass for an atheist" (155/147), for the last (*le dernier*) in the sense of the most just, as much as the least of confessors.

Before articulating a similar motif in Lyotard, let me briefly address one further central question raised by Hadot's work that will help me to situate Derrida's (and Lyotard's) meditations on Augustine more clearly. How does all of this relate to the *Christian* understanding of the ancient tradition of spiritual exercises, its specific rendering of one its central motifs—namely, the "remembrance of God"[45]—and its subsequent systematizations? In order to answer that question, it is useful to recall Hadot's periodizations and formalizations—which are based on a methodological historiographical link between philology and philosophy, Hellenism and Christianity, the Greek and the Latin (inspired by Pierre Courcelle and others)[46]—however schematic they might seem. In his view, "Christianity's acceptance of spiritual exercises had introduced into it a certain spiritual attitude and style of life which it had previously lacked. . . . In the very process of *performing repetitious actions* and undergoing a training in order to modify and transform ourselves, there is *a certain reflectivity and distance which is very different from evangelical spontaneity*. Attention to oneself—the essence of *prosochè*—gives rise to a whole series of techniques of introspection."[47] These should be distinguished from the evangelical message concerning "the announcement of an eschatological event called 'the Kingdom of Heaven' or the 'Kingdom of God.'"[48]

But things are more complicated than this formulation suggests. Although there was a "permanent survival of certain philosophical spiritual exercises in Christianity and monasticism"—exercises whose "reception" introduced a "particular tonality" into Christianity—there was also a tendency among the faithful to "Christianize their borrowings as much as possible."[49] As Hadot goes on to explain, "they believed they recognized spiritual exercises, which they had learned through philosophy, in specific scriptural passages. . . . [T]hroughout monastic literature, *prosochè* was transformed into the 'watch of the heart,' under the influence of Proverbs, 4:23: 'Above all else, guard your heart.' Examination of one's conscience was often justified by the Second Letter to the Corinthians, 13:5: 'Examine yourselves . . . and test yourselves.' Finally, meditation on death was recommended on the basis of First Corinthians, 15:31: 'I die every day.'"[50]

Yet Hadot leaves no doubt that these rationalizations were *allegorizations*, at best. The methodological and historiographical link between the philological and the philosophical (or theological), Hellenism and Christianity, the Greek and the Latin, is at once intrinsic (and close) and loose (at an infinite remove, as it were). Hadot thus concludes that "it would be a mistake to believe that these references were enough, all by themselves, to Christianize spiritual exercises. The reason why Christian authors paid attention to the particular biblical passages was that they were *already* familiar, from other sources. . . . By themselves, the texts from scripture could never have supplied a method for practicing these exercises. Often, in fact, a given scriptural passage has only a distant connection with a particular spiritual exercise."[51]

How does this link between precedent and present *present* or *represent* itself in Derrida and, as we shall soon see, in Lyotard? Although their respective reappraisals and *retractationes* are not strictly identical, and although their works are marked by a parallel *turn to religion*—which is a turning around of religion, in its own right—that leaves intact an initial difference (and, indeed, ultimate *differend*) in their reassessments of Augustine,[52] I will risk some general hypotheses here. To begin with, in both authors we find similar strategies of *appropriation by dis-*

tancing. Each of these strategies submits its absolute and absolved referent (in Derrida, the theologeme "God," Absolute Knowledge, SA, Saint Augustine; in Lyotard, the *arrive-t-il?* the *Is it happening?* of *des il y a,* of a pluralized *Ereignis*) to a certain *epochè,* rendering it hypothetical (virtual, indeed, possible) to the point of absence—one is tempted to say, indifference. Thus, Lyotard says of Augustine: "How could conversion give him light? It exempts him from nothing, it makes everything ring false, the illusory and the true" (55/79). And a little earlier in the text: "With a touch, with a fragrance, with his cry, God perhaps (or is it the devil?) immerses the creature in his presence rather than prizing it therefrom. From the dazed look of daily life, his visit remains hardly discernible, a voice emerging from the next-door garden . . . : several clues strewn among habitual signs, almost without our knowing, we poor readers" (54/78). I will return to this below.

The privileged instance—itself violent—thus seems (somewhat violently) suspended, always kept pending, held in abeyance. Perhaps this is what it would mean, "Circumfession" suggests, to *take the most careful account, in anamnesis, of this fact that in my family and among the Algerian Jews, one scarcely ever said 'circumcision' but 'baptism,' not Bar Mitzvah but 'communion,' with the consequences of softening, dulling, through fearful acculturation, that I've always suffered from more or less consciously, of unavowable events, felt as such, not 'Catholic,' violent, barbarous, hard, 'Arab,' circumcised circumcision, interiorized, secretly assumed accusation of ritual murder"* (72–73/72–73), etc.

Derrida's *retractationes* consist here in providing *post-scripts* that enable him to rearticulate, that is, allegorize, the relationship between the testimonial—or the confessional—and the more abstract, formal, or structural investigation into the *possibility,* the *condition,* and the *condition of possibility* of the event, not least in view of its temporal dimensions or modes. What is more, in this latest *retractatio* the ties with the first and most orthodox of all theological aspirations are not only severed but, equally, reaffirmed, in a singular testimony that knows no identifiable self that would give itself the law: "Here I am, peripheral and transiently, only the series of the 59 widows [the fifty-nine periods and periphrases that make up "Circumfession"] or counterexemplarities of myself, the first to have received from very high up the order" (255/236–37), a "phantom or prophet charged with a mission, heavily charged with a secret unknown to him, the sealed text of which would be in his pocket, commenting on it until he has no breath left for the 59 nations" (257/238). And yet someone—some "one"—who directs himself toward "you," "in the singular": *"when he says 'you' in the singular and they all wonder, who is he invoking thus, who is he talking to, he replies, but you, who are not known by this or that name, it's you this god hidden in more than one, capable each time of receiving my prayer, you are my prayer's destiny, you know everything before me, you are the god (of my) unconscious, we all but never miss each other, you are the measure they don't know how to take and that's why they wonder whom, from the depth of my solitude, I still address, you are a mortal god, that's why I write, I write you my god'* . . . , to save you from your own immortality" (263–64/243–44).

Lyotard's *The Confession of Augustine*

A similar itinerary, I believe, can be traced in the writings of Lyotard, from at least *The Differend* to his posthumously published *The Confession of Augustine*. Here as well, we find a condemnation of the presentness for which Augustine—and Husserl, one of Augustine's most avid readers and an early point of reference for Lyotard—supposedly stands. In the words of *The Differend*:

> Augustine's God or Husserl's Living Present is presented as the name borne by the instance [*l'instance*] that synthesizes the nows. It is presented, though, by means of the phrases in which it is presented, and the now of each of these phrases then remains to be synthesized with the others, in a new phrase. God is for later, "in a moment [*dans un instant*]"; the Living Present is to come. These only come by not arriving. Which is what Beckett signifies. Time is not what is lacking to consciousness, time makes consciousness lack itself.[53]

These passages should, of course, be read against the four other explicit references to Augustine in the book, especially in the "Aristotle Notice," which revisits—and revises?—some arguments put forward by Derrida, especially in "Ousia et grammè," in *Marges de la philosophie* ("Ousia and Gramme," in *Margins of Philosophy*). But I will leave that for now.

The whole chapter from which this discussion in *The Differend* emerges, "Presentation," is devoted to exploring an alternative—in Lyotardian parlance, *phrastic*—model for understanding time well beyond (or before) its metaphysical determinations in light of some "present instant [*l'instant présent*]."[54] "Time," Lyotard writes, "takes place with the before/after implied in phrase universes, as the putting of instances into an ordered series."[55] Time would thus be the instance that synthesizes—or rather, pretends to gather—the "nows," that is to say, instances, while forgetting its character of being itself only an instance, just another phrase, in turn.

Yet time is not only tied to the serial punctuation of phrases, each of which constitutes a virtual mini-cosmos—a singular universe—of its own. Time is also placed against the backdrop, not so much of an infinitely expanded *memoria* or a finite—recounted, narrated—*historia*, but of an oblivion that is irrevocable and, as it were, essential to the very possibility and operation of recollection (hence presentation or, indeed, confession) as such. Lyotard writes: "The presentation entailed by a phrase is forgotten by it, plunged into the river Lethe. . . . Another phrase pulls it back out and presents it, oblivious to the presentation that it itself entails. Memory is doubled by oblivion [or, rather, doubles itself by oblivion, *La mémoire se double d'oubli*]. Metaphysics struggles against oblivion, but what is whatever struggles for oblivion called?"[56]

This motif of oblivion returns in Lyotard's posthumous work *The Confession of Augustine*, based on two lectures given in 1997, only one of which was separately published,[57] and supplemented with a number of "working texts," fragmented paragraphs, sketches, and "Fac-similes." There confession is analyzed as what struggles against oblivion, but confession—and precisely this is Augustine's confession, this time in the singular!—is also what (unwittingly? sinfully? blasphemously?) contributes to oblivion and, as it were, constitutes it from within: "What a way, indeed, of asserting the fact that he is worth nothing! He had to write to save himself from oblivion, and yet through writing he forgets himself" (29/49). A little later in the book's title essay, Lyotard notes that, forgetting himself, the "first person author" is thereby precisely "the work of time: he is waiting for himself to arrive . . . postponing the instant of presence for all times" (36/56). More precisely still, the distance, the *distentio*, increases or widens as the confessions unfold and intensify: "*distentio* recurs, returns in the quick of confessive writing. The delay that this writing seeks to fill in . . . is not to be caught up. The very time taken for the proclamation of the instant of your actuality to be written down, the time taken to go through the delay again, to obtain pardon for misspent time . . .—confession aggravates the belatedness of this time lost in gaining time over time" (28/48).

It is as if Lyotard's Augustine were anticipating the paradoxical structure of the idea of the Infinite, of metaphysical desire, that Levinas finds in the spiritual exercise of Descartes' *Meditations*. Yet Lyotard's turn to this motif—of a desire that deepens, infinitizes, as it approaches the desired—goes hand in hand with a return to the libidinal-economical perspective of his early years.[58] In his rendering: "The *ipse* [or the self, *le soi*] shall not have, does not have, and did not have what it desires. It lacks being, and drugs its privation in temporal mode. It lives a mortal life, it survives, outlives itself, arranges it such that it is never on time for its objects, it *temporizes*. Temporality is its settling down, to *ipse* [*au soi*], its way of getting on with the unaccomplished, with custom, with the deferment of the act. The times decline deception, time bows and relinquishes [or resigns, *résigne*] presence" (32–33/53).

But the present instant is not only (increasingly) postponed, it has always already passed. Futurity and pastness collapse into each other to the point—a virtual point, an instant, once again—of becoming indistinguishable, nothing real, mere modulations of spirit. Lyotard writes:

> Augustine complains that the present flies so rapidly from future to past that the slightest pause is excluded. . . . So much so that none of the three temporal states in which a sign is successively presented truly *is*. Writing tails off between two abysses.
>
> Modern phenomenological thought has made these analyses famous. The temporal instances are not beings but modes according to which an object is presented to consciousness. Augustine says: to the mind, *spiritu*. He respectively names waiting, attention, and memory, the presence to mind of the future, of the present, and of the past. Annihilating acts of intention since they set up their object, diversely but constantly, as absent: not yet there, no longer there, and the there now of the present, ungraspable. Weak tensions in the night of non-being, subsiding into it. (44–45/67–68)

In the unfinished notes—the "Sendings/Envois"—added into the "Notebook [*Cahier*]," the critical perspective on the "synthesis of the nows" formulated in *The Differend* seems to have been slightly modified. Almost approvingly, Lyotard makes the confessor now say: "Of me, you know everything, having made me in an instant, having established in an instant the plan of my terrestrial journey and my peregrination (my pilgrimage) through the *peripeteia* of events, acts, and passions" (66/92). What is different is the suggestion that this instance—the "presence" forever delayed, waited for, to come—is rendered in a peculiar (and, as we shall see, highly paradoxical) way. It is praised, not through jubilation but mournfully, hardly in high spirits but almost mechanically, not theologically but nearly topologically— *theotopologically*—as is testified by the *Confessions'* last two books (XII and XIII), which speak of the "Heaven of Heavens" and the "Bible as Firmament," respectively (and do so well before this becomes a central topos in Hölderlin, the later Heidegger, Levinas, and Nancy):

> How could your incommensurability be put into work, even with regard to a poem, into my finitude, how could your atemporality be put into duration, into the *passage* of melody? . . . How could I contain you, how could my work lodge you in the minuscule *place* (*locus*) that I am? In truth, it is the space of my work, a space-time that inhabits the atemporality and aspatiality that you are, this sky that is not of the skies of the earth, but the "sky of the skies, the heaven of the heavens."
>
> To inhabit is still to say too much since the sky of skies is a non-place and a non-time. What my life and my work inhabit, my *bios* and my *graphè* at once, are the mystery of your creation. It is not you, but your *work*, this originary mystery through which, from nowhere and from time immemorial to time immemorial, time and space have been generated. Through the enigma of your appearance and withdrawal, through this "skin" that you have stretched and drawn like a veil between yourself and the world of creatures, you nevertheless diffuse your power and your knowledge. You effuse (*effunderis*) over us; your "presence" in your work, and so in mine, in my life and my book, has neither place nor moment, it is the presence of an *effusion*. You do not disseminate yourself in your creation, you gather it (*collectio*). My *confession* is not only the recital of the gathering of my life under the law of your work, it *is* this recollection that is due to you. (68–69/93–95)

Neither an emanation nor a dissemination but a gathering, without place or moment, the temporal mode of this confession is that of a delayed present, the presence of an effusion—an instant in abeyance, always pending (*en instance*)— and thus, strictly speaking, an a-, or non-, or counter-temporality of sorts. Measured against the *collectio* of the Other, the confession of the self is "a step that never advances [*le pas qui ne passe pas*]," following the signs of the "other time, without duration, the other field without horizon" (15/33).

Another section of the notes, entitled "Umbilical of Time," explains why this must be so. Like Beckett's oeuvre, as had been noted in *The Differend*, the *Confessions*, Lyotard says, "are written under the temporal sign of waiting. Waiting is the name of the consciousness of the future. But here, because it is a question not only of confessing faith in an end that awaits, that lies 'in sufferance,' but of confessing the *self* [or itself, *se confesser*], of displaying the sufferance of what has been done, waiting must go back through the past, climb back to its source, the up-stream of this faith" (70/96, trans. modified). The narrative, the "temporal intrigue" and "story of my life [*récit de ma vie*]" that follows and that "gives to the succession of events the place that is their due," as historical "facts" and "in their literal sense" (71–72/97), has a strange effect. As Lyotard observes: "Chronology reduced to itself is pure nothing, appearance and disappearance, passing away [*passage*]. The past is what is no longer, the future is what is not yet, and the now has no other being than the becoming past of the future" (72/97–98).

In consequence, Lyotard sees, the temporal mode of the confession is not only that of the evanescence of the instant, of presence, of the present instant. The reverse perspective is valid as well: "The chase after the future through the past that drives and troubles the *Confessions* is only *possible* if, in the evanescence of these times, something withholds, is maintained, immutable" (72/98). Beyond the "non-time" of the "evanescence," the "transitivity of finite being"—which is a "nonbeing," of sorts—there lies another time, an immutable time, the Time of all times, the Time of our lives, whose "hidden semiotics" (16/34) Lyotard introduces as follows:

> The plot of confessive narrative [*L'intrigue du récit confessif*] is only possible if the event *doubles up* [or doubles itself, *se double*] with another meaning, called "allegorical" by exegesis, if the *opera*, things as they are given, also constitute *signa*. It is conversion, then—since it gives us the ability to read signs in works, to read a little of divine writing in the writing of the *bios*—that justifies confession as a journey that goes backward so as to move forward. The narrative plot, which ties together times in themselves of no import, rises up from a point of time that is not in time, from a point from which time deploys its threefold move to nothingness, but which is itself never destroyed.
>
> It is the exploration of this uncanny anchoring of what happens in what does not pass by that is the concern of the entire end of the *Confessions*. (72–73/98)

The end of the *Confessions*, from Book IX and the death of Monica onward, is therefore devoted exclusively, Lyotard suggests, to sounding out the "point from which this narrative is made possible." The "epiphany of the consciousness of time" comes to substitute for the relating of "external events" (73/99), topologically, *theotopologically*, as it were. But this movement is traversed again in the opposite direction:

> The agitated movement of things is succeeded by the dizziness of the soul meditating on the peaceful umbilic of this movement, the motif of which will be resumed by Descartes with the *Cogito*. The prose of the world gives place to the poem of memory, or more exactly the phenomenology of internal time. The whole of modern, existential thought on temporality ensues from this meditation: Husserl, Heidegger, Sartre. (73/99)[59]

But again, in Lyotard's reading, in their very modernity these reflections on time— articulated in terms of a *distentio animi*, appresentation, temporal ecstasies, temporality, historicity, finitude, and freedom (the differences among these temporal modes matters little) — find their ultimate ground in a permanence, an umbilical, an anchoring, a necessity, an *atemporality* and *infinity* of sorts:

> The past is no longer, the future is not yet, the present passes by, but as things (*opera*). And yet, I am aware of their nothingness, since I can think them in their absence. There is therefore a present of the past, and this present, as long as I think it, does not pass. It is this present that Husserl will call the *Living Present*, oddly. In Augustine, this present, immanent to internal consciousness, this umbilic, from which signs become readable to me, this present, then, is like the echo in temporality of the divine Present, of his eternal today.
>
> So autobiography (if it is one) changes into cryptography: the last books of the *Confessions* devour this encrypting of the atemporal in the temporal, eat the Word become flesh and single out within the three temporal ecstasies in which it has been sacrificed and, as it were, dispersed, the kernel of permanence in which they are recollected. (73–74/99–100)

It is the assumption of this "umbilic" — namely, the presence of a permanent presence whose echo we capture — that is no longer accepted by either Lyotard or Derrida. Their confessions, which are "echographies," encrypt a different "atemporal in the temporal"; their spiritual trials and experiments solicit another response in which all reference — to addressor, addressee, and address — is *hypothesized* to the point of indeterminacy and — almost — irrelevancy. Indeed, "there can be no witness of this blow that . . . abolishes the periods, the surfaces of the archive. The tables of memory fall to dust, the blow has not passed" (8/24–25). Or again: "In truth, the blow is a *cut*, in the sense of *n*-dimensional space theory. An *n*-dimensional space-time folds around the naturally three-dimensional volume of the body" (10/27). This leaves us with a difficulty because, as Lyotard adds: "To conceive the logic of these transformations of space, Augustine cannot rely on Dedekind and Poincaré geometry" (10/27). In sum, the visitation precedes and exceeds (if such temporal and spatial metaphors are still appropriate here) the conditions of the possibility of experience in general. "The soul, cast out itself in its home, out of place and moment, intrinsically, what could it place, fix, have memorized of an avatar that abolishes the natural conditions of perception and therefore cannot be perceived as an event?" (6/22). The soul would be deprived of its very "power to gather together the diversity of instants in a single length of time [*en une seule durée*]" (ibid.). As a result of the absolute visit, the soul — the "soul-flesh," Lyotard writes — enters a "phantom state"; it "invites a fairy-story [*conte de fées*], a fable, not a discourse. . . . the rhythms of poetry" (6/23).

The "presence" of which Lyotard speaks in his reading of Augustine is thus even more convoluted than it would seem at first glance. He characterizes time as "disastrous" (33/53), as a lacking or "privation" (32/53) *of* and *in* being (rather than as Being's horizon and meaning, as Heidegger had claimed).[60] Yet tied as it is to a conception (the fissuring and filtering) of a minimal "hope," as the final words of the published part of our text confirm — we will come to that — time, the presence, is *posited* as a postulate—a *mystical postulate*—and an *originary affirmation* of sorts. Everything would come down, for us, to perceiving the difference between this affirmation and the naïveté of which Hadot, and before him Bergson, speak with so much fervor. We are dealing here with two articulations—two temporal modes—of finite humanity against the foil of an infinite Other;[61] two articulations whose essential indeterminacy is all that matters. In Lyotard's words: "Here lies the whole advantage of faith: to become an enigma to oneself, to grow old, hoping for the solution, the resolution from the Other" (55/79).

> And if, after all, I wonder, as philosophers are wont, how I can know that it is *you* that I invoke, and not some idol, then I can respond that I do not invoke you because I know you, but *so as* to know you. The invocation is a quest and search for you, you who have already found me. After all, if I believe that it is you who are in fact looking for yourself in my confession, it is because you have been preached, and because I believe this *preaching. Praedicatus* through the ministry of your son, the preacher who has announced you, speaks in advance. You have wrought through him the *advance* of your presence. My work confesses this advance, strains to be acquitted of it. Its inquest disquiets, its restlessness holds in advance its *rest*, it rests upon your announced but still concealed presence, it has as its end the quiet of your direct presence, in the sky of skies, the heaven of heavens. It has as its end its own end, the end of works, the vision of glory: as its end its becoming an angel. (69–70/95–96)

And a little further, in the fragment entitled "Contretemps":

> You are ahead of me, I run after you, caught short by your nimbleness, to recover all this time dissipated outside you. Much must be endured, so as to shorten duration; much given out, dispersed, so as to gather together. He writes on the run to recover your love, to obtain remission for the evil times, his hand lifted from the sequestered goods of pagan origin, forgiveness for heresy.
>
> The confession chokes at this pace. The breathless writing in which worldly life is restaged does not suspend this life's duration, it prolongs and repeats it. To confess the delay redounds to the passive order of delay, and increases it. Even to proclaim that I am yours, I must still be me, only be me. And that you alone are being and the sign, it must still be me who signs the confession.
>
> But who says that it must be? Who, then, is hurrying me on?" (82–83/108–09)

A definite answer to this question cannot be given, but this at least is certain: "You, the Other, pure verb in act, life without remainder, you are silent. If he encounters you, the I explodes, time also, without trace. He calls that 'god' because that is the custom [*la coutume*] of the day, theology also being a work of custom [*consuétude*]" (36/56–57). And again, while the "dreadful delay that makes the creature run after its truth in vain" and "accursed time in which the encounter with the absolute is incessantly put off" are never "abolished" (12/30) throughout the *Confessions*, throughout life, all this does not exclude "hope"—the most Christian of hopes. While life is "nothing but this: *distentio*, laxity, procrastination"—in a word, "loss of time, time of loss" (56/81)—and while each further confession adds more to sin,[62] it is, paradoxically, the infinity in the delay that allows for some hope: "So night thickens, feebly streaked by the small light of hope" (ibid.). There will always have been "a highly discreet, not to say impish, signaling of the absolute [*une signalétique bien discrète, pour ne dire malicieuse, de l'absolu*]" (16/34), "episodic flashes," "precarious moments of clarity":[63] "We mumble our way through the traces left by the absolute that you are; we spell the letters" (40/62– 63).

For all the loss of time, there is nonetheless a "credit over time," and Lyotard concludes that it is "considerable: however slender it be, this hope overturns time's course with something like an advance blow, the torsion of tomorrow in today. Listen: for by hope we are already saved" (56–57/81). He concludes by writing: "What I am not yet, I am. Its short glow makes us dead to the night of our days. So hope threads a ray of fire in the black web of immanence. What is missing, the absolute, cuts its presence into the shallow furrow of its absence. The fissure that zigzags across the confession spreads with all speed over life, over lives. The end of the night forever begins" (57/82). These are, as it were, his last words—the close of the last text he completed for publication.

A similar—not identical, but similar—hypothesized positing, postulation, and affirmation dictates the performatives, the "perverformatives," that make up the "periods" and "periphrases" of "Circumfession." As we have seen, the "constancy of God" in life—"in my life," Derrida writes—is called here "by other names," by an infinite series of nonsynonymous substitutions, "the omnipresence to me of what I call God in my absolved, absolutely private language being neither that of an eyewitness nor that of a voice doing anything other than talking to me without saying anything" (155/146– 47). This paradox of "omnipresence" as an infinite and almost infinitesimal possibility of the instant, of singular instantiation, alone— a paradox, I have argued, that is central to, but also differently articulated in the tradition of spiritual exercises—that explains the possibility, indeed the necessity and the imperative, of a belonging without belonging, of being the one who *confesses* always the last, that is to say, too late, but of being also the one who confesses the least and, perhaps, who knows, the most.

DERRIDA'S RESPONSE TO HENT DE VRIES

I was, as usual, full of admiration listening to you. If anything, I will just point to some marginal, peripheral points. For instance, the question of spiritual exercises. I would argue that "Circumfession" in its own way is also an exercise, not a spiritual exercise, but nonetheless there is something of an exercise in it. From two points of view: on the one hand, because for a long time I was dreaming of writing a great book on circumcision. In this context, when I had to write something after Geoff's "Derridabase," I had to do something. I tried to train myself to do something with the technical apparatus that I mentioned earlier, an exercise on the computer. What could I do? It was just childish exercise. That's one point of view—"Circumfession" is not a spiritual exercise, but a technical exercise. On the other hand, there is the attention paid to genre, the history of the literary genre entitled "confessions," the literary history of "confessions" from St. Augustine's opening to Rousseau; that's also an exercise. In other texts which are going to be published, I pay attention to this history of genre, that is, of an exercise. That needs to be said.

Then, secondly, Lyotard and Bataille. Of course, there would be a lot to be said, a number of common premises between Lyotard and myself. This is French history, as you realize—the publication of Lyotard's text on Augustine after his death and so on. We share a lot—but we are very different. We have different histories, different backgrounds, but common premises, among which is phenomenology. Bataille has a thinking of the instant, what he calls sovereignty, the ecstasy of sovereignty. It has to do with the instant of the erotic experience of the sacred, laughter, bursts of laughter; that's the instant. When he distinguishes his own interpretation of sovereignty from Hegel's, it's a sovereignty without mastery. I would question this, but nevertheless there is, between his concept of the sovereignty of *Inner Experience* and the question of the instant, something which could be interesting for us here. When he refers to Heidegger—since Heidegger is one of our common references here— he also denounces in Heidegger the professor. He owes a lot to Heidegger as well, but the difference between Nietzsche and Heidegger for him is that Heidegger is *Herr Professor*, with the seriousness that we alluded to this morning.

Now, the question of phenomenology, which is also something we share with Lyotard. None of these things could be intelligible without a common implication of *epochè*. All this is (for me, at least) written under *epochè*, everything, which means a number of things. First, the fictional structure of "Circumfession" under *epochè*. That is, it's an "as if," and what I'm interested in is, after the reduction, the noetic-noematic meaning of what's happening, because the suspension of the thesis of belief is part of the game. So, there is an *epochè* here, which means some fictionality, which means some spectrality too. I have been very interested, as you know, in what Husserl says about the *noema*, which is the non-real component of consciousness. I tried in some footnote somewhere to connect this non-reality of the *noema* with the spectral, with spectrality. And all this is implied in my own way of writing "Circumfession," among other things. Also, because of this, the exemplarity, the exemplary structure of these things. On the one hand, circumcision—I insist on it—is absolutely unique. It's not circumcision in general; it's *my* circumcision, a unique mark on my body, and it is irreplaceable. But on the other hand, in many texts—in "Circumfession" and in "Shibboleth," for instance—I insist on the fact that circumcision is not only Jewish. It's everywhere; it's an exemplary structure of every human experience, of every living experience, so to speak. I associate circumcision with incision, the cut, the mark—so it has, it wants to have, an exemplary structure. This would be impossible without some phenomenological reduction. So it is at the same time unique and exemplary, something I tried to do also in *Monolingualism of the Other*.

One more word—about cosmology. You are right in your answer to the question of place, of topology. Nevertheless, if we had time, I would try to show that in "Circumfession" there is some reference not only to the cosmos, but to the earth, which comes back again and again. *La terre* is being referred to in "Geoff" and the geo-logical, in the name of my mother "Georgette," in the reference to George, to *geo*. There is a constant reference to the earth, which comes back again and again until the end, until the very moment of the signature on earth. So there is everything you said but, in addition to this, the earth, the place, Geoff, the geological, the mother, Georgette. That's the "perver-formative." I'm not sure that when you mentioned the perver-formative that everyone understood what you were referring to. "Perver-formative" is a word that I coined in *The Postcard* to refer to a perversion of the performative. This causes what Werner Hamacher says also about the a-formative, so all of this is, of course, perver-formative.

I want to thank you.

NOTES

1. Jean-François Lyotard, *La Confession d'Augustin* (Paris: Galilée, 1998), "Prière d'insérer."

2. Jean-François Lyotard, *The Confession of Augustine*, trans. Richard Beardsworth (Stanford, Calif.: Stanford University Press, 2000), 3/19. All further references to this work (apart from its publicity text, which was not included in the English translation) will be given in the body of my text, with the page number of the English translation preceding that of the French original.

3. Jean-Luc Nancy, "La Déconstruction du christianisme," *Les Études philosophiques*, no. 4 (1998): 503–19; English: "The Deconstruction of Christianity," trans. Simon Sparks, in *Religion and Media*, ed. Hent de Vries and Samuel Weber (Stanford, Calif.: Stanford University Press, 2001), 112–30.

4. Lyotard, *La Confession d'Augustin*, "Prière d'insérer."

5. Jacques Derrida, "Circonfession," in Geoffrey Bennington and Jacques Derrida, *Jacques Derrida* (Paris: Éditions de Seuil, 1991), 7–291; English: "Circumfession," trans. Geoffrey Bennington (Chicago: University of Chicago Press, 1993), 3–316. All further references to this work will be given in the body of my text, with the page number of the English translation preceding that of the French original. Of "conversion," in quotation marks, Derrida speaks on page 125/119. For an extensive reading of the many motifs of "Circumfession," see John D. Caputo, *The Prayers and Tears of Jacques Derrida: Religion Without Religion* (Bloomington: Indiana University Press, 1997), chapter 6; from a different perspective, see also Hélène Cixous, *Portrait de Jacques Derrida en Jeune Saint Juif* (Paris: Galilée, 2001).

6. Not book 9, as the English translation has it.

7. On the confessional mode, see Hent de Vries, *Philosophy and the Turn to Religion* (Baltimore: Johns Hopkins University Press, 1999), 343 ff.; on the miraculous, see Hent de Vries, "Of Miracles and Special Effects," *International Journal for the Philosophy of Religion* 50, no. 1–3 (2001): 41–56.

8. Jacques Derrida, *Sauf le nom* (Paris: Galilée, 1993), 25; English: "Sauf le nom," trans. John P. Leavey Jr., in *On the Name*, ed. Thomas Dutoit (Stanford, Calif.: Stanford University Press, 1995), 40.

9. Jean-Luc Marion, *Étant donné: Essai d'une phénoménologie de la donation* (Paris: Presses Universitaires de France, 1997), 235 and 236 n. 1. See Alain Badiou, *Saint Paul: La Fondation de l'universalisme* (Paris: Presses Universitaires de France, 1997).

10. Jean-François Lyotard, *Le Différend* (Paris: Minuit, 1983), 185; English: *The Differend: Phrases in Dispute*, trans. Georges Van Den Abbeele (Minneapolis: University of Minnesota Press, 1988), 126.

11. Jacques Derrida, "Demeure: Fiction et témoignage," in *Passions de la littérature: Avec Jacques Derrida*, ed. Michel Lisse (Paris: Galilée, 1996), 13–73, 54; Maurice Blanchot, *The Instant of My Death*; Jacques Derrida, *Demeure: Fiction and Testimony*, trans. Elizabeth Rottenberg (Stanford: Stanford University Press, 2000), 15–103, 75.

12. Ibid.

13. Indeed, the following is not a bad circumscription of allegory: "I unmask and *de-skin* myself while sagely reading others like an angel, I dig down in myself to the blood, but in them, so as not to scare you, so as to indebt you toward them, not me" ("Circumfession," 240/222–23).

14. Jean Delumeau, *L'Aveu et le pardon: Les Difficultés de la confession XIIIe–XVIIIe siècle* (Paris: Fayard, 1964).

15. Cf. Jean Wahl's comment: "L'instant qui commence l'éternité prend place dans un processus long et douloureux. Durée et instant éternels sont intimement mêlés l'un à l'autre" (Introduction to Søren Kierkegaard, *Crainte et tremblement, Lyrique-dialectique par Johannes de Silentio*, trans. P. H. Tisseau [Paris: Aubier Montaigne, 1984], xvi–xvii).

16. See Hent de Vries, *Religion and Violence: Philosophical Perspectives from Kant to Derrida* (Baltimore: Johns Hopkins University Press, 2002), 182.

17. Pierre Hadot, *La Philosophie comme manière de vivre: Entretiens avec Jeanne Carlier et Arnold Davidson* (Paris: Albin Michel, 2001).

18. See Pierre Hadot, *Philosophy as a Way of Life: Spiritual Exercises from Socrates to Foucault*, ed. Arnold I. Davidson, trans. Michael Case (Oxford: Blackwell, 1995), chapter 8.

19. Ibid., 268.

20. Hadot, *La Philosophie comme manière de vivre*, 67.

21. Hadot, *Philosophy as a Way of Life*, 131.

22. Ibid. See also the quote from Marcus Aurelius in Hadot, *Philosophy as a Way of Life*, 84 and 132.

23. Ibid., 104. See also Pierre Hadot's inaugural address at the Collège de France (where he accepted the chair in the History of Hellenistic and Roman Thought in 1983), entitled *Éloge de la philosophie antique* (Paris: Éditions Allia, 2001), translated as "Forms of Life and Forms of Discourse in Ancient Philosophy," *Philosophy as a Way of Life*, chapter 1.

24. Hadot, *Philosophy as a Way of Life*, 91, 93, and 96.

25. Ibid., 122 n. 161.

26. Ibid.

27. Hadot, *Philosophy as a Way of Life*, 273, my italics.

28. Ibid., 266.

29. Marcus Aurelius, *Meditations*, 8, 54; 9, 32; cited in Hadot, *Philosophy as a Way of Life*, 99; see also the translation by C. R. Haines (Cambridge: Harvard University Press, 1999), 227 and 251, respectively.

30. Hadot, *Philosophy as a Way of Life*, 95–96.

31. Hadot, *La Philosophie comme manière de vivre*, 9, cf. 24, 27–28.

32. Pierre Hadot, *Qu'est-ce que la philosophie antique?* (Paris: Gallimard, 1995), 294–95.

33. Pierre Hadot, *La Citadelle intérieure: Introduction aux Pensées de Marc Aurèle* (Paris: Fayard, 1992), 153; English: *The Inner Citadel: The Meditations of Marcus Aurelius*, trans. Michael Chase (Cambridge, Mass.: Harvard University Press, 1998), 136. The reference is to Henri Bergson, *La Pensée et le mouvant: Essais et conférences* (Paris: Presses Universitaires de France, 1938), 168–69; English: *The Creative Mind: An Introduction to Metaphysics*, trans. Mabelle L. Andison (New York: Carol Publishing Group, 1991), 151–52.

34. Hadot, *La Philosophie comme manière de vivre*, 9.

35. Hadot, *Philosophy as a Way of Life*, 96.

36. Hadot, *La Philosophie comme manière de vivre*, 268.

37. "La philosophie n'est pas une construction de système, mais la résolution une fois prise de regarder naïvement en soi et autour de soi," cited in ibid., 29.

38. Ibid., 67.

39. Ibid., 10 and 101.

40. Paul Ricoeur, *La Critique et la conviction: Entretien avec François Azouvi et Marc de Launay* (Paris: Hachette, 2001), 133; English: *Critique and Conviction: Conversations with François Azouvi and Marc de Launay*, trans. Kathleen Blamey (New York: Columbia University Press, 1998), 86.

41. Ibid., 89/137.

42. Gaston Bachelard, *L'Intuition de l'instant* (Paris: Éditions Stock, 1931); English: "The Instant," trans. Mary McAllester Jones, in *Time and the Instant: Essays in the Physics and Philosophy of Time*, ed. Robin Durie (Manchester: Clinamen Press, 2000), 64–92. See also Gaston Bachelard, "Instant poétique et instant métaphysique," in idem, *Le Droit de rêver* (Paris: Presses Universitaires de France, 1970), 224–32.

43. Ricoeur, *Critique and Conviction*, 88/136.

44. See the interview conducted by Brigitte Sohm, Cristina de Peretti, Stéphane Douailler, Patrice Vermeren, and Émile Malet, "Derrida: La Déconstruction de l'actualité," *Passages* (September 1993): 60–75; English: "The Deconstruction of Actuality: An Interview with Jacques Derrida," trans. Jonathan Rée, *Radical Philosophy* 68 (Autumn 1994): 28–41, reprinted in Jacques Derrida, *Negotiations: Interventions and Interviews, 1971–2001*, ed. and trans., Elizabeth Rottenberg (Stanford, Calif.: Stanford University Press, 2002), 85–116.

45. Hadot, *Philosophy as a Way of Life*, 132–33.

46. Cf. Hadot, *Éloge de la philosophie antique*, 9–10/*Philosophy as a Way of Life*, 50–51.

47. Hadot, *Philosophy as a Way of Life*, 136, my italics.

48. Ibid., 137.

49. Ibid., 138–39.

50. Ibid., 139.

51. Ibid.

52. Cf. Derrida's contribution to the colloquium of the Collège International de Philosophie commemorating Lyotard, published in a volume entitled *Jean-François Lyotard: L'Exercice du différend*, ed. Dolores Lyotard et al. (Paris: Presses Universitaires de France, 2001), 177 n. 2.

53. Lyotard, *The Differend*, 77/118.

54. Ibid., 73/113.

55. Ibid., 75/115.

56. Ibid., 77/118.

57. Jean-François Lyotard, "La Peau du ciel," in *La Revue des sciences humaines*, no. 248, entitled "La Nuit."

58. Lyotard, *The Confession of Augustine*, 18–19/37–38: "The sexual is not subjected to time, if Freud is to be believed, and on occasions dispatches in its course offspring who disorganize it and are remarked within it. . . . A-temporal as it is, enemy as it is of chronological order, this powerless power would also be, so to speak, the agent, the bearer of what is recurrently deferred, making the triple instance of time, or temporal existence, what it is: the not yet, the already no longer and the now. From book XI of the *Confessions* Husserl reads off the phenomenology of the internal consciousness of time. In this book Augustine sketches out from below a libidinal-ontological constitution of temporality."

59. In this context, one should mention yet another parallel to Descartes, one concerning the motif of creation. In *Meditations on First Philosophy*, Descartes writes: "a lifespan can be divided into countless parts, each completely independent of the others, so that it does not follow from the fact that I existed a little while ago that I must exist now, unless there is some cause which as it were creates me afresh at this moment—that is, which preserves me. For it is quite clear to anyone who attentively considers the nature of time that the same power and action are needed to preserve anything at each individual moment of its duration as would be required to create that thing anew if it were not yet in existence. Hence the distinction between preservation and creation is only a conceptual one, and this is one of the things that are evident by the natural light. I must therefore now ask myself whether I possess some power enabling me to bring it about that I who now exist will still exist a little while from now. For since I am nothing but a thinking thing—or at least since I am now concerned only and precisely with that part of me which is a thinking thing—if there were such a power in me, I should undoubtedly be aware of it. But I experience no such power, and this very fact makes me recognize most clearly that I depend on some being distinct from myself" (*The Philosophical Writings of Descartes*, vol. 2, trans. John Cottingham, Robert Stoothoff, Dugald Murdoch [Cambridge: Cambridge University Press, 1996], 33–34).

60. Lyotard, *The Confession of Augustine*, 31/51–52: "The overall balance is actually disastrous. The I can try as it likes to reassure itself, putting finishing touches to the lucid taxonomy of memories. The contents of memory, however, all that can happen to the *ipse* in the course of life, reverberate with a chaotic dynamic that condenses, displaces, topples over their images into each other, disfigures them endlessly. Behind the guardian of time, supposed to watch over its order, under the wing of memory, the work of the drives persists in turning languid the seizure of events. The clear phenomenology of internal temporality covers over a strange mechanic, a grammar of the ways in which concupiscence conjugates essential frustration."

61. Cf. ibid., 27/47: "the sin of time, delay. The encounter with the act is missed from the beginning. The event comes before writing bears witness, and writing sets downs once the event has passed. Confession reiterates this condition of childhood measured against the scale of full presence: I will have been small with regard to your greatness. You, you who had no childhood, you are not transported into the oscillations of too soon and too late."

62. Cf. ibid. 56/80: "This delay from which I suffer, of which I am ashamed, that I confess to you, that I attempt, writing my confession, to make up, that I will never make up all the time that I write in time—this delay is but further drawn out by the time of confession, of writing and proclaiming." A little earlier in the text, this motif is related to that of "indifference" (*hoos mei*), of which we spoke earlier, as well as to the paradoxical logic of the more is less, less is more that defines the structure of all (metaphysical and libinal) desire: "The delay that throws the confessing I into despair is not due to a failure in its chronology; no, *chronos*, at once and in its entirety, consists in delay. Even the shattering visit of the Other, even the incarnation of grace, if it ever truly arrives, from the fact that this visit subverts the space-time of the creature, it does follow that it removes this creature from the hurried, limp course of regrets, remorse, hope, responsibilities, from the ordinary worries of life. But it is even worse than that. Delighting with your presence in such sudden ecstasy, he feels more in dissociation from himself, cleaved, alienated, more uncertain of what he is than he is usual" (ibid., 17–18/35–36).

63. Cf. ibid., 40/63– 64: "To the children of sin, the word reaches them obscured, and

the supreme light from which it emanates is absorbed into our eyes in episodic flashes, in these precarious moments of clarity whose successive appearance, like linear sequences discourse, we pursue. The true book is closed to us, the book of your truth, one in face-to-face, all at once. Undoubtedly, if we saw and heard the dazzling clamor of your wisdom without any filter, if we received it all at once, it would contort our faces, would unfix the orbit of our eyes, would turn us into a white-hot firebrand, subsiding quickly into ashes. The book in the form of the firmament filters the formidable presence of the author. Chased out of the paradise of your intimacy, we are left for memory by you the collection of your works, the world, a text of which we form as much a part as its readers. Decipherable decipherers, in the library of shadows."

Shedding Tears Beyond Being

Derrida's Confession of Prayer

John D. Caputo

I simply place my fingers or lips on it, almost every evening . . .
I touch it without knowing what I am doing
or asking in so doing, especially not knowing
into whose hands I am entrusting myself,
to whom I'm rendering thanks. But to know at least two things
—which I invoke here for those who are foreign
(get this paradox: even more ignorant, more foreign than I)
to the culture of the tallith, this culture of shawl and not of veil:
blessing *and* death. (V, 46/44–45)[1]

Beyond Being

The resources and strategies of negative theology, its "detours, locutions and syntax" (*Marg.*, 6/6),[2] have always fascinated Derrida, and that is because for Derrida, as for negative theology, our desire beyond desire is for what lies "beyond being," to use a venerable expression from Christian Neoplatonism. But what lies "beyond being" for Derrida is tears, prayers and tears, tears shed beyond being (V, 42/40), prayers sent like sighs beyond being, truth, and knowledge. That produces, on the one hand, a remarkable proximity of his work to negative theology, even as, on the other hand, it opens up an abyss between him and negative theology. I will develop this contrast by drawing the unlikely and disconcerting portrait of Derrida as a man of prayer.

In "How to Avoid Speaking: Denials" (1985), Derrida remarks that, faithful to a fault to the title of his essay, he has indeed avoided speaking of something essential. In this essay on negative theology that takes its point of departure from

Plato, Dionysius the Areopagite, and Heidegger, that is, from a massively Greco-Christian tradition, he has avoided speaking of what is neither Christian nor Greek: the Jewish and Islamic traditions of negative theology. Here as elsewhere, he finds himself speaking of foreigners in a language that is not his own. Of course, French is his "own" language and it is not "foreign," but it is not his language: "I have only one language; it is not mine."[3] This is the language which he does not have although he does not have another, as Hélène Cixous says.[4] He speaks what he calls "Christian Latin French," by which he means the language of French colonial Algeria, which is a linguistic condensation of an ancient Greco-Romano-Christian history. Hence, the one thing he has not spoken about in this essay on "not-speaking" (ne pas parler), the one thing about which he has been completely silent in this essay on mystical silence, is the very thing that is closest to him: "For lack of capacity, competence, or self-authorization, I have never yet been able to speak of what my birth, as one says, should have made closest to me: the Jew, the Arab."[5]

In a beautiful, if enigmatic autobiographical journal entitled "Circumfession" (1991), Derrida breaks this silence and professes, confesses, exposes the secret of his Algerian birth which makes of him a "little black and Arab Jew" (Circ., 57/58).[6] Or rather, it makes him the last, the least of the Jews (Circ., 146/154; 178/190) inasmuch as his relation with the Jew is both continuous and ruptured, so that he is not *simply* Jewish (or Arab or North African or French). But of all the secrets he springs on Geoffrey Bennington in "Circumfession," all of which turn around the privacy of his Jewish "circumcision" (a Latin word) in an Arab country colonized by the French, the secret that interests me here is his confession that he is privately a man of prayer, that he has been praying all his life. He wonders aloud (or in writing):

> if I ought to tell them that I pray, and describe how that could happen, according to what idiom and what rite, on one's knees or standing up, in front of whom or what books, for if you knew, G., my experience of prayers, you would know everything . . . (Circ., 175–76/188)

The private matter made public by the author of "Circumfession" is that he has been praying all along and that his experience of prayer is the secret source of "everything."

In another passage he wonders "if those reading me from up there see my tears, today . . . if they guess that my life was but a long history of prayers," for these readers have understood everything "except that I have lived in prayer, tears . . ." (Circ., 40–41/38–40). That is why he loves his prayer shawl: "A prayer shawl I like to touch more than to see, to caress every day, to kiss without even opening my eyes" (V, 44/43), a prayer shawl he has kept safe at home all his life. "Up to the end, never, whatever may happen: in no case, whatever the verdict at the end of so formidable a journey, never can one get rid of a tallith. One must never, ever, at any moment, throw it away or reject it" (V, 69/71).

But how can he, who says that "I quite rightly pass for an atheist" (*je passe à just titre pour une athée*) (Circ., 146/155), be praying? Where (*ubi*) and to whom is he to address his prayers? That is precisely what he desires to know, what he is praying to know. As he says to "G.": "You who know everything, you would tell me whom to address them to" (Circ., 175–76/188). This passage from "Circumfession" is then interrupted with a graph/graft from the *Confessions* in which Augustine asks where, had he died in sin, the prayers of Monica for his salvation would be (*ubi essent*), to which Augustine himself answers, *nusquam nisi ad te*, nowhere but with you, or, even more precisely, nowhere but toward you (*ad te*). But Derrida is at a loss to say where his prayers rise, if they rise at all, or where they drift, if they are adrift, like letters lost in the mail.

The destination of his prayers is kept secret from his readers because it is first kept from him. Where do his prayers arrive? *Nusquam nisi ad te*, he can say with Augustine, but with this difference, that Derrida does not know who this "you" (*te, toi*) is. To or with God, whom he loves, he can also say with Augustine. But then he must also ask with Augustine, "What do I love when I love you?" or when I love "my God" (*Confessions*, X, 6–7). What else can he do but make that question his own, he asks (Circ., 117/122–23). You know that I love you, he can say, but what do I love when I love you? The difficulty posed to us by Derrida's "Circumfession" is described nicely in the opening lines of Augustine's *Confessions* (I, 1). Bearing about in his body his mortality (*circumferens suam mortalitatem*), Augustine says, being but this tiniest bit of creation, still, he "desires to praise you." But must the soul first call upon you to praise you, and must it first "know you before it can invoke" you? he asks (*utrum scire te prius sit an invocare te*). "For it would seem clear that no one can call upon you without knowing you, for if he did he might invoke another than you, knowing you not. Yet may it be that a man must invoke you before he can know you?" That marks the point where their paths part, for Derrida pursues the way of *non-knowing*, of invoking without knowing, of praying without truth—for the prayer shawl has nothing to do with the veil, with the veiling and unveiling of truth. This path, which Derrida elsewhere calls the "passion of non-knowing,"[7] is precisely the path staked out by Derrida in "Circumfession" and other recent autobiographical writings. Augustine, on the other hand, casts his lot with St. Paul, who says, "But how are they to call on one in whom they have not believed?" (Rom 9:14), the same Paul who, upon finding the altar with the inscription "To an unknown god" (*agnosto theo*), told the Athenians, "What therefore you worship as unknown, this I proclaim to you" (Acts 17:23). If Paul will remove the veil that covers the Athenians eyes and reveal to them the name of the Unknown God, Derrida, on the other hand, will write an "epistle against Paul" (V, 73/77), opposing Paul on unveiling the unknown God, on unveiling men and veiling women, on resurrection, and, finally, on circumcision.

Still, has not Augustine himself gone a long way toward showing us that one needs to love something in order to know it? If so, then Derrida's path is at least quasi-Augustinian; for Derrida, loving and calling upon precede knowing, so that the prayer of "Circumfession" is a prayer "without truth" (*sans vérité*), "shedding tears beyond being" (V, 42/40). By this he means that he is invoking a God who does not belong to the order of being, truth, and knowledge, directing a prayer to a God who has nothing to do with knowing or unknowing. What lies "beyond being" for Derrida, is tears. What constitutes, if anything does, the God beyond being, or God without being, is not the *Gottheit* beyond *Gott*, not the *hyperousios* of Pseudo-Dionysius, but tears. For God is called upon in prayers and tears, which are otherwise than being, otherwise than the order of concealment and unconcealment, hiddenness and manifestation, knowing and unknowing. To invoke the name of God is to enter an entirely different order than the history of truth, to belong to a history, not of *vérité* but of *verser les larmes*, shedding tears, the way one's blood is shed.

The meaning of the name of God in deconstruction never comes down to a decision made in the order of being or knowledge, to deciding whether or not God exists; its meaning is shifted out of the circle of knowing and non-knowing, concealment and non-concealment, being and non-being, and located in a "logic or a topic" (V, 71/75) that is otherwise than knowing, in a sphere of tears *au-delà de l'être*. That is the order of the tallith, not of the veil; of the call for justice, not an inquiry into truth; the order of the heart, of blood, of faith, of circumcision, not of creedal propositions; the order, not of knowing but of doing the truth (*facere veritatem*); the order, not of things but of the event. Its meaning is not nominative, to pick out and name something somewhere, but invocative and provocative, to make something happen.

The text that most closely approaches the rhetoric and syntax of "Circumfession" is *The Post Card*, which is another text addressed to "you," where we are also unsure of who is being addressed. So it is no surprise that the text of "Circumfession" contains italicized grafts from a notebook that Derrida was keeping in the 1970s and 1980s, at the time of the composition of *The Post Card*. In the final entry in "Circumfession," Derrida writes:

> . . . resurrection will be for you, *"more than ever the address, the stabilized relation of a destination, a game of a-destination finally sorted out, for beyond what happens in the P.C., it is now the work to dispatch it that must win out, toward the secret that demanded, like a breath, the 'perversity' of the P.C., not to be finished with a destinerrancy which was never my doing, nor to my taste, but a still complacent and therefore defensive account of the Moira"* (7-6-81) (Circ., 290/313–14)

He lacks the "salvation" and "resurrection," the stable destination taught by the "grand masters of the discourse about the resurrection, Saint Paul or Saint Augustine," and he seeks a "quasi-resurrection," that is, a "return to life" that would consist in an event to come that would "open up a new era" (V, 35/32) otherwise than Pauline resurrection (V, 26/22). Life will have been so short—and late will this quasi-resurrection come; *sero te amavi* (V, 35–36/33). Being a little lost, his "Circumfession" is like a postcard gone astray, beset by *destinerrance*, sent off only to arrive heaven knows where, addressed to the "secret," which is not to be identified with the *deus absconditus*, which is in fact a more assured destination and the stuff of a *docta ignorantia*. For the secret kept from him is that there is no Secret Truth, that we are circum-severed from the Truth (Circ., 291/314), deprived of *vérité* and *savoir absolue;* and so he does not know to whom to pray, his condition of non-knowing being more adrift, more radical, than the prayer of a negative theologian to the *deus absconditus.*

In the spirit of his epistle against Paul, one might imagine Derrida defending the prayers the Athenians offer to the unknown God where this altar is meant to keep the name of God safe from knowledge. The God to whom he prays in "Circumfession" is unknown (*ignotus*) but not ignored. Neither an epistemic puzzle we cannot solve nor the divine abyss of negative theology, the name of God draws us beyond knowing and unknowing, leads us outside the circle of hidden and revealed, to the order of the tallith, beyond being and without truth. The Messiah of whom he dreams, for whom he prays and weeps as he caresses his tallith, the one whom he calls to come, "comes to strike dumb the order of knowledge: neither known nor unknown, too well known but a stranger from head to foot, yet to be born" (V, 34/31). "My white tallith belongs to the night, the absolute night" (V, 80/85; cf. Circ. 83/84). The coming of his Messiah is not a matter of truth (*vérité*) and manifestation, but it represents instead a verdict (*vere dictum*) without verity or truth, for the Messiah belongs to the order of the order, the order of the command, of the Law, which is a demand for justice. His Messiah belongs to the "culture of the tallith," of the prayer shawl whose fringes remind us of the Law, and not to the culture of the veil (V, 44/42– 43, 73/77), to the long history of veiling and unveiling, of appearing and not- appearing, that stretches from Plato to Heidegger, which is the Greco-Christian history of truth (V, 34/31). He is "fed up" with this trope of the veil, infinitely weary of that "tiresome, tireless, tired out" history of concealment and unconcealment, driven to "tears beyond being," to dreaming of justice beyond being's truth and unconcealment (V, 42/39 – 40). His call to "come" is a call for justice, a prediction of the verdict of justice, foretelling in the sense of calling for a justice to come. Residing "beyond any truth as ontological revelation" (V, 79/83), it has nothing to do with foreseeing the future.

But is it possible to pray to God in an absolute night? Can one kiss one's tallith and pray to God, or, like a certain Augustine, to "you," if I do not know who you are, who this "you" is? Would that still be a prayer, really a prayer?[8]

The Wounded Word

In "The Wounded Word," Jean-Louis Chrétien describes the structure of praying to an unknown God that is of some help in this matter. He cites a verse from the French poet Jules Supervielle:[9]

> How surprised I am to be addressing you,
> My God, I who know not if you exist,

Chrétien describes this as a prayer to a virtual God, a "watered-down" God, as Supervielle himself says, but not a virtual prayer; it is a real and actual prayer, belonging properly to the religious order, "with the virtual character of the God to whom it says 'you' constituting a moment in its religiosity."[10] An "actual prayer" directed toward a "virtual God," a "virtual you": but what, or who, pray tell, is that? A real and earnest prayer, heartfelt, unfeigned, and full of tears, directed to God, *s'il y en a*. Is this perhaps something of an "anonymous prayer" on the model of Rahner's anonymous Christian, the prayer of someone who is praying to God even though he does not know that it is God to whom he prays? And what if there is no God, *s'il n'y en a pas*? Then it is a prayer directed somewhere, who knows where (God knows where!), but a prayer nonetheless.

This is a thin and diluted prayer, Chrétien observes, a more robust form of which is to be found in the prayer of the father of the child possessed by a demon in the gospel of Mark, "I believe, help my unbelief" (9:24), which is both a prayer for prayer and an act of faith in faith. This remarkable formula from the New Testament recognizes that all faith proceeds from faithlessness, and all prayer proceeds from an inability to pray, so that to pray that one be able to pray constitutes indeed a most authentic prayer. A prayer is a performative act—the very act of directing one's words to God *is* the prayer—with a unique reflexivity, so that to pray for the prayer itself, to pray that one be able to pray is already to pray. Indeed, this would be so even if one is not so sure that one believes in God, *especially* if one is not sure one believes in God, which also means that one is not sure one does *not* believe in God. When Derrida is asked why he says "I quite rightly pass for an atheist" instead of simply saying that he *is* an atheist, he responds by saying that he is not, in fact, sure that he *is* an atheist. This is what others say about him, and perhaps they are "right"—in the order of cognitive assertions and creedal assent—but he is not so sure himself that he is one. That is, that he is *one*. For there is a certain *sic et non* that goes on within him, within all of us, such that we are each inhabited by advocates of opposing sides, and the one will not give the other any rest. Accordingly, while he kisses his tallith and prays *viens, oui, oui*, he cannot be sure of the destination of his prayer, for his prayer is *"destinerrant,"* sent on a journey that may very well go astray like a lost love letter.

For Chrétien, prayer arises from a destituted, de-constituted subject, a subject dispossessed of subjective authority, suppliant and in need of help. But what subject has less authority than the one who, lost in prayer, does not know to whom he or she is praying, who prays, "Oh God, if there is a God," or even *"Dieu qui n'est pas, pose ta main sur notre épaule"* (Oh God, who is not, put your hand on our shoulder).[11] When would the destitution of the praying subject, the "nudity" of the voice in prayer, as Chrétien puts it, be greater? When would the voice in prayer be more in need of prayer? When would the prayer for prayer, and hence prayer itself, be more intense?

Prayer, as Chrétien argues, is the very element or stuff of religion: where there is prayer, there is religion; and where there is religion, there is prayer. But can there be a religion and a prayer without God? If that is so, as Chrétien argues, would it not follow that it is the prayer of a religion without religion, a prayer *sans*

Dieu in a *religion sans religion* of the sort that Derrida describes in *The Gift of Death* (*Donner la mort*)?[12]

The bareness and the barrenness of the prayer to the unknown God lays bare the intentional structure of prayer in a way that no other prayer can, for it exposes the structure of prayer as an act directed at someone, at "you," even and especially if one has no assurance that there is such a "you." This prayer enacts a kind of phenomenological reduction of the real existence of an *ens reale*, or an *ens realissimum*, which has been bracketed in order to lay bare the structure of the intentional act. The directedness of prayer to "you" holds so radically that it holds even if one has no assurance that someone is listening, reducing the one who prays to praying that someone be there to hear the prayer, so that one is praying for the prayer itself. The intentionality of the act does not require that someone indeed be there, or be known to be there, but that the prayer be directed to someone, if they are there. Indeed, and this in virtue of its performativity, there would be prayer as long as one is praying that there be someone to whom to pray, as long as one send one's prayers to someone, whoever and wherever they are, to someone of uncertain destination. Prayer, even in its most classical and orthodox forms, arises from the groundless ground of praying that there be someone who hears our prayer. *Domine, exaudi orationem meam:* O Lord, *hear* my prayer; *et clamor meus ad te veniat:* and let my cry come unto you. Whenever we say *oremus,* let us pray, we are saying, let us preface our prayer with a prayer; before we even begin praying let us begin praying for our prayer; let us begin with a prayer that there be someone who hears. The uncertainty does not dissipate the prayer but constitutes it in the first place and intensifies it, for that is the very reason to pray in the first place and all the more reason to keep on praying, to pray like mad, to pray that our prayers "to heaven go" (*Hamlet,* III, 3). The very uncertainty that seems to make it impossible to pray is what makes it necessary, what reduces us to prayers and tears.

Like the law of inverse proportions that governs the structure of faith according to Johannes Climacus, the objective (or destinational) uncertainty of the prayer raises to a fever pitch its subjective intensity, its prayerfulness. While the prayer to the virtual God may be a "thin" prayer when measured by the doctrinal standards of the actual and concrete historical faiths, it is for that very reason a profoundly passionate movement of the heart (*inquietum est cor nostrum*). The thinness has to do with the determinacy of the doctrinal content of the prayer and the identifiable determinacy of its destination. But a more robust prayer by this standard would not be a more prayerful prayer, more of a prayer; it would be a *more determinate* prayer, a prayer marked by more constants and fewer variables, by more proper names and fewer pronouns. A more robust prayer would be safer, having a more secure place within a rich and determinate historical tradition of texts and prayers and names for God. For a Christian, for example, it would join itself with Jesus' prayer to the Father in the Spirit and insert itself in the long history that ensues from Jesus' prayer. It would be, in short, less lost.

The prayers that emanate from the author of "Circumfession," on the other hand, are the adrift, *destinerrant,* a-destinal prayers of someone deprived of salvation and resurrection; his prayer is more aporetic, more uncertain of its outcome, more exposed to encountering the very opposite of what he is praying for. His prayer lacks a determinate and identifiable destination, is deprived of the inherited vocabularies of age-old prayers, and is radically exposed to failure, even to something fearful. The Messiah for whom he prays is both desired and feared, awaited and not awaited. Waiting for the Messiah for him is like a defendant awaiting a "verdict" (which is a good "nickname" for the Messiah) of a jury in a trial. The verdict lies in an unforeseeable future which befalls us like death, for the future does include death, which means that it is a future that we are waiting for and postponing.[13] He is waiting for justice, waiting to hear the verdict, but then again, if it is going to go against him, he does not want to hear, so that he does not want what he wants (V, 27/25). I do not know what is to come when I call for the coming of the *tout autre.* When I pray, "Come," when I ask, "When will you come?" I am worried that someone is really going to show up, and worried about who, worried about what will be demanded of me, worried that the Messiah will not be at all what I expected (which is, of course, just what is to be expected of the *tout autre*). One should always be careful about what one prays for, lest one's prayers be answered. So when I say or pray, "When will you come?" that longing ("How long, O Lord, how long?") always comes admixed with fear and a desire for deferral, for the Messiah is both a promise and a threat. The call *"viens"* is a *contretemps,* a single gesture in which "the other is made to come, allowed to come, but his coming is *simultaneously* deferred."[14] Still, does being more "lost" and exposed, more lacking in salvation, diminish the need for prayer? And should not every prayer be admixed with a fear of what we are getting ourselves into? Must we not always divest ourselves of our own preconceived ideas about who God is and what God has in mind for us when we pray? Must not our intention always be to renounce our own intention? Must not our desire be to renounce our own desire? "Not what I want but what you want" (Mark 14:36). Does not all this intensify and provide the very conditions of prayer?

Let us look at things from Derrida's point of view. The movement by which one determines the destination of prayer as the "God" of the inherited biblical faiths is an attempt to still or arrest this indeterminacy and destinerrancy; but such a determination must always be inscribed within the more radical translatability and determinability that affects all language in virtue of *différance.* For it would always be possible to determine otherwise what is called "God" in the concrete biblical faiths, always possible to ask what I love when I love my God. That is why Derrida says of his mother that she must have known that the "constancy of God in my life is called by other names" (Circ., 146/155). What gives constancy in Derrida's life is subject to irreducible plurality and translatability, whereas in the inherited religious traditions this constancy goes under the constant name of "God." From Derrida's point of view, the determinacy of the direction of the prayer is a way of trying to appropriate the secret, to make it one's own, to utter its secret name, revealed only to the believers or insiders, instead of confessing more radically its

unknowability. On Derrida's point of view, we would never be authorized to determine the secret, to arrest the play, to still the endless translatability of the various names to which we pledge our troth. Where would we be situated when we
attempted such a thing? How would we have gained access to such a standpoint?
In that regard, Derrida's "Circumfession" is more radically confessional than Augustine's *Confessions*, his word more wounded. For when Augustine confesses his
wounded and mortal nature, he is also confessing/professing a faith in which these
wounds would be bound up. But Derrida confesses the secret, the non-knowing,
the destabilized and destitute state of his confession, his confession without a confessional bond. His is a confession without confession, a confession of the "without," of the *sans*, by which his heart and flesh are marked, *sans voir, sans avoir,
sans savoir, sans s'avoir.*

I would argue that the unknowing in this prayer to the unknown God is a
structural element of prayer itself, of *any* prayer, the most classical prayers of the
faithful included; it is not restricted to certain poets or philosophers who may as
a contingent fact rightly or wrongly pass for atheists. For inasmuch as prayer is
inscribed within the movement of faith—Lord, I believe, help my unbelief—there
is a moment in every prayer where it finds itself thrown back on itself, finds itself
praying for the prayer itself, praying that there is some point to prayer, praying
that there is someone to hear our prayers, praying that our prayers find someone
who hears them. There is, furthermore, always and essentially something unknown about the one to whom we pray, an uncertainty about their response, an
irreducible uncertainty about the future, which is why we are praying rather than
confidently forecasting a successful outcome. That ring of unknowing is a condition of prayer that is not only found in those who rightly pass for atheists but is
also a mark of prayer itself, even and especially the most saintly prayer, the passionate prayer that issues from that passion of non-knowing called the dark night
of the soul. At that point in mystical prayer, the soul comes to question whether
she believes in God, or believes in prayer, having reached a point where she has
to pray to be able to pray, pray to be able to believe in prayer, pray to be able to
believe at all.

The point of prayer, its intentional aim, is God, if there is a God; in prayer,
one stands *coram deo*, before God, like Augustine in the *Confessions*. In *Being and
Time*, Heidegger distilled the structure of the *coram deo* in Augustine into what
we might call analogously a *coram morte*, a being before death (*Sein zum Tod*), a
running forward into death (*Vorlaufen in den Tod*), which he treated as a "formal
indication" of the one-to-one relationship of the soul with God in the *Confessions*, a text that was mediated to him by Luther and Kierkegaard. Augustine's *coram
deo* is for Heidegger an ontic specification, a de-formalized instantiation, of this
formal indication. But in my view, Heidegger's formal indication leaves out something crucial. Far from formalizing the *coram deo*, Heidegger has transformed it
into something of an entirely different form and truncated its intentional type. For
his formalization has omitted the very intentionality of the *coram deo*, that is, of
the prayer. The discourse (*Rede*) of Dasein standing before death, being brought

back before its own death, is a soliloquy, a dialogue of Dasein with itself, an examination of its conscience in which Dasein makes itself ready to hear the call of
conscience, in which Dasein calls out to Dasein to return to itself. The wound of
mortality, the wounded word that Dasein speaks to itself standing before death, is
the wound of a being that has to pull itself together from its dispersion, its scat-
tering abroad (*Zerstreuung*), which is the *distensio animae* that Augustine describes
in Book X of the *Confessions*. That wound is healed in authentic resolve, which
corresponds to Augustinian *continentia*, the gathering or self-collecting of the soul,
its ability to abide within itself. But when in *Being and Time* Dasein collects and
recollects itself, when it gathers itself together into an authentic resolve, that self-
centering constitutes a certain self-possession or autonomy that Marion rightly describes as a kind of "autarchy" or self-rule. The wounded word of prayer, which
is the very structure of the *coram deo*, on the other hand, is the wound of a being
torn outside itself and directed to another, to "you," whose help it seeks, whoever
this you is, even if I do not know if this you exists, especially if I do not. The
wounded voice is a voice of supplication, an-archic, not autarchic, deprived of
being an origin, *sans voir, sans avoir, sans savoir, sans s'avoir*. Prayer is a dialogue,
not a soliloquy, in which abyss calls to abyss.

In "Circumfession," Derrida has preserved the intentionality of the prayer,
the intentional structure of the address, of the *confiteor*, the confessional mode
that is turned to "you." The fifty-nine periphrases of "Circumfession" are so many
words cut by the wound of circumcision, "that wound I have never seen" (Circ.
66/66), a "virtual," "unmemorable" and "indecipherable" wound (Circ. 271/293),
which strikes down the proud heart, which circumcises the heart and the word,
the ear and the tongue. His tallith, he says, does not protect him and make him
invulnerable but "recalls me to the mortal wound" (V, 62/64), that he is under
the law, laid claim to by the call of the other, that he is circumcised. The tallith
is like the cloth wrapped around the wounded infant penis; "the tallith hangs on
the body in memory of circumcision" like a detached prepuce (V, 68/70). The
words he speaks in "Circumfession" are not the self-possessed words of radical and
erect resoluteness, not the words of a being which has become transparent to itself (*Erschlossen*) and resolute (*Entschlossen*) about its ownmost course of action.
They are rather the words of one who is lost and adrift, cut, cut loose, and cut
down to size; words deprived of erection and resurrection, not so much incisive
as incised words, not self-possessed but confessional, circumcised, circum-fessional.
Circumcision is what makes him write (Circ., 188–89/202), the writing that is
incised on his body and inscribed on his soul, the inscriptions of his stylus reproducing and reinscribing the incisions of the mohel's blade.

The difference between "Circumfession" and a negative theology is not that
negative or mystical theology is inscribed in prayer whereas "Circumfession" is a
memoir of an atheist to himself. Rather, they are both constituted by movements
of prayer—that is the surprising thing that unites them—but the prayer of the negative theologian has a determinate and identifiable destination, *à Dieu*, where the
name of God is a constant historical and biblical name, the name that has been

handed down to us by the Scriptures and tradition. That is a name that is both un-nameable and omni-nameable, as Meister Eckhart says, a name that contains the perfection of every name within itself and by that very fact both excites and ex-ceeds every name we send God's way. The name of God is the name we must save because God is everything save the name, *sauf le nom*, by which God is addressed. The God of negative theology is not simply unknown, for the negative theologian, who takes her bearings from an historical faith, knows to whom she directs her prayers, *nusquam nisi ad te*. If the God of negative theology is called unknown, this is meant as a compliment, as praise, and it is to be taken strictly in the sense of the cloud of unknowing and the learned ignorance. We know that it is to the God of Abraham and Isaac to whom we pray, and we know that we can never know this God. But we know this God whom we do not comprehend is more intimate to us than we are to ourselves, and we know that if something is comprehended, then it cannot be God whom we comprehend. There is nothing higher, nothing greater we can know about this unknown God than that.

But the name of God in Derrida is more desert-like and radically adrift than the God of negative or mystical theology; the absolute night of his white tallith is not the dark night of the soul in John of the Cross. His prayer is, for all that, not less actual, not less real, not less earnest and heartfelt, not less full of tears. It is fully actual within an order that is otherwise than knowing and being, an order of shedding tears beyond or without being, where the whole order of knowledge, of the very distinction between knowing and unknowing, has been struck dumb (*V*, 34/31). He does not love his tallith less than an orthodox believer, but his prayer is less determinate, less clear about its destination, not able to be identified with any of the historical names of God that are handed down to us by the Abrahamic religions. But that indeterminacy does not undermine the prayer; it intensifies it, leaving his word wounded, suppliant, and errant in a radical and disturbing way; his is the prayer of a desert wanderer, a white tallith in an "absolute night" (*V*, 80/85), a circumcised word, where circumcision means to be "severed from the truth," *sevrée de la vérité*, cut off, circum-severed from the truth, awaiting a *verdict sans vérité*. Of the two men who went up to the temple to pray, his prayer would be rather more like the one who does not feel fit to pray (Luke 10:18), which is more and not less of a prayer. The more unfit one feels for prayer, the more un-able, the more prayer is prayer. He lacks the "truth" about God in the sense of lacking any theology or dogma, and in the sense of being unable to identify him-self with a determinate historical community of faith, with a fixed textual and in-stitutional faith tradition. But over and beyond that cognitive indeterminacy, *au-delà de l'être*, the very idea of God, the meaning of the name of God, resides in an order that is otherwise than truth and being. Derrida's prayer will always main-tain a certain ironic quality inasmuch as he will always maintain a certain *ironic distance* from the name of God, because the name of God for him is endlessly translatable, "the constancy of the name of God" for him going under many names. But at the same time, and for the same reason, it will always be in earnest, bathed in the blood and tears of existence.

Différance and the Name of God

We can shed some light on the question of the meaning of the name of God for Derrida if we briefly mark an interesting evolution that this name has undergone in his work. The name of God first appears in Derrida's early writings under the theme of the "reduction" or the "effacement" of the trace, the "lifting" of the trace in favor of "full presence." What begins in Platonism, he says, culminates in "infinitist metaphysics":

> Only infinite being can reduce the difference in presence. In that sense, the name of God, at least as it is pronounced within classical rationalism, is the name of indifference. . . . We must not therefore speak of a "theological prejudice," functioning sporadically when it is a question of the plenitude of the logos; the logos as the sublimation of the trace is *theological*. (*OG*, 104/71)[15]

The name of God, which is the "theological" name par excellence, at least the "rationalist" pronunciation of it, is taken to be something that must be effaced in the name of God's utter transcendence of every name or concept. The name "God" arises from "speech dreaming of plenitude," from a dream of "life without *différance*" (*OG*, 104/71), from a dream of presence without *différance*, of which classical negative theology is a case in point. To seek such pure and perfect transcendence is, as with Levinas's "dream of a purely heterological thought," to pursue a thought unconditioned by a subject and unencumbered by any horizon, which is a dream that "must vanish *at daybreak*, as soon as language awakens" (*ED*, 224/151).[16] The name of God should be a self-effacing trace, like a comet that burns itself out and disappears as it streaks across the sky of language. Negative theology knows that the straightest way to the Godhead beyond God, to the God beyond the trace, is to take the detour of the apophatic (*ED*, 398 n. 1/ 337 n. 37), for God is infinite, ineffable, and inconceivable (*Marg.*, 6/6).

    To be sure, Derrida's point in all this is critical and delimitative. It is not to consign the name of God to the rubbish heap of illusions, although that is a conclusion drawn by both his (secularizing) admirers and (religious) critics alike, but to bring this name down to earth. He does not deny that this name has reference but seeks to reinscribe it in *différance*. It is not as though there is some sort of negative ontological argument lodged deep in deconstruction, in virtue of which the very idea of *différance* would disprove the existence of God and discredit negative theology. But Derrida insists that whatever reference this name has is a function of difference, of the system or chain of differences within which it is inscribed. That means that it cannot be insulated from an irreducible translatability into other names that could do service for it. The name of God, like every name, is a nominal "effect," which means, of course, an effect of lettering but not a literal effect, because *différance* is a quasi-transcendental condition of nominal unities of meaning, not a real, entitative or transcendent cause of equally real or transcendent entities. The name "God," like every name, acquires significance by the differential relations within which it is always and already inscribed—God/human, God/world, God/gods, infinite/finite, eternal/temporal, and so on. It is inescapably inscribed within the multiple systems—syntactical, semantic and pragmatic, phonic and graphic, social, historical, institutional, and gendered—by means of which it is forged as a certain linguistic, historical, and nominal unity. Whatever the nominative power of this name, whatever the real or entitative status of its referent— and Derrida is not saying, and he is not authorized to say, one way or the other, what that is—the name "infinite" is a finite name, the concept "inconceivable" is quite conceivable, and the name "ineffable" is very speakable. Rather than bringing discourse to a halt, these are among our very best words, supplying the stuff of the most beautiful, poignant, and soaring discourses, giving rise to the most stunning and audacious sermons and treatises. I never tire of pointing out that "Meister" Eckhart, that master of mystical silence and ineffability, whose prayer to God was to rid him of God, was the greatest preacher of his day in the Order of Preachers, and one of the veritable creators of the modern German language, a master of *Lesen und Leben*.

But we would be missing something important in Derrida's early writings if we did not see that, beyond critique and delimitation, he has been stirred in an affirmative way by this discourse on God in negative theology. He has, of course, and this is what has drawn most of the attention in the literature, very considerable regard for the strategic resources of negative theology. He has always admired its "detours, locutions and syntax," the extraordinary economy with which it enacts the self-effacing trace and the "rarefaction of signs" (*Sauf*, 41/48).[17] For this is a language that would exceed language, a "sweet rage against language" that operates "at the edge of language," (*Sauf*, 63–64/59–60), upon which he does not hesitate to borrow (*Marg.*, 6/6). For Derrida, the language of negative theology is a wounded word, driven by passion to go where we cannot go, to name the unnameable God:

> —It is this passion that leaves the mark of a scar in that place where the impossible takes place, isn't it?
> —Yes, the wound is there, over there (*Sauf*, 63–64/59–60)

The scar left behind on the language of negative theology is the wound inflicted by the impossible.

I would emphasize, however, that the early Derrida's interest in this name has another side, less mystical than prophetic, less Neoplatonic than biblical, more Jewish than Christian, more religious than theological, which also makes its first appearance in the early writings. I refer to his fascination with the evocative discourse of Levinas on the *tout autre* in "Violence and Metaphysics," an essay that it would be a mistake to reduce to a simple critique of Levinas. Let us entertain the "hypothesis," he says at the end of this essay, that "this experience of the infinitely other" is to be called "Judaism," which represents a kind of "non-philosophy" or "absolute empiricism" that comes to "solicit" the "autistic syntax" of Greek philosophy: "Therefore nothing can so profoundly *solicit* the Greek logos—philosophy—than this irruption of the totally other (*tout autre*)" (*ED*, 26/152). The issue of this solicitation is for Derrida a fruitful aporia, a productive impossibility. We find our-

selves faced *both* with the necessity to speak and articulate, to conceive and phi-
losophize, to have recourse to the categorial system handed down to us by the
Greeks—how could we avoid that and why would we want to?—*and* at the same
time with the necessity to disturb that conceptuality, to open it up from within to
the outside, to awaken it from its autistic dream. Both of these at the same time,
both Greek and Jew, living in the difference between the Greek and Jew, being "attached to both the philosophers and the prophets," as Levinas says. This is achieved,
not in a reconciling *Aufhebung*, but in the mutual solicitation and incessant dis-
turbance of the Greek by the Jew and of the Jew by the Greek, of the one by the
other. "Jewgreek is greekjew. Extremes meet." "Are we Jews? Are we Greeks? We
live in the difference between the Jew and the Greek, which is perhaps the unity
of what is called history" (*ED*, 227/153).

So the affirmative point that emerges from a deconstructive analysis of the
name of God, even in Derrida's early writings, is to welcome the shock that "Judaism" delivers to "philosophy," to open Greek logos to its other, to "circumcise"
the logos of the philosophers and so open philosophy to its outside, like the circumcised ear and the circumcised heart in Jeremiah:

> See, their ears are closed [uncircumcised],
> they cannot listen. (Jer 6:10)

> For all those nations are uncircumcised, and all the house of Israel is
> uncircumcised in heart. (Jer 9:25)

In Derrida, circumcision cuts both ways—it is both the literal defining inscription
that marks the Jew off from the peoples (*goyim*), and it is the figure of welcoming
the other that cuts open the circle of the same. Like his tallith, his circumcision
is literal, not merely a figure indifferent to its literality, which is what divides him
from St. Paul (*V*, 72/75–76). Unlike Heidegger, who thinks that the name of God
closes down questioning and stops the question of Being in its tracks, for Derrida
the name of God is the open-ended name of the *tout autre*, a name that disturbs
and solicits the Greek logos and keeps it turned to the other for which it cannot
be prepared.

The Promise

That is why a careful and theologically sensitive reading of Derrida's early writings, of which there is not an oversupply, would not have been surprised by the
force and saliency with which the name of God would resurface in his later writings, in particular in "Circumfession." What I wish to emphasize here is that in
"Circumfession" the name of God is not a theological name:

> Well, I'm remembering God this morning, the name, a quotation, something
> my mother said . . . to quote the name of God as I heard it perhaps the first time,
> no doubt in my mother's mouth when she was praying, each time she saw me
> ill, . . . I heard her say, *gràce a Dieu, merci Dieu*, when the temperature goes

> down, weeping in pronouncing your name, . . . I'm mingling the name of God
> here with the origin of tears . . . (Circ., 112/117)

The name of God is mingled with prayers and tears, mingled like water and wine. It is not a theological word but a religious one, especially if, as Chrétien argues, the defining feature of religion is prayer. It does not function nominatively, to pick out an entity, but invocatively, to call upon and provoke an event. The name of God does not belong to "the logic or the topic of the veil," to the order being, presence, and truth, as he says in "A Silkworm of One's Own," but to the order of the tallith, of prayers and tears (V, 71/75). The name of God in "Circumfession" does not pick out an object of metaphysical theology, nor the subject matter of rationalist metaphysics; it does not have to do either with ontic truth of entities or the ontological truth of Being. It is the name of "you," *te, toi,* "my God," not of a dream of full plenitude and presence. It does not name this "you" as an entity, but calls upon it. "God" is not an *ens realissimum,* but an addressee to whom I direct my prayers and tears, by whom I am always already addressed and solicited, "my God."

Now if this name does not signify the dream of presence without *différance,* it is no less a name forged by dreaming. But far from being a dream from which we "awaken" at the dawn of language, it is the dream *of* language, language's own dream of the coming or the incoming of the other, which is the very promise by which language is provoked, the promise of which language dreams, which is accordingly the dream that fires deconstruction, which constitutes deconstruction. For what else is deconstruction but a dream of the coming of the other, indeed, a prayer for the coming of the Messiah? In the final passage of the text of *Circumfession,* which also contains an allusion to the *sero te amavi,* which is the epigraph of "Silkworm," Derrida writes:

> you have spent your whole life inviting calling promising,
> hoping sighing dreaming,
> convoking invoking provoking (Circ., 290–91/314)

Deconstruction is the dream and desire for the coming of the other: *Viens, oui, oui.* He is always saying, praying, Amen, yes, yes, to the coming of the *tout autre.* Yes, I said yes. Amen. Yes, to the justice to come, to the democracy to come, to the gift to come, to the forgiveness to come, to the hospitality to come, to the friendship to come. As such, deconstruction is structured around a prayer which in its most economical form reminds us of the final words of the last book of the New Testament. Like every prayer, Derrida's prayer is what Chrétien calls a wounded word, a notion explicitly articulated by the cut of circumcision, whose decisive, or incisive, character is summed up in this final passage of "Circumfession." He has been "hoping sighing dreaming":

> what, the witness, you my counterpart, only so that he will attest this secret truth,
> i.e., severed from truth, i.e., that you will never have had any witness, *ergo es,*

in this very place, you alone whose life will have been so short... (Circ 290–91/314–15)

Sevrée de la vérité: the cut in Derrida's circumcised word is this severed truth, this severing of him from the truth, the sign by which he carries about his mortality, as Augustine said, *circumferens suam mortalitatem*. His prayers arise *de profundis*, from the depths of the cut, which opens a desire for the coming of the other, for prayer "opens the religious dimension, and never ceases to sustain, to support, and to suffer it," as Chrétien says,[18] even as his prayers are directed toward the secret from which he is cut off, "convoking invoking provoking" the unknown God. *Abyssus abyssum invocat.*

Cut off from the truth, praying for the coming of the *tout autre*, for the fulfill-ment of the promise, he prays to remain faithful to the promise. But what is this promise, and who is promising what to whom? In what can he have faith? For what and on what basis does he hope? What does he love when he loves his God? We are awash in questions.

The promise, as I construe it, is the promise that is inscribed in language it-self, the promise language makes to which we are always already responding. This promise is not a particular speech act, as when one person promises something definite to another person, but the very promise of language itself. In this sense:

> "a language is promised," which at once precedes all language, summons all speech and already belongs to each language as it does to all speech.
>
> The promise of which I speak . . . and of which I am now proposing that it promises the impossible but also the possibility of all speech; this strange promise neither yields nor delivers any messianic or eschatological *content* here. There is no salvation here that saves or promises salvation.
>
> But the fact that there is no necessarily determinable *content* in this prom-ise of the other, and in the language of the other, does not make any less indis-putable its opening up of speech by something that *resembles* messianism, sote-riology, or eschatology. It is the structural opening, the messian*icity*, without which *messianism* itself . . . would not be possible.[19]

Language is opened by the promise of a language to come, and our speech comes always and already in response to such a promise; our language comes to us as the in-coming of the other. But we are not in a position to determine in advance any specific content, to hold up a determinate ideal or program. The "given lan-guage," the language given us, is astir with many gifts, made restless (*inquietum*) with words of an elemental "donatative" force, words like *gift* and *forgiveness*, *hospitality* and *friendship*, *come* and *welcome*, *yes* and *amen*, *justice* and *democ-racy*. These given words, our least bad words for something to come, come in re-sponse to a promise inscribed in language itself. Our hearts are restless, and we will not rest until we can recall a call that never was present, until we welcome a future that will never come, which is an impossible future, the future of *the* im-possible. But that restless heart is not consigned to hopelessness; on the contrary, that indeterminacy belongs to the very structure of the promise. This restlessness describes the groaning of history and language to bring forth the "event," the *événe-ment*, the *évenir* of the in- coming (*l'invention*) of the wholly other, that is, of the unforeseeable future (*l'avenir*). For history and language move about in the am-bience of the promise, of the space opened up between the absolute past and the absolute future.

The author of "Circumfession" does not and cannot determinately identify what he desires, but his desire is aroused (*tu excitas, ut laudare te delectet*, I, 1) by something that stirs in those words in particular, which are not chosen arbitrarily—he does not dream of a monarchy to come, or an enmity to come. Something is promised to us by them; something calls to us from afar. They come to us from of old, from an ancient memory, from a time out of mind, and they summon us to a future to come. To be sure, these are our words, but we do not have them; they have us, and we speak in answer to their call. Our words are at bottom the words of the other in us, the other who addresses us. Such words call to us, and we an-swer, "*Viens, oui, oui*," come, yes, come; but our "come" comes second, as an an-swer, a second yes, *oui, oui*, to the call addressed to us in these words, which is the first yes, the yes that language calls to us, *tu excitas*, the yes that language is, the promise that language is. That means that for Derrida the prophetic and messianic texts of the three great religions of the Book, all of which turn on a messianic com-ing, as well as the philosophical eschatologies of Hegel, Marx, and Heidegger, are more definitely and determinately destined sendings, directed at a more assured, that is, a more fixed and identifiable destination.

But the author of "Circumfession" is a little more lost, a little less assured, a little more adrift, a little more confessional, a little more deprived of salvation, kissing and caressing his tallith, shedding tears beyond being. Periphrasis 59 con-tinues, and these are the last words of the book:

> . . . the voyage sent, scarcely organized, by you with no lighthouse and no book, you the floating toy at high tide and under the moon, you the cross between these two phantoms of witnesses who will never come down to the same. (Circ 290–91/314–15)

He does not know to whom he is praying, which means he does not know by whom the promise of the future has been made, if it has been made by anyone at all, or whether the promise does not arise in some middle-voice operation that gets itself made in the given language, in what is handed down to us by language and tra-dition, coming from a past that was never present, promising us an unforeseeable future. He does not know who to thank for

> a gift for which thanks should be given to goodness knows what archaic power. . . . The day I would know to whom gratitude must be rendered for it, I would know everything, and I would be able to die in peace. Everything I do . . . resembles a game of blindman's bluff . . . [he] holds out his hand like a blind man seeking to touch the one whom he could thank for the gift of a language, for the very words in which he declares himself ready to give thanks.[20]

His prayer lacks the security of an assured destination, the fixity of a definite point of arrival, but that lack is an opening that intensifies its passion, impassioning it with the passion of the impossible, with the passion of non-knowing. To be sure, there is a considerable passion when passion has a determinate destination, when we set our hands to the plow with a fixed goal and do not look back (Luke 9:62). But there is no less passion, and perhaps there is more, at least there is a different passion, in this passion of his that is not quite sure of how to proceed or where it is heading, a passion that is thrown back upon itself and gropes like a blind man in the dark, which risks getting lost, which *is* a little lost. Getting lost is what he risks, but his risk is no more risky than the opposite risk, which is the danger to which they are exposed who, thinking themselves to know the way, risk getting complacent, self-assured, dogmatic, or routinized. But when we do not know where we are going, or how things will turn out, then the tensions are tightened, the stakes raised, and the passion pushed to its highest pitch, in accord with the law of the raising of subjective intensity first formulated by Johannes Climacus.

Sero te amavi

It is not so much a question of his faith in his tallith, Derrida says, but of his tallith's faith in him. Happily, his tallith is very understanding and forgiving of his inconstancies:

> I love the peaceful passion, the distracted love my tallith inspires in me, I get the impression it allows me that distraction because it is sure, so sure of me, so little worried by my infidelities. It does not believe in my inconstancies, they do not affect it. I love it and bless it with a strange indifference, my tallith, in a familiarity without name or age. As if faith and knowledge, another faith and another knowledge, a knowledge without truth and without revelation, were woven together in the memory of an event to come, the absolute delay of the verdict, of a verdict to be rendered and which is, was, or will make itself arrive without the glory of a luminous vision. My white tallith belongs to the night, the absolute night. (V, 79–80/84–85)

He is a man of prayer, a man of the tallith, who has a tallith of his own, not because it belongs to him but because he belongs to it. His tallith does not keep him safe or make him invulnerable, but it reminds him of the wound of his mortality, the open-endedness of his aspirations and the uncertainty of what is to come. That is why one should never, never get rid of one's tallith, even as one must never be late for prayer (V, 69/71, 65/67). That is why, every night before going to bed, he places his hand on his tallith and presses it to his lips.

Our tears are sent beyond being, drawn beyond being; we weep and pray for what, beyond being, beyond truth, calls up our tears. Our hearts are restless, *inquietum est cor nostrum*, with an incessant aspiration for the impossible, *viens, oui, oui*, astir with hope in the promise of an unforeseeable event. To invoke the name of God, which he associates with tears (Circ., 112/117), is not to name a being or a non-being, something known or not known. The name of God does not have a nominative power for him but an invocative one; it does not name something but calls for an event (*événement*), something to come (*à venir*), something to be done (*facere veritatem*). The name of God draws us outside the closed circle of being and truth into an open space without borders, where tears are shed beyond being, into a desert place where the distinction between knowledge and non-knowledge is struck dumb, luring us like a love that we will have always loved so late, *sero te amavi*, life having always been too short (V, 35–36/33). The prayers of circumfession are prayers of "peaceful passion" and its love is a "distracted love." Its prayers and tears are sent beyond being, like sighs lovers send God knows where for their future, for something futural, for the coming of something wholly other, even as they steel themselves for the threatening promise of what is to come, for the open-ended possibility of the absolute surprise.

NOTES

This essay previously appeared as "Tears Beyond Being: Derrida's Experience of Prayer" in *Théologie négative*, ed. Marco M. Olivetti (Padua: CEDAM, 2002), pp. 861–80, and is here reproduced with permission of CEDAM.

1. V: Hélène Cixous and Jacques Derrida, *Voiles* (Paris: Galilée, 1998); English: *Veils*, trans. Geoffrey Bennington (Stanford, Calif.: Stanford University Press, 2001). This book contains a short piece entitled "*Savoir*" by Cixous on the severe myopia from which she suffered from birth, which was cured by laser surgery, and her subsequent and unexpected mourning for the loss of her myopia, her lifelong companion; and a second longer piece by Derrida entitled "A Silkworm of One's Own (Points of View Stitched on the Other Veil)" ("Un Ver à soie: Points de vue piqués sur l'autre voile"), which deals with his lifelong companion, another veil, which is not a veil at all, but a white tallith, a prayer shawl.

2. *Marg.*: Derrida, *Marges de philosophie* (Paris: Éditions de Minuit, 1967); English: *Margins of Philosophy*, trans. Alan Bass (Chicago: University of Chicago Press, 1982).

3. Derrida, *Monolingualism of the Other; or, The Prosthesis of Origin*, trans. Patrick Mensah (Stanford, Calif.: Stanford University Press, 1998), p. 1 et passim. This essay is an extended meditation on this phrase.

4. Hélène Cixous, *Portrait de Jacques Derrida en Jeune Saint Juif* (Paris: Galilée, 2001), p. 9.

5. Derrida, "Comment ne pas parler: Dénegations," in *Psyche: L'inventions de l'autre* (Paris: Galilée, 1987), p. 562, 562 n. 13; "How to Avoid Speaking: Denials," in *Derrida and Negative Theology*, ed. Howard Coward and Toby Foshay (Albany: SUNY Press, 1992), pp. 100, 135–36 n. 13.

6. Circ.: "Circonfession: cinquante-neuf périodes et périphrases," in Geoffrey Bennington and Jacques Derrida, *Jacques Derrida* (Paris: Éditions du Seuil, 1991); the number following the slash is the page number of the English translation by Geoffrey Bennington: "Circumfession: Fifty-nine Periods and Periphrases" in Geoffrey Bennington and Jacques Derrida, *Jacques Derrida* (Chicago: University of Chicago Press, 1993). For commentaries, see John D. Caputo, *The Prayers and Tears of Jacques Derrida* (Bloomington: Indiana University Press, 1997), §18; Cixous, *Portrait*; Gideon Ofrant, *The Jewish Derrida*, trans. Peretz Kidron (Syracuse, N.Y.: Syracuse University Press, 2001); Jill Robbins, "Cir-

cumcising Confession: Derrida, Autobiography, Judaism," *Diacritics* 25 (1995): 20–38; Elisabeth Weber, *Questions au Judaïsme* (Paris: Desclée de Brouwer, 1996). Citations of the Latin text of the *Confessions* are from *Loeb Classical Library* (Cambridge: Harvard University Press, 1916), vol. 26. I am using the translation of the *Confessions* by F. J. Sheed (Indianapolis: Hackett, 1970).

7. Derrida, *Cinders (Feu le cendre)*, a bilingual edition, trans. Ned Lukacher (Lincoln: University of Nebraska Press, 1991), p. 75.

8. In Derrida's account of prayer, as distinguished from his practice of prayer in "Circumfession," prayer is composed of two elements: (1) a pure invocation of the other as other, any other, God, for example; (2) an element of praise, which inevitably involves a predicative content. One never finds invocation in its purity but always mixed with a predicative element, which makes it Christian, Jewish, etc.; see "Comment ne pas parler: Dénegations," p. 572; "How to Avoid Speaking: Denials," p. 110; for commentaries, see Caputo, *The Prayers and Tears of Jacques Derrida*, pp. 38–39, and Hent de Vries, *Philosophy and the Turn to Religion* (Baltimore: Johns Hopkins University Press, 1999), pp. 135– 41.

9. Jean-Luis Chrétien, "La parole blessée: Phénoménologie de la prière," in *Phénoménologie et théologie* (Paris: Criterion, 1992), p. 41; English: "The Wounded Word: The Phenomenology of Prayer," trans. Jeff Kosky in *Phenomenology and the "Theological Turn": The French Debate* (New York: Fordham University Press, 2001), p. 147. "Voilà que je me surprends à t'adresser la parole / Mon Dieu, moi qui ne sais encore si tu existes." Jules Supervielle, *La fable du monde* (Paris: Gallimard, 1950), p. 39.

10. Chrétien, "Blessée," p. 42; "Wounded," p. 147.

11. Yves Bonnefoy, *"La Lumière, Changée," Poèmes* (Paris: Mercure de France, 1978), p. 211.

12. Jacques Derrida, "Donner la mort" in *L'Éthique du don: Jacques Derrida et la pensée du don* (Paris: Métailié-Transition, 1992), p. 53; English: *The Gift of Death*, trans. David Wills (Chicago: University of Chicago Press, 1995), p. 49.

13. See Derrida, *Sur Parole: Instantanés philosophiques* (Paris: l'Aube, 1999), p. 54.

14. See Derrida, *Politiques de l'amitié* (Paris: Galilée, 1995), pp. 197–98; English: *Politics of Friendship*, trans. George Collins (London and New York: Verso, 1997), pp. 173–74; and *Deconstruction in a Nutshell: A Conversation with Jacques Derrida*, edited with a commentary by John D. Caputo (New York: Fordham University Press, 1997), pp. 24–25.

15. *OG: De la grammatologie* (Paris: Éditions de Minuit, 1967); English: *Of Grammatology*, corrected edition, trans. Gayatri Spivak (Baltimore: Johns Hopkins University Press, 1997).

16. *ED:* Jacques Derrida, *Écriture et la différence* (Paris: Éditions de Seuil, 1967); English: *Writing and Difference*, trans. Alan Bass (Chicago: University of Chicago Press, 1978).

17. Derrida, *Sauf le nom* (Paris: Galilée, 1993), pp. 41– 46; English: *On the Name*, ed. Thomas Dutoit (Stanford, Calif.: Stanford University Press, 1995), pp. 48– 60.

18. Chrétien, "Blessée," 41/"Wounded," 147.

19. Derrida, *Monolingualism of the Other*, pp. 67– 68.

20. Ibid., p. 64.

six

Heidegger

Reader of Augustine

Philippe Capelle

I have been asked to discuss the relationship between Heidegger and Saint Augustine, and more precisely, to give an account of Heidegger's reading of Saint Augustine's work in order to determine the influence of this reading on the development of his own thought. This question is not new but has been addressed many times since Otto Pöggeler's famous book, *Der Denkweg Martin Heideggers* in 1963.[1] I have recently organized two academic meetings in Paris on this subject, focusing on specific issues such as the theme of *memoria* in Augustine and its rendering by Heidegger. To this purpose, it would be quite useful to build a typology of the various commentaries—although I am aware that it is impossible in the framework of a lecture. This difficult task would enable us to distinguish the different strategies at work and emphasize the aims that they serve.

However, the issue that I would like to concentrate on here is the relation between Heidegger's thought and that of Augustine, his *Confessions* in particular, which I address from a systematic point of view. What does "systematic" mean here? First of all, it implies an exhaustive account of the genesis of this relationship and a consideration of the questions that provided the context for Heidegger's investigation of Augustine. But "systematic" also means a correct understanding of the level at which this encounter between the two occurred.

Clearly, the recent publication of some of Heidegger's previously unpublished works justifies and urges a fresh reading of his oeuvre. Not so long ago the "Letter on Humanism," settling his accounts with Sartre, was the center of interpretation; since then, the publication of several texts by the young Heidegger, where most of the references to Augustine figure, has displaced attention to a period of unsuspected richness, which I believe supports my hypothesis that the relation between philosophy and theology in the thought of Heidegger is threefold:

1. First, it is revealed as a contrast between philosophy and Christian theology. Ontology as a science (while distancing itself from all *Weltanshauung*) erupts in rigorous fidelity to the abyssal philosophical adventure and is anchored only to the folly of the question of "Being." Ontology stands opposed to Christian theology, an ontical science founded on the *positum* of faith in a crucified God. Nevertheless, the "answer" and the "security" (the shelter) it offers leaves the ontological search intact. Heidegger's 1927 lecture, the first part of his 1935 course, and the letter dated August 8, 1928, recently published as part of his correspondence with Blochmann, should all be read within this perspective.

2. The second topic reorganizes the relation between philosophy and Onto-theology. Both philosophy and theology (whether Christian or philosophical theology) develop within the dimorphic structure of Western metaphysics. Metaphysics proceeds from a betrayal of ontology in favor of "foundation," or "ground," which is expressed by theology as "a Being-Theos." At the origin of this betrayal lies the confusion between two conducts of thought—one in search of the general features of beings, and the other trying to designate their raison d'être. This confusion gives rise to Onto-theology and its epochal variations. Whereas the first "topic" considers Christian theology a possibility, the second one denounces the progression of its historic compromise with metaphysical determination.

3. The third and final topic, "the thought of being and waiting for God," debates whether the possibility of a divinity lies beyond any Christian or anti-Christian reference and can only be conceived in the Opening-up of Being. This god, the "last god" (*Letzte Gott*), does not arrive like a resolution from above, like the new subject of a compelling revelation; but on the contrary, it belongs to the ever-present transcendence of the Dasein, the transcendence of the Being, a temporal diffusion of the *Ereignis*. The words do not summon this god; as witness to human distress over his absence, the world carries the mysterious trace of its presence in anticipation of its possible advent. It is a *waiting* without *desire* since it has no *measure*, which is only possible "in between" (*Zwischen*) the moment common to the Dasein and the god, which never leaves the transcendence of Being.

It would be impossible to assign a distinct period to each of these three topics since *each one coincides with a new commencement of vigorous thinking that coexists with the others*. We can say that Heidegger's approach to Augustine's *Confessions* belongs to the first topic or, to be more precise, it prepares the way for it. The Protestant world in which Heidegger learns to read Augustine turns him toward primitive Christian experience as the experience of factical life. But the conceptual device elaborated during this period will foster the diagnosis of Onto-theology.

So we have to start from the beginning in order to understand the writings that Heidegger dedicated to Augustine, *Augustine and Neo-Platonism* (1921) and *The Concept of Time* (1924). This means we have to understand as much as possible the phenomenological program laid out in the lessons that immediately preceded the course on Augustine, specifically the *Einleitung in die Phänomenologie der Religion* from 1920–1921.[2]

I. A Phenomenology of Religion

The 1920/1921 winter-semester course, *Introduction to the Phenomenology of Religion*, is best described as an attempt to theorize the comprehension of religious life from a phenomenological point of view. Such theorizing is sustained by a commentary on a number of passages from the New Testament.

This attempt proceeds from the formulation of some fundamental questions pertaining to the essence of philosophy. What do we call *introducing* to philosophy? How do we *introduce* to philosophy? We can use this expression only insofar as philosophy springs from the experience of factical life. Here "experience" should not be misunderstood as synonymous with "experiential," a term that implies exteriorization; on the contrary, it wants to express "the totality of both the active and passive stances of men and women towards the world in its deepest singularity." The concept of "world" is threefold: (1) as environment (*Umwelt*), that is, that which comes to be encountered by us, that which we come upon, or rather, which comes upon us; (2) as with-world (*Mitwelt*), the world of others; and (3) as the world of oneself (*Selbstwelt*).[3]

"Facticity" designates that which imposes itself upon us; therefore, to experience factical life amounts to confronting "the features that impose themselves,"[4] that is, life as it constitutes the tenor (*Richtung*) of all experience. Factical experience also manifests a complete "indifference" (*Indifferenz*) toward experience and builds its self-sufficiency (*Selbstgenügsamkeit*) on this indifference.

Heidegger creates a few carefully chosen concepts, and the sole purpose of this complex conceptual structure is to account for that which, prior to any theorization or any given value, presents itself within the experience of factical life as "significance" (*Bedeutsamkeit*). Ultimately, we cannot grant any pertinence to the dichotomy between "realm of facts/realm of significations" since each of the terms is relative to the tenor of factical experience as it unfolds within a seminal "significance." Therefore factical experience itself offers another site for conceiving the act of "philosophizing" as well as for conceiving religious phenomenality.

The confrontation that interests Heidegger takes the form of a fundamental debate about whether the philosophy of religion "emanates from the religious sense or, on the contrary, whether religion is immediately captured in such an *objective* way that it finds itself encased in the straightjacket of philosophical disciplines."[5]

This question had already been introduced, albeit in embryo, in the 1918 course on medieval mysticism, but here it receives a clear-cut answer, against Troeltsch: philosophical disciplines that deal with religion do not in fact derive from religion but treat it as an ob-ject (*Objekt*). Although Troeltsch indeed broke new ground by going so far as to analyze *belief* (*Glaube*) in the existence of God as an archetypal phenomenon of religion, he nevertheless reinserted belief into the system of connections among real objects, in compliance with the unifying requirements of reason.

Hence, a return to the question Heidegger identified straightaway: Is a phenomenology of religion sufficiently equipped to think out religion in its irreducible factuality, or does it too belong to a scientific-objective dynamic of integration? This question will be dealt with and developed by turning to the problem of historicity.

At this point, Heidegger not only leaves behind all philosophies of history but also the principle that governs them, the attempt to *find protection* against history's *cura*. This dismissal is achieved through the scrutiny of three emblematic paths: (a) the Platonic path in which the meaning of temporality unfolds and is accomplished in the supratemporal; (b) the path of radical abandon, represented mainly by the positions of Simmel and Spengler, according to which the historical world, inasmuch as it is "the only fundamental reality, the only *effective* reality,"[6] finds itself drawn up into the objective process of things happening";[7] and finally, (c) the path that results from a compromise between the two preceding ones and that tends to find value in the relation between the two worlds: here "the values of 'we' are given only in a relative feature but through which the absolute shows through."[8] However, if we take a closer look at these three paths, we realize that Platonism dominates the others: whether life tries to protect itself *against* history (first path), or rather *with* history (second path), or indeed, *starting from* history (third path), it nevertheless obeys the principle of referring to an absolute that interrupts history.

Consequently, even before the course on *Augustinus und der Platonismus*, a rift opens up out of which historicity receives a concept adequate to counter the multiple efforts of secularization: the concept of *Bekümmerung* (care, concern). As I said before, this concept is forged here without any explicit reference to Augustine; it expresses the categorical refusal to integrate *care* (*concern*) as an object of history. The factical-being to which the concept refers is not blind: it entails a meaning that remains to be elucidated, which requires a new concept of time furnished by the "formal indication" (*formale Anzeige*).[9] With this notion that will become pivotal until well after *Sein und Zeit*, Heidegger wants to foster a new way of considering the object: not according to its quiddity, its essence, but according to the fact of its being given, not its ontic place, but its ontological determination. This task consists of experiencing "the inaugural temporality in factical experience, in total abstraction from pure conscience and pure time."[10] We will reach the ultimate sense of time only if we follow the path that originates from this founding experience.

At this point Heidegger conducts a series of exegetical studies of the New Testament. They provide him with a testing ground at the intersection of the basic methodological requirements of phenomenology and the effort to understand the factical experience of life under a new light in an original way supported by phenomenology. Against the classical philosophies of religion that constantly objectivize religion and, more profoundly, against tendencies to secularization, this ex-

ercise in phenomenological explication brings temporality back to the heart of
the religious act, at least as far as Christian tradition is concerned. "The Religiosity (*Religiosität*) of primitive, original Christianity stems from the life experience
of this original Christianity and it coincides with this very same experience. . . .
The factical experience of life is historical. Christian Religiosity experiences temporality as such."[11]

The phenomena of proclamation of faith, and of eschatological determination are therefore each apprehended as coextensive with the temporal experience
of factical life. What is announced here, aside from the dismissal of philosophies
of religion, is indeed a turning point in phenomenology, by which phenomenological intentionality is gradually grounded in the being as Being-there, factually
present, and consequently in which the outline of a radical phenomenology of religion can be discerned.

II. Augustine and the Abandon of Facticity

To understand the summer semester course *Augustinus und der Neuplatonismus*,
we have to take into consideration two interconnected elements: the context of
phenomenological research that we have discussed so far, and the teeming of ideas
within the revival of Protestant theology. Elsewhere, I have tried to draw attention to the influence of Protestant theology on Heidegger; it represents an in-
valuable source for his philosophy not only as a young man but also during his
maturity.[12] We can gather evidence of this influence by considering the course
of 1921. The first clue comes from the treatment of medieval mysticism. In the
1918 course, Heidegger had conducted a study of this movement that he had interpreted as a protest against both scholastic theology and ecclesiastical practice.
In 1921, Augustine inspires him to establish a link between that revival movement and Luther's process of formation. A second clue to Heidegger's position-
ing of himself within Protestantism is the fact that he stigmatizes the Catholic
world for betraying Augustine to the advantage of "an Augustinianism already
adapted to Church doctrine."[13]

Subsequently, the question turns to the bearing of Augustine upon Christian
tradition. Heidegger thoroughly examines the methodologies of historical research
as employed by Ernst Troeltsch, Adolph von Harnack, and Wilhelm Dilthey. He
shows that each one of them conceives historical analysis as an inquiry into Augustine's heritage in Western culture. According to Troeltsch, as Heidegger sees
it, the fact that Augustine has tried to establish an ethical consonance and harmony between the calls of Christian life and the demands of culture would explain the cultural survival of Christianity beyond its original Judeo-Hellenistic
foundation. Harnack, for his part, specifically underscores Augustine's contribution to the dogmatic shaping of the Church. As for Dilthey, he perceives Augustine's effort to place revelation in an historical perspective as the start of a process
leading to the modern consciousness of history. These three models — Troeltsch's
universal history of culture, Harnack's *history of dogma*, and Dilthey's *history of*

science—and the motives behind their construction are all tarnished by the same flaw, that is, the search for an objective progression in Christian history. By examining the relation between Augustine and neo-Platonism, Heidegger does not intend to single out arbitrarily a special case allowing access to a supposedly "objective" history of the relation between Greek thought and Christianity. This is utterly impossible for the fundamental reason that we are implicated in the very history of the encounter between Augustine and neo-Platonism, and therefore we can neither control nor objectivize this history. The idea that the analysis of the historical development of Christianity in its successive periods might provide a hermeneutic key to Christian faith is not sound. We can easily see what is at stake here: we have to think of the relation between Augustine and neo-Platonism from the factical position that makes us contemporary with this relation.

Thanks to Augustine, through a phenomenological interpretation of Book X of the *Confessions*, Heidegger pursues his effort to thematize factical life and clarify the concept. "Facticity" does not mean "factuality" (*Tatsächlichkeit*), that is, the simple, plain contingency of objects in the world of experience, as we find at the beginning of Husserl's *Ideen*. Facticity is tied to Augustine's *facticia est anima*, to the basic original constitution of that which is there and which is thought of as such. But at the same time, we are going to see that Heidegger's reading of Augustine is ambivalent.

In order to show this, I turn to §9 "The astonishment over memory" (*Das Staunen über die memoria*), where Heidegger analyzes the concept of memory. He emphasizes that memory exceeds everything that the human "mind," or personal identity, can grasp: "*Penetrale amplum et infinitum!* All this belongs to me distinctively and I do not grasp it. . . . That which the mind does not grasp from within itself, where should it be?"[14] Heidegger emphasizes both the non-coincidence of the mind with itself and the fact that it is thrown into the insecurity pertaining both to Augustine's problematization of time and to the essence of Heidegger's commentary. For Augustine, this non-coincidence makes possible two dispositions of the spirit *curare* (*Bekümmertsein*): man can choose between two directions: he can turn away from good; or he can actively listen to that which inhabits him, exceeds him, and constitutes his memory. Heidegger elaborates the concept of facticity within this domain and goes so far as to comment on three modes of *tentatio* that bring about a dispersion of life: *concupiscentia carnis, concupiscentia oculorum, ambitio saeculi*,[15] as well as *molestia* (worry).[16] These remarks will form the premises of the analysis of Dasein in *Being and Time*.

It might be surprising that Heidegger does not carry through his analysis to the second orientation that Augustine considers: going beyond facticity. But it is easy to understand why he does not. For Augustine, it is memory, exceeding the limits of the human mind, that is open to the presence, in each person, of the interior Word. Through this Christian concept of memory, Augustine has been able to build a bridge, albeit in a critical manner, to Platonic and Neoplatonic theories of reminiscence and *anamnesis* in particular.[17] Heidegger draws up his overall diagnosis of Augustine's thought from this angle: by resorting to Greek philosophy, Augustine has abandoned the facticity of life and sacrificed it to metaphysics. The entire structure of the course on Augustine, the way it is organized, reveals the question that Heidegger considers paramount: it is not the temporalizing of the soul in its different modalities that preoccupies him but the facticity of life. On this point (*souciance*, concern), he finds that Augustine's conceptual system drifts away from facticity; although he approaches the latter within the analysis of *curare*, he later forsakes it. This infidelity is manifest in the way he presents the *fruitio Dei*; this *fruition*, by seeking to rest in God, *Summum Bonum*, robs facticity of its ontological and historical solicitude. In the end, Augustine is criticized for trying to think of memory without time, for having taken away its drive toward completion to the advantage of an immutable consistency.[18]

I will consider the remaining topic from two aspects: ontological time, and the difference between Augustine's *intentio* and Heidegger's *verlaufen*.

III. A New Concept of Time

The lecture "The Concept of Time" (*Der Begriff der Zeit*),[19] delivered in 1924 before the Marburg Theological Society, unquestionably marks the most symbolic moment in the transition from a young, Catholic Heidegger to a mature one. The main themes of *Being and Time* are present in embryo. From now on, time will no longer be conceived from "a theological point of view," that is, starting from eternity and going "from eternity to time." From now on, one should adopt the philosopher's point of view: the philosopher does not believe in God and therefore has resolved *to understand time in terms of time*."[20] The lecture is neither theological nor strictly speaking philosophical; it intends to elaborate a concept of time in keeping with the facticity of the "being-there" of humankind.

The trivial question "What is time?" points from the beginning to a comprehension of events within a spatial and continuous structure—not unlike Aristotle, who associates this notion with that of the alteration of Being. "Since time itself is not movement, it must somehow have to do with movement."[21] A preferable way of formulating this question might be "Who is time?" This question points to the original intimacy between temporality and Dasein. In Augustine's *Confessions* we find a first attempt to thematize this intimacy: "*In te, anime meus, tempora metiorn; noli mihi obstrepere: quod est*" ("So it is in you, my mind, that I measure periods of time . . . in you, I affirm, I measure periods of time").[22] Unfortunately, Heidegger continues, "Augustine left the question hanging at this point"; he assigns to human existence, to the "I," the relation to time: "*Ipsam metior cum tempora metior.*" The present consciousness is what I am measuring, not the stream of past events which have caused it. "When I measure time, that is what I am actually measuring."[23] The "Being-there" coincides with oneself "in the temporality of its most extreme possibility: one's death. This coincidence is accomplished in the movement of Dasein "running ahead to its past." "Running ahead seizes the past as the authentic possibility of every moment of insight, as what is now certain."[24] Thus the relation between Dasein and authentic time is established in these terms: "Being futural . . . gives time, because it is time itself."[25] The time of "Being-there" is neither being-present in the now, nor possibility as potentiality.

IV. Augustinian *intentio* and Heidegger's *Vorlaufen*

Unfortunately, the previous approach does not do justice to the Augustinian concept of time, nor does Heidegger concede what he borrows from it. It is grounded on the binomial relation to time expressed by *distentio-intentio*. In the *Confessions* we read, *"Video igitur quandam distentionem"* (I therefore see that time is some kind of extension)[26] and further on: *"Ecce distentio est vita mea"* (See how my life is a distention).[27] The concept of *distention* in Plotinus signifies the "temporalizing" of man, as it is subject to the constant, irreversible, everyday flowing of time. This notion is coupled with the very Augustinian notion of *intentio* that designates eschatological anticipation. While *distentio* defines a "negative" relation to time, a submission, *intentio* fixes a "positive" relation, an appropriation of time. In the first instance, man is "temporalized"; in the second, he "temporalizes."

We can say more. According to Augustine, the temporalizing of man is coextensive with the movement of conversion to God the Creator: "'Forgetting the past' and moving not towards those future things which are transitory but to 'the things which are before' me, not stretched out in distraction, but extended in reach, not by being pulled apart but by concentration. So I 'pursue the prize of the high calling' where I 'may hear the voice of praise' and 'contemplate your delight' (Ps. 25:7; 26:4) which neither comes nor goes."[28] As we see, these concepts cannot be understood independently of their existential foundation, that is, Christian conversion.

Here we can perceive how Heidegger moves away from Augustine. What the latter names *intentio*, the direction toward the promised God of eternity, the former calls *Vorlaufen*, the running ahead toward the mortal destiny of the being-there. This displacement is brought about by confusion between the two perfectly distinct notions of *distentio* and *aversio*. In the *Confessions*, *intentio* is an act of radical conversion, while *aversio* is the temporality of sin and *distentio* is the temporality of what we can call "human finitude." By entering the time of God, which is eternity—*intentio*—man rejects *aversio* and goes beyond *distentio*. For Heidegger the temporality of *intentio*, once it breaks away from eternity, is the temporality of the extreme possibility of Dasein: being towards death. The shift from the *intentio* of Augustine to the *Vorlaufen* of Heidegger is the indication of a formal appropriation of the Augustinian notion of "anticipation," but it is also an indication of an essential departure from the hermeneutics of the call of God to the hermeneutic of the call of death.

V. Critical Remarks

I would like to conclude with two remarks. The first one concerns Heidegger's reading of *memoria* in Augustine's work. You will remember that this concept plays a crucial part in allowing the soul to open up to eternal truth, but Heidegger con-

siders this concept to be over-determined by the notion of *anamnesis* borrowed
from Platonism and neo-Platonism. This is a misunderstanding, and Heidegger
misses the point along two lines. First, what he does not see, or perhaps what he
does not pay enough attention to, is the fact that in Book X, chapter 5 of the *Confessions*, Augustine associates memory with Scripture, and with Saint Paul in particular. When he writes, "There is something of the human person which is unknown even to the 'spirit of man which is in him,'" he is clearly inspired by an
excerpt from the first letter to the Corinthians: "For now we see in a mirror, dimly,
but then we will see face to face" (1 Cor 13:12, NRSV). Although eternal truth is
not entirely present to the human spirit, it is nevertheless not entirely absent from
it. This is the reason why—and this argument is conclusive—"memory," inasmuch
as it represents the habitation of the Verb in the human spirit, can be understood,
within Augustine's logic, as a notion of factical life. The resistance that prevents
Heidegger from accepting eternity as a notion relevant to factical life—the lecture of 1924 that we have investigated does presage the phenomenological rejection of the notion of eternity in *Being and Time*—can be attributed to the fact that
he assimilates it to speculative metaphysics. It is true that by identifying eternity
as the aim of *intentio*, that is, as quietude, the rest that interrupts and puts an end
to unrest, Augustine fulfills his project to go beyond temporality. But does this mean
that, since Augustine's concept of eternity attempts to exceed the concept of temporality, it can only be an alternative to it? We have to give a negative answer, and
this negative answer makes room for a phenomenological recovery of eternity on
the basis of the Augustinian notion of memory.

The second point on which Heidegger misses Augustine's project is linked to
the stake inherent in patristic tradition since Justin concerning the relation between proclamation of the faith and the Greek heritage. We have to remember
that the church fathers had a generally positive relation with this heritage; it allowed and fostered a renewed reading of Greek philosophy. A perspective of completion used to determine the hermeneutical link between the Old Testament and
Christ is transposed with extreme care, most of the time, to the relation between
various figures of Greek philosophy on one side and the advent of the truth in
Christ on the other.

The second remark concerns what I have expressed by the notion of "ambivalence." Heidegger maintained an ambivalent relation to theology; this ambivalence is a constant feature of his itinerary, a reminder of his theological provenance. "Herkunft bleibt stets Zukunft" (Provenance always means future). We find
an expression of this ambivalence in a letter written to Elisabeth Blochmann in
1928, where he says of his students: "I have freed more than one from theology.
Nevertheless, if these young men have found their interior freedom this way, it is
a good thing."[29] This ambivalence is obviously not psychological but stands as an
indication that even when he progressively leaves theology behind, his thought is
still nourished by it. To this end it is always useful to distinguish between Heidegger's *roots* in a Catholic background; his *debt* vis-à-vis the schemata of Catholic,
and more especially Protestant theology; and his *provenance*, which registers the

move (sustained by theology) toward a system of thought striving to achieve its independence.

This paradox can be clearly understood if we turn to what I have briefly mentioned previously: the "formal indication," as it is defined by §13 of the 1920–1921 winter course *Introduction to the Phenomenology of Religion*. In contrast to the act of *generalization* that holds in the region of things, *formalization* considers the object as given, as being there. Therefore, the formal indication does not pronounce a judgment on the content of the object; it is part of the phenomenological analysis as a methodological moment. "Formal" refers to the phenomenon detached from any theoretical determination. Along the way to the redaction of *Being and Time*, the expression "formal indication" will be riveted to the ontological foundation. We can say that Heidegger applied formal indication to Augustinian conceptuality, and even though he did not do justice to the constituent features of Augustinian thought—nor by extension to Christian theology—he nevertheless honored the Augustinian claim of the contemporaneity of the subject in the act of truth and truth itself.

Translated by Anna Allais and Susan Emanuel

DERRIDA'S RESPONSE TO PHILIPPE CAPELLE

I want to thank you very warmly for your paper. Of course, I share with you the conviction that the reading of these texts, these old but new texts by Heidegger, should transform the perception that we have of his itinerary, and that is a conviction I deeply share with you. Now, to be brief, my question is, when Heidegger said in 1928, "I freed more than one from theology," my question is, did he free himself from theology? When, at the end of your wonderful lecture, you analyzed the ways in which Heidegger moves away from Augustine, couldn't we say that this transfer from what you call the analytic of the call of God to the analytic of the call of death means that, in fact, we can always retranslate this transfer? Everything in Heidegger, then, could be re-translated into Christian, Catholic, or Protestant theology so that in fact, moving away means continuing the same, not moving away, being true while being untrue to this heritage. That is my assumption, that he remained deeply Christian despite his denial. Even the concept of destruction, his *Destruktion*, which—Jack Caputo taught this to me—comes from Luther's *destructio*, means that, in fact, the Christian tradition remains stronger than everything.[30] You can always operate the other way around, that is, to re-translate Heidegger despite his denials into Christian concepts, and then nothing will change.

Capelle: Yes, I thank you very much for this decisive question. In *Of Spirit: Heidegger and the Question*, you try to imagine a conversation between Christian theologians and Heidegger.[31] You conclude by saying that you are not really in the same position as Christian theology, and that you are not Heidegger, but that we today live exactly at the point where we can understand where we are. That means there is a position where it is possible to understand Christian theology independently of Christian theology. That is very important. So my question was, at the end of my text, about whether this kind of transfer is compatible with, is honest about, theology. Is it possible to be a theologian and accept that? I would say "yes." But the question is for the theologian to accept the irreducible position of being able to understand theology while not being a theologian. That is the question. Heidegger tried to say that "I would like to understand theology, I would like to know where theology is." Nevertheless, I would resist, and I think you will agree that it is not a good idea, to give a theological interpretation of Heidegger. Because Heidegger doesn't struggle with theology but wants to get at another point, to understand, from an ontological point of view, what theology *is*. I think that is not an opposition for the theologian. It is does not involve a meditation that would build a new theology. I think it is not an opposition, and I think you will agree. At the same time, I would say the Christian theology has the right to protest against, particularly concerning the texts which thematize the onto-theology, the abusive re-appropriation of several axes of its Tradition and its Systematics. Thank you for this important, difficult question.

NOTES

1. Otto Pöggeler, *Der Denweg der Martin Heideggers* (Pfullingen: Neske, 1963); English: *Martin Heidegger's Path of Thinking*, trans. Daniel Magurshak and Sigmund Barber (Atlantic Highlands, N.J.: Humanities Press International, 1987).

2. *Einleitung in die Phänomenologie der Religion*, GA 60 (Frankfurt am Main: Klostermann, 1995), 1–156.

3. GA 60, 11.

4. GA 60, p. 9.

5. GA 60, p. 27.

6. GA 60, p. 46.

7. GA 60, p. 43.

8. GA 60, p. 44.

9. GA 60, §13.

10. GA 60, p. 65.

11. GA 60, p. 80.

12. See §§1–3 and 12–21 of my book *Philosophie et théologie dans la pensée de Martin Heidegger* (Paris: Cerf, 1998; 2nd ed., 2001).

13. GA 60, p. 159.

14. GA 60, p. 182.

15. GA 60, §§ 13–15.

16. GA 60, § 17.

17. Saint Augustine, *Confessions*, X, 10.

18. GA 60, pp. 247–48.

19. *Der Begriff der Zeit* (Halle: Niemeyer, 1989); English: *The Concept of Time*, trans. W. MacNeill (Oxford: Blackwell and Cambridge University Press, 1992).

20. *Concept of Time*, p. 1.

21. Ibid., p. 3.

22. Augustine, *Confessions*, Book XI, chapter 27.

23. *Concept of Time*, p. 6.

24. Ibid., p. 15.

25. Ibid.

26. *Confessions* XI, 23, 30.

27. Ibid., XI, 29, 39.

28. Ibid.

29. M. Heidegger and E. Blochmann, *Briefwechsel 1918–1969* (Stuttgart: Deutsche Schillersgesellschaft, 1989), p. 26.

30. Jack Caputo, in turn, was taught this by John Van Buren, *The Young Heidegger: Rumor of the Hidden King* (Bloomington: Indiana University Press, 199), pp. 161– 62.

31. Jacques Derrida, *Of Spirit: Heidegger and the Question*, trans. Geoffrey Bennington and Rachel Bowlby (Chicago: University of Chicago Press, 1989), pp. 110–13.

seven

The Form of an "I"

Catherine Malabou

To Kevin Hart

Facticity or machination? *Faktizität oder Machenschaft?* Heidegger inscribes the meaning of confession in Saint Augustine between these two ways of making. In fact, in the expression "to make the truth" (*veritatem facere*) that opens Book X: "I desire to make (or bring forth) [the truth] in my heart, before Thee in confession, but also in my book, before many witnesses," Heidegger classifies as equivocal the ontological signification of the verb *facere*: "to make," "to do," "to bring forth."

In indicating this equivocality, which, from one language to another—*facere, faire, machen,* make, *Macht,* machine—manifests the ambiguity of the ontological status of confession, I am already making an avowal. I confess my incapacity to speak of "Circumfession" without a witness, or, as Derrida says, "with no lighthouse and no book."[1] I need here, I confess, a lighthouse and a book: Heidegger's *Phenomenological Interpretation of Book X of the Confessions,* undertaken in a course he gave in 1921.[2] This interpretation will have important repercussions for *Being and Time,* in a certain way for the *Beiträge,* and also for Derrida's "Circumfession."

"To make or bring forth the truth": Derrida's text is itself also haunted by this formula. We find its first occurrence in the ninth "period "or "periphrasis" of "Circumfession." "To make the truth," Derrida says, cannot simply mean "to tell it," if "to tell the truth" presupposes "information," "presentation," a manner of "bringing to knowledge" something that "is" (Circ., 49/48). Further on: one can "speak truthfully" without "bringing out the truth" (56/56); further on still: "one can always describe or note the truth without avowal" (99/101).

My first question is this: Is Derrida's understanding of "bringing forth the truth" indebted in some way to the double hermeneutical possibility brought to light by Heidegger? On the one hand, according to Heidegger, *facere*, "bringing forth" refers back to facticity: a "self" would only confess in order to understand and to make understood, that it is "there," "thrown." On the other hand, *facere* means "to machinate, to fabricate, to make." Thus understood, confession would only be one more metaphysical gesture, complicit in the philosophical enterprise of the auto-fabrication and auto-verification of the ego, an enterprise that Heidegger characterizes in the *Beiträge* as being *"ohne Scheu,"* without modesty.

The "cir-" of "circumfession" both surrounds confession and holds it at a distance. Can this "cir-" allow itself to be contained in the ontological alternative which permits Heidegger to tilt confession either in the direction of existential analytic (in this sense, "cir" would be another way of saying *da*), or else in the direction of the metaphysical tradition to be deconstructed (thus, "cir" would mark a manner of surrounding which bids adieu to the thing thus circumscribed)? Or does it announce the opening of a completely other possibility of understanding?

My second question: life. If "bringing forth the truth" consists neither of informing, nor of presenting facts, nor of recounting one's life, then what life, what sense of life, is at issue in confession? If, as Derrida says, "my life is neither a content to be hidden, nor an interiority of the solitary self" (Circ., 212–13/228), then what can the "turn toward itself" of life implied by every confession mean? I turn again to Heidegger. For him, it is not truly a life, but the very being of life that confesses. Confession is always the phenomenon of life's being; in fact, it reveals the following:

> *Je mehr das Leben lebt; je mehr das Leben zu sich selbst kommt* (the more life lives, the more life reaches itself).[3]

Heidegger situates this speculation of life upon itself between facticity and machination (or staging). Again, a double hermeneutical possibility is open here. On the one hand, interpreted according to facticity, this circle of life is nothing other than the deployment, in confession, of the possibilities of Dasein's existence. On the other hand, understood differently, this circle prefigures the economy of the will to power, and this is already indicated by the Nietzschean accents of its formulation. Confession would reveal that life wills itself. My question on this point is this: When Derrida speaks of alliance, of the return of life upon itself in confession, of the movement of "turning around," of the ring, of the band, is he inscribing this circularity in the ontological horizon of such a distinction between life and life? Or on the contrary, does the "what will have been most alive in me" of "Circumfession" (14/12–13) appear as irreducible to the question of meaning understood as the meaning of being, which for Heidegger determines the understanding of life? To what extent does Derrida's book succeed in removing the confession, as a philosophical and literary form but also as a religious practice, from the authority of the ontological questioning which, in a certain sense, deprives it of a future?

The meaning of my title: "The Form of an 'I,'" depends on these questions. Heidegger is particularly attentive, in his course given in 1921, to the phenomenon of "temptation" (*tentatio*), presented by Augustine in Book X in all its richness and diversity. The analysis that Heidegger proposes prefigures the elaboration of Dasein's decline (falling, *Verfallenheit*) in *Being and Time*. The word *Verfallenheit* had not yet appeared in 1921, although Augustine had proposed it in Latin. It is a question of *defluxus*, the supine form of *defluere*, which means "to slide," a verb Augustine uses in this declaration: "Yes, abstinence reassembles us and leads us back to the unity which we had lost when sliding into the multiple (*a quo in multa defluximus*)."[4] The three principle forms of temptation—concupiscence of the flesh, concupiscence of the eyes, and concupiscence of secular ambitions (glory, love of praise, pride)—appear as inevitable threats of sliding. Yet it is these threats that, according to Heidegger, reveal existence to itself, or factical life (*faktische Leben*) to itself.

"In the 'sliding' (*im defluxus*), factical life constructs for itself, based on itself and for itself, a completely determinate direction of its possibility. . . ."[5] This "determinate direction" is nothing other than *care*. In 1921, Heidegger prefers *Bekümmernis* rather than *Sorge* (which appears only twice in the text) to translate the Latin *cura*. According to Heidegger, the apparently contrasting double possibility of sliding and care is contained in *molestia*, "worry, trouble, torment, bother." Heidegger turns *molestia* into the *Grundstimmung*, the fundamental form, of the affect of confession.[6] Insofar as it originally gives the subject to itself, *molestia* reveals facticity, the weight of the self, which makes itself felt in the constant appeal of sliding and fall: "*Molestia: ein Wie des Erfahrens, eine Beschwernis und Gefährdung des Sichselbsthabens*" (*Molestia*: a how of experience, a weight and a burden of having-oneself).[7]

Never, in his interpretation of Book X, does Heidegger mention avowal, fault, asking for pardon. If confession before God and before men has, as he says, a "motive," it is permitting Dasein (the word appears in the text) to discover its possibilities of existence, to feel its *Geworfenheit* (thrownness). Commenting on chapters 36–38 of Book X, Heidegger considers in minute detail Augustine's affirmation: "We are led, by certain demands of human society, necessarily to make ourselves love or fear men."[8] Heidegger sees in this "human society," not the domain of mundane affairs, but the world itself, the world in its phenomenological sense: *die Selbstwelt* (the world of self).[9] The "there." As for the "necessarily" (in "we are led necessarily to make ourselves love or fear men"), it is understood as the very sense of facticity. "*Necessitarium*," writes Heidegger, "indicates the *Faktizitätsinn*."[10] *Molestia* is an equivocal affect: on the one hand, it is desire for the world, desire to love, desire to fear. On the other hand, *molestia* is the fear of being nothing but desire. Due to this fear of "being nothing more," it seeks its own transcendence or transgression and thereafter becomes authentic care. This propels confession toward its proper destiny: the search for the love and the fear of God.

For Heidegger, if a confession before God and before men reveals something, it is less a guilty act, a deed, or an event than the very facticity of existence. Confession, more than a *was*, reveals a *Wie*. Everything happens as though the self knew nothing of itself before confessing, as if the very decision to confess gave birth to what there is to say, gave birth to the self itself as care. Care is the true gift of God. By means of confession, existence avows its own facticity. To return to our opening question, the expression "to bring forth the truth" cannot mean to convey information or to make known.

"*Molestia* is nothing objective (*ist kein Objektstück*), but rather describes a how of experience (*ein Wie des Erfahrens*), and as such we characterize it as the how of the experience of facticity (*das Wie des faktischen Erfahrens*)."[11] The bringing forth of truth is less an operation, a production, than a letting-be, a *Gelassenheit*, which alone can lead to happy life. There is a delay—a delay which is, for Heidegger, not yet a difference, between the self before and after a confession: "Very late did I love you, O beauty so old and so new, very late did I love you."[12] Confession is the revelation of the delay that divides the tempted soul while binding it to itself, full of the worry of *molestia*. Confession is also the delivered soul, which attains the happy life. Now, between the moment before and after confession, what the subject gains, according to Heidegger's strange declaration, is a *form*, the very form of the self, the *form of an I*. This is how he interprets the "very late did I love you": "*aber ich selbst war nicht in der Form, ich hatte nicht das Sein, das echtes Sein eines Selbst ist*" (but I myself was not in the form, I did not have being, the authentic being which is a self).[13] Heidegger opposes this form to *deformis*, an adjective used by Augustine, who declares: "*deformis irruebam*" (disgraced, I threw myself about).[14]

Deformis means "disfigured, disgraceful, deformation," but also "without form." Thus, the authentic form of the Self, for Heidegger, is that of Being. God gives to the self who confesses its form, that is, the very form of its facticity. The form of the I is its Being. Thus, to make out the truth is to form the self, to reveal to it what Heidegger in *Being and Time* calls its structural whole. Confession would be a sort of auto-analysis or existential auto-analytic. Still, at the moment when he interprets the "making" as a sort of passion, if not a creative passivity, Heidegger announces the necessity of deconstructing confession: "*Zur Destruktion von Confessio X*," he writes in an appendix,[15] thus opening a program that he left unaccomplished. In this appendix under this heading, he notices the insufficiently "radical" (*radikal*) aspect of the Augustinian analysis, this lack of radicality in the face of Being, understood as deafness to the question of Being. The whole thought of the present and of presence that Augustine puts to work—the present of memory, the presence of the happy life, the present of daily worry—is never, Heidegger declares, anything but modalities of *Vorhandensein* (being present).

It is relatively easy to lay out the basis of this deconstruction of confession if we turn to Heidegger's later works, such as the *Beiträge*. Although they do not refer directly to Augustine, they allow us to clarify the reading Heidegger proposes in 1921. To deconstruct confession amounts to disturbing this "form of the I" which presents itself through a certain aspect of itself as the constitution of the being (*Seinsverfassung*) of Dasein, that is, as facticity. To the extent that, for Heidegger, this facticity always has its declension in the present, it appears, through another aspect of itself, as one more machination (*Machenschaft*) of the ego or of the subject of metaphysics. In this sense, there would be very little difference between the self of confession and the I of Descartes's *Discourse on Method* or even the consciousness of Hegel's *Phenomenology of Spirit*. There is the same preoccupation in each case: to bring forth the truth, that is, to fabricate it, to create its motor, to machinate its effectiveness. In the history of metaphysics, consciousness of self (*Ichbewusstsein*) gives the measure of being-oneself (*Selbstheit*). *Machenschaft*, Heidegger writes in the *Beiträge*, "speaks of the domination of making and of what is made."[16] This domination, which rests upon a certain understanding of Being, has governed the philosophical tradition since the beginning. From the very beginning, Beinghood (*Seiendheit*) has been understood through the bringing forth or of the "makeability" of the being (*Machbarkeit des Seiendes*). A true being is that which is capable of making-itself-from-itself (or bringing-itself-forth-by-itself, *Sich-von-selbst-machen*). Every unfolding, every accomplishment, including those of *physis* itself, is thus interpreted in the history of philosophy on the basis of self-fabrication, of *technè*. An original solidarity ties together *idea, technè*, and *poiesis*. This solidarity constitutes *Machenschaft*. Present at the dawn of Greek philosophy, receiving its fundamental form in Aristotle's *Physics*, machination will not cease (until the Nietzschean will to power), transforming everything while remaining the same. Its biblical-Christian (*christlich-biblisch*) determination is another fundamental moment in its history, conferring the meaning of creation.[17] These analyses show that the self of confession, in learning of its facticity, fabricates it at the same instant. It creates itself by itself.

The self gains its effectiveness to the extent that it speaks to God. Equally, the form of a self or of an I is understood as the result of an ideal technique, that of auto-organization. Forgive me for taking so long to get to "Circumfession." I have discussed the Heideggerian interpretation of "bringing forth the truth" so as to signal its apparent proximity with that of Derrida. For Heidegger as for Derrida, remember, *veritatem facere* (to make the truth) does not mean to recount the facts. I return to the ninth period of "Circumfession":

> [M]aking truth has no doubt nothing to do with what you call truth, for in order to make an avowal, it is not enough to bring to cognition, to make known what is, for example to inform you that I have brought death, betrayed, blasphemed, perjured, it is not enough that I present myself to God or you, the presentation of what is or what I am . . . , "truth" then, having never given rise to avowal, to true avowal, the essential truth of avowal having therefore nothing to do with truth, but consisting, if, that is, one is concerned that it consist and that there be any, in asked-for pardon, in a request rather, asked of religion as of literature, before the one and the other which have a right only to this time, for pardoning, pardon, for nothing. (49–50/48–49)

In a certain way, Derrida recognizes in this declaration that the ontological difference, older than truth, watches over confession, and even confesses it. Being confesses the confession, purifies it; a confession is only true, and brings about the true, only if it avows that it cannot and must not avow anything. Nothing of a being, nothing which would emphasize *Vorhandensein*. Derrida affirms that making the truth is addressing an original request for pardon. This pardon has no object in the world, no sure addressee. He seems to install at the very heart of confession a division between authentic confession and an improper or pre-ontological confession. The authentic confession is the pardon for nothing in particular, a sort of ontological confession in some sense. And the improper confession is the confession of something, some thing in particular. In this sense, "Circumfession" appears as a sort of ontological absolution given to confession itself.

A second possible proximity between Heidegger and Derrida, connected to the first, is the interpretation of "bringing forth" based on facticity. For a long time, I understood the request for original pardon uttered by the author of "Circumfession" as "pardon *for* being-there," "pardon *of* being-there," pardon for being Dasein, that is, pardon for being there where I am, pardon for being this Dasein there, pardon for being a Dasein in general. This requested pardon reveals, at the same time, to the Dasein who requests it, the very fact of being, facticity. "You see, I'm here," says the author to his mother. "Ah, you're here," she replies to him (Circ., 121–22/127).

For a long time, I interpreted circumcision itself, or what Derrida says about it, the reason for which he says something about it, as a mark, an inscription (singular and at the same time comparable to every other inscription) of facticity. Is the "crime of [his] circumcision" not described by Derrida as a "kickoff" (73/74) or as the "*es gibt*" of a "stroke of the gift" (129/136)? I am thinking also of this passage, which affirms that circumcision is nothing other than that which is done: "*Kar*: to do (*faire*) in Sanskrit, the thing done as sacred thing, what happens in circumcision, what is done, outside language, without sentence, the time of a proper name, the rest is literature" (115–16/120–21). As for the mother, my "mother," is it not she as well, the name given to facticity, to "my" own? She who threw "me" into the sea, who ejected "me": this "volcano I tell myself I'm well out of," says Derrida (78/80). I then asked myself if "Circumfession" was not the existential analytic of a new age. Does one see there too a son, a man, a father, constantly tempted, haunted by desires and spirits, gnawed at by a sort of *molestia* without limit? "You cannot," Derrida declares to himself, "economize on your torment" (120/126). You have, as Augustine said, a heart "overburdened with poignant cares."[18] And one notices that this torment and this care manifest themselves most often through the fear of that which falls: this "fault [which] fell upon me like life itself, like death" (276/299) and through the fear of falling. Does the latter not speak of being haunted by *Verfallenheit*? If throughout his life Derrida has asked himself what "to turn around" means, he has also constantly interrogated the very possibility of the fall, the fall which appears here precisely as the possibility of sliding: "and later in the night, the words 'counterfeit coin,' in English, come to be associated with the word 'slip' in the same sentence, to denounce when I wake what I am doing here, missing my mother or letting her down" (243/262). Missing, sliding, *defluere*—are we not very close here to the fallenness of Dasein?

I could give other examples which would show that "Circumfession" brings forth its truth while writing the very facticity of existence. And certainly such a reading would not be wrong, strictly speaking. Still, it does not "bring out" the "truth." This is because Derrida has always known, perhaps since his very birth, that *Faktizität* and *Machenschaft* are the same and that the ontological difference, for that reason, most often plays at being dead, and that it is sometimes difficult, even impossible, to reanimate it. It is the machine itself that says so. It is the machine itself that reveals the impossibility of distinguishing, even in the time of an analytic, between facticity and machination. In "Circumfession," the machine is first of all the Geoff theologic program (*théologiciel*), the implacable "Derridabase," the techno-poetics of a corpus without citation, that is, without the legal appearance of the Dasein of the author. But the machine is also the involuntary mechanics of the agony, the dying life or the living death of his mother. This impassive life, this outstretched body, lets facticity itself be seen, the factical being of facticity. The mother is nowhere else but there. Caught in the vice of these two machines—the computer and the vegetative life—the "I" who writes here declines to interrogate any further the onto-theological structure of the confession. He knows it too well to distribute the premiums of authenticity or to refuse them. The onto-theological structure of confession is no longer any help to him.

What can ontology really do in the face of a certain agony: does a Dasein who vegetates still have a comprehension of its Being, or is it not precisely merely a mechanism? This alternative, in the end, has no meaning. That a Dasein should be able to falsify facticity by losing the sense of Being while still remaining there, that it should be able to machinate its facticity without dying—this kind of existential monstrosity opens an unsuturable breach into ontological questioning. Being does not *say* everything, that's why one *writes*, Derrida has always confided. Whence the fact that the "I" of confession could only have the form of a sentence: "I have been seeking myself in a sentence, yes, I, and since a circumbygone period at the end of which I would say I and which would, finally, have the form of what I have turned around" (Circ. 14–15/13).

Form of Being or form of a sentence? It is by speaking of life, of the relation between confession and life, that we see unfold the dynamic of the mis-step carried out by "Circumfession" with respect to the question of being. As I suggested at the outset, confession for Heidegger reveals the very law of life to the mortal: "The more life lives, the more life reaches itself"; in a word, life, in living, accomplishes itself. The same ontological ambiguity which spreads its shadow over the sense of "making" in "making the truth" weighs upon this circle. Another pair is superimposed onto the facticity-machination pair, strictly dependent on it and formed, according to Heidegger, out of existence (*Existenz*) on the one hand, and "lived experience" (*Erlebnis*) on the other. "The more life lives, the more it reaches itself"; this program opens a double exegetical direction once again. Simultaneously it announces both the possibility of an authentic grasp of existence by itself, and the organization, in the metaphysical sense of the term, of spirituality. The subject, in accumulating lived experiences, realizes life in the biological sense of the term. It auto-fabricates like an organism.

"The more life lives, the more it reaches itself." Heidegger's formula means that the more existence accomplishes the directions of experience (*Erfahrungsrichtungen*), the more it clarifies the "historical" (*historisch*) sense of facticity. Heidegger concludes: "[T]he more life lives, the more it reaches to its Being." The "more," he adds, is its "measure" (*Maßtab*) in the "direction of the Being of life itself."[19] In this way, in and through confession, "the whole of the concrete factical situation," which is "the radical possibility of the fall" reaches the proper Being of life, or in other words, finds its ontological direction and anchor.[20] Later, Heidegger will renounce the interchangeable use of the words "life" and "existence." The concept of life, applied to Dasein, will no longer mean anything but "lived experience" (*Erlebnis*). *Erlebnis* refers to the effectivity of events, to the real of experience, a real which *Being and Time* counts as curiosity, ambiguity, and preoccupation (*Besorgen*). Furthermore, as the *Beiträge* shows, lived experience is the accomplice of machination as much as the product. Precisely, sections 66, 67, and 68 of the *Beiträge* are entitled "*Machenschaft und Erlebnis.*" The two concepts work together to produce the logic of certainty, this certainty consisting in the unity of the "I think" and the "I live."

Lived experience, Heidegger says in section 61, has always given, in the West, the measure of justice and truth. Read in this light, the declaration of 1921, "[T]he more life lives, the more life reaches itself," can no longer be understood as the expression of facticity or finitude but as the affirmation by a thinking subject of its power of absolute domination. Heidegger shows in his *Nietzsche* that the will to power signifies first of all life "which comes to itself." In this sense, as paradoxical as it might seem, every confession would already have had its interests tied up with the will to power. In refusing to confide or confess to lived experiences, real events, acts and gestures, thus protecting himself against curiosity, Derrida also seems to establish a distinction between "life" and "lived experience": "I do not give to be seen or heard the detail of each of the transgressions, and I'll never do so, each of those that your curiosity wants to see, know, archive" (Circ., 99/103). He seems to distinguish between what he calls his life, or the "whole of his life," and the lived events in which it consists, these inadmissible events which are his crimes, his blasphemies, his betrayals ("perjures"), his deceptions. These are excluded from the live writing, which prefers to avoid them, by transforming them into concepts and depriving them of sensible content. The fundamental events confessed in the book are not lived ones. For example, circumcision, which determines a life, an alliance, cannot strictly speaking be a lived event.

This difference between *Leben* or *Existenz* and *Erleben* must again be called ontological. No sooner is this difference hinted at than it is abandoned. Certainly, in "Circumfession," it is a question of nothing other than life, of the life that sees itself dying, of survival. Certainly, in "Circumfession," it is a question of nothing other than life as alliance, return, ring: "the form of the Ring, return upon itself in the alliance, alliance for a new departure," says Derrida (237/256). Certainly, in "Circumfession," it is a question of nothing other than the possibility of rendering life to itself by means of writing. But very quickly, from the very beginning, Derrida refuses to distinguish, at the heart of the word "life," at the heart of the word "autobiography," between the existential avowal and the desire for domination. The two always go together, and indeed, one sees how, in the book, the fragility of the spoken word (*parole*) is endlessly doubled by this fantasy of power which always secretly motivates a confession:

> I am still so young; the unforgettable power of my discourses hangs on the fact that they grind up everything including the mute ash whose name alone one then retains. . . . (252–53/273).

Impossible, here again, to distinguish between facticity and machination. Life is finite, which is why it calculates. Perhaps one only confesses in order to cash in on the benefits of an existence, and even on the benefits of mourning:

> Mourning capitalizes, it accumulates, it stocks up, saving loves me, a work that no longer has to work, like what I am staking here and meaning is working all alone at my reserve, simultaneously put ahead and put to one side, a stake in any case. . . .[21]

In this speculation of life on itself, facticity or machination, life or lived experience, authenticity or calculation, honesty or strategy of confession, gain and loss, one recalls Derrida's affirmation in *Otobiographies* about the eternal return: "[N]othing returns to the living."[22] An affirmation that in a sense simultaneously ruins metaphysics and the "other thought," which seems assured by the possibility of its survival.

I will end by insisting on a motif that seems to gather together the proximity and infinite distance of two writings of confession: that of Heidegger and of Derrida. This motif is "therapeutic treatment (harassment), relentlessly pursued" (*acharnement thérapeutique*). It is named in the 34th period of "Circumfession":

> We euthanize ourselves in asking what a living woman would think if she saw death coming, whereas my mother had, when she was alive, before her lethargy, demanded from the doctor cousin, who told us this later, that he should never let her live in this way, never practice on her what the doctor is accusing us of, therapeutic harassment (*acharnement thérapeutique*), as though—[23]

The sentence is not completed; it remains, without punctuation, in suspense. Therapeutic harassment characterizes, in a pejorative manner, the zeal of the doctors and the entourage to keep alive a terminally ill person in an incurable coma, or sufferers of dementia. Confronted by his mother, kept alive at all costs, the author of "Circumfession" turns endlessly around the sense of this harassment, simultaneously a duty and a crime. *S'acharner* in French—to harass or to pursue relentlessly—means literally, in hunting vocabulary, "to flesh out"; one garnishes a decoy with flesh in order to excite the dogs and train them for the hunt. By extension, *l'acharnement*, this relentless pursuit, designates tenacity, stubbornness, animosity, or the furor of repetition. Therapeutic harassment, a way of garnishing the dying person, or the survivor, with flesh, is what inscribes, in "Circumfession," a mark as decisive as that of circumcision: that of the impossibility of slicing the difference between authenticity and inauthenticity in the making of existence. Therapeutic harassment bears witness to what Derrida has been thinking for so long under the name of the undecidable. Surely such harassment poses an undecidable ethical problem, for no one, not even God, can decide rigorously whether one should continue to make a dying person live or let a dying person die—a living dead, a living person already dead.

Therapeutic harassment renders equally improbable the difference between preoccupation (*molestia*) and care (*cura*). *Therapeuein* in Greek means "to treat, to take care, to care for." But when it is harassing, therapy becomes that extreme form of solicitude which comes close to guilt and sin, since it deprives the other of their death. As a medical and familial machination, a hospital poiesis and prosthesis, therapeutic harassment maintains a factical facticity of the dying person, which can no longer fall under the law of being or of ontological difference. Once again, an "immortal mortal," "too human inhuman," "the dumb god, the beast" (Circ., 78/80)—is that, strictly speaking, a Dasein?

To save life, to keep alive, to help to live or survive, to take upon oneself the tears of she or he whom one prolongs in this way, to receive their confession, to give them the last sacrament, is this to unburden them of their death, is it to steal the soul that they no longer have, to deprive them of their resolve? These questions, again irreducible to ontological determination, are endlessly present in "Circumfession." And who among us does not have to confess the existence, in their family or their close circle, of one of these "fortuitous victim(s) of the modern sacrifice" (271/293) to use Derrida's admirable expression? Who among us could say exactly what the culpability is that accompanies such a sacrifice? Who among us could decide the ontological regime of this sentence: "She seems not to be suffering," enunciated in the sixteenth period of "Circumfession" (79–80/82)?

The more one thinks about it, the more the idea, even the concept, of therapeutic harassment, to the extent that it allows itself paradoxically to be disincarnated, that is, to be theorized, traverses the whole text like a leitmotif. For example, is circumcision the fruit of such a harassment? Can one not detect, in its age-old practice, this original hygienic obstinacy, this harassment that "makes bleed" (208/224), as Derrida calls it when describing this excessive, cruel care with remarkable meticulousness? And today, when there remains in Derrida's words "so little" Judaism (279/303), why continue to harass oneself with circumcision? Care for facticity or machinic preoccupation? Obviously, it is impossible to answer. If one goes still further, could one ask whether philosophy, religion, and in particular, in Christian religion, the very practice of confession does not survive solely due to a comparable harassment, a generalized harassment, the same zeal to treat, which at one blow destroys by wanting to save? Would therapeutic harassment be the *Aufhebung* of postmodernity?

To conclude, I must once again ask pardon for having taken Heidegger here as a witness, for relentlessly pursuing as a witness that particular witness who has never confessed as one would have expected him to do. But at the same time, how to "bring forth the truth" without him? How can one not be attentive to his mistrust with regard to autobiographic onto-theology? Given this mistrust, how can we deny the courage of Derrida, who affirms anew this "form of theology as autobiography" (Circ., 84/87) that is confession? Is this also a kind of harassment? No doubt. And from the start, harassment is a device of temptation. No doubt *molestia* is itself a harassing animal. At the same time, there cannot be novelty, alterity, even *Gelassenheit* perhaps, without harassment.

Derrida is harassed by the theologic program which pursues him. And this provokes him to invent a counter-example for himself, an unheard of event, a surprise, an other religion, and an other "form of I." He succeeds in making a "sublime I" speak—an "I" which, strictly speaking, remains below the threshold of consciousness and of the unconscious as well. The form of this "I" is foreign to that of the *cogito* or to the being of the self. This "I" indeed mimes, without ever confusing itself with the self of a survivor maintained in limbo by harassment, that place where souls await their deliverance. If you like, such an "I" is indeed a substance but not a subject. Rather, it is a consistency, similar to that of blood, the "fluid and slowly stretched substance" (Circ. 187/201), which tries, as one says in French, to *prendre*, to "take," that is, to coagulate, to solidify. An "I" which, in "Circumfession," takes the form of the only sign of life manifest in the survivor, the blood, the circulation of the blood, which sometimes still wells up from the scabs. The "I" takes the form of the life of the other, as if it ended up by being disinterested in itself—these are also Derrida's words—in order to become a piece of (the other's) body, one of the other's scratches, one of the other's wounds. The very opposite of an interiorization. An entirely other care.

My grandmother lasted for seven years, first in a state of dementia, then in a vegetable state in an old folks' home, a service pompously called "palliative care." When I went to see her, I couldn't help thinking of Plato, telling myself that her soul had taken flight, that the dearest wish of every soul is to take flight, and that what I had before my eyes was a body deserted by a soul finally blessed. I suffered, in that I admired Plato with all the force of my reason and heart and yet was not able to believe him. "Circumfession" has obviously not stitched up this rip between faith and reason, but it has oriented this rip differently: If it is not possible to deliver the souls of survivors which will doubtless remain forever in limbo, is it at least possible to receive from them, as one collects from blood, something like a confession? Which, paradoxically yet necessarily, must invent itself? A birthing of souls for the second time: I can only, Derrida says, "harass myself, call myself into question, me, a whole life long, to make her avow, her, in me" (Circ., 73/74).

Given that one of the less-known meanings of confession is also "praise," allow me to confess, that is, to praise "Circumfession," for having given to the "I" of confession this hitherto unknown form, irreducible both to its metaphysical form and to its existential form. No longer "I am" but "she is me."[24]

DERRIDA'S RESPONSE TO CATHERINE MALABOU

I have two confessions to start with. First, I have read the text twice, once in French before coming here and once in English last night. But by reading it now, I have the feeling of reading it for the first time. I have just discovered a lot of things that I was blind to before. That's a strange experience, and I enjoyed the text even more. The second confession, and this is a confession to Philippe Capelle also, when I wrote "Circumfession" I did not know—and I still haven't read—Heidegger's text on Augustine's *Confessions*. So had I known this text, perhaps I would have would have done something else or inscribed the text differently. But the fact is, and I confess it, that it is a discovery for me that Heidegger had written on confession and precisely on this *facere veritate*. When I tried to discuss this expression by Augustine, I had no idea of Heidegger's discussion, which means two things. First, I should have done so; I should have known. On the other hand, what I'm doing with this, making the truth, I think, has nothing to do with Heidegger's meditation, which is very inspiring and very interesting.

Having expressed my gratitude and my admiration for this text by Catherine Malabou, I must say that my first reaction had to do with my astonishment concerning the status of the text. Of course, everything she says is right, and this comparison is necessary and should be developed. But the first thing I would have to speak to is the essential difference in status, as regards the tone and the scenario of this *Auseinandersetzung* with Augustine. Yesterday I was thinking that Heidegger never tried to praise anything written in Latin, not to my knowledge. Of course, my experience of the language in this text and of my reading of Augustine had to do with the French and the Latin, first of all. And of course, if we had the time, I could show how the Latin is here indispensable, how Augustine's Latin and the French Latin roots are in the way I write. Second, as to the status, of course "Circumfession" is a fiction in which the "I" is to some extent fictional. I know of no text by Heidegger in which the discourse is fictional, in which Heidegger says "I." If it happens, it's exceptional. It is the I of the professor, of the lecturer, but he never says I. Not to speak of tears and laughter. What is constant in "Circumfession" is the experience of weeping "with" Augustine, something that Heidegger never pays attention to, and of laughter. There is no sign of laughter, no interest in laughter in Heidegger, not that I know of. Not to speak of the sexual dimension of the text.

Now, before coming back to this question of sexuality, yesterday we were addressing the question of literature. Heidegger didn't like "literature" precisely as something rooted in Latin. He liked poetry in German or in Greek, but literature—what we call literature, strictly speaking—was to him inauthentic. To that extent, I'm sure that these texts of "Circumfession," first of all, could not be read by Heidegger. That's my constant rule in a cer-

---

Editors' Note: As Professor Malabou was unable to attend the conference in person, Jacques Derrida read her paper in her absence and then offered the following commentary on it.

tain way. I'm constantly accompanied by Heidegger, watched by him; and I always do my best to disconcert him in me, to disobey him, and to write something he wouldn't be able to read. And I think this is the case. We can have a lot of commentaries, analyses—and Catherine does a wonderful job of this—but at some point, we must ask, why is it that Heidegger could not read such a text, or would simply dismiss it as just so much exhibition, literature, narcissism? We know what he would have said, confronted with such a text. So I constantly counter him, try to write what he's against, what is counter to, or irreducible to, Heidegger's machinery. Because there is a machinery interpretation of Heidegger. There is a machine; there is a program. My question is: what could disappoint or disarm Heidegger's program? And this text, among others, is written in this spirit. Even in the book I wrote with Catherine Malabou, *La contre-allée*, I insist on precisely this ghost of Heidegger, which is constantly persecuting me. I say, well, I'm writing *contra*, and I have a lot of pages about *contra* and *gegen* Heidegger.[25]

Now, I want to just read a passage in which Heidegger is named in "Circumfession," if you allow me to quote myself. By the way, "Circumfession" was written with a machine, with a computer, and with an arbitrary rule coming from the computer: where the computer tells me this paragraph will be too long, I just stop. I obey the computer. Imagine Heidegger doing that. So, in this machinery there are layers within the text—different dates, different types of text, different rhetorics—and I explain this in the book. What I'm going to quote is a text taken from diaries that I had written years before, in the late 1970s, in view of this book on circumcision. I say this, and Heidegger is named here:[26]

> *now delicately detach the ring of flesh around my foreskin* . . .

Imagine Heidegger reading this!

> *. . . and put it on the lady's finger, you know the iconography of Catherine of Siena, and if I graft, will it be a naturalization of the symbolic seal or the condition of an ineffaceable pact for the only philosopher to my knowledge who, accepted—more or less—into the academic institution, author of more or less legitimate writings*

That's me.

> *on Plato, Augustine* . . .

Augustine is named here.

> *. . . Descartes, Rousseau, Kant, Hegel, Husserl, Heidegger, Benjamin, Austin* . . .
> *. . . will have dared describe his penis, as promised, in concise and detailed fashion, and as no one dared, in the Renaissance, paint the circumcised penis of Christ on the incredible pretext that there was no model for it, come off it, now if I do not invent a new language (through simplicity rediscovered) another fluid, a new SENTENCE [une nouvelle phrase], I will have failed in this book, which does not mean that that's the place to start, on the contrary, you have to drag on in the old syntax, train oneself with you, dear reader, toward an idiom which in the end would be untranslatable in return into the language of the beginnings, learn an unknown language, Elie, I call you, break down the wall, intercede for the intercessor that I am, you, for the third circumcision before the first, not the second, that of Easter in the plains of Jericho,* . . .

I could also quote another passage in which this question of making the truth could be elaborated. At the time I was interested in the question of bearing witness, in the experience of testimony, and in the fact that to bear witness doesn't mean simply to report something—the truth—but, under oath, to say something that one is the only one able to bear witness to, or attest to. That is, you make the truth because of the performative and because you are speaking under oath, a non-constative statement. That's why, in this context, I came back again and again to this difference between telling the truth and making the truth. But I was not relying on making the truth; I was not relying on the truth that was made. I was just trying to demonstrate that this originality of making the truth was, of course, open to perjury, to invention, and to lying. So it was a question about the truth of a very different style from Heidegger. As I was saying the day before yesterday, these suspicions about the constative or theoretical dimension of the truth, *homoiosis*, or, as Heidegger would say, as revelation, *aletheia*, which is also constative, these suspicions about the constative dimension of the truth do not mean that I trust the performative, that I rely on the performativity of the truth. As I said the day before yesterday, "Circumfession" is under the law of interruption. I didn't know—and this is true—I didn't know, while I was writing "Circumfession," after having read the "Derridabase," whether my mother would die before the end and interrupt me in the middle of a sentence. I was just expecting and not expecting an event which wouldn't, which couldn't, depend on me. So this experience of the event, precisely, which defeats the constative as well as the performative, was the rule of the writing of "Circumfession"—as well as the computer, which gave me the order to stop at the end of a period, of a paragraph.

I wanted to say also that at the very beginning of "Circumfession," in a style that is very different from Heidegger, I asked the question about the history of confession, of the institution called "confession," in Christianity. Of course, as you know, there is a wide and general meaning of confession, but there is also a specific institution called "confession," as you know better than I. But when Augustine wrote his *Confessions*, there was no such institution. So I referred to this at the beginning of the "Circumfession." I did research on the history of the institution called "confession."[27] Heidegger was never interested in this history as far as I know.

Catherine Malabou, at the beginning of her paper, confesses that she has and needs a witness, that she takes Heidegger as a witness. So I wanted to go back to what I say about making the truth in relation to witnessing, to the idiom of bearing witness or taking someone as a witness. I am going to read a passage that Geoff knows is, more than any other, untranslatable. Nevertheless, I'm going to read the translation and go back to the French text, in Period 11:[28]

> No point going around in circles, for as long as the other does not know, and know in advance, as long as he will not have won back this advance at the moment of the pardon, that unique moment, the great pardon that has not yet happened in my life, indeed I'm waiting for it as absolute unicity, basically the only event from now on, so the only event will be being pardoned from now on, no point going around in circles, so long as the other has not won back that advance I shall not be able to avow anything if avowal cannot consist in declaring, making known, informing, telling the truth, which one can always do, indeed, without confessing anything, without *making* truth . . .

I interrupt my quote here just to say, to mention a point on which I would perhaps disagree with Catherine Malabou. This is the only point where I would perhaps disagree with her, although it's not that simple—it's not simply a disagreement. She says, more than once, that I am interested in the ontological dimension of a confession to the extent that, like Heidegger, I confess nothing, that I insist on the confession which would not refer to any determined event, fact, deed, or so on. That is not true, and that's one of the differences between Heidegger and the meditation of such a text. Because, of course, "Circumfession" is precisely full of events, of dates, of singular and unique happenings, and reference to crimes. Even if I don't give details, I refer to determined crimes and faults, and events, and aggressions, and lies, and perjuries, and so on. So, it's not ontological in that sense. That's the point on which I would partially disagree with her. Then I continue this quote:

> . . . without *making* truth (*sans faire la vérité*), the other must not learn anything that he was not already in a position to know.

That was my assumption. For a confession to be a confession worthy of the name, you have to assume that the other knows already, because knowing is not the point. That's why God is required—God as the one who knows everything. If I confess something to someone who doesn't know my crime, then my confession might look like or sound like a report, that is, just an act of letting the other know. Whereas when the other knows what the crime is, confessing doesn't mean to report; it means, I'm guilty; I admit I'm guilty; I ask for forgiveness. This is an act of love in the Christian tradition. So the other should know. He is, as Lacan would say, *supposé savoir*, he is supposed to know, for an act of confession to be worthy of that name, which is a strange implication.

> . . . the other must not learn anything that he was not already in a position to know for avowal as such to begin, and this is why I'm addressing myself to God, the only one I take as a witness . . .

That's the name of God: just "witness."

> . . . without yet knowing what these sublime words mean, and this grammar, and *to*, and *witness*, and *God* . . .

And here, my dear Geoff, you had to fail, because what is here indispensable is the reference to the word *prendre, apprendre*, which is untranslatable. Let me read the French now:[29]

> . . . il faut que l'autre n'apprenne rien qu'il ne soit déjà en situation de savoir pour que commence l'aveu comme tel, et c'est pourquoi je m'addresse ici à Dieu, le seul que je prenne à témoin

That is, take as a witness

> sans savoir encore ce que veulent dire ces mots sublimes

"without yet knowing what these sublime words mean, and this French grammar." Geoff suppressed "French," the word "French." He was right to do so, but the fact is, French is suppressed here.

> cette grammaire française, et *à*, et *témoin*, et *Dieu*, et *prendre*,

And "take," *prendre* becomes take, *prendre Dieu*, "take God."

> et non seulement je prie,

Then there is this unique French association between *prendre* and *prier*. "*Je prie*" means "I pray" but also "I took [*je pris*], I took as a witness." So this is untranslatable:

> comme je n'ai jamais cessé de le faire dans ma vie, et le prie, mais je le prends ici et le prends à témoin,

"take him as a witness"

> je me donne ce qu'il me donne c'est-à-dire le *c'est-à-dire* de prendre le temps de prendre Dieu à témoin pour lui demander non seulement, par exemple. . . .

So this is, in a certain way, the same thing one does with the word *pour* in French and in other languages. I won't bother you any more with these quotes. But even if no other event in that text were referred to—but there are a number of such events—this recourse to, or this use of, the most untranslatable French idiom is itself an event; in itself, that is, it is unique, and it happens just once in such a text. The body of the idiom cannot be erased or cannot be suspended, put into brackets. That's why I never try to erase the eventness of the event.

   Now, a last word. Of course, my relationship to Augustine in this text is very different from Heidegger's. No doubt. I'm at the same time full of love and sympathy for Augustine, but at the same time I reject everything coming from him. It's a double; it's very ambivalent. At the same time, I try, in my own way, to deconstruct a number of Augustine's assumptions in this text. I can't demonstrate this right now—it would take too long—but in its way it is a deconstruction of Augustine, but very different from Heidegger's, if only because it's a non-Christian deconstruction. As has been shown,[30] even when he deconstructs or tries to deconstruct Augustine's *Confessions*, Heidegger refers to a tradition which is Luther's tradition of *destructio*. I try, not simply from a Jewish point of view, but from another point of view, another kind, another style of deconstruction. It's not a Jewish deconstruction, but it's a deconstruction which starts from somewhere else. As you know, if you read this text, of course, the question of Judaism is very complex for me. I never present myself as a Jew, but there's this problem of circumcision, this sentence and "the last of the Jews," which means the worst one. This will be the last word. I apologize for being so long. As I said, Heidegger never pays attention, never praises anything, written in Latin, in Roman Latin, which is for him the fall of thinking. But he doesn't pay attention to anything coming from a Jewish tradition either, be it purely Hebraic or Hebrew, or from Jewish thinkers. That would be one more point for reflection. So, I'll stop here. Thank you.

NOTES

   1. "Circonfession," p. 291; "Circumfession," p. 315. Hereafter page references to "Circonfession" are given in the text, first to the French edition in Geoffrey Bennington and Jacques Derrida, *Jacques Derrida* (Paris: Le Seuil, 1991), and second to the English edition in Geoffrey Bennington and Jacques Derrida, *Jacques Derrida*, trans. Geoffrey Bennington (Chicago: University of Chicago Press, 1993).
   2. *Gesamtausgabe: Phänomenologie des religiösen Lebens* (Phenomenology of Religious Life), volume 60, section 2: Augustinus und der Neoplatonismus, Hauptteil, p. 175: Phänomenologische Interpretation von Confessiones Liber X. Hereafter referred to as GA 60.

3. GA 60, p. 242.

4. *Conf.*, X, 29, 40.

5. GA 60, p. 207.

6. *Molestia.* To my knowledge, Book X contains only a single occurrence (X, 28, 39: *quis velit molestias et difficultates?*).

7. GA 60, p. 244.

8. *Conf.* X, 36, 254: "*itaque nobis, quoniam propter quaedem humanae societatis officia necessarium est amari et timeri ab hominibus.*"

9. GA 60, p. 229.

10. Ibid., p. 230.

11. Ibid., p. 231.

12. "*Sero te amavi, pulchritudo tam antiqua et tam nova,*" *Conf.* XXVII, 38.

13. GA 60, p. 204.

14. *Conf.* X, XXVII, 38.

15. GA 60, Anhang 1, p. 247.

16. "Des Machens und des Gemächtes," *Beiträge zur Philosophie,* GA 65, p. 67.

17. Ibid., p. 67.

18. Circ., second citation of Augustine, end of section, p. 107/112.

19. GA 60, p. 243.

20. "radikale Möglichkeite des Abfalls," GA 60, p. 245.

21. Circ., p. 154, beginning of section 32; 165.

22. *Otobiographies: L'Enseignement de Nietzsche et la politique du nom propre* (Paris: Galilée, 1984), p. 44.

23. Circ., p. 167, end of section 34; 178–179.

24. Cf. "about she who is all over me" (Circ. 140/148).

25. Jacques Derrida and Catherine Malabou, *Voyager avec Jacques Derrida—La Contre-Allée* (Paris: La Quainzaine Littéraire, Collection Voyager Avec, 1999); English: *Counterpath: Travelling with Jacques Derrida,* trans. David Wills (Stanford, Calif.: Stanford University Press, 2004).

26. "Circonfession: cinquante-neuf périodes et périphrases," in Geoffrey Bennington and Jacques Derrida, *Jacques Derrida* (Paris: Éditions du Seuil, 1991), pp. 109–11; English: "Circumfession: Fifty-nine Periods and Periphrases," in Geoffrey Bennington and Jacques Derrida, *Jacques Derrida* (Chicago: University of Chicago Press, 1993), pp. 114–16.

27. See "Circonfession," periphrasis 17, pp. 84–88; English: pp. 86–91.

28. Circ., 56–57/55–58.

29. Circ., 56–57/57–58.

30. See John Van Buren, *The Young Heidegger: Rumor of the Hidden King* (Bloomington: Indiana University Press, 1994), pp. 161–62.

Time, Evil, and Narrative

Ricoeur on Augustine

Richard Kearney

I want to concentrate here on two of Paul Ricoeur's texts on Augustine's *Confessions*. First, the opening chapter of volume one of *Time and Narrative*—entitled "The Aporias of the Experience of Time in Book XI of Augustine's *Confessions*," and second, an article written in 1985 entitled "Evil: A Challenge to Philosophy and Theology."[1]

These are by no means the only places where Ricoeur looks to Augustine, but they are in my view two key writings that bring together some abiding issues for Ricoeur—namely, *time, evil,* and *narrative.* In my conclusion, I will suggest that the resolution of this problematic triad points to a horizon of *pardon:* a theme which was, of course, crucial for Augustine, and which Ricoeur has chosen to explore in the Epilogue to his most recent book, *La mémoire, l'histoire, l'oubli.* The fact that his reflections on pardon are conducted in energetic and respectful dialogue with Jacques Derrida make them of additional interest here.

I. Ricoeur on Book XI of Augustine's *Confessions*

Ricoeur makes it clear from the outset that his main aim in the opening chapter of *Time and Narrative* is to show (1) how Augustine's analysis of time is highly aporetical; and (2) how it points ultimately to some kind of narrative eschatology.

The aporia derives from the basic existential fact that two temporal directions of the human psyche work in antithesis—namely, the *distentio animi* and the *intentio animi.* Whereas the former (*distentio*) denotes the soul's character of dispersal and fragmentation over past and future, the latter marks the soul's countervailing movement of intensification and concentration. While Augustine will look to a religious faith in the Eternal to convert the *distentio* into *intentio*, Ricoeur initially seeks to bracket out this theological horizon. He resolves instead to interrogate Augustine's aporia of time from a more strictly phenomenological perspective. With this in mind, Ricoeur will go on to compare the Augustinian opposition between *distentio* and *intentio* to the Aristotelian pair of *peripeteia* (temporal vicissitude) and *muthos* (narrative emplotment) in chapter 2 of *Time and Narrative*.

Ricoeur begins with Augustine's question in Book 2 of the *Confessions:* "What then is time?" (*Quid est enim tempus*) (XI, 14, 17). Unlike the cosmological thesis of Plotinus and the Platonists, who seem to know what time is, Augustine opens his meditation with the famous avowal of ignorance: "I know well enough what it [time] is, provided that nobody asks me; but if I am asked and try to explain, then I am baffled" (XI, 14,17). He then proposes what Ricoeur terms a "psychological" response to the skeptical attitude to time, but this never fully succeeds— as we shall see—in overcoming the existential aporia. At most, Augustine will eventually intimate some kind of "poetical"—as opposed to "theoretical"—response to time.[2] But we will return to this in more detail below.

The first aporia that Ricoeur identifies in the *Confessions* is *the being and the nonbeing* of time. Augustine begins with an analysis of our ordinary language discourse. How, he asks, can the *positive* character of verbs attributed to time such as "to be," "to occur," "to take place," be reconciled with the *negative* character of adverbs such as "not yet," "no longer," "not always" ? In short, how can time be said to *be* since the future is always *not yet*, the past is always *no longer*, and the present is always *not always?* But if the present moment cannot have indefinite duration, what can hold out against the skeptical collapse of the existence of time into nonexistence? And how, if time does not exist, can we continue to attribute measures to it, as when we say, for example, that time is long or short, or that it crawls or flies? (XI, 15, 18).

It is in response to these skeptical questions that Augustine comes up with his innovative thesis of the "threefold present." Ricoeur spends considerable time on this, realizing that it contains the seeds of a cogent phenomenology of time. Since past, present, and future cannot be said to exist if taken as three separate moments, Augustine proposes to take them together as modifications of each other. In other words, if we cannot consider the past and the present to exist as such, we must rethink them as temporal qualifications which can exist in the present. Past, present, and future must thus be reconsidered as qualities existing *within* the soul as implied by our experience of narrating the past and expecting the future. Past and future are not, therefore, to be seen as "things in themselves" but rather as signs (*vestigia*) by means of which the soul has a memory of things gone or a preperception (*praesensio*) of things to come. "It might be correct to say that there are three times, a present of past things, a present of present things and a present of future things. Some such different times do exist in the mind, but nowhere else that I can see" (XI, 20, 26). Augustine concludes, accordingly, that the acts of memory, attention, and expectation constitute the three horizons of time as "seen" through the enlarged present: "I can see (*video*) three times and I admit that they do exist" (XI, 20, 26).

Ricoeur asks at this point if Augustine, by incorporating remembrance and anticipation into the "extended and dialectical present," has not here resolved the ontological aporia of time. By linking our experience of the threefold present to that of psychic distension, has he not, in Book XI, sketched out the basics of a phenomenological psychology, prefiguring the Husserlian analysis of retention/pretention and the Heideggerian description of retrieval (*Wiederholung*) and fore-understanding (*Vor-Verstandnis*)? Is this not "the stroke of genius of Book XI of Augustine's *Confessions*," asks Ricoeur, "in whose wake will follow Husserl, Heidegger and Merleau-Ponty"?[3]

But, Ricoeur goes on, in thus replacing the old cosmological basis of time with an account which locates this basis *within* the human soul, understood as *distentio animi*, Augustine has not *really* solved the problem. He has merely displaced it from "outside" to "inside" the psyche. Instead of time being split between being and non-being in the sense of external metaphysical substances, it is now our inner soul which finds itself cleft. As Ricoeur makes clear, Augustine's thesis of the threefold present does not ultimately resolve the enigma, for in order to make sense of it, he must retreat from any attempt to locate the three temporal moments somewhere in space (*where*, he asks, are future and past things to be found?) and redirect our attention instead to two contrary directions of the human soul, namely *distention* and *intention*.

The *distentio animi* is vividly translated by Ricoeur as a "tearing apart" (*TN*, 18) or "bursting asunder" (*TN*, 20), conveying the way the human mind is stretched in opposing directions. Taking the example of the simple recitation of a verse, Augustine writes: "The scope of the action which I am performing is divided (*distenditur*) between the two faculties of memory and expectation, the one looking back to the part which I have already recited, the other looking forward to the part which I have still to recite" (XI, 28, 38). And, paradoxically, the more actively the soul seeks to engage itself in the intensifying action of the threefold *present*, the more it finds itself split and spread out, that is, non-coincident. Or as Ricoeur notes: "[T]hat the soul 'distends' itself as it 'engages' itself—this is the supreme enigma" (*TN*, 21). Ricoeur sums up this enigma as follows: "Augustine's inestimable discovery is, by reducing the extension of time to the distention of the soul, to have tied this distention to the slippage that never ceases to find its way into the heart of the threefold present—between the present of the future, the present of the past, and the present of the present. In this way he sees discordance emerge again and again out of the very concordance of the intentions of expectation, attention, and memory" (*TN*, 21). And the implications of this apply not only to the recitation of a verse but, as Augustine himself insists, to a "man's whole life of which his actions are parts" and, by extension, to the "whole history of mankind, of which each man's life is a part" (XI, 28, 38).

Here we find the blueprint for that hermeneutics of narrative identity which is to become the preoccupation of Ricoeur's three-volume *Time and Narrative*.

"The entire province of narrative is laid out here in its potentiality," claims Ricoeur, "from the simple poem, to the story of an entire life, to universal history" (*TN*, 22).

What is simply adumbrated by Augustine in the *Confessions* will be explored in detail by Ricoeur in the subsequent chapters of his work. More precisely, it is in response to the discordance-concordance enigma of temporal existence laid bare by Augustine, that Ricoeur proposes the practice of narrative emplotment—first announced in Aristotle's *Poetics*. But Ricoeur insists that such a response operates at a poetic, not speculative, level.

The reason that Augustine ultimately feels compelled to place his phenomenology of time within the context of a poetic hymn to eternity is, Ricoeur argues, not simply a matter of Christian apologetics. There is something in the very matter of the being/non-being aporia that calls out for some kind of eschatological (Derrida might say "messianic") response. Ricoeur relocates this pointer in the fact that as we move toward a psychological solution to the aporias of time, we confront a further and even deeper puzzle (*aenigma*)—how are we to give unity and identity to a human soul divided between its temporal dispersal over time and its unquenchable desire for constancy and perdurance? It is by way of seeking some response to this puzzle that Augustine includes his investigation of time within a poetical meditation on the eternal Word. There is "something missing," says Ricoeur, "from the full sense of *distentio animi*, which the contrast with eternity alone can provide" (*TN*, 22).

But what exactly does Ricoeur mean by this? He seems to be saying that by thinking about time *in contrast to eternity* we learn to re-situate speculation about time within the horizon of a limiting idea that invites us to reflect simultaneously on *what is time* and on *what is other than time*. Augustine considered eternity superior to time in that it is something that exists that was *not created*. Eternity is "forever still" (*semper stans*) in contrast to temporal things that are "never still." Or to put it in another way, for Augustine the divine Word (*Verbum*) remains, while human words (*verba*) perish. *Verba* are in fact "not at all, because they die away and are lost" (6:8). The more Augustine confesses his faith in eternity, therefore, the more Augustine marks time with the stigma of non-being and negation. As Ricoeur says, paraphrasing Augustine, "We must think of 'nothing' in order to think of time as beginning and ending. In this way, time is, as it were, surrounded by nothingness" (*TN*, 25). It is in this context of juxtaposing eternity with the non-being of temporality that Augustine speaks of God as having all his years "completely present to him all at once because they are at a permanent standstill (*simul stant*)." Eternity is described as being "supreme over time because it is a never-ending present, since God is at once *before* all past time and *after* all future time" (XI, 13, 16). The metaphysics of presence could hardly be more plainly stated.

Ricoeur underlines a number of salient points at this crucial point in the argument. First, Augustine does not merely *think* about the eternal as an abstract presence; he *addresses* it as a personal "Thou." And it is in light of the infinite perfection of this divine Other, spoken to in the second person by a first person, that we sense our temporal existence, *qua distentio animi*, to be a "lack or defect in being" (*TN*, 26). The absence of eternity in our lives is experienced negatively by Augustine, not just as a limiting idea of abstract thought, but as a gaping gulf of sorrow at the very heart of our existence. Time is experienced in the interiority of our own nothingness. We feel ourselves to be creatures hemorrhaged by the non-being of distention—this deep scar marking out the "ontological difference separating the creature from the creator" (*TN*, 27). In this manner, claims Ricoeur, the experience of distention is raised to the level of "lamentation"—a *pathétique of time* which calls in turn for a *poétique of narration* transcending the arguments of reason. In short, it is the narrative form of the *confessio* which, in Ricoeur's words, brings "lamentation to the level of language" (*TN*, 27).

This is pivotal for Ricoeur. He makes it clear that for Augustine this appeal to the confessional narrative of lamentation is not just *any* kind of narrative. It is narrative with a difference, and narrative that makes a difference—narrative geared toward an eschatological hope in things to come. In spite of the fact that we find ourselves "torn asunder" in our creaturely existence, "deprived of the stillness of the eternal present," and laid waste by distractions (*distentio est vita mea*); even though we are given over to dispersal into the many, like the aimless wandering of the old Adam, we are, for all that, still capable of seeking after the *intentio* of the inner self united with its Maker (XI, 29, 39). *Intentio*, as the appropriate confessional response to *distentio*, is thus construed as the "hope of the last things," the hope that one may leave behind the old Adam and "forgetting what one has left behind, look forward (*non distentus sed extentus*) . . . to an eternal goal . . . not distracted by other aims (*secundum distentionem*) but intent upon this one purpose (*secundum intentionem*)" (Phil 3:12–14).[4]

The confessional narrative of lamentation is thus, in the concluding passages of Book II, supplemented by a narrative of praise galvanized by the belief that our temporal *distentio* may indeed be somehow healed by an eschatological *intentio*. This expresses the hope that time itself may, in spite all our phenomenological and empirical evidence of dispersal, approximate to eternity. How? By returning into the inner self and listening to the inner *Verbum* of unity. For, Augustine suggests, to engage with this divine language of interiority is to learn from the eternal Word and, heeding divine teaching, redirect our lives from the fallenness of non-being toward a new quest for reconciled being. "Between the eternal *Verbum* and the human *vox*," as Ricoeur comments, "there is not only difference and distance but the relation of teaching and communication. . . . The teaching, we could say, bridges the abyss that opens up between the eternal *Verbum* and the temporal *vox*. It elevates time, moving it in the direction of eternity" (*TN*, 29).

But Ricoeur is quick to point out that this does not signal some kind of mystical or otherworldly repudiation of time. We should not read the conclusion to Book XI as some rehabilitation of the moment of Plotinian ecstasy recounted in

Book VII. Even the conversion experience of Book VIII and the ecstasy of Ostia recounted in Book IX never eliminate the temporal condition of the soul. Nor are they intended to. On the contrary, says Ricoeur, these keynote experiences "only put an end to wandering, the fallen form of the *distentio animi*. But this is done in order to inspire a peregrination that sends the soul off again on the roads of time. Peregrination and narration are grounded in time's approximation of eternity, which, far from abolishing their difference, never stops contributing to it" (*TN*, 29).

In other words, it is, paradoxically, when we attend to the still and steadying character of the eternal Word that we fully realize just how distended and scattered our temporal lives are. But this very difference-in-comparison may in turn accentuate our realization that it is the same eternal Word which created "both past and future time" (11:13). Thus anchoring the dialectic of *distentio* and *intentio* in the larger dialectic of time and eternity, Augustine underscores the fact that it is in the very midst of our experience of temporal dispersal that our desire for some eschatological reconciliation emerges.

The reconciliation remains in the future, of course; it is expressed in narratives of hope, desire, and faith, which point forward to a promised land that is not yet, a messianic era that transcends the here and now.

All this, Ricoeur concludes, makes for an "intensification" and "deepening" of time, rather than its "abolishment." For it is from our insights into the experience of time that our longing for eternity arises; it is from acknowledging the difference between creature and creator that we may address the latter as our most intimate and distant Other. The *Confessions* may thus be said to intensify our awareness of this complex dialectic between time and eternity, disclosing the fact that our temporal existence is itself a complex dialectic of narrative dispersal and recovery.

Ricoeur extrapolates the following key conclusions for his own thesis on the relationship between time and narrative: "If it is true that the major tendency of modern theory of narrative—in historiography and the philosophy of history as well as in narratology—is to 'dechronologize' narrative, the struggle against the linear representation of time does not necessarily have as its sole outcome the turning of narrative into 'logic,' but rather may deepen its temporality. Chronology does not have just one contrary, the a-chronology of laws or models. Its true contrary is temporality itself. Indeed it was necessary to confess what is other than time in order to be in a position to give full justice to human temporality and to propose not to abolish it but to probe deeper into it, to hierarchise it, and to unfold it following levels of temporalistion that are less and less 'distended' and more and more 'held firmly,' *non secumdum distentionem sed secundum intentionem* (XI, 29, 39)" (*TN*, 30).

In light of this conclusion, we may say that Augustine's *Confessions* prefigure the blueprint for Ricoeur's own hermeneutic interpretation of the relation between the aporetics of time and the poetics of narrative, an interpretation which he scrupulously and rigorously unfolds in the subsequent chapters and volumes of *Time and Narrative*.

II. Time, Evil, and Narrative

The second text that I wish to look at here is Ricoeur's reading of Augustine's theory of evil. This text, entitled "Evil: A Challenge to Philosophy and Theology," traces the genealogy of the Western understanding of evil in which Augustine plays a key part. The pivotal link between the Augustinian notions of *time* (discussed in Book XI of the *Confessions*) and *evil* (discussed in Books VII and VIII) is that both expose us to an experience of "non-being." Indeed, Augustine defines evil in the *Confessions* (and elsewhere) as the lack of being or deficiency of good (*privatio boni*). In view of Ricoeur's claim in his *Time and Narrative* reading of Augustine—discussed above—that it is the limiting idea of eternity which "strikes time with nothingness" and reveals how our souls are dispersed over the non-being of what is no-longer and not-yet, we are faced with a deep conundrum: how do we, as temporal beings, deal with evil if our own very being is in part made up of non-being?

Before examining Ricoeur's answer to this question, let me say a few words about his presentation of the Augustinian view of evil. Augustine's account of evil is, in Ricoeur's view, innovative in relation to previous treatments of the problem and (like his treatment of time) deeply aporetic. It is innovative to the extent that it tries to combine the human and non-human aspects of evil in terms of a new metaphysical concept—namely, *malum* as *nihil* or *privatio boni*. Augustine develops this new speculative position in response to the gnostics, more particularly, the Manichees, under whose sway he had personally come as he admits in Books V and VIII of the *Confessions*. Whereas the Manichees had taught that evil is a substance implanted in the cosmos, Augustine replies that it is a perversion of the human will and therefore something which we are—at least partially—responsible for (Books VII and VIII). His question is this: "Where does evil comes from, if God made all things and because he is good, made them good too?" (Book VII, 5). Since for Augustine "the Creator and all his creation are both good," it follows that evil must be something human beings bring into the world by their own actions. As such, it is a *human* product. And since everything that God creates "is" and "is good" (*ens et bonum convertuntur*), the evil generated by the perverted human will is actually a *deficiency* of what is. So it is by way of countering the gnostic view that evil is a cosmological substance that Augustine reinterprets the biblical notion of punishment (*poena*) for human sin (*peccatum*) and invents the category of "nothingness" (*nihil*). In short, for Augustine, if there is evil in the world, it can only be the result of humans turning away from the good being of God toward a lack of being.

Ricoeur commends Augustine's advocacy of a radically *moral* vision of evil. He approves the attempt to replace the genealogical question *Unde malum?* with the question of willful human wrongdoing, *Unde malum faciamus?* This marks,

Ricoeur believes, a significant departure from the more anonymous accounts of evil previously proposed by mythic, gnostic, and even neo-Platonic explanations. The novelty of Augustine was to have clearly articulated the view that the causes of evil are not to be found in cosmogony but in some form of *willed* action—the sins of the "bad will." Ricoeur especially appreciates the deeply existential and anthropological character of the Augustinian innovation; but this does not prevent him from recognizing that it brings new problems and paradoxes.

Foremost amongst these, for Ricoeur, is the problem of "just suffering." The Augustinian account leads ineluctably to a penal view of history where no one—in theory—suffers unjustly. Everyone gets their reward, and all pain is a recompense for sin. Responsibility, by this view, must be commensurate with accountability. But this is not, of course, what experience bears out. Suffering befalls many *innocent* people; while happiness is often the lot of *wicked* people. The notion of punishment proportionate to wrong-doing is not always sustainable—or convincing. In other words, if evil is something we as humans *do*, we cannot deny that it is also *done to us*: something we suffer, something inherited, something already *there*.

The major difficulty here, as Ricoeur sees it, is how to reconcile (a) Augustine's somewhat extreme hypothesis of *moral* evil with (b) the need to give sin a "supraindividual" and historical-generic account in order to explain how suffering is not always justly apportioned as retribution for individual sins (for in countless cases it is clearly excessive). It is precisely in response to this difficulty, Ricoeur suggests, that Augustine sought to reinterpret the Genesis tale of Original Sin in order to rationalize this apparently irrational paradox: namely, we are responsible, but not *entirely* responsible, for evil. Ricoeur sums up the Augustinian account thus: "By conjoining within the concept of a sinful nature the two heterogeneous notions of a biological transmission through generation and an individual imputation of guilt, the notion of original sin appears as a quasi-concept. . . ."[5] But the aporia remains. If sin is, even in part, an historical-genetic inheritance going back to Adam and repeatedly evidenced in our temporal nature as dispersed finite beings, then how can we avoid the trap of predeterminism? If, on the other hand, sin is an individual act freely chosen by the perverted human will, how can we explain the absurd fact that in a universe ostensibly created as "good" by God, the innocent suffer and the wicked prosper? There seems no solution.

Ricoeur argues that these Augustinian speculations on Original Sin were to exert a profound influence on subsequent philosophical and theological theories, from the Middle Ages right down to more modern thinkers like Leibniz, Hegel, and Kant. Leibniz tries to resolve the Augustinian aporia by proposing the principle of Sufficient Reason to explain the judicious balancing of good with evil in the "best of all possible worlds." This balancing act of retribution and compensation, attributed to the infinite mind of God by Leibniz, is dialectically humanized by Hegel and the German Idealists. Hegel's "cunning of reason" silences the scandal of suffering by subsuming the tragic into a triumphant logic where all that is real is rational. And it is here, Ricoeur says, that the hubris of systematic speculation reaches its untenable extreme: "The more the system flourishes, the more its victims are marginalized. The success of the system is its failure. Suffering, as what is expressed by the voices of lamentation, is what the system excludes."[6] The explanations of speculative reason are utterly insensitive to the particular agony of evil. They ignore the horror suffered. The System does not weep.[7]

On the other hand, Ricoeur is equally wary of the mystical irrationalism which declares, against Augustine, that God is not only beyond being but beyond all questions of good and evil to the point of being a pure "superessential" nothingness. Certain apophatic mystics can bring us so far down the *via negativa* that we are struck dumb before the sublimity of the absolute. (Or as Derrida remarks on the apophatic surpassing of good and evil: "Evil is even more devoid of essence than the Good. Let us draw, if possible, all the implications of this strange axiom.")[8]

No version of theodicy—rationalist or mystical—Ricoeur argues, can provide a convincing answer to the protest of unjust suffering: *why me? why this particular victim?* This is a recurring protestation echoing through the testimonies against evil from Job and Gethsemane to Auschwitz and Hiroshima. And it surfaces dramatically and eloquently in the agonizing query of Ivan Karamazov—why does this innocent child have to suffer this evil? Dostoyevsky's Grand Inquisitor scene would suggest that no speculative account can explain this enigma away. At best, suggests Ricoeur, we might look for a more ethical and practical—rather than theoretical—response to this enigma.

As philosophers, Ricoeur recommends that we start with the debunking of "rational theology" and theodicy in part three of Kant's *Critique of Pure Reason*. Here Kant moves from a purely speculative explanation of evil (in terms of metaphysics) to moral-political action rooted in human decision. And in so doing, argues Ricoeur, Kant liberates the insight that evil is something which *ought not to be* and needs to be struggled against. By de-alienating evil and making it a matter of contingency rather than necessity (cosmogonic, theological, metaphysical, or historical), Kant retrieved the anthropological aspect of the original Augustinian account, bringing us face to face, once again, with our human responsibility for action. But Kant goes further than Augustine in freeing us from metaphysical speculation on evil. He seeks to remove evil from the realm of both metaphysics and mystique, thereby diminishing some of its captivating power. And in this wise, Kant enables us to see that evil is not a property of some external demon or deity, nor indeed some original ontological property inherited from "our First Parents," but a phenomenon deeply bound up with human acts. With the arrival of Kantian ethics, Ricoeur notes with approval, evil ceases to be a matter of abstract metaphysical accounting and becomes instead an affair of human practice and judgment. Kant, in a word, *re-anthropologizes* evil.

But the aporia of evil is not so easily resolved. Even Kant, as Ricoeur is compelled to concede, could not ultimately ignore the paradoxical character of evil. For if he clearly called for a response within the limits of practical human reason, he could never completely deny some residual inscrutability (*Unerforschbarkeit*)

in the matter. This he called "radical evil." At one point, indeed, Kant even admitted that there might be "no conceivable ground from which the moral evil in
us could originally have come."[9]

There is indeed no solution. The lament of *Why? Why me? Why my beloved
child?* remains as troublingly enigmatic as ever. Augustine's bewildered cry, *Unde
malum faciamus?* still goes unanswered. Ricoeur thus terminates his genealogical
critique of evil, from Augustine to Kant, by noting that victims of evil cannot be
silenced with either rational explanation (theodicy) or irrational submission (mysticism). Their stories cry out for other responses capable of addressing both the
humanity and the *alterity* of evil.

III. Three Modes of Response

Finally, I want to briefly review three ways in which Ricoeur attempts to respond
to the double Augustinian aporias of *time* and *evil*—sharing as the latter do a common contact with the *nihil*. Ricoeur's attempts, sketched out in a number of books
and essays, may be roughly regrouped under the following headings: (a) Practical
Understanding, (b) Working-Through, and (c) Pardon. I will, by way of conclusion, say a few words about each in turn.

Practical Understanding

Practical understanding is the name Ricoeur gives to that limited capacity of the
human mind to *deliberate about* or *reflect on* the enigma of evil. He draws here
from a number of precedents, notably Augustine's confessional narrative (as opposed to his speculative metaphysics), but also Aristotle's "practical wisdom"
(*phronesis*), and Kant's model of "reflective indeterminate judgment." What these
models share is an ability to transfer the aporia of evil from the sphere of theory
(*theoria*)—proper to the exact knowledge criteria of logic, science, and systematic speculation—to the sphere of a more practical art of understanding (*technè/
praxis*): a practice which allows for an approximative grasp of phenomena: what
Aristotle calls "the flexible ruler of the architect." Where speculative theory, epit-
omized by theodicy, explained evil in terms of ultimate causal or genetic origins,
practical understanding is geared toward a more hermeneutic comprehension
of the singular and contingent characteristics of evil—while not abandoning all
claim to quasi-universal criteria (that would account for at least a minimally
shared sense of evil). Such practical understanding operates on the conviction
that evil is something that must be actively *contested.* In that sense, it resists the
fatalist archaeologies of evil—mythical and theodical—in favor of a future-
oriented praxis.

For Ricoeur, the ultimate response (though by no means a solution) offered
by practical understanding is to *act against evil*. Instead of acquiescing in the fate
of an origin that precedes us—including Adam's original sin—action turns our
understanding toward the future in view of a *task* to be accomplished.

The moral-political requirement to act does not, therefore, abandon the legitimate quest for some model (however limited) of reasonable discernment; in fact, it solicits it. For how could we *act against* evil if we could not *identify* it, however approximately, that is, if we could not *in some way* and in fear and trembling discern between good and evil? In this respect, the genuine struggle against evil presupposes a critical hermeneutics of suspicion. And such hermeneutic understanding would fully respect Kant's insistence on a practical reason, which embraces the quasi-impossible task of thinking the unthinkable. (And does so, in Ricoeur's words, with the "sobriety of a thinking always careful not to transgress the limits of knowledge.")[10]

Such a critical understanding of evil might never surpass the provisional nature of Kant's indeterminate judgment. But it at least judges, and in a manner alert to both the singular alterity of evil and to its quasi-universal character as grasped by the *sensus communis*. It is not exact or adequate judgment, I repeat, but a form of judgment for all that, based on the practical wisdom conveyed by confessional narratives and driven by the hunger for moral justice.

We may say, accordingly, that practical judgment is not only "phronetic" but "narrative" in character. In proposing such an ethical role for narrative, Ricoeur seems to be forging some kind of strategic alliance between Aristotelian *phronesis* and Kantian *Urteilung*, on the one hand, and Augustinian *confessio* on the other. This plea for a narrative model was already prefigured, as we saw, in Augustine's response to the aporia of time (as being and non-being) in terms of a narrative poetics of hope. But we could enlarge this response to include the very genre of the *confessio* itself as a singularly narrative account of the great conundrums of time, evil, and creation. For if it is true that Augustine engages in speculative metaphysics in this work, especially Book XI, it is equally true that these arguments are themselves framed by the overall confessional form of narrative (a far more narrative form, let it be noted, than either Aristotle's *Poetics* or Kant's *Critiques*).

Ricoeur's reasoning here is that while morality often speaks abstractly of the relation between virtue and the pursuit of happiness, it is the task of confessional narrative to propose various fictional figures that comprise so many *thought experiments* which may help us see connections between the ethical aspects of human conduct and fortune/misfortune. Poetical expressions—like those of Augustine in the *Confessions*—can dramatically illustrate how reversals of fortune result from a specific kind of behavior, as this is re-enacted in the "plot" of his life and that of many of his acquaintances. And at a broader level, it is thanks to our familiarity with the particular types of emplotment inherited from our culture or civilization that we may come to better relate virtues, or forms of excellence, with happiness or misfortune.[11] These "lessons" of poetry, as Ricoeur calls them, constitute the "universals" of which Aristotle spoke, and which we today might more properly call approximate or "quasi-universals" of a lower degree than those of purely theoretical thought and logic. And so, Ricoeur suggests, we may speak of some kind of "phronetic understanding," where narrative and interpretation have their proper place, in contrast to theoretical understanding, which is the domain of science and metaphysics proper. One of the most appropriate methods for treating the fundamental aporias of time and evil so powerfully articulated by Augustine in the *Confessions* is, it appears, narrative understanding.

Working-through

But Ricoeur goes further. If narrative understanding addresses the action-response to evil, it sometimes neglects the *suffering*-response. Evil is not just something we *struggle against*; it is also (as noted above) something we *undergo*. Something that befalls us. To ignore this passivity of evil suffered is to ignore the extent to which evil strikes us as shockingly strange and disempowering. It is also to underestimate that irreducible alterity of evil which Augustine could not but acknowledge in spite of his rejection of the gnostic notion of evil as a cosmic substance. Evil may indeed be "nothing," but it is still "something" we suffer as well as something we choose. And precisely as something endured it needs to be worked through. One of the wisest responses to evil is, Ricoeur suggests, to acknowledge its traumatizing effects and work-them-through (*durcharbeiten*) as best we can. Practical understanding can only redirect us toward action if it has already recognized that some element of alterity almost always attaches to evil, especially when it concerns illness, horror, catastrophe, or death. No matter how prepared we are to make sense of evil, we are never prepared enough; and the sense is always inflected with senselessness. That is why the "work of mourning" is so important as a way of not allowing the inhuman nature of suffering to result in a complete "loss of self" (what Freud called "melancholia"). Some kind of catharsis is necessary to prevent the slide into fatalism that all too often issues in despair. The critical detachment brought about by cathartic mourning elicits a wisdom which turns *passive lament* into the possibility of *active complaint*, that is, *protest*.[12]

The role played by narrative testimony is, Ricoeur repeats, crucial here — whether it be that of political victims generally or of specific survivors of the Holocaust and other extreme traumas. For such narrative remembering may invite the victim to escape the alienation of evil, that is, to move from a position of mute helplessness to speech- acts of revolt and (where possible) acts of self-renewal. (Augustine's own *Confessions* are, of course, a micro -model of such renewal.) Some kind of narrative working-through is necessary, it seems, for survivors of evil not to feel crippled by guilt (about the death of others and their own survival), or to succumb to the syndrome of the "expiatory victim." What the catharsis of mourning-narrative offers is the realization that new actions are still possible *in spite of evil suffered*. Confessional catharsis may thus be said to detach us from the obsessional repetitions of the past and free us for a less repressed future. For only thus might we free ourselves from the disabling cycles of retribution, fate, and destiny: cycles which — as Augustine knew all too well from the Manichees — *estrange* us from our power to act. (The Manichees instilled the view that evil is overpoweringly alien, that is, irresistible.)

This is not to suggest that Ricoeur thinks evil can be magicked away, or cordoned off into some hinterland from which we, now purged and purified, would remain forever after immune. Mourning, for Ricoeur, is not a way of instituting

a new sacrificial dialectic of us versus them. On the contrary, it is a way of learning to live with the monsters in our midst so that by revisiting and renaming
them, we might outlive them. If monsters arise when reason sleeps, as Goya says,
then confessional narrative might be seen as a certain kind of reckoning with
unjust and unmerited suffering. Not that it can ever provide a solution. The evil
of suffering can never be explained away by *confessio*—for that would be to return to the "rationalization" of theodicy and its secular equivalents. At best, confessional narrative serves as a necessary, but never sufficient, condition for an
ethical and practical resistance to evil. There are, of course, many *non-narrative*
criteria of judgment and protest that are equally indispensable for a more complete response—ranging from a phenomenology of the face *à la* Levinas, to a
discourse ethic *à la* Habermas, to an existential pragmatism *à la* Dewey or Sartre,
to a religious intuitionism *à la* Bergson, to a deconstructive hope for justice *à
la* Derrida and Caputo.

All that Ricoeur is claiming for confessional catharsis here is that it offers one
step, amongst others, that may be taken in face of the paralyzing lure of evil: a lure
before which the gnostic and theodical accounts remain helpless. In sum, working-through the experience of evil—narratively, confessionally, cathartically—may
enable us to take, however provisionally, some of the allure out of evil, so that we
can begin to distinguish between possible and impossible modes of protest. In this
sense, working-through is central to a hermeneutics of action, for it resolves to make
evil *resistible*.

Let me cite, in summary, some emblematic examples. If Moses had not compelled the sublime numen of the burning bush to say its name and explain its
pledge to history, Moses might have perished on the spot. If Christ had not confronted and debated over forty days with the demons in the desert, he might not
have survived his three posthumous days in hell on the eve of resurrection. If Mi-
larpa, in Buddhist legend, had not faced his monster head on and spoken to him
face to face, he might never have left his cave. Or to give an example from our
contemporary film culture, *Apocalypse Now*, the epic retelling of the horror of
Vietnam based on Conrad's *Heart of Darkness*: without the narrative catharsis
brought about by Captain Willard's final exchange with his nation's sacrificial
monster, Kurtz, he would not have been able to resist evil. It is only by listening
patiently and acknowledging the evil for what it is, that Willard can eventually decline Kurtz's tempting offer to replace him, and walk on.

Pardon

Finally, there is the difficult issue of forgiveness. I conclude with this, recalling that
it is in the very nature of a certain kind of *confessio* to call out for pardon. Against
the "never" of evil, which rules out pardon, Ricoeur—following Augustine—
recommends that we think of the "marvel of a once again" which might make the
impossible possible.[13] But the possibility of forgiveness is a "marvel" precisely because it surpasses the limits of rational calculation and explanation. There is a certain gratuitousness about pardon due to the very fact that the evil it addresses is

not part of some dialectical necessity. And here Ricoeur rejoins not only Augustine but Derrida. Pardon is something that makes little or no sense before we give it. *Before* it occurs it seems impossible, unpredictable, incalculable in terms of the economy of exchange. So it requires a leap of faith, of trust—but not a *completely blind* leap. And this is where confessional-phronetic understanding, attentive to the particularity of specific evil events, joins forces with the practice of patient working-through to ensure that past evils might be prevented from repeating themselves and give way, instead, to future possibilities of non-evil. Confessional narration can help us make the impossible task of pardon a bit more possible. That is why amnesty is never amnesia: the past must be recollected, reimagined, rethought, and worked-through so that we can identify *grosso modo* what it is that we are forgiving. The cult of the "immemorial" sublime should, I suggest, be resisted. For if pardon (for us humans) is indeed beyond reason—as Augustine recognized in the *Confessions*—it is not without a certain awareness. Or to put it in Pascal's terms, pardon has its reasons that reason cannot comprehend. Only a divinity could forgive indiscriminately. And there may indeed be some crimes that God alone is able to pardon. Even Christ had to ask his Father to forgive his crucifiers: "Father forgive them for they know not what they do." Presumably the "man" in him found it impossible; he couldn't do it himself.

But here ethics approaches the threshold of religious hermeneutics. And it does so, bearing in mind Derrida's timely warning: "I believe it necessary to distinguish between forgiveness and this process of reconciliation, this reconstitution of a health or a 'normality,' as necessary and desirable as it would appear through amnesties, the 'work of mourning,' etc. A 'finalized' forgiveness is not forgiveness; it is only a political strategy or a psycho-therapeutic economy."[14] Derrida does add the telling admission that he himself "remains 'torn' between a 'hyperbolic' ethical vision of forgiveness, pure forgiveness, and the reality of a society at work in pragmatic processes of reconciliation."[15] Here Derrida seems to concede that between his own version of "impossible" pardon and Ricoeur's notion of "difficult" pardon, there may not be an unbridgeable divide. Perhaps such pardon is only *quasi-impossible*—especially if one believes, as Augustine certainly did in his *Confessions*, that infinite forgiveness can somehow traverse at moments the limits of finite forgiveness.

In light of the above, I tender this hypothesis. By transforming our experience of distention, alienation, and victimization into a response of protest and forgiveness, might not a hermeneutic practice of *confessio*—inspired by Augustine, Ricoeur, and Derrida—offer us some kind of answer, however tentative, to the challenge of evil?

NOTES

1. P. Ricoeur, "Evil: A Challenge to Philosophy and Theology," first published in English in the *Journal of the American Academy of Religion* 53 (1985): 635–50; reprinted

in P. Ricoeur, *Figuring the Sacred* (Minneapolis: Fortress Press, 1995). Originally published as a short book in French entitled, simply, *Le Mal* (Geneva: Labor et Fides, 1986).

2. Here is Ricoeur's own statement of intent as he embarks on his reading: "A constant thesis of this book [*Time and Narrative*] will be that speculation on time is an inconclusive rumination to which narrative activity alone can respond. Not that this activity solves the aporias through substitution. If it does resolve them, it is in a poetical and not a theoretical sense of the word. Emplotment (*la mise-en-intrigue*) replies to the speculative aporia with a poetic making of something capable, certainly, of clarifying the aporia (this will be the primary sense of Aristotelian *catharsis*) but not of resolving it theoretically. In one sense Augustine himself moves toward a resolution of this sort. The fusion of argument and hymn in Part 1 of Book XI—which I am at first going to bracket—already leads us to understand that a poetical transfiguration alone, not only of the solution but of the question itself, will free the aporia from the meaninglessness it skirts" (*Time and Narrative*, vol. 1 [Chicago: University of Chicago Press, 1984], pp. 6–7).

3. Ricoeur, *Time and Narrative*, vol. 1, p. 16. Hereafter cited in the text as *TN*.

4. Quoted in ibid., pp. 27–28.

5. Ricoeur, "Evil: A Challenge to Philosophy and Theology," p. 254.

6. Ibid., p. 257.

7. See William Desmond, *Beyond Hegel and Dialectic: Speculation, Cult and Comedy* (Albany: SUNY Press, 1992), p. 231.

8. J. Derrida, "Comment ne pas parler," in *Psyché: Inventions de l'autre* (Paris: Galilée, 1978), p. 571.

9. I. Kant, *Religion within the Limits of Reason Alone* (New York: Harper Torchbooks, 1960), p. 38.

10. Ricoeur, "Evil: A Challenge to Philosophy and Theology," p. 259.

11. P. Ricoeur, "Life in Quest of Narrative," in *Paul Ricoeur: Narrative and Interpretation*, ed. D. Wood (London: Routledge, 1991), p. 23.

12. P. Ricoeur, "Memory and Forgetting," in *Questioning Ethics*, ed. R. Kearney and M. Dooley (London and New York: Routledge, 1999), pp. 5–12.

13. P. Ricoeur, *La Mémoire, l'histoire, l'oubli* (Paris: Le Seuil, 2000), pp. 574f.

14. J. Derrida, *On Cosmopolitanism and Forgiveness* (London and New York: Routledge, 2001), p. 50.

15. Ibid., p. 51.

nine

Arendt's Augustine

Michael J. Scanlon

Hailed as the "first modern man," Augustine is certainly holding his own with the postmoderns. He features in the work of Heidegger, Wittgenstein, Lyotard, Derrida, and quite amply in the writings of Hannah Arendt. In 1996 Arendt's 1929 dissertation was published in English translation as *Love and Saint Augustine*. This event occasioned different points of view on the ongoing relationship between Arendt and Augustine. Commentators on her work questioned the extent of the influence of St. Augustine on her writings. Some found little influence; others found an extensive, lifelong influence of the one she called her "friend." As a political theorist, Arendt was drawn to Augustine, who shared her concern with human action in an ambiguous world. She did not share Augustine's theological vision of God's grace, but she found enough in his philosophical thinking for her purposes. She was aware of the fact that Augustine wrote long before any clear distinction between philosophy and theology emerged, and she knew that Augustine's "philosophical" anthropology was the fruit of his Christian faith; faith not only precedes understanding but is its very condition—"understanding is the reward of faith."[1] Without hesitation, she followed Augustine in replacing the philosophical ultimate, Being, with the biblical Creator, the Source of Augustine's *caritas*, which she renders as "neighborly love."

From Augustine Arendt created her central metaphor, "natality"—"new beginnings." Augustine overcame the Greek understanding of cyclical time with his insistence that the Incarnation was the radical *novum* in history. But the initial novelty in the world was the creation of the human being as freedom—freedom is not just something the human being enjoys; the human *is* freedom, the source of "new beginnings": *initium ut esset, creatus est homo, ante quem nemo fuit* (that a beginning be made, man was created).[2] Opting for natality empowered by *car-*

itas rather than mortality as the spring of action, Arendt employed Augustine to overcome the influence of her mentor, Heidegger. Agreeing with her two major philosophical teachers, Heidegger and Jaspers, that death is the ultimate "limit situation," Arendt followed Augustine, who basically agreed with her mentors but who refused to stop at this limit. Reflecting on mortality led Augustine to transcend the fear of death by moving toward the ultimate Limit, the Creator of life. Embracing the Augustinian *caritas,* Arendt transcended both of her philosophical mentors in discovering herself as coinciding with the discovery of God.

The Arendt text that supplies the focus for my paper is the last one she wrote for publication, *The Life of the Mind,* volume 2: *Willing.* There she celebrates Augustine as the first philosopher of the will and the Romans' "only" philosophical mind.[3] But Augustine's philosophy of the will was constructed on a theological base, the discovery of the will in the writings of St. Paul. Thus, we may say that if Athens discovered the mind, Jerusalem discovered the will.

In resonance with Arendt's claim, I will offer an overview of Augustine's philosophical/theological anthropology, which is centered on human conation, the infinitely erotic structure of human desire, the infinitely restless human heart. The distinctive theology of the Western Church is a long commentary on the third article of the creed, a theological anthropology focused on human conation as empowered by the Spirit of Christ. In this sense it is a theology of freedom as the fruit of grace, inspired by St. Paul's discovery of the will as transformed by the self-communication of God in the Spirit. As Christopher Dawson observed: "Theology in the West found its centre and principle of organization in the doctrine of Grace, and the Christian Life is the Life of Grace."[4] At the source of this tradition is, of course, Augustine, who translated the language of Paul into the language of a theology destined to become official doctrine in the Church. To retrieve Augustine's anthropology in dialogue with Hannah Arendt, I will employ his own favored language, the language of human conation: will, person, grace, freedom, love, history.

Will

All commentators on Augustine's anthropology concur on the centrality of the human will as a key to his thought. *"Quid sumus nisi voluntates?"* (What are we but wills?).[5] Human conation consumed his interest and gave to all his writings a passionate ring. Throughout his life he felt profoundly the insatiable élan of the *cor inquietum.* For him this desire is an intimation of God. This constitutive *eros,* this hounding hunger reveals human finitude while it may engender hope for a fulfillment it cannot reach by itself.

Augustine's discovery of the "inward life," focused on the will, was the beginning of a new era in the history of thought.[6] While the discovery of mind is properly attributed to the Greeks, the exploration of the will demanded different soil. Mind presupposes order, but will wants novelty. "Will implies future, but the Greeks had a cyclical view of time."[7] "To Israel must be attributed the discovery of history as the realm of meaning."[8] For Israel history had meaning because it was the sphere of the divine epiphany, and this evaluation of history was intensified by the emergence of eschatology in the prophets. Eschatology in both of its biblical forms—prophetic and apocalyptic—anticipated the future as ultimately the time of the fulfillment of the divine promise. And it was faith in this tradition that led the Christian philosopher Augustine to break the spell of the Greek cyclical view of time for subsequent Western thought. For Augustine the Incarnation meant that the definitive *novum* had occurred once and for all in the midst of history. Now Christian *memoria* looks forward to its consummation at the end of history. Memory becomes anticipation, and the longing of the will for beatitude reaches out in hope for the future fulfillment. So completely did this religious vision transform his mind that "wherever Augustine speaks of three tenses, he stresses the primacy of the future."[9]

Augustine's early work, *De libero arbitrio*, is at once a theodicy and a theological exploration of the relationship between the will and the question of the moral self. For Augustine *the* choice of the will is for or against God, a choice which determines the moral quality of the will. Moral evil results from the choice against God. "But let us be careful to understand how exactly evil is rooted in the will, for it is two different, although not entirely unrelated, things to say that the deficiency is in the act willed or to say the deficiency is in the willing will itself. And for Augustine it is clearly the latter that he is worried about."[10] More will be said below on impotency of free will in relation to Augustine's notion of freedom in grace.

Person

Augustine's discovery of the will is further developed as the discovery of personality. The will is "the inmost core of the human person."[11] To understand the Augustinian "will" as synonymous with what we name as "person" is of fundamental importance for our contemporary task of developing a postmodern anthropology over against the modern rational/autonomous self. Personhood emerges as the historical self-enactment of will, and it is personhood in this sense that Augustine explores with his understanding of the "soul." The Augustinian "soul" is not Aristotelian "substance"—nor is it the Cartesian "ghost in the machine." It is what is referred to today as the "subject," but the subject as derived from and dependent upon the God of the Bible. Unlike the medieval debate between Thomistic intellectualism and Scotistic voluntarism, Augustine does not regard the different dimensions of human interiority as separate spheres "but as aspects of one and the same act, inseparably united with one another."[12] For Augustine "the soul is the living whole of personality, whose life is a unity, and which by its self-consciousness is certain of its own reality as the surest truth."[13]

In this interpretation of will and soul in the language of personalism, Augustine sounds very modern, for in some ways the modern period saw the further development of this cast of thought but in a direction toward an individualism of the "private self," which is contrary to Augustinian "interiority." So aware was Augustine that he had discovered the radically new self-understanding of Christian anthropology that he perceived the basic inadequacy of the "ontic" categories of Greek cosmocentric thought to express this spiritual interiority. He recognized the need for a new language to explore and express human consciousness and freedom—what Karl Rahner called "ontological" language.[14] However, with Augustine these new categories of internality are only in the process of coming into existence.[15]

It can be said that Augustine mediated to the West the biblical understanding of the human being as person. Several theologians and some philosophers have concurred on the thesis that what we know today as the personal structure of existence emerged in Israel during the time of the prophets.[16] Some theologians have employed Jaspers's notion of the "axial age" as a heuristic to specify Israel's understanding of the newly discovered individual or self.[17] Jaspers described the millennium before Christ as the "axis" of world history because during that time individual consciousness as we know it today emerged for the first time among many ancient peoples.[18] These different peoples gave different interpretations to the newly discovered self. For the Greeks the self was identified with reason. For Israel the self was described in the language of will and responsibility. The prophets proclaimed Yahweh as the God of freedom, the eminently Personal One, beyond all human manipulation. Through prophetic eschatology Yahweh revealed the divine freedom as indictment and promise.[19] Divine fidelity became a promise of future salvation for those who heeded Yahweh's call to ethically responsible selfhood. This prophetic form of eschatological hope created that religious concern for the future wherein responsible will and selfhood could appear. Human personhood is discovered as the anthropological correlate to the revelation of a Personal God:

> It is the unconditional character of the biblical God that makes the relation to him radically personal. . . . The God who is unconditional in power, demand, and promise is the God who makes us completely personal in our encounter with him. It is not that we first know what person is and then apply the concept of God to this. But, in the encounter with God we first experience what person should mean.[20]

The Personal God of the prophets was revealed as the Will for justice, mercy, and love. This "ethical monotheism" aligns true worship of God with the works of justice in a community of persons. With the end of prophetic activity in late Judaism, the Torah became the central religious symbol. The Law was the revelation of the divine will, and obedience to the Law was the mark of the responsible Jew.

For Christians the Law reaches its goal (its *telos*) in Jesus, in whose words, deeds, and destiny divine and human personhood find their definitive epiphany.[21] The meaning of Exodus 3:14 coincides with that of Genesis 1:26—the *tetragrammaton* is fulfilled in the *ikon*: ". . . the splendor of the gospel showing forth the glory of Christ, the Image of God" is the fulfillment of the divine promise, identical with the Divine Name, "I will be for you what I will be for you."[22] In light of God's self-revelation in the person of Jesus, personhood for Christians becomes discipleship.

Augustine mediated this biblical understanding of personhood to the West — a mediation whereby Christianity conquered the Greco-Roman world.[23] Reason is transformed by faith as the latter becomes the condition for reason's access to the truth. Augustine presents God, not as "an object to be known," but as "the principle of self-conscious life."[24] God, *intimior intimo meo*, is the Whence of human personhood. As Charles Cochrane so lucidly observed, Augustinian Trinitarianism flows from this experience of consciousness grounded in God — the *praxis* of personhood (being, knowing, willing) reveals its Source in the dynamic personhood of God (Being, Wisdom, Power).[25] For Augustine the Trinity describes the divine life of the Personal God, and, quite significantly, he registers a reluctance to speak of the Trinity as three "persons."[26] As Paul Tillich pointed out, Augustine "is one of those responsible for our present-day inclination to apply the term, *persona*, to God, instead of applying it individually to the Father, Son, and Holy Spirit.[27]

The first philosopher of the will is the theologian of personhood. The religious roots of this personal structure of existence are further clarified in Augustine's theology of grace.

Grace

As Augustine rehearsed in his own experience the prophetic breakthrough to personhood, he became more and more profoundly convinced of the precarious situation of the responsible self. With Jeremiah he felt the need for a "new covenant," written by God on the heart, a new divine empowerment from within the human spirit (Jer 31:33). With Ezekiel he hoped for a new heart, a heart of flesh to replace the heart of stone, when God would put the divine Spirit within the people (Ezek 11:19). But with Paul, Augustine believed that this prophetic longing had been answered through Christ's gift of the indwelling Spirit. The struggling Augustine had found himself described in the seventh chapter of Paul's epistle to the Romans. But with his conversion he found himself described by the redemptive power of the Spirit of Christ, celebrated in the eighth chapter of the same epistle. The development of this theology of grace (this pneumatology) was to be his destiny.

Pelagianism, with its optimistic understanding of the power of free will and moral effort, was the context for Augustine's distinctive theology of grace.[28] Much of this theology became the official doctrine of the Western Church through Augustine's insistence at the Council of Carthage in 418 (the acts of this council were subsequently approved by Pope Zosimus) that Pelagianism was a moralistic reduction of the gospel. From his own intense experience of moral impotency before his conversion, Augustine realized that the gospel is the "good news" that

God saves us; that Christ is our Redeemer and not merely a Revealer; that the gift of the Spirit is empowerment for the future and not merely the forgiveness of past sins.

Augustine constructed the basic categories of the Western theology of grace. Against Pelagianism he insisted that original sin had rendered free will powerless in regard to salvation. True freedom came from the power of the grace of the Holy Spirit liberating the human heart from its bondage to itself. However, in his hyperbolic rhetoric on the necessity and gratuity of salvific grace for a humanity in universal bondage to sin, Augustine engendered an excessive pessimism in the West, especially as regards predestination. Indeed, with Jean Guitton, "we may wonder to what degree Christianity still suffers from St. Augustine's pessimism."[29] But despite our need to modify and mollify Augustine's teaching through a more hopeful recollection of God's universal salvific will, there is much in his theology of grace to guide our reflections on present Christian discipleship.

Augustine is the witness to the divine initiative with his notion of "prevenient grace" (*gratia praeveniens*), endorsed as doctrine at the Second Council of Orange in 529 against those later known as the Semi-Pelagians. In no way, however, is pessimistic predestinationism essential to the notion of prevenient grace. It can be used to describe the human condition as embraced from the beginning by God's universal salvific will. It was so used by the Catholic philosopher Maurice Blondel—and in the theology of Karl Rahner it became the famous "supernatural existential." God's self-offer comes first to all, and this offer is nothing less than the universal prevenience of the Spirit.

Augustine's teaching on "operating grace" (*gratia operans*)—"what God does in us without us"—again emphasizes the divine initiative and the primacy of grace in our salvation. It is this teaching that a later Augustinian friar, Martin Luther, will radicalize as "grace alone" (*gratia sola*). Augustine complemented his doctrine of operating grace by his notion of "cooperating grace" (*gratia cooperans*)— "what God does in us with us." This is the teaching that will be elaborated by Thomas Aquinas.[30]

The contemporary consensus on the primacy of *praxis* demands an understanding of grace as the ground of freedom, understood as historical self-determination. The call of Pelagius for moral effort was correct, even though his reduction of grace to free will is unacceptable. The primacy of *praxis* requires that we finally overcome the traditional—and very unfortunate—juxtaposition of "grace and free will" wherein God is portrayed as vying with, or efficaciously overcoming, human freedom. Two examples will clarify what I mean. Jean Guitton describes beautifully the inner working of the "divine art" in disposing people for faith, but he so emphasizes the gentleness of God that he is led to the unhappy phrase "while leaving freedom intact."[31] Again, in praise of Augustine he states that "no one has striven so much to grasp God's immanence, so respectful of human freedom."[32] While Guitton means to emphasize God's action as the working of love rather than force, his references to human freedom can be misleading. One might interpret the divine action as contending with human freedom rather than as constituting it. To-day we must retrieve the Pauline teaching that freedom is the fruit of grace: "Where the Spirit of God is, there is freedom" (2 Cor 3:17).[33] As Antoon Vergote sagely reminds us, "While grace and freedom may be affirmed together, they cannot be thought together."[34] Vergote shows how Augustine finally arrived at this position of affirming a simultaneous but distinct divine and human activity in his *Retractationes*: "Thus the one and the other (faith and good works) are ours by reason of the will's freedom, yet the one and the other are given by the Spirit of faith and love."[35]

Augustine's *libertas christiana* describes persons living in the community of the Spirit of Christ. Augustine clearly distinguishes between free will (*liberum arbitrium*) and freedom (*libertas*). In this life, free will implies the possibility of doing evil, whereas freedom designates the one whose will is confirmed in good through grace. The full flowering of freedom is eschatological, but it is anticipated now in the grace of the Spirit.[36] As the best of the Catholic tradition always affirmed, God does not act "alongside of" but in and through human action. Christian discipleship is grace-enabled *praxis*, which is authentic freedom. Historical consciousness has made us aware today that history is not the sweep of time in which people are caught—it is the concrete result of human conation. History is the content of eternity, while eternity is the issue of history. With Walter Kasper, historically conscious Christians with faith in cooperating grace can dare to say: "History is entirely subject to God's promise and yet is wholly entrusted to human responsibility."[37]

In his classic *Christ and Culture*, H. Richard Niebuhr portrays Augustine's thought as an illustration of his preferred model, "Christ, the Transformer of Culture." Indeed, Augustine "himself is an example of what conversion of culture means." In his theology of creation Augustine delights in the divine ordering of the world, and in his theology of redemption he celebrates the divine ordering of what has become disordered by sin. But, unfortunately, his pessimistic doctrine of predestination kept Augustine from fully developing the transformationist theme. "He was led to embrace a dualism more radical than that of Paul and Luther."[38]

Love

Hannah Arendt's work on Augustine's understanding of neighborly love recalls a long history of the conflict of interpretations on this theme. "Medievals, moderns, or contemporaries, we must all contend with the legacy Augustine bequeathed to us, and find it a somewhat mixed bag."[39] In terms of the main thrust of his theological anthropology, love is the redemption of the will; love is the whence and whither of personhood; love is the enactment of freedom in grace. But in terms of the concrete execution of his theology of love, Augustine evoked a hermeneutics of suspicion that has never abated. On the one hand, Augustine enjoyed the company of his friends. Thus, "Augustine is really a Christian philosopher of community."[40] "Of a love which has no interest at all in establishing friendship Augustine has no knowledge."[41] On the other hand, according to Jaspers, "Augustine knew the passion of friendship but not the loyalty." Because he knew loyalty only to God and the church, Augustine displays "inhuman" traits which "repel" us. His almost fanatical ecclesiocentrism is "a symptom of the process that was to make Christian love so ambiguous a concept in the eyes of all mankind. . . ."[42] In sum, in his reflections on love Augustine seems both warm and cold. Here a critical hermeneutics of retrieval is in order.

All of Western spirituality has been formed by Augustine's teaching on the primacy of love: "We love God and our neighbor from one and the same love, but we love God for the sake of God, and ourselves and our neighbor for the sake of God."[43] That statement is very clear, and from the perspective of many people today it sounds rather cold. Even though Augustine describes the experience of love in the warm rhetoric of ardor and passion, he seems to want to save all this passion for God alone. While love of neighbor is never omitted, it is often expressed in the sober language of duty and obligation—of obedience to the divine command. But in regard to love of neighbor there is significant development in Augustine's thought, a development so significant that it demands further elaboration below.

As we have seen, on human relationships Augustine sounds ambivalent. He can recall with peerless poignancy his grief at the death of a beloved friend in his youth. He can extol the values of community. He is delighted by good conversation. Individual persons are important. But at the same time, he is convinced that "in the sojourning of this carnal life each one carries his own heart, and every heart is closed to every other heart."[44]

Often criticized as a most inappropriate context for the discussion of love of others is Augustine's (in)famous *uti/frui* (to use/to enjoy) distinction: God is to be enjoyed; creatures are to be used.[45] The either/or nature of this distinction forces Augustine to speak of "using" others—a contradiction of his own personalism, for persons are never means but always ends. To explain this anomaly we must recall the predominant meaning of the word *caritas* in Augustine. Even though he knew love as benevolence toward the other as end, "for the most part he tends to think of love in appetitive terms, of *caritas* as our 'appetite for the beatitude' we shall enjoy in the vision of God."[46] Since God alone is the ultimate satisfaction of the restless heart, God alone can be loved for God's own sake. People must be loved as fellow pilgrims limping toward the eternal city. Thus, to "use" others is to serve others in and for God. During our earthly pilgrimage we move in darkness, each one hidden from the other. We are shut off from one another; the body hides the soul; the face is mere surface; our words conceal as much as they reveal. In the City of God, however, "we shall rest and we shall see, we shall see and we shall love, we shall love and we shall praise. Behold what we shall be in the end without end. For what else is our end except to reach the kingdom which has no end."[47]

Eudaimonism is the general context for the development of the Augustinian theology of love. In his study of the notion of self-love in Augustine, Oliver O'Donovan shows how authentic self-love is identical with the love of God. Love is the active pursuit of happiness, and God is our happiness. Love of neighbor is helping others in pursuit of the same goal. "In practical terms love of neighbor is evangelism."[48] O'Donovan discusses the "false step" of the *uti/frui* distinction, but also shows how Augustine "recovered" from it. After 397 it is not used again. After 400 something new appears—self-love as opposed to the love of God: "Two loves have built two cities. . . ."[49] For Augustine, to live is to love—what is needed is the right ordering of love, and he finds that ordering in loving in and for God. This reordering of human love is accomplished by God Who Is Love. Commenting on Romans 5:5, Augustine states that the "love of God shed abroad in our hearts is nothing other than the Holy Spirit who sheds it."[50] Here is the core of the gospel for Augustine. The grace of Christ is the Holy Spirit, and Christian spirituality is the victory of the immanence of divine love liberating the heart turned in on itself for the authentic love of God, self, and neighbor.

In terms of a retrieval of Augustinian spirituality for today, it would be interesting to relate Augustine's theology of love to that of Karl Rahner, who is the most famous of recent theologians who identify love of neighbor with love of God. First of all, Rahner would agree with Augustine that we love God and neighbor from one and the same love, the divine love that has been infused into our hearts by the Holy Spirit, God's self-gift. But would Augustine agree with Rahner on the unity of the object of love—that loving neighbor is loving God? A positive answer to this question has been given rather recently by the Augustinian scholar, Johannes van Bavel, O.S.A. Van Bavel discovered an evolution in Augustine's thought wherein he moved from asserting a strong distinction between love of God and love of neighbor to an insistence on the practical primacy of love of neighbor. Indeed, in 407 Augustine went so far as to make a "daring inversion" of 1 John 4:8 and 16, "God is love," into "Love is God." Among the far-reaching consequences of Augustine's inversion, van Bavel mentions two: the first is that love is so much of one piece that it cannot be split up (it does not matter where our love begins, from God, from Christ, from neighbor, the outcome will always be the same); and the second is that love for neighbor is the absolute condition for love for God. This theology of love is not reductionist (Creator and creature are not identified). It is based on a radical interpretation of the Incarnation. Thus can van Bavel correctly claim that in his theology of love Karl Rahner "closely follows Augustine's line of thought."[51]

As illustrated above, there has been much criticism of Augustine's theology of love as coldly theocentric. But this criticism has not recognized a development in his theology. The Augustinian tradition is in debt to scholars such as Johannes van Bavel who show how the mature thought of Augustine on love of God and love of neighbor resonates with the most significant recent developments in Christian spirituality wherein love of neighbor has become the central theme (e.g., work for social justice, peace, and all current forms of liberation theology). The mature

Augustine would certainly resonate with the words of Karl Rahner: "Only one who loves his or her neighbor can know who God actually is."[52]

History

We share with Augustine, says Guitton, "his most profound intuition, his conception of existence in time."[53] Like all Christians, Augustine believed that ultimate truth was disclosed in the historical event, Jesus Christ. In line with the Latin patristic tradition he inherited (Tertullian, Cyprian, Ambrose), Augustine sought to relate the unfolding events of his time to the events of salvation history recorded in the Scriptures.[54] For the Fathers of the fourth century *the* event which demanded theological interpretation was the unexpected Constantinian recognition of the Church and its sequel, the Christianization of the Roman Empire. Eusebius of Caesarea in the East and Ambrose of Milan in the West are the clearest illustrations of that theological interpretation known as "imperial theology" — the first positive political theology in the history of the Church. Eusebius's reception of Constantine was unrestrained in its enthusiasm — the emperor was hailed as the Vicar of Christ and common bishop of the faithful! Less enthusiastic, but no less positive was Ambrose's relationship with the Emperor Theodosius. Ambrose exemplifies the sacerdotal mentality of the Western Church — Theodosius was indeed the emperor, but as a Christian, he was subject to the authority of the bishop, Ambrose. While the imperial theology of the East embraced "caesaropapism," that of the West chose "papocaesarism." The consequences of these different options describe the struggles between throne and altar in subsequent church history.

Common and central to both forms of imperial theology is the notion of the *tempora christiana* ("Christian times"). According to this notion, the Christian era dawned with Constantine. It seemed that the period of the New Testament was to be a rehearsal of Old Testament salvation history. As Exodus-Sinai was followed by the conquest of Canaan and the Davidic monarchy, so the cross and resurrection of Christ initiated a movement culminating in the conquest of the Roman Empire with Constantine as the new David. This was indeed a political theology of glory! Today we rightly tend to be very critical of such religious legitimations of political power. But for the theologians of the fourth century, the Church was far more than an institution alongside other social institutions (the typically modern conception of religion). The Church was "a new *people* taking shape in the course of history, which happened according to God's design that had been determined long ago. Thus the rise of that people to prominence was inevitable."[55]

The early Augustine accepted the imperial interpretation of the *tempora christiana*. However, the collapse of the Christian Empire, signaled by the sack of Rome in 410, rendered this imperial theology implausible. After 410 Augustine rejected the central tenet of imperial theology as he was forced to develop his own theology of history. In his mature thought, Augustine insisted on the "homogeneity" of all time after Christ.[56] History continues only in order that conversion to eternity might happen for God's elect in time. The divine promise is life eternal, not progress in history. Thus, Christian concern for the political order is utterly pragmatic: "[T]he heavenly city . . . while in its state of pilgrimage, avails itself of the peace of earth, and, so far as it can without injuring faith and godliness, desires and maintains a common agreement regarding the acquisition of the necessaries of life, and makes this earthly peace bear upon the peace of heaven."[57] With this sober assessment of the state, all religious aura is removed from political arrangements. The redemptive work of God's grace is confined to the interiority of the individual person. Progress is limited to the process of sanctification. Augustine did not identify the kingdom of God with the Church; the kingdom is *manifest* in the Church[58]—an early form of the contemporary understanding of the Church as *sacrament* of the kingdom. For Augustine, salvation is redemption *from* the perpetual perishing that is history—it is not the redemption *of* history. The fulfillment of Christian hope is transhistorical in God's eternity beyond history.

This Augustinian theology of history has been dominant in the Church down to our own day. When the medieval monk Joachim of Fiore presented his vision of the dawning of the "third age of the Holy Spirit" within history, Thomas Aquinas turned to Augustine's teaching on the finality of Christ (and thus, the homogeneity of all time after Christ) to condemn it.[59] And when the liberal theology of the nineteenth century, which had interpreted divine providence in terms of progress in history, became pathetically implausible in light of the horrors of the twentieth century, Karl Barth resuscitated the Augustinian theology of history for his "neo-orthodox" reaction.[60] There is no such thing as inevitable progress in history— the lesson Augustine continues to teach us.

Augustine is "the founder of the Western philosophy of history."[61] He initiated historical consciousness, for in his reflections on memory and time in the 10th and 11th books of the *Confessions*, "he did succeed in establishing the temporality of the subject."[62] He broke the Greek cycle and gave us the linear sequence of unrepeatable events ruled by divine providence. But Augustine was unaware of our contemporary radicalization of historical consciousness. He did not see history as determining and determined by human freedom. For him eternity was the always already "finished" realm waiting to receive elected pilgrims. For many of us today eternity is "unfinished"—it is coming to be in time—it is the fruit, the grace-inspired issue of history.[63]

A Postscript on a Shared Metaphor

One of Augustine's favorite metaphors is the "abyss." He often uses it to refer to the profoundly inscrutable ways of God, but he also uses it to refer to the chaotic depths of the restless human heart—*homo abyssus est.*[64]

Employing Augustine's "conative" anthropology, Hannah Arendt often uses the same metaphor to describe the inscrutable depths of the human heart. If our attainments are always finite, there is, however, something "infinite" about our outreach. Limited by the perpetual perishing of our temporal condition, we reach out for the unending rest of eternity in God. Like Augustine, Arendt experienced the human abyss. She entitled the *Willing* volume of *The Life of the Mind* "The Abyss of Freedom and the *novus ordo seclorum*." She poignantly describes her Augustinian self in terms of the "dark 'abysses' of the human heart . . . subject to time and consumed by time, but not its quintessential being that adheres to it. To this quintessential being I belong by virtue of love, since love confers belonging. . . . In finding God [man] finds what he lacks, the very thing he is not: an eternal essence."[65]

If the term *postmodern* can be used historically to describe the West after 1914, the end of the modern ideology of progress, we can say that Arendt's work as a political philosopher addressed the abysmal world scene of the early postmodern period. To do so, she chose the premodern Augustine as her favorite dialogue partner because there is something about his work that continues to address us as we search for a "hope against hope" in a time that she, Augustine, and we would call abysmal.

NOTES

1. Augustine, *In Joan.Evang.*, *Tract xxix. 6: intellectus merces est fidei.*

2. Augustine, *De civitate Dei*, 12, 20.

3. Hannah Arendt, *The Life of the Mind*, vol. 2: *Willing* (New York: Harcourt Brace Jovanovich, 1971), p. 84.

4. Christopher Dawson, *Medieval Religion* (New York: Sheed & Ward, 1934), p. 36.

5. *De civitate Dei*, 5, 9.

6. Arendt, *Willing*, p. 85.

7. Ibid., p. 18.

8. Cf. Mircea Eliade, *Cosmos and History* (New York: Harper Torchbooks, 1959), pp. 102ff.

9. Arendt, *Willing*, p. 109.

10. Eric Springsted, "Will and Order: The Moral Self in Augustine's *De Libero Arbitrio*," *Augustinian Studies* 29, no. 2 (1998): 85.

11. Wilhelm Windelband, *A History of Philosophy* (London: Macmillan, 1914), pp. 280–81.

12. Ibid., p. 278.

13. Ibid.

14. Karl Rahner, *The Foundations of Christian Faith* (New York: Seabury Press, 1978), p. 302.

15. Windelband, *A History of Philosophy*, p. 302.

16. Cf. Eric Voegelin, *Israel and Revelation*, vol. 1 of *Order and History* (Baton Rouge: Louisiana State University Press, 1956), pp. 422, 430, and 485 on Jeremiah; cf. also William Thompson and David Morse, eds., *Voegelin's Israel and Revelation* (Milwaukee, Wis.: Marquette University Press, 2000), esp. pp. 140–63; and Stephen McKnight, ed., *Eric Voegelin's Search for Order in History* (Baton Rouge: Louisiana State University Press, 1978).

17. Cf. John Cobb, *The Structure of Christian Existence* (Philadelphia: Westminster

Press, 1967), especially chapter 9; reprint by University Press of America, 1990, with special preface; William Thompson, *Christ and Consciousness* (New York: Paulist Press, 1977).

18. Karl Jaspers, *The Origin and Goal of History* (New Haven, Conn.: Yale University Press, 1953), pp. 140ff.; Hannah Arendt illustrated the "axial age" as the time "when, for the first time, man becomes (in the words of Augustine) a question for himself" in her *Men in Dark Times* (New York: Harcourt, Brace, & World, 1968), pp. 88–89.

19. Old Testament eschatology has two basic forms, "prophetic" and "apocalyptic." Prophetic eschatology envisions a fulfillment of the divine promise ("new covenant," "new David," etc.) within history but with significant discontinuities with the present. Cf. Donald Gowan, *Eschatology in the Old Testament* (Philadelphia: Fortress Press, 1986).

20. Paul Tillich, *Biblical Revelation and the Search for Ultimate Reality* (Chicago: University of Chicago Press, 1955), p. 27.

21. Romans 10:4; here, as commentators have pointed out, *telos* means end in the sense of goal.

22. 2 Corinthians 4:4 as the eschatological revelation of Exodus 3:14. On the current understanding of YHWH (the *tetragrammaton*), see André LaCocque and Paul Ricoeur, *Thinking Biblically: Exegetical and Hermeneutical Studies* (Chicago: University of Chicago Press, 1998), pp. 307–29.

23. The West at the time of Augustine can be described as Graeco-Roman in line with Horace's famous words on the victory of Rome over Greece: "the captive that captured her rude conqueror" (*Graecia capta ferum victorem cepit et artes intulit agresti Latio*), as quoted in J. Wright Duff, *A Literary History of Rome* (London: Ernest Benn, 1960), p. 79.

24. Charles Cochrane, *Christianity and Classical Culture* (London: Oxford University Press, 1957), p. 408.

25. Ibid., p. 407.

26. Augustine, *De Trinitate*, 9, 12.

27. Paul Tillich, *A History of Christian Thought* (New York: Simon & Schuster, 1967), p. 116.

28. "Pelagianism" is Augustine's interpretation of the teaching of Pelagius. From the perspective of our contemporary hermeneutical consciousness we must distinguish between the pastoral intent of Pelagius the reformer and his polemical reception by Augustine. For an overview of some contemporary reassessments of Pelagius, see Piet Fransen, "Augustine, Pelagius and the Controversy on the Doctrine of Grace," *Louvain Studies* 12, no. 2 (Summer 1987): 172–81; Augustine never denied free will, but he found that "to will and to be able are not the same," *Confessions* 8, 5.

29. Jean Guitton, *The Modernity of St. Augustine* (Baltimore, Md.: Helicon Press, 1959), p. 79.

30. Augustine, *De gratia et libero arbitrio*, 33.

31. Guitton, *Modernity of St. Augustine*, p. 16.

32. Ibid., p. 19.

33. On this passage F. W. Dillistone observes: "There is, I think, no more pregnant sentence in the New Testament on the work of the Spirit than Paul's in II Cor. 3:17" (*The Power of Symbols in Religion and Culture* [New York: Crossroad, 1986], p. 198).

34. Antoon Vergote, "Finding God: A Matter of Recovering or Discovering? Reflection on Augustine's Teaching," *Louvain Studies* 12, no. 2 (1987): 111.

35. Augustine, *Retractationes* I, 23, 2–3, as quoted by Vergote, "Finding God," p. 110.

36. Cf. Etienne Gilson, *The Christian Philosophy of St. Augustine* (New York: Random House, 1960), pp. 323–24, n. 85.

37. Walter Kasper, *An Introduction to Christian Faith* (New York: Paulist Press, 1980), p. 186.

38. H. Richard Niebuhr, *Christ and Culture* (New York: Harper Torchbooks, 1956), pp. 206–17.

39. Robert O'Connell, *Imagination and Metaphysics in St. Augustine* (Milwaukee, Wis.: Marquette University Press, 1986), pp. 25–26.

40. Mary T. Clark, *Augustinian Personalism* (Villanova, Pa.: Villanova University Press, 1970), p. 1.

41. Oliver O'Donovan, *The Problem of Self-Love in St. Augustine* (New Haven, Conn.: Yale University Press, 1980), p. 127.

42. Karl Jaspers, *Plato and Augustine* (New York: Harcourt, Brace & World, 1962), pp. 113, 118, 114. Jaspers, Arendt's dissertation director, was rather negative on the Augustinian theology of love!

43. Augustine, *De Trinitate*, 8, 7, 10; 8, 8, 12.

44. Augustine, *Ennarationes in Psalmos*, Psalm 55, 9.

45. Augustine, *De doctrina christiana*, 22, 20.

46. O'Connell, *Imagination and Metaphysics*, p. 26.

47. Augustine, *De civitate Dei*, 22, 30.

48. O'Donovan, *Problem of Self-Love in Augustine*, p.112.

49. Augustine, *De civitate Dei*, 14, 28.

50. Quoted in O'Donovan, *Problem of Self-Love in Augustine*, p. 130.

51. See Johannes van Bavel, "The Double Face of Love in Augustine," *Louvain Studies* 12, no. 2 (1987): 116–30.

52. Karl Rahner, *The Love of Jesus and the Love of Neighbor* (New York: Crossroad, 1983), p. 71.

53. Guitton, *Modernity of St. Augustine*, p. 7.

54. See Lloyd Patterson, *God and History in Early Christian Thought* (New York: Seabury Press, 1967), pp. 3–30.

55. Wolfhart Pannenberg, *Human Nature, Election, and History* (Philadelphia: Westminster Press, 1977), pp. 63–64.

56. See R. A. Markus, *Saeculum: History and Society in the Theology of St. Augustine* (Cambridge: Cambridge University Press, 1970).

57. Augustine, *De civitate Dei*, 19, 17.

58. Pannenberg, *Human Nature, Election, and History*, p. 68.

59. Thomas Aquinas, *Summa Theologiae*, IaIIae, q. 106, a. 4.

60. See Langdon Gilkey, *Reaping the Whirlwind* (New York: Seabury Press, 1976), p. 219.

61. Jaspers, *Plato and Augustine*, p. 101.

62. Stephen Crites, "The Narrative Quality of Experience," in Stanley Hauerwas and L. Gregory Jones, eds., *Why Narrative? Readings in Narrative Theology* (Grand Rapids: Eerdmans, 1989), p. 73.

63. Karl Rahner, *Foundations of Christian Faith*, p. 437.

64. In *Ennarationes in Psalmos*, commenting on Psalm 41, Augustine explores the abyss that the human being is. The source of this metaphor is Genesis 1:2 ("The earth was a formless void, and darkness covered the face of the deep—*faciem abyssi*").

65. Hannah Arendt, *Love and Saint Augustine* (Chicago: University of Chicago Press, 1996, p. 162.

ten
Reading like Angels

Derrida and Augustine on the Book
(for a History of Literature)

Mark Vessey

Ellipsis (1): Literature and Testimony

Derrida with his finger on the sixth seal of Blanchot's Apocalypse:

> In memory of its Christian-Roman meaning, "passion" always implies martyr-dom, that is—as its name indicates—testimony. A passion always testifies. But if the testimony always claims to testify in truth to the truth for the truth, it does not consist, for the most part, in sharing a knowledge, in making known, in in-forming, in speaking true. As a promise to *make truth*, according to Augustine's expression [*Conf.* X.i.1], where the witness must be irreplaceably alone, where the witness alone is capable of dying his own death, testimony goes always hand in hand with at least the *possibility* of fiction, perjury, and lie. Were this possi-bility to be eliminated, no testimony would be possible any longer; it could no longer have the meaning of testimony. If testimony is passion, that is because it will always *suffer* both having, undecidably, a connection to fiction, perjury, or lie and never being able or obligated—without ceasing to testify—to become a proof. (DM 27)

The possibility of *fiction* is a condition for the truth-claim of *testimony*, a possi-bility that is also a living passibility, since not even a martyr's death can prove the truth of what is asserted. This (un)truth condition of testimony, Derrida argues, is common to all our mortal experience and utterance, both to what we call litera-ture and to what we may think of as other-than-literature:

> Here, in any case, the border between literature and its other becomes unde-
> cidable. The literary institution has imposed itself; it has also imposed the rigor
> of its right to calculate, master, neutralize this undecidability, to make *as if*—
> another fiction—literature, in its possibility, had not begun before literature . . .
> (DM 92)

As testimony labors under suspicion of falsehood, so "literature" bears the burden
of being named under an external law, of being no more than a name, of being a
name without the thing, of not being. That is the ultimate passion of literature:

> There is no essence or substance of literature: literature is not. It does not ex-
> ist. . . . No utterance, no discursive form is intrinsically or essentially *literary* be-
> fore and outside of the function it is assigned or granted by a right [*un droit*],
> that is, a specific intentionality inscribed directly on the social body. . . . Its pas-
> sion consists in this—that it receives its determination from something other
> than itself. Even when it harbors the unconditional right to say anything . . . its
> *status* is never assured or guaranteed permanently. . . . This contradiction is its
> very existence, its ecstatic process. (DM 28)

These theses on literature are familiar to us from other writings by Derrida.
What is singular about their expression here in *Demeure*, aside from the num-
bering of passions suggested by his host in Louvain, is the historical juncture indicated, on the one hand, by the citation (DM 23–25) of Ernst Robert Curtius's
1948 book on *European Literature and the Latin Middle Ages* and, on the other,
by the joint reference to Augustine's *Confessions* and to an understanding of martyrdom that dates from the persecution of Christians under the Roman Empire.
Martyrdom and confession are cognate forms of Christian testimony. Before Augustine's time, the role of *confessor* was understood to be heroic. To "confess" the
Christian faith was then to suffer all but the extremity of death itself. With the
ending of intermittent persecution by the Roman state, Christian confession assumed new heroic forms, prominent among them the civil death of monastic life.
The monks, like the martyrs before them, carried their testimony to the physical
and legal limits of Roman *civitas*. These are just a few elements of the history
that Derrida evokes as having "counted greatly in the institution and the constitution of literature, in its relation to religion and politics" (DM 21), in order to
pose the larger question of the (in)dissociability of that institution from *Latin-
Roman-Christian* culture.

To put the question this way is certainly to differ from Curtius, who, as Derrida points out (DM 24), modeled his ideal totality of European literature on Roman citizenship under the Empire, but then made Latin "literature" an unreflect-
ing translation of Greek *grammatike* and Homer its founding hero. Curtius's Latin
literature is thus not only hellenized but largely un- or dechristianized. He gives
notably short shrift to Augustine's *Confessions*. Only as an afterthought does he
consider how "preoccupation with the Bible and the rise of Christian writing"
could have influenced (Latin, European) "literary theory," by which he meant

poetics.[1] By insisting on the *Latin* letter of literature, Derrida would reassert its relation to Rome and Latin Christianity. He would even, perhaps, make space in a
book-to-come for a few pages, in a chapter on literature, on the "thinker of the
end of history and absolute knowledge" (DM 83) who wrote that sometimes paradoxical treatise in twenty-two books (or chapters) on Roman citizenship, Latin
letters, and Christian Scripture, *The City of God.*

But if the question "concerning the Latin-Europeanness of literature" (DM
22) entails a revision of Curtius, does it not also imply a "retractation" (in the Augustinian sense of revision or self-correction) of Derrida? In the "history of writing" proposed in *Of Grammatology*, there is only one epoch of the (metaphorical) book, one "idea of a totality of the signifier" variably repeated from Plato to
the Enlightenment and beyond, a single continuity of metaphysics, theology, and
encyclopedism — all decently Greek words, like philosophy and grammatology —
which subsumes all "historical" differences that may here and there be detected
in the representation of writing, "however important in fact [they] might be" (G
15; cf. DM 104–8). It is less than clear, on first consideration, how another chapter on literature, that endlessly enigmatic (no)thing with its inalienably Latin name,
is to be inserted in the already immense book of Derrida's writing on writing. What
would it mean, after the letter of *Grammatology*, to investigate the "literality of lit-
erarity, *insofar as the latter is close in its destiny to the European heritage of Christian Rome*" (DM 23, my italics displacing Derrida's)?

The postscript to *Demeure* (104–8), closing the gap that a hostile critic once
claimed to make between Curtius and Derrida, and the preamble in the same
text, in which Derrida opens Curtius's history of European literature to deconstruction, may not entirely cancel each other out. We are confronted both with
a *question of literature* that would not be exhausted by the ancient opposition of
natural to artificial writing or by the modern definition of the "text," and with the
prospect of a theory of literature that would make specific "historical" reference
to Rome and Latin Christianity. If there were a piece of writing by Derrida that
already joined the two halves of this ellipse, he might have referred to it in *Demeure*. If there is a text on the subject among works of his not yet published, lost,
or still to be written, we should expect to find its conclusions accounted for in
the great code of Geoffrey Bennington's "Derridabase." Failing those possibilities, there remains the chance of an encounter with Augustine, the chance of
Derrida's "Circumfession."

We shall continue our pursuit of this lost manuscript, indirectly.

Enigmas of the Great Code

English literature had its theorist of the total book long before Mallarmé began
dreaming of *le Livre*. His name was William Blake. "The Old and New Testaments," Blake wrote and inscribed, "are the Great Code of Art." It is one of the
aphorisms that coil around his engraving of Laocoön. The final phrase was
adapted by the Canadian literary critic Northrop Frye for a book on "The Bible

and Literature." A maker of books with his own hands, several of them called *The Book of* . . . , Blake knew that a sacred code was first and literally a *codex*, an artifact of folded sheets bound in a pair of covers. Frye's aim was to establish a *literary-critical* basis for the unity and totality ascribed to the texts of Christian Scripture, the book(s) of the Old and New Testaments. Ancient histories of the biblical canon and the production of Jewish and Christian sacred books did not concern him. The Bible of Christian observance, he grants, had its name from a Greek plural diminutive noun (*ta biblia*, "the little books"). Perusal of its contents could lead one to think that it was "thought of as *a* book only because it was contained for convenience within two covers." What matters to the critic, however, is that it "has traditionally been read as a unity." The Bible exists, says Frye, "if only because it has been compelled to exist." Elsewhere he gives a rough account of the process. Yet even a work that has been forced into being must, if it is to be *read* as a whole, possess some internal shape and coherence. That is Frye's major claim. A genuine Higher Criticism would show how compelling already were the objects of compulsion. Meanwhile, anyone who takes up the Book and reads it from beginning to end will discover "that at least it has a beginning and an end, and some traces of total structure. It begins where time begins, with the creation of the world; it ends where time ends, with the Apocalypse, and it surveys history in between, or the aspect of history it is interested in, under the symbolic names of Adam and Israel."[2]

In stating this, as he was well aware, Frye wrote in the spirit of Augustine. The beginning, middle, and end phases of the biblical grand narrative are the subject matter of the first, second, and third tetrads of the second part of *The City of God* (Books XI–XIV, XV–XVIII, XIX–XXII). The unity and uniqueness of Christian Scripture, assumed by *The Great Code*, were likewise Augustine's point of departure in the great work of his late years: "What we call the City of God," he wrote at the outset of Book XI, "is vouched for by that scripture [*scriptura*] which . . . by the guiding power of supreme providence stands above the writings [*litterae*] of all peoples." Augustine's redescription of the City of God, begun already in the later books of his *Confessions*, inaugurates the singular Writing and capital Book of Latin Christianity.

Northrop Frye was a traditional literary critic. He calls criticism "the conscious organizing of a cultural tradition." That was the work of his *Anatomy of Criticism* (1957). Anyone who begins to read the *Anatomy*, at either end, quickly discovers that Frye's common sense of (this) literature makes the Christian Bible the "definitive myth," "central encyclopaedic form" or "single archetypal structure" in relation to which other texts and stories in the culture have their meaning. Hence the aptness of Blake's aphorism. "All my critical work," Frye remarks in the introduction to *The Great Code*, "has revolved around the Bible" (xiv). Conversely, his Bible turns out to be a work of criticism, an anatomy in its own right, another conscious organizing of (the same) cultural tradition. This conscious *organizing*, like the compulsion in the contexts quoted above, is both objective and subjective. It denotes an external and an internal power, the force of an exegesis applied to a body of texts from outside to fix their meaning *and* the meaning of a form already immanent in the texts themselves. These are the terms in which Frye evokes the interplay of literary idiom and literary institution.

The Great Code: The Bible and Literature was published in 1983, amid a flourishing of newer, transatlantic styles of literary theory in North America. A decade and a half later an English critic was ready to treat Frye (who died in 1991) as a figure from the past. "It is interesting to speculate," writes Brian Vickers, "what might have happened to literary theory," had Jacques Derrida and a few other Parisian intellectuals of recent reputation not existed. Would the "archetypal-scriptural approach of Northrop Frye" have won out instead?[3] Sparing Frye and Derrida the distortions of a triumphalist "losers' history" of literary theory, let us see what happens if we pursue the comparison.

Frye himself pointed to an area of common interest when he spoke of "many issues in critical theory . . . ha[ving] their origin in the hermeneutic study of the Bible." At the close of the introduction to *The Great Code*, in an uncontentious aside, he footnotes the opening chapter of Derrida's *Of Grammatology*. The point of his first two chapters, he has said, will be to show how a study of myth and metaphor can answer the question: What is the literal meaning of the Bible? "The general thesis is that the Bible comes to us as a written book, an absence invoking a historical presence 'behind' it, as Derrida would say. . . ." If this formulation does not sound quite Derridean, it is for a good reason, at least as far as Frye and other Christian readers are likely to be concerned. The startlingly *untranscendent*, *historical* presence here in question is that of a divine "word" made doubly human in the body of Christ and in the letter of the Bible. According to Frye, the traditional application of the phrase "word of God" to both Christ and the Bible is more than just "a dubious syllepsis." The Bible is not content to refer to God as something existing in another world and time. It brings God into ordinary historical and material reality, through the letter of history in the strict sense ("it is our only real contact with the so-called 'Jesus of history'") and, more powerfully, through the letter of metaphor, including the kind of historically expanded metaphor known as "typology," which links the two Testaments in a single, harmonious presentation of the one God of (the new) Israel, incarnate in Christ.[4]

Frye's Christocentric, Protestant biblical exegesis is an instance of a more general attempt in recent years to speak of the Bible in the language of Literature, and vice versa. Scholars with other religious and literary-theoretical commitments, or professing none, have taken other tacks. What many of their approaches have in common, even if it is not always made explicit, is an assumption of the *givenness*, not to say canonicity, of a particular body of sacred writing. Another giant Blakean, and as impassioned an exponent of the literary canon-as-encyclopaedia as Frye, makes the point in passing in the preface to a book designed to release part of the "biblical" narrative from an alleged tyranny of the greater codes of Jewish and Christian tradition. Although named *The Book of J*, as if to attest (by exploiting) the residual appeal of such comprehensive titles, Harold Bloom and David Rosenberg's edition of the presumed earliest strand of the Pentateuch—

called "J" in biblical scholarship after its choice of "Yahweh" (in German, Jah-weh) for the name of God—is at heart a protest against a certain religious con-ception of *the* book. "Many contemporary literary critics of the highest distinc-tion," writes Bloom, "have turned their labors of cognition and description upon the [Hebrew] Bible, but almost without exception they chose to deal not with J but with R, the triumphant Redactor, who seems to have been of the Academy of Ezra, insofar as it existed. To that diverse company of eminent readers—Northrop Frye, Frank Kermode, Robert Alter, and Geoffrey Hartman among them—the Bible is the received Bible of the normative traditions. Perhaps there can be no other Bible."[5] Had he pushed his survey a little beyond the Anglo-American or-bit and the company of scholars professedly writing on the Bible and Literature, Bloom could have made some notable additions to the modern school of Ezra. For it is also a characteristic of much of the most incisive French writing from what can now be thought of as the classical "time of theory"—the period from the early 1960s, say, to the early 1970s—that it takes the (or a) Bible as a given and longstanding unity.[6] Certainly this is true of Derrida, even if there is more day-light between his grammatology and Frye's conception of an archetypal scripture than the latter's codicil lets appear.

Here is Derrida in almost his own words:

> The good writing has therefore always been comprehended. Comprehended as that which had to be comprehended: within a nature or a natural law, cre-ated or not, but first thought within an eternal presence. Comprehended, there-fore, within a totality, and enveloped in a volume or a book. The idea of the book is the idea of a totality, finite or infinite, of the signifier; this totality of the signifier cannot be what it is, a totality, unless a totality constituted by the signified preexists it, supervises its inscriptions and its signs, and is independent of it in its ideality. The idea of the book, which always refers to a natural total-ity, is profoundly alien to the sense of writing [as Derrida will expound it]. It is the encyclopaedic protection of theology and of logocentrism against the dis-ruption of writing, against its aphoristic energy, and . . . against difference in general. If we distinguish the text from the book, we shall say that the destruc-tion of the book, as it is now under way in all domains, denudes the surface of the text. That necessary violence responds to a violence that was no less nec-essary. (G 18)

"The destruction of the book . . ." After Hegel, Mallarmé, Nietzsche, Heidegger, and Blanchot, of what book can Derrida here be speaking if not (also) of the Chris-tian Book par excellence, the upper-case, superior, or simply "good" writing of Latin Scripture, from whose millennial surveillance an upstart vernacular writing (*écriture*) was now at last to be sprung, in the new "opening" of grammatology? The very word that promises to undo the book—*text(e)*—owes its currency to the Latin Bible, the book in contact with which the word *textus* first came to mean "text" in the traditional, pre-(post)structuralist sense of an ideal totality of visible verbal signifiers. So far as it can now be pinned down, that premodern textual turn seems to have occurred within a short time of Augustine's death, and in milieux sensitive to his work. To the opening of one grammatology in late-twentieth-century France, we may conjecture, there answers (before the event) the opening of another in late-fourth-century North Africa.

Although Augustine is not named in *Of Grammatology*, a place could easily be made for him a page or two before the passage just quoted, between the lines of Rabbi Eliezer on the unexscribable Torah of memory and those of Galileo and Descartes on the Book of Nature. In other, nearly contemporary writings of his, Derrida is less reticent about the (early) Christian, Pauline and neo-Platonic, components of the "theological" or "metaphysical" epoch that he sees extending overall from Plato to the present. On one occasion (WD 11), he calls a church father to witness—but not Augustine, even though, we now know, no church father came before the author of the original *Confessions* in the readings of Jacques Derrida. Encouraged by a later exercise in the same genre, we may wonder by what unconscious circumlocution Derrida omits the name of Augustine at this point in *Of Grammatology*. If the violence that reveals the surface of the *text* is indeed a necessary response to another that lays writing under the law of the book, there can be few places where that primal, recurring act of "biblical" violence is more graphically figured than the moment early in Book XI of the *Confessions* when Augustine calls on God to "circumcise his lips" and make the Scriptures his "chaste delights" (*Conf.* XI.ii.3). This prayer may be almost as close as we can now come to the original compulsion of the Great Code. (It is only a breath or period away from the chapter whose title makes Derrida's first citation in "Circumfession" [XI.i, misnumerated in the English edition of *Jacques Derrida*].)

The writers who appear in the absence of Augustine from *Of Grammatology* are haled there by Derrida to attest the long-term continuity in Western culture of a figure of thought that sets a fallen, literal, material writing against its imagined analogue in an ideal, transcendent realm, the latter being regularly identified with the "theological" Book (of Nature, the Law, the Heart, etc.). "There remains to be written," wrote Derrida in 1967, "a history of this metaphor that always opposes divine or natural writing to a human inscription seen as laborious, finite and artificial" (G 15). Laboriously, sometimes exquisitely, that many-handed history of writing is being written. One of the most substantial contributions to it is Eric Jager's recent study of *The Book of the Heart*, which acknowledges Derrida and gives Augustine his due.

In Jager's lucid analysis, Augustine is seen opposing divine and human writing in order to accommodate each to the other. The narrative of his spiritual growth in the *Confessions* "begins with his recognition of the divine law written on the heart, continues with his heart-centered reading of Scripture, and culminates in his new role as an author writing from his heart to edify a literary public." In all these areas, Augustine's metaphorics of the book sustains a lively tension between inner and outer, spirit and letter, spirit and flesh. "Although [he] regards the inner word . . . as a mental and even nonverbal entity, his metaphors of interior writing," Jager reminds us, "often have a bodily aura. . . . In the *Confessions*, writing on the heart belongs to a cluster of fleshly metaphors that includes [the Pauline image of] the 'circumcised' heart." Similarly, in relating his conversion by Scripture, Augustine makes deliberate play with the technology of the *codex* or spine-hinged book. His codex "is more than a practical convenience; it is a psychological symbol as well," the symbolism deriving from the fact that a codex is a "container having an interior and an exterior . . . an enclosure that can be opened and closed. . . . Augustine's sudden opening of the codex—a gesture more precise and binary than the slow unrolling of a scroll—results in an inward flood of light that suggests a heart finally opened to God's word." Later, calling upon his readers to "hear" his confession by laying their ear to his heart (*Conf.* X.iii.4), Augustine makes the "written text serve . . . as a bodily surrogate for the author himself." (In a miniature from a fifteenth- century manuscript of the *Confessions* now in the British Library, he stands at a desk with an opened codex, holding his heart and a pen.) For this extraordinary facility in psychosomatic metaphors of writing and the book, as for other elements of his "theory of the written word," Augustine seems to have been particularly indebted to Ambrose of Milan. One of that churchman's greatest achievements, Jager shows, "was to collect, combine and allegorize biblical writing metaphors to create a coherent theology of writing, a Christian grammatology." After Augustine, and largely as a result of his influence, these tropes became part of the lingua franca of the West.[7]

For all its emphasis on the morally positive value ascribed to embodiment and materiality in Augustine's textual metaphorics, and despite its careful marking of places where writing in human flesh or upon the unfleshed skin of a parchment codex appears as *good* writing, *The Book of the Heart* does little to disturb Derrida's thesis of the prevailing disparagement in Western culture of empirical inscription in favor of its transcendent double. If anything, it reinforces it. By showing how Augustine exploited the resources for a distinctively Christian, biblical, and incarnational grammatology already laid up by such writers as Origen and Ambrose, Jager makes it easier for us to understand why a thinker who was as devout in his logocentrism as this Platonically minded Christian also felt free to confess such an affection, such a headlong passion, for the fallen letter—in the books of the Platonists, the books of the astrologers, the books of Cicero and Virgil, the books of the Christian Scriptures, and not least in the books of his own authorship, to whose literal, physical "retractation" (in the *Retractationes* or "Revisions") he gave some of his last hours on this earth. (The Latin noun *tractator*, before it became the normal term for an interpreter of texts, meant a masseur.) Only an Augustine thus held, if in no wise torn, between the immanence of God in the letter and the presence of God beyond it could appeal as he would to generations of Western Bible-readers down to the time of Erasmus and Luther.[8] Only this Augustine would lend himself equally to the grand narrative of Derridean grammatology and to Northrop Frye's calculated misprision of Derrida.

After reading *The Book of the Heart* we may also more easily understand why the book of the *Confessions*, despite its author's manifest desire to refer the signs of his laborious life to a foreknown, supervisory totality of the (theological) signified, has more than once been taken to conceal *writing* in the Derridean, post-

structuralist sense, and therefore treated (tractated) with all the violence necessary to destroy the book and denude the surface of a text. And why not? If Roland
Barthes and others could uncover *text* in the Torah, the very letter of the Jewish
Law, and if the rabbis were already doing the same thing by Augustine's time,[9]
there must be a good chance that Augustine's prose-poem of himself and the Holy
Scriptures can be loosed from the institutions and intentions that governed its inscription near the end of the fourth century.

   If Derrida himself were to take that chance, what would be at stake?

Prière d'insérer: *The Double Exposure*

Three images that repeat one another in multiple sequence, each made as if to
be the frontispiece of a separate volume, all interleaved in a single book like so
many post cards. Double portrait of one who writes and (one) who does not (Figures 1–3).

   A reader who begins at the beginning of *Jacques Derrida* by Geoffrey Bennington and Jacques Derrida and turns one page at a time comes first (11) upon
the "Post Card or *tableau vivant*" of a writer at his word-processor (J.D.), hands
fleetingly at rest on the keyboard, eyes trained to a screen that slants away from us
but fronts the gaze of the one who stands behind him (G.B.), whose right hand
rests with what looks like gentle pressure on the other's chair back and whose left
points to a text displayed on the monitor, the two men caught at a moment "during the preparation of these pictures—and of this book." Or caught mimicking it
(Figure 1).

   It is a moment with a powerful sense of *déjà vu* for any reader over the shoulder of Jacques Derrida, who is himself, we are reminded by the scatter of books
on his desk in the photograph, a prodigious reader of other writers—that is, if he
is not *two* readers. For a few pages earlier, Bennington has suggested that "[o]ne
can imagine Derrida as very modest, entirely occupied by reading and re-reading
his predecessors with minute attention, determined to spend the time it takes over
the slightest detail, the slightest comma, guardian of the letter of the old texts, putting nothing forward that he has not already found written by an other, scarcely
our contemporary—and this is true. But one can also imagine him, on the contrary, as immodesty itself, forcing these same old texts to say something quite different from what they had always seemed to say . . . our most contemporary contemporary" (Db 6).

   In fact, if there is an immodest gesture in the photographic image before us,
it is the one made by Bennington, jabbing his left finger at a text we take for Derrida's (he is at the keyboard) but which, to judge from the level indicated on the
screen, is more likely to be the superpositititious "Derridabase" compiled by G.B.
Derridean as Bennington's ostensive immodesty may be, it is ostensibly of another
kind than he would have us ascribe to Derrida, consisting as it does in this book in
an attempt, not to make the writer's texts "say something quite different from what
they had always seemed to say," but to make them say (again) everything they have
always seemed to say before and (already) everything they might say hereafter.

Post Card or *tableau vivant*: with Geoffrey Bennington at Ris Orangis,
during the preparation of these pictures—and of this book,"a hidden pretext
for writing in my own signature behind his back" (*Derridabase*, p. 316f).

Fig. 1. Geoffrey Bennington and Jacques Derrida, *Jacques Derrida*, trans.
Geoffrey Bennington (Chicago: University of Chicago Press, 1993), p. 11.
Photograph © Suzanne Doublet.

Bennington's immodesty, we realize, is the collusive and contractual counterpart of Derrida's modesty, a style of reading so programmatically faithful to an author's texts as to lay them more open than ever to the event of surprise from the pen of "an other"—the author himself, in this event. So it is that the refusal to quote verbatim, literatim from Derrida's writings, though sharply at odds with the latter's own practice, becomes the sign of a diabolical if not damnable fidelity (Db 316). By keeping the letter of these texts out of play, suppressing the singular unpredictability of their effects, Bennington makes them readable in a way that lowers their potential as "texts" in Derrida's sense. He says as much on the page opposite the image in view, when he invokes Derrida's concept of the "re-mark" (Db 10), the figure whereby a text, doubling or folding itself *as text*, exceeds the reader's ability to thematize its contents and thereby confine it to a world otherwise and already known.

Even before we consider *its* contents more closely, the "Post Card or *tableau vivant* [of Jacques Derrida]: with Geoffrey Bennington at Ris Orangis" offers to mark and re-mark the present text in just such a fashion. The word *tableau* (qualified as *vivant*) and the omission of the author's name seem calculated to recall Derrida's own reluctant placing of Mallarmé (specialist of literary *tombeaux* or *tableaux morts*) within a chronologically predetermined *Tableau de la littérature française: de Madame de Staël à Rimbaud*. Mallarmé it was, as Derrida there quotes him (AL 112), who said that "[t]he one who would call himself his own contemporary is misinformed," a claim and disclaimer repeated with slight variation on Derrida's behalf by the man now commissioned to place him in another publisher's series of "Les contemporains" (Db 8; cf. **13**). This Mallarméan allusion without citation comes at the end of the first section of "Derridabase," as Bennington sets Derrida speculatively in the uncontemporary company of "Plato and a few others, at Heliopolis, in Egypt" (Db 8). The next word in his text is "Remark," the title of the section into which the *tableau* will be inserted and an advance reference to the theory of the "re-mark" elaborated by Derrida (in "The Double Session") on the basis of texts of Plato and Mallarmé. Meanwhile, in the lower "internal" margin of the same page, in both the French and English versions, the name of St. Augustine appears for the first time. In these contexts, the picture of the unnamed writer "with Geoffrey Bennington at Ris Orangis" may appear not so much contextualized as dramatically misplaced.

That is not all. When we stop to consider it, the referral of the image on this "Post Card" to a time "during the preparation of these pictures—and this book" becomes at least doubly preposterous. For one thing, the anaphora of "*these* pictures" (among which *this* picture will be either the second, third, or fourth in the order of printed reproduction, depending on whether or not we count the portrait of Derrida on the book's title page and the other on its cover) has no prior referent: there is no mention of pictures in the preliminary contract between G.B. and J.D. (p. 1), nor can they have any place in the program of a "Derridabase" that we know to have been devised at a time before personal computers (or PCs) were able (like postcards) to carry photographic images. Excluded by contract and program, pictures might claim a right of entry before the "law of the genre" for biographical series of modern writers like "Les contemporains" (319–22). But that law would only license them to appear in the "second round" of the book, as in fact they do in considerable number; it would not cover their insertion amid the pages of "Derridabase" and "Circumfession," texts to which they are evidently external, both because their captions sometimes quote them and because these full-page illustrations, counted but unnumbered in the serial pagination, interrupt the split-page layout ordained for the body of the book—*preordained* for it, in fact, since this was already the format used for the French translation (super-text) and Latin original (base-text) of the "bilingual edition (Garnier, 1925) in which, so long ago," Derrida came upon the *Confessions* of Augustine (Db 8; 1). The dash in "these pictures—and this book" thus marks a disjunction no less physical than the conjunction retro(pro)spectively asserted by the "and" that follows it. At best, *this* photograph taken "during the preparation of these pictures" may be said to inaugurate a series that has no sanction before its own belated ("Post") appearance.

There is a further spatio-temporal difficulty entailed by this picture taken "during the preparation . . . of *this book*." The caption indistinctly combines a present entity comprising this photograph ("this book") with a past time when this (same) book, whatever idea was then had of it, must not have included this photograph, as a condition of its being possible for the photograph to be taken. Strictly speaking, then, the "book" of the photograph is not *one*. Like a preface, or more exactly like a frontispiece, the image with its caption presupposes the completeness of the work that it is called to complete. The "Post Card" of J.D. and G.B. is impossibly both inside and outside the book of which it is (not) a page, a paradox resolvable—if ever—only by treating it either as a misplaced frontispiece or as what it purports to be but materially cannot be, namely, a postcard *inserted* in a book . . .

Anyone can play this solitary game of cards. It is the hands-on, interactive, readerly distraction to which Bennington invites us as soon as the simulated "duel" of the "first round" is over (319), a game at which "Derridabase" should by then have made us proficient, at the risk of guaranteeing that the only tricks we ever take have already been won by someone else. ("Loosing," in fact, may turn out to be the name of the game.) Specifically, to find ourselves dealt a hand of cards by this book, to experience the *écartement* or separation of its tightly bound and written pages that is brought about by such inserted leaves, may be partly to re-perform—as always, with a difference—Derrida's dealing with texts of Mallarmé in "The Double Session," where the word "insertion" is said to "mark the breaking through of theater into the book, of spacing into interiority" (D 234). In the present case too, the *jeu de cartes* is a *jeu de théâtre*. The *tableau vivant* of J.D. "with Geoffrey Bennington at Ris Orangis" is staged as well as inserted, a fact which may contribute not a little to the difficulty of our closing the volume on it. Like its Mallarméan precursor, the Derridean book offers no protection against the supplementarity associated with theatrical and other kinds of re-presentation in the classical theory of mimesis. On the contrary, it (re-)marks it. Mallarmé cited by Derrida: "A book, held in our hand . . . makes up for all theaters [*supplée à tous les théâtres*], not by casting them all into oblivion, but by imperiously calling them to mind" (D 235).

As it happens, the theatrical supplementarity of such a book is enacted upon us with extreme economy in the image in view, which begins multiplying even before its caption is read. Downstage on the writer's desk, upstaging and invisible to G.B. and J.D., propped against a stack of books directly in front of the spectator's eye, is the "original" postcard image of Socrates writing before Plato, the image reproduced on the cover of Derrida's *Post Card*, focal point of the "Envois" (viz. postcards) collected in that earlier volume, ultimate "pretext" for Bennington's conceit of "writing in [his] own signature behind [Derrida's] back" in this one (Db 316, already cited 11) (Figure 2).

A full-page reproduction of the same double portrait, from a thirteenth-century Latin fortune-telling book, appears toward the end of *Jacques Derrida*, captioned with a quotation from *The Post Card*: "Socrates writing, writing before Plato . . . like the negative of a photograph waiting twenty-five centuries to be developed—in me, of course . . ." (365 = PC 9). In the earlier work, the writer of the postcards (J.D., as he will eventually sign them) greets the discovery of *this* image on a postcard from the Bodleian Library in Oxford as a quasi-apocalyptic event, announcing the catastrophe of a world-drama plotted on the theoretical exclusion of writing in favor of the "presence" of speech. To find Socrates, who (for Nietzsche and others) famously wrote nothing, depicted as scribe or secretary to Plato, taking dictation from him: what was this if not graphic corroboration of the theses of *Of Grammatology* and *Dissemination*? The friends who led Derrida to the Bodleian shop could have predicted, even programmed his reaction (PC 20).

But the "Envois" of *The Post Card* are more than incidentally a postscript to earlier texts of Jacques Derrida. The "epoch of the letter" (PC 62) is understood not only as a long history of the marginalization of writing in Western philosophy and annexed institutions but also, most pressingly, as the present possibility of a future held out by "letters" as correspondence-with-an-other. "To whom do you think [Socrates] is writing?" the writer of the postcards asks the beloved correspondent whose own letters we never see, except inasmuch as *these are her letters*, being addressed to her. "To whom do you think he is writing?" we read in a letter that reaches us without being addressed to us by name. "For me it is always more important to know that than to know what is being written; moreover I think it amounts to the same, to the other finally" (PC 17). The "law of the letter" is death and love, love-in-death, courtly as it is evangelical:

> In the beginning, in principle, was the post, and I will never get over it. But in the end I know it, I become aware of it as our death sentence: it was composed, according to all possible codes and genres and languages, as a declaration of love. In the beginning the post, John will say, or Shaun or Tristan [. . .]
>
> you understand, within every sign already, every mark or every trait, there is distancing, the post, what there has to be so that it is legible for an other, an other than you or me, and everything is messed up in advance, cards on the table. The condition for it to arrive is that it ends up and even that it begins by not arriving [. . .] The condition for me to renounce nothing and for

Cover of *The Post Card* (Socrates and Plato, frontispiece of *Prognostica Socratis Basilei*, 13th century, Oxford, Bodleian Library, ms. Ashmole 304, fol 31 v°). "Socrates writing, writing before Plato . . . like the negative of a photograph waiting twenty-five centuries to be developed—in me, of course . . . Socrates, he who writes—sitting, bent, docile scribe or copyist, Plato's secretary, I guess. He is in front of Plato, no, Plato is *behind* him . . . but standing . . ."

Fig. 2. Bennington and Derrida, *Jacques Derrida*, p. 365, quoting Jacques Derrida, *The Post Card: From Socrates to Freud and Beyond*, trans. Alan Bass (Chicago: University of Chicago Press, 1987), pp. 9–10. *Image used by permission of the Bodleian Library, University of Oxford.*

my own love to come back to me, and from me too be it understood, is that you are there, over there, quite alive outside of me. Out of reach. And that you send me back [. . .]

Example: if one morning Socrates had spoken for Plato, if to Plato his addressee he had addressed some message, it is also that p. would have had to be able to receive, to await, to desire, in a world to have *called* in a certain way what S. will have said to him [Derrida here uses the respectively lower- and upper- case initial letters from the names of Plato and Socrates in the Bodleian image]; and therefore what S., taking dictation, pretends to invent—writes, right? p. has sent himself a post card (caption + picture), he has sent it back to himself from himself, or he has even "sent" himself S. *And we find ourselves, my beloved angel, on the itinerary.* Go figure out then if you, at this very moment, in your name

this is the catastrophe [. . .] (PC 29–30; emphasis added, unpunctuated gaps in the original, new ellipses marked by square brackets)

With a theatricality that is all of the book, the writer of these letters deals his readers the cards, complete with blanks, which—on condition of their own desiring it—will put each in the way of reading like the "beloved angel" of the address, that is, of repeatedly calling into being what can only be (said) with(out) her or him.

Yet even such an angelically solicitous and solicited reading, because it too belongs to the "epoch of the letter," trembles on the edge of catastrophe; to read faithfully to the end of this correspondence is to set it on fire (PC 256). Meanwhile, the possibility of reading and writing, of loving and finding one an other, depends critically on the deferral of a particular (viz. general or universal) reading of the Post Card: "For the day that there will be a reading of the Oxford card, the one and true reading, will be the end of history. Or the becoming-prose of our love" (PC 115). The crisis comes with the delivery of a letter from a specialist in *Kunstgeschichte*. According to this authority, there can be no question of Plato's giving or Socrates' receiving dictation: the one (p.) simply exhibits the other (S.) to an invisible audience, *Voilà le grand homme!* The Bodleian image is revealed as a *tableau* with a theatrical life of its own but without the life of a correspondence. It is of a piece with "literature," no longer a postcard (PC 9). Unsendable. Unplayable. Institutional. "The becoming-prose of our Socratic novel [*roman*], I am giving it a symbolic birthplace: *Zentralinstitut für Kunstgeschichte*" (PC 173).

Voilà le grand homme! That is the reading which, transferred to the "Post Card or *tableau vivant*" of G.B. and J.D., will put an end to any romance of "Circumfession" before it can begin, before either party has time to find the "vein" of the other (2). The danger is made greater, we may think, by Derrida's electing to inscribe his own text in the place on the page once filled (Garnier, 1925) by the Latin prayers of a saint.

Of several pictures of Augustine intercalated in *Jacques Derrida*, one above all seems designed to capture the (im)modesty of a duel that also means to be the continuation of a correspondence. In the order of the book's dealing (357), it is both the fore- and after-image of each of the two other illustrations we have been considering (Figure 3).

Chronologically (going backward in time) and bibliologically (going forward in the book) *this* picture of Augustine occupies a place between the contemporary portrait of Derrida with Bennington and the purported frontispiece (PC 209) from the thirteenth-century *Prognostica Socratis* (here 365). The caption to it begins: "Saint Augustine, Frontispiece for *The City of God* (16th century). With copyist's instruments in his hand, like the Socrates in *The Post Card*, Saint Augustine seems to be writing to the dictation of the angel behind him . . ." What flights might this woodcut have inspired in the *epistolier* of "Envois"? The present caption simply confirms Augustine's place within the "epoch of the letter" illustrated by the Oxford postcard. Even so, the testimony of the frontispiece is at least double. By writing like the Socrates who did not write, this Augustine makes another negative (in the photographic sense) of the "positive" image of writing due to be developed in a later century by and in Derrida. At the same time, by writing only under angelic inspiration, eyes staring at a point outside his page, hands hardly belonging to him, he colludes in a classically "Platonic" abjection of human writing in the face of the transcendent writing of the divine book-as-*logos*. In short, he figures both the long history of Western (metaphorical) writing and its recently prophesied "closure." The final words of the caption, a quotation, exploit this dual signifying potential in terms that implicitly link Augustine's *Confessions* with the auto-hetero-epistolography of *The Post Card*. There is no grammatical subject for the phrase "sagely reading others like an angel" (citing **45**). The inferred reader may be Augustine (subject of the image), Derrida (subject of the quoted phrase in its original context), or an other. It is the uncertainty of the encounter (Db 15).

There are other images of Augustine scattered or disposed throughout *Jacques Derrida* (17, 109, 149, 195). If this one holds our attention, it is not only because it repeats the motif of the reader over the shoulder. It also stands in a place of priority, at the beginning of the section headed "Bibliography," opposite the rubric for the first chronological listing of Derrida's publications: "1. Books" (356). Even without knowing that Augustine was one of the first Latin authors to draw up a list of his own works in order of their composition (in the *Retractationes*), or that he began his inventory with the category of books (*libri*), we may be struck by the homology (or heterology) that now sets a beginning reader of Derrida in the situation of the dictating angel who was formerly Geoffrey Bennington, only with this difference: whereas G.B. was resolved to "begin somewhere" without appealing to chronology, the reader who has traversed J.D.'s *curriculum vitae* in words and pictures (324–53) is more likely now than ever to be interested in tracing an "intellectual itinerary" across his oeuvre (Db 14). Minimally, then, the placement of the image draws attention to the chronological and bibliological dispersal of a writer's texts and thoughts, and to the correspondent act of assembling them (under a single proper name) that is the repeated work of every editor, biographer, and reader—even, or especially, of the reader whose final act of devotion is to commit them to the flames. Because it depicts an Augustine of *The City of God*, rather

Saint Augustine, Frontispiece for *The City of God* (16th century). With copyist's
instruments in his hand, like the Socrates in *The Post Card*, Saint Augustine
seems to be writing to the dictation of the angel behind him: "sagely
reading others like an angel" (*Circumfession*, 45).

Fig. 3. Bennington and Derrida, *Jacques Derrida*, p. 357.
Image courtesy of Roger-Viollet.

than the saint of the *Confessions* already sagely (*sagement*, well-manneredly) circumscribed by Derrida, this belated frontispiece provokes once more the very questions about "the identification and delimitation of an [authorial] corpus or a work" that were suspended at the outset of "Derridabase" (Db 9) on the grounds that Derrida's own work (e.g., PC 83ff. on the *corpus platonicum*) puts them constantly in play.

Who is writing the author's works in the repeated scene of frontispiece or postcard? The wager of the four-handed *jeu du hasard et de l'amour* entitled *Jacques Derrida*, if not also (but perhaps also) of the one assigned in our bibliographies to Jacques Derrida, seems to turn on the chance of an individual's *not* being sole author of his or her (own) work: an eventuality that for Derrida, as we shall see again in "Circumfession," is at once necessary, desirable, and full of risk.

How does the case stand between him and Augustine?

A Fold in the Letter: Writing before Plato

The caption in our text assimilates the Augustine of a sixteenth-century printed book to an earlier manuscript and scribal Socrates because he has "copyist's instruments in his hand" and "seems to be writing to the dictation of the angel behind him," as the Bodleian S. can be thought to have written before p. That is the romantic and romanesque construction put on the image by the book of *Jacques Derrida* and by the books of Jacques Derrida. Loosed from those contexts, however, the same image can be shown to recapitulate a series of figures *within* the epoch of the letter that Derrida imagines extending, as if without extension or differentiation, from Plato to Mallarmé.

If we refer to the *Zentralinstitut für Kunstgeschichte* again, this is the history we learn:

> From the ninth to the twelfth century and to a lesser degree in the thirteenth century, authors [in the illustrations of Latin manuscripts] were customarily shown dictating their works. God as the true author of Holy Scripture was depicted whispering to Old Testament prophets and dictating [in the guise of an angel or symbolic figure] to the evangelists serving as secretaries taking down the spoken word. The church fathers of antiquity and the early Middle Ages, Saint Augustine, Saint Jerome, Gregory the Great . . . were drawn either as scribes recording divine dictation [e.g., from angels or a dove representing the Holy Spirit] or as authors in their own right dictating to secretaries. Secular authors, too, like Horace . . . were similarly presented dictating their works.
>
> In the thirteenth century, scenes of literary composition began to change. The evangelists were no longer exclusively shown taking down dictation, but were often portrayed silently copying the divine text from an exemplar usually held by an angel . . . Similarly, Saint Jerome, depicted throughout the twelfth century both as a dictator and as a scribe taking dictation, was in the fourteenth and fifteenth centuries regularly painted writing his own works. Authors of antiquity, frequently portrayed in the fourteenth and fifteenth centuries, were also shown writing their own compositions.

> In the late Middle Ages, both ancient and contemporary authors were typically
> drawn sitting at a desk surrounded by a complex of lecterns and book shelves
> designed to hold reference materials and drafts . . . The new furnishings were
> invented to accommodate authors who composed drafts in their own hand-
> writing and compiled citations from easily consulted reference aids.[10]

The historical record reveals that the icon of the *doubly auto-graphic* author,
inscriber of his own thoughts with his own hand, is a late medieval invention. Transposed to the images and captions of *Jacques Derrida*, this institutionally authorized chronology reshuffles the cards on our table. The Socrates of the thirteenth-
century Bodleian fortune-telling book now foretells the rise of a new idea of literary
composition as the conjunctive act of a single person's mind and hand, supplanting
an older iconology that consistently distinguished between the mind of an author
who spoke but did not write, and the hand of a scribe who had neither thoughts
nor words of his own worth setting down. Already in the medieval artist's vision,
Socrates begins to assume a modern author's rights. To imagine him taking dictation from Plato, or to wonder whether the name-labels have been misapplied
(so that p. would properly have been taking dictation from S.), as the writer does
in *The Post Card*, is indeed to romanticize the history of art.

The alternative prose-history of writing figures will impinge, as soon as we
let it, on our view of the frontispiece of Augustine as author of *The City of God*.
In woodcut illustrations of the earliest printed editions of their works, ancient
Christian writers strike the pose of the author *nouveau style*, composing their own
works in their own hand. For example, the 1489 Amerbach edition of Augustine's
The City of God shows the saint seated on a monastic library-bench, writing at a
desk that doubles as a book-chest: here is a learned author whose literary inventions are nourished by other men's published works, even if lines radiating from
his head also suggest the assistance of a higher power. Occipital effulgence aside,
this is the same figure cut by and for Latin and vernacular writers from Bocca-
ccio to Erasmus and beyond. In a modern company of authors that by then already includes other church fathers, the Augustine of the frontispiece chosen for
Jacques Derrida wears a slightly old-fashioned look. There are no signs of a reference library (unless the demons are carrying it off), and the winged creature
perched at the cleft of the bishop's miter looks like the survivor of a bygone age
of dictatorship. Saving historical appearances, we could suppose that this angel's
role is the same as that of the Bodleian Plato behind Socrates, not to dictate but
to tell an invisible audience, *Voilà le grand homme!* Or we could suppose that
the angel was summoned here expressly to oppose the demons in the drama of
Augustine's two cities (as in the lower register of the woodcut in the Amerbach
edition). These would be decent hypotheses of *Kunstgeschichte*. But they fall dis-
appointingly short of the romantic plot of *Jacques Derrida*, in which Augustine,
by seeming to write "to the dictation of the angel behind him," mysteriously
prefigures the reading style of "Circumfession," if not also of "Derridabase." Sus-
taining that local legend, even for the time of a chance encounter, requires the

revival of a figure of scribal authorship older than any directly represented by our postcards.

Derrida's epoch-bearing Augustine must be mistakable for a scribe, like his counterpart the Oxford Socrates. There is a deep (not to say Derridean) irony in this doubling of parts. As we shall see, in art historical terms only one of the two "scribes" in the pictures could model the role in time for the other to play it, and the *precursor* is Augustine. Whatever Augustine the convert may have owed to the books of the Platonists, Augustine the author *writes* before Plato.[11]

To resume and complete the chronology outlined above: the church father depicted as "scribe recording divine dictation" was common in Western book-art between the ninth and twelfth centuries. His biblical double, the "evangelist serving as secretary taking down the spoken word [of God]," can be traced in extant artifacts as early as the middle of the sixth century and may have made his debut some generations before that, perhaps in the fourth century. Figures or putative portraits of authors (philosophers, poets) had a long history in earlier Greek and Roman visual and plastic art, and Christian artists were clearly influenced by prior conventions. In one respect, however, Christian visual representations of the "author" innovate strikingly on pagan models: they show their subjects pen-in-hand, as if in the act of inscribing the texts attributed to them. That pose, so familiar to Western spectators from the Renaissance onward, is virtually unknown to authors depicted in the classical tradition.

In classical iconography, literary creativity is symbolized by the presence of an author's muse at his side or of a book-roll in his hand; it is rarely if ever associated with the mechanical action of writing. Where individuals appear pen- or stylus-in-hand, they are almost always of subaltern status: slaves, children doing their lessons, trades people with their tools, women, stenographers. There is no suggestion that they are "authors." In reality, Greek and Roman authors must often have written with their own hands during the process of composition; the literary record is full of allusions to their doing so, even if many of the references (e.g., in elegiac poetry) are highly artificial and formulaic. The visual record, by contrast, presents only an idealized vision of creative inspiration (the muse) and finished literary work (the book). The poet in classical iconology is thus *agraphic* and subject to a double law or "passion" of literature: compelled by a power above himself, he finds words (of his own) that are then set down in writing by another, lesser mortal than he.

The image of the Christian writer taking divine dictation *in his own hand*, which enters the visual repertoire in later antiquity, significantly alters the balance of this classical figure of (poetic) authorship. The replacement of the pagan muse by a symbol of the Holy Spirit may have been an automatic reflex; a similar substitution is found in the invocations of Christian epic poetry from the time of Constantine onward. Less easy to naturalize, at our remove in time, is the lowering of the status of the human author (now figured as scribe) and the raising of that of the scribe (henceforth endowed with the name and functions of an "author"), which ran counter to a well-established habit of separating the higher musical or liberal arts from the lower or mechanical ones. Exactly when, where, and how this innovation was made is not easy to determine from surviving monuments, the earliest of which already reflect established norms. We can hypothesize that the first authors to be manifested as scribes in Roman art were the biblical evangelists, and that the portrayal of later Christian writers in the same guise was a secondary development. A sixth-century fresco from the Lateran shows a Latin church father, presumed to be Augustine, depicted in the style of a Roman man of letters, teaching from an open codex, book-roll in hand to denote authorship, but still without pen or other scribal encumbrance. Only in the Carolingian period does the figure of the church father as divinely inspired scribe seem to have become widely used in Western book illustration. Then, if not before, Augustine was to be seen *receiving* dictation. Not until several centuries later, as images of literary inspiration-and-inscription began to take a recognizably modern form, centered on the individual person of the author, would "authors of antiquity" (Socrates among others, then Plato) appear in the act of writing with their own hand.

Art history need not be fatal to romance. The Augustine of a sixteenth-century frontispiece can be placed in a historically reconstructed series of writing figures, then dealt back into the hand of *Jacques Derrida*. The game of divination by the book may even gain from it. The Augustine who "seems to be writing to the dictation of the angel behind him," we now see, is no ordinary phantom invented by Bennington and Derrida at Ris Orangis. He is the print-age avatar of a scribal-authorial persona of long date, a palimpsest-figure whose twin historical identities are simultaneously legible, interchangeably "original" and "supplementary," in the tracery of a single woodcut. Such a reading entails no catastrophe. It does, however, add a further twist to the play of simulacra between p. and S., J.D. and G.B., St. Augustine and the angel, by switching the polarity of the phrase "like the Socrates in *The Post Card*." If *this* Augustine is like *that* Socrates, it is not only because he comes after him. It is also, to an extent that the texts of Jacques Derrida may seem to have concealed, because the Latin bishop taught the Greek philosopher to write.

Unless those texts are saving this surprise until last.

Reading on the Skin, in the Machine: "Circumfession"

"above all do not believe that I am quoting more than G." (**45**), writes Derrida after quoting Catherine of Siena (patron saint of scribes), *ne croyez pas surtout*. Of the many things his "Circumfession" might invite or incline us to believe, this could seem one of the hardest. After all, it is the privilege of the sur-text, of G.'s text *surtout*, the supremely top-heavy "Derridabase," to dispense with literal quotations from Derrida's work, whereas the inferior text by Derrida himself is almost from the start a tissue of transcriptions *à la lettre*—in Augustine's case, in the original Latin (**40**)—of texts from other contexts. Having read G.'s commentary, we shall perhaps allow that these questions of context and quotation are more complicated than they are sometimes taken for (Db 85–86, 152). Even so, the immediate case of Augustine remains highly particular. By choosing the (non-)genre of (*cir-*)confession for the subversion of G.'s "theologic program" (**28**), Derrida seems to hint that his own writing, at this time (January 1989–April 1990) and in this place ("at the bottom of this book," "here below" [4]), has a uniquely intimate relation to the text of Augustine, if there is any (i.e., "text" of Augustine, or text that is strictly his). The present period (45) supports and challenges that inference in two ways: by offering a statement on Derrida's "normal" reading practice, and by a demonstration of his intertextual style of writing in "Circumfession." It proceeds with an extract from Derrida's notebook-sketches for the autobiographical *Livre d'Élie*, or "Book of Elijah"—the work referred to in the subtitle of *Jacques Derrida* as in preparation, itself called after the "secret name" Derrida associates with his circumcision (16–17, 35)—and another from the last of the *Libri confessionum* of St. Augustine, a.k.a. SA. According to the rule of these pericopes, text and quotation follow one another paratactically. The English translation by Bennington is scrupulously literal, the only significant variants occurring between the French and English versions adopted for Augustine's Latin. (We mark our own cuts with double square brackets.) Here is the rest of the period:

> . . . above all do not believe that I am quoting any more than G., no, I am tearing my skin, like I always do, I unmask and *de-skin* myself [*je me démasque et désquame*] while sagely reading others like an angel, I dig down in myself to the blood, but in them, so as not to scare you, so as to indebt you toward them, not me, "how to circumscribe, the edge of the text, those are words to avoid so that the totality of the lexicon, bearing the marks of my other texts, a little more than 50 words, should be impossible to find in 'circumcision,' if that is the title [[. . .]]" (10-18-77), I do not know SA, less than ever, I like to read right on the skin of his language, my chosen one for a year, and like an angel but unlike angels, is this possible, I read only the time of his syllables, *et ibi legunt sine syllabis temporum, quid velit aeterna voluntas tua. legunt, eligunt et diligunt; semper legunt et numquam praeterit quod legunt* [. . .] *non clauditur codex eorum* ("They read there, without temporal syllables, what Thy eternal will desires. They are reading, choosing, and loving; they read forever, and what they read never passes away [. . .] Their book is never closed, [nor is their scroll rolled up]" [XIII.xv.18]).

Fools rush in where angels fear to read. We may as well begin here ("chance or arbitrariness of the point of departure" [10]), since it is the point to which we shall find ourselves returning. Augustine's language is Derrida's "chosen one for a year," *mon élue pour un an*. The phrase echoes at both ends, first with the secret name of Elijah, *Élie*, interpreted by Derrida as the sign of his own "election" (*Élie . . . celui qu'on élit* [16]; cf. *electos* [24], *genus electum* [48]) and secondly with the sound of Augustine's angels (*un an . . . un ange . . . des anges*). Though we shall hesitate to call it fateful (59), the choice of this Christian Latin author, in this year, cannot be entirely random, any more than it can be perfectly calculated (55). Suppose that a certain elective affinity has twinned Augustine with Derrida. Why Augustine? Why *Confessions*? Why now? Even with all the time and space of the world here below (21, cf. *Conf.* XII.xxxii.43), we should not expect to get to the bottom of this question.

There are fifty-nine periods in "Circumfession," one for each year of Derrida's life at the time of writing. Already in the first, he speaks of a lifelong dream of "another language" that will flow like blood from a vein. Later (22), a paragraph quoted from his notebooks (dated 1976) makes the discovery of that medium ("a new language . . . another fluid, a new fluid, a new SENTENCE") the goal of *The Book of Elijah* or "Circumcision," but predicts that it will not be easily reached: "[one must] drag on in the old syntax, train oneself with you, dear reader, toward an idiom which in the end would be untranslatable in return into the language of beginnings" (cf. 57: "in the beginning the *logos*"). This laborious passage of writer and reader through the old language of logocentrism is evoked in the same period by a list of names of authors whose texts Derrida has already traversed in his own: "'Plato, Augustine, Descartes, Rousseau, Kant, Hegel, Husserl, Heidegger, Benjamin, Austin.'" Austin and the others, granted. But Augustine? Where are Derrida's texts on Augustine before 1976? (This reader may have overlooked them. Only God or a liar will claim to have read all the works of Jacques Derrida, except in the future perfect tense [27].)

After the missed opening in *Of Grammatology*, it will be a long time before Derrida comes to Augustine in writing, a long time before he comes to *Confessions*. The time of *Confessions* (397– 400) in Augustine's own life (354– 430) was around the present period (45) in Derrida's. Even though Augustine never confessed "in the modern sense of the word," in relation to the ancient Christian regime of penitence (17) where full confession of sins was often made only *in articulo mortis*, he did so in advance ("converts himself quite early on" [33]). By the time he was fifty-nine, the final period of "Circumfession," Augustine was embarking on *The City of God*, the book which perhaps more than any other would encompass his lifetime's thought and which would occupy him until almost the end of his life. The only work that he began of his own accord after completing *The City of God* was the *Retractationes*, a recapitulation of all that he had ever written, left (how else?) unfinished at his death. Late as it may seem in one respect, Derrida's engagement with Augustine is thus strikingly premature in another. Augustine "does not recount his death" (33) in the *Confessions*, or anywhere else: that task would be left to his first biographer. "Circumfession," pursuing under cover of *Jacques Derrida* the project of a still unwritten *Book of Elijah* ("the name of he who on my death you will call Elie" [35]), is auto-thanato-graphical from the outset ("I posthume as I breathe" [5]; "dying is the word I discover at the age of 59" [39]; *je me donne ici la mort* [53]). If yet another title were needed, and not reserved for Blanchot, this text of Derrida's could also be called *The Instant of My Death*.

Having "initialized" (53) his on-screen encounter with Augustine in a footnote to the first period, Derrida (3) launches his response to the all-knowing "theologic elaborated by Geoff who remains very close to God" by making it appear as though (*comme si*) the author of *Confessions* could once have found himself in a similar case, "want[ing], by force of love, to bring it about that in *arriving* at God, something should happen to God," and finding it necessary to contrive this event "in *writing*, precisely, after the death of his mother." Precisely? *Justement?* Quite the contrary. (For other insufferable instances of *comme si*, see 41. This is the language of "circum-*ci*-sion" [40].) The first part of the comparison is obviously forced, improbable, strictly unhistorical and atheological. Nothing, we know, will ever happen to the God of Augustine's *Confessions*, who is by definition as impassible in his divinity as he is omniscient, unless Derrida can make it happen in *his* writing, and then the God in question will no longer be Augustine's any more than the writing will be his. Here, surely, is an instance of Derrida's habitual forcing of "old texts to say something quite different from what they have always seemed to say" (Db 6, a few pages earlier). Except that a large share of the responsibility for it has been passed to us as readers: "Geoff . . . who you [*vous*, the second-person address that Derrida uses for the unknown reader] would be tempted to compare to Augustine's God." Thus are "we" dragged into the syntax of this latest traversal of a text of the *logos*. The more plausible half of the comparison, between the death of Monica (commemorated in *Confessions* IX) and the impending death of his own mother Georgette, Derrida promptly disclaims ("not that I dare link what he says about confession with the deaths of our . . . mothers, I am not writing about Saint Georgette"), before going on to develop a parallel between the two women's lives.

And so begins the second "duel" (**5, 32**) of *Jacques Derrida*, the one conducted within the "internal margin" of "Circumfession" as distinct from that carried on between the main text ("Geoffrey Bennington's book" [vii]) and the margin: the *agon* of Derrida and Augustine, J.D. and SA. We shall not confuse the tones of the two encounters. Derrida claims to love Geoff (**2, 6**) the way Augustine claimed to love God. Augustine he professes only to "venerate and envy," and even then only *d'autre part* ("elsewhere," Bennington jealously translates). This interlinear contest of uncontemporary "compatriot[s]" (**9**), like other histories of twins (**27**), cannot end until one or other has been excluded, even if he is preferred (**52**). It is (a) writing to (the) death, *écriture à mort* (**43**), and we the reader are in it for the duration.

How then are we to read "Circumfession"? The original contract envisages an electronic version (Db 14), which would facilitate nonlinear access to the text. Lacking that or any kind of index, we are subject to the rhythmic, periodic "compulsions" of Derrida's personal scripture. He himself speaks of an inescapable "whirlpool, the experience of a confession which no longer has anything to do with truth." After Augustine, confession becomes a literary genre, confessional texts have family resemblances, "where[as] one must confess that . . . this story doesn't look like anything [*cette histoire ne ressemble à rien*], nothing has shifted since the first morning on the threshold of the garden" (**26**). We are in another region of unlikeness, or would be if this confession of generic eccentricity were any more reliable than Derrida's other confessions. If it is true at all, it is so only in his own, ostensibly anti-Augustinian sense of "making a truth" that would otherwise not appear (**9, 11**). For there is already a resemblance between the narrative parataxis of "Circumfession" and Augustine's (admittedly more grammatical) manner of interweaving the story and prayer of his *Confessions* with excerpts from Latin Scripture. Just as one may read the *Confessions* with and against the book of Psalms (for example), so one might try to read "Circumfession" with and against its primary non-Derridean source or "support." Which of course is what we shall now proceed to do.

Even the most cursory indexing of Augustinian passages cited by Derrida yields a curious datum. Of thirteen books of *Confessions*, the only one not represented by at least one quotation in "Circumfession" is Book VIII, in which Augustine recounts his "conversion" in the garden in Milan in 386. That event, we recall, occurs as the last of a series of book-related accidents (the random opening of a codex of St. Paul), the higher, providential sense of which it is the purpose of the *Confessions* to expound. Book VIII reveals the "theologic program" of Augustine's life as now narrated; it is the hinge on which the work turns. Derrida's intermittently encompassing transcription excises it. We open his copy of *Confessions* at Book VIII and accidentally discover a blank.

The logic of this act of atheological divination is spelled out in the surface-text of "Circumfession," in lines on the still-to-be-written *Book of Elijah*: "'. . . if this book does not transform me through and through, if it does not give me a divine smile in the face of death . . . it will have failed'" (15). The book that Derrida is preparing is one of self-transformation or conversion like Augustine's *Confessions*. But this ("Circumfession") is not it, not yet, even if in some sense—scarcely legible to Derrida himself, let alone to us—the conversion has already occurred (26, 41). Herein may lie one of the truths of Derrida's disavowal of the analogy between his mother and Augustine's. In relation to the texts of their sons, Derrida's mother is the more powerful figure. In the *Confessions*, the story of Monica's life and death is incorporated as the sequel (Book IX) to a conversion she herself has witnessed (VIII.xii.30); she is a character in a narrative that owes its sense and structure to an event that she prayed for but could not have brought about. For the author of "Circumfession," the future death of Georgette Derrida, who will have understood nothing of her son's religion (30), promises to shape a text that has as yet no circumference, is still uncircumcised: "for never will the man flayed alive that I am have written like this, knowing in advance the nonknowledge into which the imminent but unpredictable coming of an event, the death of my mother . . . would come to sculpt the writing from outside, give it its form and its rhythm from an incalculable interruption" (39). The secret sense of Derrida's conversion or (second) circumcision is thus placed *hors texte*, in a future perfect tense, rather than textually enfolded after the fashion of Augustine's conversion in the codex of St. Paul, in *Confessions*. It is still to come, like "the book" that he is preparing. Proclaiming himself "the last of the Jews" (30, 36), the last among the last to be converted, Derrida "the last of the eschatologists" also contrives to be more eschatological (15) than Augustine. Is it any wonder he prefers the company of angels?

After Book IX with its narrative of Monica, the next most favored part of the *Confessions* in Derrida's use of it is the concluding Book XIII. He treats the two books differently, however. While citations of the former are generally quite short and appear throughout "Circumfession" (3, 8–10, 21, 29–30, 37, 49), those from the latter include some of the longest excerpts in the work and are concentrated toward its end (**43, 45–48, 50–51, 59**). When citations of the preceding Book XII are also taken into account (**38, 42, 44**), a sharper distinction emerges: the two areas of *découpage* barely overlap. If we bracket an extract from IX.xii.33 that partly repeats an earlier citation (**49, 9**: *confiteor tibi in litteris*, "I confess to you in writing"), the parting of Derridean periphrasis from the "Book of Monica" exactly marks (**37/38**) its joining with Augustine's exegesis of the beginning chapter of the Jewish and Christian Bible(s) in *Confessions* XI–XIII.

That the figure of Augustine's mother should make way in "Circumfession" for his engagement with Scripture may be partly explicable in terms of the parallels established by Derrida between "1. the theologic program of SA, 2. the absolute knowledge [*savoir absolu*] or geologic program of G., and 3. the presently present survival" of his own mother (**14**). Like G.'s database, the living figure of Georgette Derrida (known as "Geo" [**3**] / Geoff / geo-logic) represents the foreclosure of Derridean *écriture*, its premature reduction to an original matrix (Lat. *mater*) or grammar (*grammaire, mère*) (**5, 9–10**) as if to a pre-existent *logos*. The equivalence of this geo- or Geo-logic to "absolute knowledge" extends, by a play of initial letters, to St. Augustine (SA, *savoir absolu* [**10**]), whose God we may already have been tempted to assimilate to Geoff (**3**), if only because Derrida's writing over the years has encouraged us to assimilate all kinds of metaphysical, metalinguistic discourse to a common "Western" logocentrism, of which Augustine's supposed "theologic program" would be merely another, if outstanding, example. But what are we to understand *Augustine's* theologic program to be? Apart from taking for granted a (presumably uncontroversial) "theological" reading of the *Confessions*, Derrida offers few hints on this subject for the first two-thirds of "Circumfession." The situation changes as he turns his attention to Augustine's later books. From then on, we can follow the course of a textual encounter.

Rash assumption, seemingly ruled out in advance by the very period at which we mean to begin! "it is impossible to follow my trace [writes Derrida] . . . I never write or produce anything other than this destinerrancy of desire, the unassignable trajectories and the unfindable subjects but also the sign of love, the one gaged on this bet . . . *and you try to calculate the itinerary of texts*" (**38**, italics mine). We do. And we should not feel rebuffed. Invited, rather. Forbidding as it sounds, the language of this ban is less than a hair's breadth from the lover's discourse of "Envois" in the *Post Card*, the published work of Derrida's most often cited in "Circumfession" (**9, 13, 27; 89**) and perhaps the one most readily aligned with it. The "beloved angel" and corresponding reader of "Envois" has a counterpart right here in the figure from a solitary, unattributed quotation of William Blake: "'I beheld the Angel who stretched out his arms embracing the flame of fire and he was consumed and arose as Elijah. This Angel, who is now become a devil, is my particular friend'" (**38**). The quotation ends there, cutting off the second half of Blake's sentence: "we often read the Bible together in its infernal or diabolical sense, which the world shall have if they behave well." This is the penultimate line of *The Marriage of Heaven and Hell*, a work much concerned with "Bibles or sacred codes" and contrary ways of reading them. Into the space of the missing phrase, Derrida transcribes the desire for a freely flowing style of writing once expressed by Augustine in the guise of Moses, author of the book of Genesis (38 after *Conf.* XII.xxvi.36–37). Again, the original reference to the Bible is excised. The ensuing excerpt from the notebooks develops the theme of liquid writing in terms recalling the first period of "Circumfession": "'always the question of the continuum, I write in Latin because the *uum* mimes the fluid and slowly stretched substance, the one that I desire to keep, desire *as* what is kept, keeping not being the object but the continuum of desire, a writing without interruption which has been looking for itself for ever, looking for me across the cut. . . .'" Across the cut, as if from the other side of the division that gathers and disperses all Derrida's writing: "'circumcision remains the thread [*fil*, alarmingly rendered "threat" by a typo in the English translation] of what is making me write here'" (cf. 14: circumcision is the thread that joins / cuts across the periods of the notebooks and the theologic triptych of "Circumfession").

Blake the poet-engraver was fully as conscious of the physical media in which he worked as Bennington and Derrida are of their Macintosh computer and its accessories (11, 35, Db 315; 26, 53, 59). To expunge "the notion that man has a body distinct from his soul," he wrote in the *Marriage of Heaven and Hell*, he would print "in the infernal method, by corrosives . . . melting apparent surfaces away." There is something of that infernal spirit in Derrida's writing from below in "Circumfession." In the cramped but cursive minuscule of these *bas de pages*, as in the earlier "Envois" of the *Post Card*, the ancient theological and metaphorical opposition between "divine or natural writing" and "human inscription seen as laborious, finite and artificial" (G 15) mysteriously dissolves. In its place, set over against the looming menace of "Derridabase," is the dream of a writing that will be at once fully human, materially inscribed, and perfectly fluid (1, 3 . . .). The "language of Augustine," Derrida's chosen one for a year, turns out, surprisingly, to be one of the languages of the dream. Having tapped the fluid metaphors of a scriptural-textual style (*texendi sermonis modus* [38]) evoked in *Confessions* XIII, Derrida turns back for three periods to Book V (39–41), then finds the vein again. A passage from the notebooks enables him to join the hands of his mother and St. Augustine:

> "Rediscover the (lost) taste for holding the pen, for writing well in a sense I have mistreated, reworked, lost a long time ago [[. . .]] rediscover an easy, offered, readable, relaxed writing" (10-14-77), oh how fine her hands are, my survivress, she had such beautiful handwriting, that can be said in the past, quite different from mine, and very legible, stylish, elegant, more cultivated than herself, I wonder if that's possible, and how to speak of her and SA without participating in their chirography, from the lowest part of my body and to the tips of my fingers, without even feeling the resistance the support must have opposed to both, but no more to you, G., nor to me, and I wonder again what can have happened when my writing changed, after thirty years, then again later, when machines took it over. (42)

We have it on good authority that Derrida is no machine-breaker, has never been the least nostalgic for a time before the typewriter or word processor, carries no brief for "manuscripture" (Db 313; 26). Whence then this sudden passion for *la plume de ma mère, la plume d'un père*? The co-handedness of St. Augustine and Georgette Derrida can have nothing directly to do with the "theologic program" they both differently represent, since the latter's handwriting has not survived her illness, is already a thing of the past. Of Augustine's handwriting, so far as anyone knows, not a jot survives. In any case, he dictated most of his works, including, probably, the *Confessions*. The figure of Augustine as divinely inspired penman, writing in his own hand, is a latter-day fiction as we have seen. Yet the writer of "Circumfession" wants to feel the pressure of the material surface on which Augustine wrote (*le support*, a paleographical term lost in translation), the very skin of the parchment into which he supposedly opened the vein of *his* compulsive writing. In the same breath, he assumes for his own text the polysemic quality claimed by Augustine for Moses' (**42**, citing *Conf.* XII.xxxi.42).

If any doubt remains about the intricacy of Derrida's writing with the later books of the *Confessions*, it should now quickly dissipate. Eight of the next nine periphrases (**43–48, 50–51**) treat passages from Books XII–XIII, almost every one of them bearing on issues of textuality. We shall read on for a few more periods before returning in good time to the anniversary at which we began (**45**) and the company of angels (or "Angels" [**53**]).

The dream of writing outside the machine can easily be interpreted as a desire to elude the division that writing otherwise makes, or that otherwise makes all writing (**14**), namely, "circumcision" (**38**). Thus Derrida, in the period that begins "I invent the word *dhavec* this day," writing again from the site of

> infinite separation, the initial and instantaneously repeated i.e. indefinitely postponed divorce from [*d'avec*] the closest cruelty which was not that of my mother but the distance she enjoined on me from [*d'avec*] my own skin thus torn off, in the very place, along the crural artery where my books find their inspiration, they are written first in skin, they read the death sentence held in reserve on the other side of the screen for in the end since the computer [*enfin depuis l'ordinateur*] I have my memory like a sky in front of me, all the succor, all the threats of a sky, the pelliculated simulacrum of another absolute subjectivity, a transcendence which I would finally do with as she would like, she who wants my death, "the sublime scission, the bottomless bet: to learn how to love— [[. . .]]" (10-14-77) (**43**)

What is written as if breathed in the skin is then instantly torn off, set on the other side of a screen that rises like the sky of another skin. The English words render the hard edge of the scab, *escarre* ("bedsore" in Bennington's version, moribund yet still-living flesh of Derrida's mother), itself already ringing in French with the *eschaton* he has chosen for his device (**15**). A pulse or two later, he will testify to "the painful pleasure of an obsessive ideomotor drive, a scene of tearing off skin" (**44**), and talk of unmasking and desquamating himself (*je me démasque et desquame* [**45**]). This compulsive self-flaying is the life-in-death of writing for Derrida, a painful "digging down," de-surfacing or de-layering that seems to be the only way of protecting himself, in the total absence of protection, from the death that is to come and that already affects the writer in every text skinned from him (Db 50–51). The capital SENTENCE Derrida dreams of writing (22), a sentence without period, would not only defy the commands of his computer (35) and make obsolete all possible future editions of "Derridabase" but also cancel the original, handwritten (!) death-sentence of Augustine's God (55: *chirografum*, citing *Conf.* VII.xxi.27 = Col 2:14). In the meantime, the same machine that enables him to write without resistance also confronts him, across its screen, with an artificially advanced (7) memory of his own death: all his texts are stored, inventoried, ordered there, as if at last (*enfin*) in the "Complete Works of Jacques Derrida" that by definition (genre, title) he will not live to see and that will never bear his signature . . . unless by some hyper-eschatological, supremely contrary, counter-exemplary, self-contradictory stroke he succeed in affixing it now (10, 36–37, 48, 50; cf. 6 and especially Db 148 – 66: "The Signature"). Would not that be the "sublime scission," the stroke to make an end at once of all pen- and key-strokes as of all endings and beginnings: circumcision without cut, de-aspiration of *dhavec*, writing as pure *jouissance* (44), circling of the *cum* (37), in and by "Circumfession"?

That is certainly a way of short-reading Derrida, among many. We should cleave more tightly, if we can, to the other skin that is the text of Augustine, as it flashes on this screen, fleshes beneath this pen. If we can. For we have come to a place of extreme friction between surfaces. Pursuing the period that we keep cutting at our peril,

> I do not [says Derrida] have the other under my skin, that would be too simple, the other holds, pulls, stretches, separates the skin from [*d'avec*] my sex in her mouth, opposite or above me, she makes me sperm in this strange condition, it's my condition, on this suspended condition that I write to death on a skin bigger than I, that of a provisional and sacrificed spokesman who can't stand it any more, caelum *enim* plicabitur ut liber *et nunc sicut pellis extenditur super nos. sublimioris enim auctoritatis est tua divina scriptura [. . .]* sicut pellem *extendisti firmamentum libri tui, concordes utique sermones tuos, quos per mortalium ministerium superposuisti nobis. [. . .]* Cum hic viverent, non ita sublimiter extentum erat. nondum *sicut pellem caelum* extenderas, nondum mortis eorum famam usquequaque dilataveras. ("For 'the heavens shall be folded together as a book,' and now it is stretched over us like a skin. Indeed, Thy divine Scripture is of more sublime authority [. . .] Just so, Thou has stretched out the firmament of Thy Book like a skin, Thy wonderfully harmonious words which Thou hast imposed upon us [. . .] while they were living here below, it was not so sublimely extended. Thou hadst not yet spread out the heaven like a skin; Thou hadst not yet broadcast the renown of their death in all directions" [*Conf.* XIII, 15, 16] [43])

Folded like a book! If the promised *Book of Elijah* or "Circumcision" was to bear no mark of Derrida's other texts (43), then *pli* ("fold") would be among the first words proscribed from its lexicon. For "it is within the fold and blank of a certain hymen that the very textuality of the text is re-marked" (D 246), and no moderately retentive reader of Derrida will forget that he has already written on a more subtle membrane than the sky of Augustine's "divine Scripture." But now he speaks in the first person, and of a sacrifice never demanded of Mallarmé, most ceremonious of poets in self-sacrifice. The greater skin on which Derrida is writing (himself) to death in *this* book has been stretched out by one who went before him, almost as if sent before him, his provisional but not prophetic or providential spokesman (*porte-parole provisoire*), a writer who can no longer speak for himself or stand by what he has written, being no longer up to anything (*qui n'en peut plus*), being no contemporary of Derrida's. Being dead. Dead as the writers of divine Scripture were by the time God stretched the skin of their text like a firmament over the living. Dead and famous. (*Voilà le grand homme!*)

As "a book, held in our hand" may "make up for all theaters" (Mallarmé), this is a scene of exceptional pathos. Only a reader wholly insensible of the romance of writing described in the *Post Card* or—which may come to the same thing— convinced of his or her own immortality can be unmoved by it. By the same token, we may think, the man who writes and transcribes these words must love the writer Augustine (as well as loving to read his books, his language [**23, 45**]). Yet he never says he does, at least not here, and will claim in a moment not even to know him, to know him less than ever (**45**). Augustine defines the "condition" of Derrida's text without ever being party to it, like the mother who makes him write but never reads a word of what he has written (**44**). The real intimacy, now as before, is with G., in the "*aparté* of a confessional where we are in for nobody, changing skin every minute to *make* the truth, each his own, to confess without anyone knowing" (**44**). That is, *inter alia* and among other readers, to confess what Augustine could never know and would be surprised to find his own texts declaring, for example in this period: "'And for me (and I am saying this from my heart, without any fear), were I writing something aimed at the highest authority [*si ad culmen auctoritatis aliquid scriberem*], I should prefer to write in such a way that each man could take whatever truth about these things my words suggested, rather than put down one true opinion so plainly as to exclude other opinions'" (*Conf.* XII.xxxi.42).

The author of the *Confessions* is here again speaking for Moses, a writer whose words were indeed to have the "highest authority," that assigned by Augustine exclusively and definitively to the book(s) of Holy Scripture (*sublimioris enim auctoritatis est tua divina scriptura* [**43**]; cf. XIII.xxxiv.49: *et solidasti auctoritatem libri tui*, the last Latin phrase cited in "Circumfession" [**59**]). The inference that Augustine meant his own "texts" to be interpreted in the same fashion as Moses' or other biblical writers', though strictly irrefutable in his absence, is literally a *contresens* or misreading—one, moreover, that "re-marks" the very questions of textuality and reading posed by the passage in question. The final paragraphs of Book XII of the *Confessions* contain one of Augustine's most eloquent statements on the undecidability of the sense of individual passages of Scripture, the honor owed to the human authors of Scripture, the love owed each other by interpreters of Scripture, the univocality of the Truth disclosed by Scripture as a whole, and the transcendence of that Truth with respect to all human writing, including Scripture. If he misses the sense intended by Moses, he prays, may he at least "say what your Truth wills to reveal to me through the words of Moses" (XII.xxxii.43). It would be hard to find a more concise and determined expression of the (theo)logic principle that Derrida has spent most of his life writing around, trying to "de-termine" (44). J.D. loves SA. *Contresens*. If that sentence cannot make Augustine's computer crash, it may yet cause Derrida's hand to tremble.

In the event, it is Derrida's system that crashes first: "the flight, a noise of wings, the angel that last night took hold of my computer, dooming once more invention to dispossession" (45). Once more, because the plot of his first (unpublished) novel, written when he was fifteen, concerned the "theft of a diary," making a sequel or prelude to the *histoires de manuscrits perdus*, more or less novelistic or romanesque, later catalogued in *Demeure*. Was this night's visiting angel a "particular friend," a demon in disguise, or a plain demon like the ones carrying off the books in the frontispiece to one sixteenth- century edition of *The City of God*? It is from Augustine, author of *The City of God*, that Western readers learn that trick of telling good angels from bad. Like Blake, who found Milton to be both "a true Poet and of the Devil's party without knowing it," Derrida retains and blurs the difference, playing the devil himself, greeting all strangers as angels. Writing from below, he upsets the separation of infernal and supernal: "my computer I've nicknamed *subjectile*, like I'd baptized my attic, where I stock the skizzes of my circumcision, *my sublime*, my upside downs, for I have neither up nor down" (26). How can the *sub*lime be what is above, unless there is something higher above it? *Sublimior, sublimiter* are the terms Augustine uses to fix the height of Scripture, above the earth and under heaven. Derrida's *subjectile* simulates the "absolute subjectivity" of a divine sky-writing; thanks to this "high-tech" simulacrum, he is able to "reconstitut[e] the partitioned and transcendent structure of religion . . . in the internal circumcision of [his] 'life'" (26, 43). The writing-machine is where he strips himself naked, not to be seen like Augustine (11; cf. *Conf.* VIII.vii.16; IX.iv.8), but to dream of another language and another skin, "dreaming of him [Augustine] who dreams of the place of God, burning it up in his prayer and going up toward it like ivy *scriptura vero tua usque in finem saeculi super populos extenditur*" ("Thy Scripture extends over the peoples until the end of the centuries" [*Conf.* XIII.xv.18]). It is here in the machine that he experiences "the furious repulsion that attracts me right up onto a skin [*à même une peau*]," where he slides between his skin and another's "the thin blade of a writing knife" (46). Amid all this carnal excitement, the insertion of the blade seems a gesture of the utmost gentleness and tact. Is there no edge to Derrida's knife, no point to his pen?

Dreaming in the machine, dreaming of the body, ready to sperm. Skin to skin with Augustine, skin to skin with a "little girl allowing herself distractedly to be buggered," the writer confronts a sudden check: "'Do I lie? Do I bring confusion by not distinguishing the clear knowledge of these things in the firmament of

heaven from the bodily works?'" (47). The question was Augustine's first, anticipating an objection to his allegorical reading of the creation story in *Confessions*
XIII. Was he not confusing the eternal sense of the creation, as it would be understood by the Creator himself and his angels, with its unfolding sense in human
time? The issue is central to the traditional conception of a unified Christian Scripture, according to which every valid meaning of a biblical passage, even the most
figuratively derived, depends on the literal, historical truth of the gospel revealed
in Christ. Whatever God and his angels may know from eternity, human understanding (like reading) takes place in time, and the Christian *sense* of time begins
with Christ as incarnation of the *logos* who was "in the beginning" (John 1:1). Augustine is one of the founders of the tradition and answers accordingly. But his answer, and hence already his question, is "too Catholic" for the Jewish Derrida, too
clear about the binary of the "figural and the other [i.e., the literal]," which for
him is just another formula for the subordination of all human knowledge to an
absolute *logos*: "that means, follow carefully [*vous*, readers], that you [*tu*, Derrida]
never write like SA." We are following as closely as we dare, though still cutting.
What follows? To "go beyond" the disagreement with Augustine, as he says he always does in such cases, Derrida collapses the Latin writer's hierarchy of knowledge into a quasi-universal realm of resemblance: "you look more and more like
your mother." Imagine saying that to Jesus! For Augustine the pretended *pas au-
delà* is worse than none, could only count as a step back (**46**: "I never like the play
of words with no beyond"). That is not the end of their difference or even necessarily its beginning. "One date," we are reminded, "is enough to leave the geologic program behind." On the face of it, the circumcised Jew below controls all
the dates, all periods, while Augustine dreams only of a timeless signified above.
Appearances are distracting. Slipping his knife into this fold of the *Confessions*,
Derrida severs Augustine from the date on which all others hang for him: that of
the coming of the *logos* as Christ, the beginning of Christian time and Christian
Scripture, the folding-point of time itself. Taking the question of *opera corporalia*
out of its literal context in the work, he refuses the datum of the double, fleshly
and textual, incorporation of the Word, conceived by Augustine as a single work
of the Spirit over time (*Conf.* XII–XIII). Capital period (**47**). While we look the
other way, Derrida smoothly cuts the thread of Augustine's *Confessions*, buggers
his whole system.

    The contest is as good as over, though Derrida will pluck at a few more pas-
sages of Book XIII before he is done. It may be clearer now what has been at stake
all along. The "spirit" in the machine is legion, and that is why (writes Derrida,
gathering his demonic selves for the next period) "I stand against Augustine" when
he asserts the underlying unity of the meanings signified by the divine Spirit in
Scripture (**48**, citing *Conf.* XIII.xxiv.36). "Stand against" conveys the idea of legal
testimony at the cost of a literal metaphor: *je m'inscris en faux contre SA*, Derrida
writes. I deny Augustine's truth. I forge a testimony against him. Against Augustine I register myself a fake. I falsely inscribe my name in the place of Augustine,
in the place of one already dead. What could be plainer than this proliferating

sign of dis-authentication? The "countertruth" or "counterexample" of himself that Derrida seeks to multiply in "Circumfession," the "countersignature" that in contradiction of a lifetime's writing he strives to set on his posthumous *opus*, will be produced in the first instance by his forging of the signature of the author of the *Confessions* ("Jacques Derrida").

Why Augustine? Why *Confessions*? Why now? The *Confessions*, as Derrida's quotations sufficiently show, marks the point at which an idea of the transcendent book, the Book of God, *liber signatus*, the Book whose Author signed and sealed it once and for all time in the perfect unity of its truth, enters (a) history. Enters that history and makes it too: Christian history, the history of a Christian nation, the history of the West, the Western history of truth. Augustine's book is the book par excellence of the Book, the book of the History of the Book, the program of the Great Code. Circumscribe the *Confessions* in an infernal or Derridean sense, and how many other histories, books, truths might now at last be free to appear? To begin with, there would be the pocket apocalypse of Jacques Derrida, last of the Jews, of which no one, not even he, knows anything yet: "*Vos autem*, genus electum [*Conf.* XIII.xix.25], you [*tu*] are waiting for an order from God who, calling your mother back to him to give you the starting signal, the race and history beginning at this point, finally allows you to speak, one evening you'll open the envelope [*tu ouvriras le pli*], you'll break the seals like skins, the staples of the scar, unreadable for you and for the others, and which is still bleeding, so that finally ceasing from eyeing your pocket they may enter at dawn the terrible and sweet truth you bear" (48).

Of course this is not the end. It never is. But it is far enough beyond any writing of Augustine's for us to have come at this point. Circling back to our first period ("above all do not believe that I am quoting more than G." [45]), we shall no longer be puzzled by Derrida's desire to read in a different manner from Augustine's angels, marking "the time of his syllables" and the intervals between them. We should perhaps have known that he could not suffer Augustine's book to remain eternally open, unfolded like the Book of God. "The virginal foldings of the book are . . . exposed to the kind of sacrifice which caused the crimson-edged tomes of ancient times to bleed. I mean they invite the paper-knife, which stakes out claims to possession of the book" (Mallarmé).

Ellipsis (2): Confession and Countersignature[12]

Having reached the end of the ten books of *Confessions* that he wrote "about himself" (*de me*, he says in the *Retractationes*), Augustine addresses the one whom he considers to be the inspirer of his work and whom he calls God. "Why, then," he asks, "do I tell Thee the detailed story of so many things?" (Under cover of a chapter title, this is the first literally Augustinian encounter of Derrida's "Circumfession.") Augustine answers: "Certainly, not for Thee to learn them through me, but to arouse my feeling of love toward Thee, and that of those who read these pages, so that we may all say: 'Thou art great, O Lord, and greatly to be praised'" (*Conf.*

XI.i.1). Unable to indebt God to him, since this God has already signed off on a timeless book that includes all the events of the writer's life, Augustine indebts himself again and his readers in advance. He and they will con(tra)fess each other, confessing God together in a hymn of praise that anticipates the eternal unison of the blessed, beyond all human authorship and countersignature. The circle of strictly Augustinian confession or circumfession is always closing on that eschatological, ultimately uneventful event. So it does now, over three more books (XI–XIII) "on the Holy Scriptures [*de scripturis sanctis*], from where it is written 'In the beginning God made the heaven and the earth' as far as the sabbath rest" (*Retr.*). We have seen how closely at times Derrida reads the second and third books of this trinity. From the first, Book XI, he cites only the opening paragraph, as partly quoted above, and its Latin title from the edition (Garnier, 1925) in which he first read the work (1, 3, 15, 17). As in the case of the omitted Book VIII with its multiple narrative of divination and conversion by book, this refusal to read "beyond the beginning" (DM 104) of Book XI may be less than random.

Consider what Augustine now goes on to say to his God, as he turns from the books he has written on himself to the books of the inspired prophets and evangelists:

> Behold, I have told Thee many things [*Ecce narravi tibi multa*] . . .
>
> But when can the voice of my pen be adequate to the task of proclaiming all Thy encouragements, all Thy terrors, consolations, and guidances whereby Thou hast brought me to the point of preaching Thy Word and administering Thy sacrament to Thy people? And if I am adequate to the task of setting them forth in orderly detail, then time's drops are precious to me. Now, I have for a long time been developing an ardent desire to meditate on Thy law and to confess to Thee the extent of my knowledge and lack of skill in it. . . .
>
> O Lord my God, be attentive to my prayer . . . From all temerity and all lying, *circumcise my lips*, internal and external. Let the Scriptures be my chaste delights. . . . For Thou didst not will so many pages of dark secrets to be written in vain. . . . Let me confess unto Thee whatever I shall discover in Thy books . . . and consider the wondrous things of Thy law, from the very beginning, when Thou didst make heaven and earth, unto the perpetual reign of Thy holy city with Thee. . . .
>
> May it be pleasing in the sight of Thy mercy for me to find grace before Thee, so that the inner parts of Thy words may be opened unto me as I knock. I beg it through our Lord, Jesus Christ, Thy Son, the Man of Thy right hand, the Son of man Whom Thou hast confirmed for Thyself, as Thy Mediator and ours before Thee. . . . I beseech Thee through Him Who sits at Thy right hand and intercedes with Thee for us, in whom are hidden all the treasures of wisdom and science. These do I seek in Thy books. Moses wrote about Him: He says this Himself; the Truth says this.
>
> Let me hear and understand how "in the beginning" Thou didst "make heaven and earth." (*Conf.* XI.i.1–3, 5; emphasis added)

As much as the accidental/providential book-opening in Book VIII, this is a cardinal moment in and for the *Confessions*, as the author's intention and ours shifts decisively from the story of Augustine to the letter of (the) Scripture(s). *Institui animum intendere in scripturas sanctas*, Augustine wrote of his first encounter with that text, "I decided to turn my mind to the Holy Scriptures" (*Conf.* III.v.9). We understand now that it was a decision more than once renewed, an intention repeatedly deferred, dis-tended, postponed most recently by the act of "confession" in its primary Augustinian sense of narrative self-declaration: *narravi tibi multa*. (Unlike Derrida's "Circumfession," Augustine's *Confessions* is generically plural.) Only when *that* confession has been broken off can Augustine begin another, which he calls *confessio scientiae*, a confession of knowledge which (like the former confession of himself) is also an admission of ignorance: the declaration of what he discovers in Scripture, beginning at the beginning.

Whatever Augustine's motives may have been for supplementing the narrative of himself with an interpretative re-narration of Scripture, we usually assume that the decision to begin at the beginning of Genesis would have been a natural if not obvious one for him. There are good reasons for that opinion. In a manual *On Catechizing the Uninstructed*, apparently composed around the same time as the *Confessions*, he recommends starting with the creation story. He had already written at length on Genesis in a tract against the Manichees and had recently begun a literal commentary on the same text, so the choice was economical. He tells us in the prologue to the *Confessions* that God had inspired his own faith in him through "the ministry of a preacher" (I.i.1), possibly a reference to Ambrose, bishop of Milan, who preached a set of sermons on the days of the creation that Augustine could have heard in 386 or 387, later published as a book. Now that Augustine himself had been "drawn to preach [God's] word to his people," an exegetical essay in more or less the same genre would round out his *Confessions* in a well-mitered style, *satis episcopaliter* (V.viii.23, referring to Ambrose). "Augustine as bishop" is the title James O'Donnell gives to the preamble to Book XI in his recent commentary.[13]

Yet this was to be no routine episcopal performance. The ministry of the Word-in-Scripture that the author of the *Confessions* now proposes to himself far exceeds the normal scope of catechism or sermon. Not in vain, he surmises, were *so many* pages written with dark secrets (*tot paginarum opaca secreta*). More than the first chapter of Genesis is in view. The long-delayed *confessio scientiae* is meant to embrace, even if it cannot comprehend, all God's books (*libri*), all his Scriptures (*scripturae*), his whole law (*lex*) with its many inward meanings and hidden treasures (*secreta, abdita, interiora, thesauri*). The field of discovery is vast and deep. But not limitless. For limits are also set. "Let me," says Augustine, "consider the wonders of your law, from the beginning when you made heaven and earth [*ab usque principio*] until the everlasting kingdom with you in your holy city [*usque ad regnum tecum perpetuum*]." Because the day after the six days of creation prefigures the sabbath rest of the saints, he is able already to reach the far term of this consideration in the exegesis of Genesis 1 that fills *Confessions* XI–XIII. The whole order of creation and the promise of eternity are compassed in a hebdomad in three books, at the end of the last of which Augustine returns to his point of departure, asking, seeking, knocking (XIII.xxxviii.53). Nearly thirty years later, at the close of the third tetrad of the second part of *The City of God*, he would reach the same point again, having traversed the entire "sacred history" from Genesis to Revelation. Even then the tongue of his pen would not be stilled.

The story that Augustine unfolds in the last three books of the *Confessions* and the last twelve of the *City of God*, *ab usque principio . . . usque ad regnum perpetuum* (from the beginning of time until the kingdom without end), is the narrative Scripture (singular and with a capital S) of Latin Christendom and its successor states. As such, and with good warrant from Augustine himself (*Civ.* XI.i.1), it has traditionally been set over and apart from the aggregate of other stories and texts preserved and used in literate cultures descended from Roman Christianity or from what Curtius called *Romania*, the Latinity of the Roman Empire in the West as it gave way to the new "nations" and languages of medieval Europe. The latest expression of this felt difference, still classic and current despite many revisions since its advent with "scientific" biblical criticism in the eighteenth century, is the contraposition of Scripture and Literature or, more common nowadays, the Bible and Literature. We noted some of its most recent and influential forms in an earlier section of this essay.

Bible/literature. Book/writing. Truth/fiction.

Three or innumerable binaries, a single stroke of parting.

A parting around which Derrida may seem to have been turning all his writing life.

A parting already marked by Augustine, if only by implication, in the first period of Book XI of the *Confessions*, and curiously unremarked in "Circumfession," despite the violence of the prayed-for act. *Circumcide labia mea*, "circumcise my lips." In future, our histories of literature may begin again here.

DERRIDA'S RESPONSE TO MARK VESSEY

Derrida: First, a footnote. I was impressed by your eloquent and elegant scholarship and I am very grateful. I learned a lot. The footnote has to do with two texts that I wrote and which, with no scholarship at all, would go in your direction. Probably you don't know it because it hasn't been published in English. *The Gift of Death* was first published in English, but in the French version,[14] which appeared after the English version, there is a chapter in which I try in my own preliminary way to question the biblical or Christian genealogy of literature. It has to do with the secret and forgiveness. I try to show that it is as if the question of literature, modern literature—not only in the seventeenth and eighteenth centuries but in the nineteenth and twentieth centuries—asks for forgiveness for having forgotten or betrayed the Christian origin of literature, of writing, the way you have wonderfully explained to us. So that's one way I try to go in your direction and show how convinced I am by your demonstration. The second is an essay that has just appeared called "The Typewriter Ribbon," in which I discuss the literary genre of confession from Augustine's *Confessions* to Rousseau.[15]

Question (from the floor, unidentified). First of all, I want to say that I enjoyed your presentation, and I learned very much about the Latin Middle Ages and the configurations of literature. I'm not quite sure if I was exactly satisfied with your definition of what literature is. Is it something that can be confined to oral literature? Is it something that can be confined to anything in print? That is the first part of my question. The second part is related to the quotation, "Is there an institution of literature apart from Rome, Christianity, and Europe? Nothing is less certain." I'm wondering if you are isolating the very nature and act of literature and excluding other types of religious writings. There are Babylonian writings, Sanskrit, Confucianism, etc. I know that you're containing this, in a sense, with Augustine's *Confessions*, but I wanted to know how you juxtapose, or how you would compare, what I conceive to be literatures in terms of a global context? I'd like to hear your thoughts on how you align these other types of literature in the context of European literature, restricted to religious writings.

Mark Vessey: Yes, thank you. My certainty of the unlikelihood of there being any other kind of literature than, let us say, the European kind, is initially the confidence of Jacques Derrida's uncertainty on this point. I'm keen to share both certainty and uncertainty, because it seems to me that if one is willing to pose and at least begin to try to answer, not the whole question of literature, but the question of the name of literature, then the irrefutable datum that literature is a Latin word presents a number of interesting possibilities. Now, part of the excitement and provocation of what Derrida said at Louvain lies in the heresy of suggesting that what we properly mean by literature is somehow confined by what is Roman, Latin, Christian, European. There is a *défi* in that definition, which I was trying to take up. I did not intend to answer, or even ask, unless by citing, the question "What is literature?" You can consult the "Derridabase" to see what Derrida makes of that and similar "What is . . ." questions. I was not offering, nor would I want to offer, even under pressure, a definition of literature that could cover the range of phenomena that you're indicating, though I might recognize many or all of those things as legitimate objects of literary study. I'm concerned here mainly with the question of the name of literature and with the determinants, or putative determinants, Latin, Roman, Christian and European, of that name—and with how Derrida's reading of Augustine's text might enable us to reckon with them. That's a dusty answer, but the bigger question that you're asking is one I don't really feel able to address. I may as well admit that now. But Professor Derrida can probably save me from this kind of rough paraphrase.

Derrida: I don't think it's only a question of name. Of course, the question of name matters, but it's more than a question of name. I would argue, running the risk of saying something which sounds Eurocentric, that there is no non-European literature. It is not only a question of name. It is the same with philosophy; there is no philosophy outside Europe. I don't say this in a Eurocentric move. There are a number of writings, of works, which are perhaps more interesting than literature itself, outside of Europe. But they are not, strictly speaking, literary. It is not only a question of name; it's a question of institutions, of sets of axioms, of norms—and the same goes with philosophy. Not just any thought, any thinking, is philosophical. There are, outside of Europe, ways of thinking which are perhaps more decisive, deeper, more important than philosophy, but they are not philosophical. Even in Europe, what one calls Greek poetry is not literature. What one has to take seriously is not only the word *literature* but the whole set of axioms, institutions, presuppositions—a number of things that constitute the concept of literature, which has no meaning outside of Europe. Now, the fact that today in global space we have Chinese literature or Japanese literature means that, in fact, this concept, with the whole set of axioms and nouns and presuppositions, even the Christian ones, have been exported or have been globalized. But

210 Mark Vessey

the concept, the name of the concept, of literature is, strictly, not only European but Christian. I try to show then that, of course, in what is called the secularization of literature — there are a number of people who would disagree with me — you find the signs of this guilt, this implied "asked for forgiveness" for having precisely broken, interrupted, the Christian memory that you so powerfully reconstituted. So not only is this not Eurocentric, but it's a matter of drawing the limits of Europe. Literature is something European. Now we have to account for the fact that it has become a global phenomenon. That is a major issue not only for literature but also for philosophy, for international law, for a number of such things. The starting point would be the recognition of this history, the history that you reconstituted.

Vessey. Thank you for helping me to have the courage of someone else's convictions.

NOTES

References to English translations of the works of Jacques Derrida in the text follow the abbreviations in the Bibliography in Geoffrey Bennington and Jacques Derrida, *Jacques Derrida*, trans. Geoffrey Bennington (Chicago: University of Chicago Press, 1993) 355–56, with the addition of:

DM   *Demeure: Fiction and Testimony,* translated (with Blanchot's *The Instant of My Death*) by Elizabeth Rottenberg (Stanford, Calif.: Stanford University Press, 2000). French: *Demeure: Maurice Blanchot* (Paris: Galilée, 1998).

Citations of Bennington and Derrida's *Jacques Derrida* distinguish where necessary between the text of Bennington's "Derridabase" (Db) and that of Derrida's "Circumfession"; boldface numerals refer to the numbered periods of "Circumfession"; unmarked numerals refer to pages where there is no split between upper and lower text. Phrases are now and again interpolated from the original French edition (Paris: Seuil, 1991). References to Augustine's works employ the customary Latin abbreviations for the *Confessions* [*Conf.*], *The City of God* [*Civ.*], and *Retractationes* or "Revisions" (*Retr.*). To match the style of *Jacques Derrida*, Roman numerals have been used for the book and first-order chapter divisions of Augustine's major works and translations of longer passages from the *Confessions* have been taken from the version in the series Fathers of the Church, by Vernon J. Bourke (Washington, D.C.: Catholic University of America Press, 1953).

1. Ernst Robert Curtius, *European Literature and the Latin Middle Ages*, trans. Willard R. Trask (Princeton, N.J.: Princeton University Press, 1953), pp. 42, 16, 74, 446.

2. Northrop Frye, *The Great Code: The Bible and Literature* (Harmondsworth: Penguin, 1990 [originally published in 1983]), pp. xii–xiii. See also his *The Secular Scripture: A Study of the Structure of Romance* (Cambridge, Mass.: Harvard University Press, 1976), pp. 19–20, and *Words with Power: Being a Second Study of "The Bible and Literature"* (Harmondsworth: Penguin, 1990).

3. Brian Vickers, "Derrida and the *TLS*," *Times Literary Supplement*, 12 February 1999, p. 12, purportedly a review of John D. Caputo, ed., *Deconstruction in a Nutshell: A Conversation with Jacques Derrida* (New York: Fordham University Press, 1997) and another book.

4. *The Great Code* xxxii, pp. 76–77. See now John David Dawson, *Christian Figural Reading and the Fashioning of Identity* (Berkeley: University of California Press, 2002).

5. Harold Bloom and David Rosenberg, *The Book of J* (New York: Grove Weiden-

feld, 1990), p. 13. Cf. Edward W. Said, *The World, the Text and the Critic* (Cambridge, Mass.: Harvard University Press, 1983), pp. 290–92.

6. Patrick French, *The Time of Theory: A History of* Tel Quel *(1960–1983)* (Oxford: Clarendon Press, 1995). See my "The Early Christian Book between History and Theory," in the proceedings of a conference on "The Early Christian Book" held at The Catholic University of America, June 6–9, 2002 (forthcoming).

7. Eric Jager, *The Book of the Heart* (Chicago: University of Chicago Press, 2000), ch. 2.

8. Christopher Ocker, *Biblical Poetics before Humanism and Reformation* (Cambridge: Cambridge University Press, 2002).

9. Daniel Boyarin, *Intertextuality and the Reading of Midrash* (Bloomington: Indiana University Press, 1990).

10. Paul Saenger, "Silent Reading: Its Impact on Late Medieval Script and Society," *Viator* 13 (1982): 388–91, emphasis and paragraphing added.

11. Fuller detail and references in my "From *Cursus* to *Ductus*: Figures of Writing in Western Late Antiquity (Augustine, Jerome, Cassiodorus, Bede)," in Patrick Cheney and Frederick A. De Armas, eds., *European Literary Careers: The Author from Antiquity to the Renaissance* (Toronto: University of Toronto Press, 2002), pp. 47–114.

12. See also "Derridabase," s.v. "Signature."

13. James J. O'Donnell, *Augustine: Confessions,* 3 vols. (Oxford: Clarendon Press, 1992), 3:253.

14. Jacques Derrida, *Donner la mort* (Paris: Galilée, 1999).

15. See Jacques Derrida, "Typewriter Ribbon: Limited Ink(2)," in *Without Alibi,* ed. and trans. Peggy Kamuf (Stanford, Calif.: Stanford University Press, 2002), pp. 71–160.

eleven
Augustine's Unconfessions

James J. O'Donnell

The reading practices of moderns when confronted with Augustine's *Confessions* are extraordinarily consistent and extraordinarily idiosyncratic. To find a way to talk about Augustine and his self-representations that breaks the crust of that familiar set of practices even a little, I will choose to begin by reading a bit of Augustine's presentation of a fragment of the life of his friend Alypius.[1]

One day when meditating on his school exercises in Carthage, Alypius was walking in the forum and came upon—Augustine will have us believe—a crime scene. Another student, perhaps one of those *eversores* ("wreckers") of whom Augustine did not approve,[2] had taken an axe to the lead grating over the tiny cells in which the silversmiths of the artisans' quarter had to work. No one should envy those workers their difficult and probably toxic work in cramped quarters or the draconian discipline to which they were subjected, but they had their own solidarity and loyalty to their trade. So when they heard the would-be thief trying to break in, they set up an alarm. The thief dropped his axe and ran.

At this moment, Alypius comes along (so the story goes), finds the axe, and picks it up with a wondering look on his face. The silversmiths and the authorities converge on the spot, and Alypius is more or less arrested.

By any reasonable standard of ancient justice, this should have put paid to Alypius's career right there. Found *in flagrante delicto*, his prospects for future health and safety, let alone career success, were dim.

But Augustine assures us that Alypius was the right sort, and lucky besides. The civil servant who had the title of "architect" of the forum happened along (no doubt from habitual haunts nearby), recognized Alypius as someone he knew, and listened to his story. Because Alypius had this connection, investigation followed and the real culprit was tracked to his lair where a slave boy, no doubt fearing the

swift application of judicial torture, happily "dropped a dime"[3] on the young master of his employer's house—he recognized the axe, and Alypius was off the hook.

I do not see that any reader of Augustine's *Confessions*, ancient or modern,
has ever paused to doubt the truth of this story for a moment. Let us pause.

If this were not Augustine telling us the story, and if it were not Alypius of
whom he spoke, would we be so certain? Is there anything we *know* of Alypius
that makes it impossible to imagine that he was himself the culprit? Are we so
confident in the veracity of ancient slaves and the integrity of the Roman judicial
process that we can be sure that the sight of an angry judicial mob at the front door
would not impel a frightened slave boy into perjury against a master he may have
had no special reason to love?

The question of Alypius's guilt should remain open and the story an intrigu-
ing one. He would not be the first distinguished attorney with a complicated case
of adolescent miscreancy to explain away. But Augustine's narrative, artfully constructed of self-accusation and excuse, has proven impermeable to assault. The
only piece of narrative that has ever undergone assault on grounds of truthfulness
is the fragment of time in the garden in Milan when he hears the child's (or the
angel's?) voice urging him to "take up and read." For an autobiographical narrative with heavy theological overtone, written by a man with a suspect past and enemies of several sorts, that gullibility—the word is not too strong—is astonishing.
Augustine may very well be making his own kind of truth out of his past,[4] but his
truth need not be our truth—and at the very least *should* not become our truth so
unreflectively.

But art and history are on Augustine's side. He who writes a dense, vivid, and
sophisticated narrative will very often be taken seriously. When the same writer
acquires, over a thousand years, a reputation as a philosopher and theologian of
the first rank, he assures himself a broad and friendly readership. His halting, frus-
trated, difficult autobiographical text will be taken as the ideal first-person correlate of the genre of hagiography and read as though it were a particularly privileged version of that kind of text. The holiness of the author will be assumed at
the outset rather than tested throughout, and the self-serving narrative will come
to dominate all narrative of the writer's life.[5]

But generalization fails in the case of Augustine because he is a case beyond
generalities. He is the most prolific surviving writer from the ancient world[6] and,
apart from epistolary Paul, the most ancient writer of immense and continuous
religious reputation from his own time to ours. The story of his early life did not
always dominate the conversation,[7] but in modern times, the story looms astonishingly large in all discussion of his work and thought. The two books that tell us
something about Augustine that are most widely read and distributed are his *Confessions*, of course, but second only to the *Confessions* must be Peter Brown's thirty-
five-year-old biography, *Augustine of Hippo*.[8]

There are several other narratives of Augustine's life available, but none with
the prestige and staying power of Brown's marvelous book. It was in many respects
the first modern critical biography of Augustine and, together with Courcelle's

1950 *Recherches sur les Confessions de saint Augustin,* brought Augustinian study
to the point that New Testament study had reached in the late nineteenth century: that is, post-hagiographic, open to the complexities and contradictions that
inhere in a variously textured body of evidence surviving nearly two millennia,
and thus marked by assertions that could seem impious to those devoted to an earlier and less critical style of biography. Augustine sprang to life on those pages from
birth to death, vividly portrayed and beautifully evoked, entirely human and yet,
if anything, more remarkable for having achieved what he did without a halo securely bolted to his head.

At the same time, as I have shown elsewhere,[9] even in Brown's biography (and
a fortiori in other studies of that generation and even this), the *Confessions* remain
a dominant and pervasive force. Typically in modern narratives of Augustine's life,
something like 40 percent of the narrative covers the period roughly covered by
the *Confessions*—and the remaining 60 percent is devoted to the period of Augustine's life in which the achievements that gave him claim to our attention were
made. Augustine the bishop and writer deserves our attention, but Augustine-the-
confessed dominates the view. More remarkably still, it is precisely the most artful and contested of stretches of *Confessions* narrative that remain the most powerful in the modern biographies. Brown himself, in the chapter on "Conversion,"
treats the garden scene from Book VIII of the *Confessions* by no more and no less
artful an approach than to present without comment a slightly abridged translation of the crucial passage from the *Confessions*.[10] Such a procedure burkes all
question of whether the account is correct on the small scale (did these events
happen exactly that way on that day in that garden?) but even more whether the
implicit narrative pattern of a life changed around that moment is to be taken at
face value. It remains the assumption, in short, of all modern biographers—hostile,
friendly, and merely attentive—that a "conversion" in Milan, on *or about* the time
of 386, is the central and most powerful explanatory fact about Augustine's life.
Augustine would be pleased that we agree with him so readily.

But perhaps we should not. Perhaps Augustine, in telling this story about himself, had interests and purposes he could not avow. Perhaps this retrospective story,
which first appears almost a decade later in something like its *Confessions* form,[11]
is creating a structure for the past that is not irrefutable.

To make that suggestion, however, is to play out the game of biography on a
traditional level—a contest over narratives. To be fully alert to the possibilities, we
need to realize that the genre of biography itself powerfully compromises with the
confessional style itself in ways that make it harder, not easier, to see what Augustine is up to. The biographer today shares a fundamental set of principles with
Augustine. In short, I will characterize these thus:

1. The human personality is at its best single, unified, and subject to rational
    control.
2. A successful human life is marked by the assertion of coherence and con-
    trol over what often seems, particularly in rambunctious youth, a welter

of conflicting desires, impulses, and velleities. (Failure to achieve such integration is a fundamental failure in such terms.)

3.   It is therefore appropriate to use a linear, reductionist narrative of the consecutive transformations of that single personality-entity (Augustine would more compendiously say "soul"/*anima*) over time, measured against the criterion of unity/disunity, control/incoherence.

These principles surely animate Augustine's *Confessions,* I believe just as surely animate Brown's biography,[12] and, I would argue, are to be found at the heart of the wide array of biographies that now unreflectively pour forth from our scholarly and unscholarly presses. The debunkers and the rebunkers (by such I mean those who make biography by recovering the reputation of neglected American presidents) share these principles and these practices wholeheartedly.

In a series of reflections that have taken place, quite literally, in the presence of Jacques Derrida, it is surely possible to argue that such a metaphysical hypostatization of the personality demands to be questioned and tested if not discarded outright. My venture in that direction will take the form of presenting multiple narratives of the same Augustinian life-stretch. I think my own preference for the more unfamiliar of those narratives will become clear, but I should not let that authorial prerogative dominate. I genuinely mean to show that the same evidence and the same life can and does generate multiple narratives — and will have generated them in Augustine's own time. To know the life of Augustine, I argue, requires us to know this multiplicity of narratives and not merely to craft a single privileged one.

If you go to Tagaste — modern Souk Ahras — you will find that there is no secure trace of Augustine to be found. When a group of European and American scholars were taken there by our Algerian hosts at the memorable "Universalité et Africanité" conference of April 2001, the charabancs full of curious visitors were taken to a small hilltop in the center of the town and there disembarked to see a large and wizened olive tree on the hilltop.[13] It was this very tree, legend recounts, under which Augustine loved to sit and meditate.

There is no textual authority for this story. The only tree under which we know him to have sat on any account is the fig tree in Milan that recalls a similar tree in John's gospel.[14] But Tagaste plays a crucial and understudied part in the evolution of Augustine's mature life and his narratives of the way that life came about.

Here is the first version of a narrative of that development:

> On returning to Africa from Milan, Ostia, and Rome in 388, Augustine entered monastic retirement on his family property in Tagaste, building a community of like-minded men, studying philosophy and Scripture, and communicating with a few like-minded souls elsewhere — notably his friend Nebridius, in similar retirement near Carthage.
>
> It was by chance some three years later in 391 that Augustine, who had avoided visits to cities that might be looking for bishops lest he be drawn, unwilling and unworthy, into such a calling, was visiting Hippo to recruit a gov-

ernment bureaucrat (*agens in rebus*) for the monastic life when the congregation there—under the urging of their aging and originally Grecophone Bishop
Valerius—laid hands on him and forced him to accept ordination as *presbyter*
(priest). Staggered by the events and thought of his own unworthiness, Augustine wept inconsolably but accepted his fate. He asked Valerius for a few months
of respite from his new duties in order to study the Scriptures, but soon settled
in to the clerical routine and surroundings that would accompany him all his
life.

So far, so good. Let me try again in a slightly different key.

Augustine was a man who failed and failed again until chance and opportunism made him a success. He had left Africa all aglow with enthusiasm
and ambition for a career in the great world, and for a while the gods smiled
on him. He made his way to Rome and thence to Milan, where his appoint-
ment as imperial professor of rhetoric was a remarkable coup for a young man
with a strange foreign accent. His whole family came to join him there, to see
where his career might lead—a provincial governorship seemed the least of his
ambitions.

But something went wrong. Suspicious claims of illness, a sudden withdrawal to the country, a resignation sent in weeks later, and his disappearance
from the Milanese scene marked the end of his career. It took a year for him to
make his way back to Africa, and when he did, he went to ground on his family's own and not very impressive property in Tagaste. There he lived the life of
a country squire, filling the idle hours with literary activity of no very impressive sort, talking to his friends. He performed the duties of a member of the
local senate with the indifference customary in his type—always looking to minimize the financial outlays that would go with that kind of citizenship. Two or
three years later, his son Adeodatus died, leaving the father without an heir for
the property, and at that point Augustine's religious leanings got the better of
him. He is next seen selling his property and slipping away to Hippo to take up
duties as a minor cleric in the schismatic church of the Caecilianists there. In
so doing, he managed—like many others in his time—to evade the duties of
citizenship and senate membership, but it was unlikely that he would amount
to anything in his new and obscure role.

That reading is less attached to the *Confessions* and Augustine's other later
accounts, but is a little distanced from the man and his own experience. It sounds
like what someone would say who knew him only formally and did not much care
for his religious enthusiasms.[15]
May I make one more venture?

The events of 386–87 in Milan marked Augustine as a familiar type of
eccentric in his world: the lettered member of the upper classes fallen heavily under the spell of Platonic idealism. That his particular form of this enthusiasm took him to the threshold of the Christian church was unusual, though
not so very unusual in the circles around Ambrose in Milan. The retirement that
followed was controversial—some would think it cowardly and weak-spirited,
others would praise its unworldliness. His time at Tagaste was marked, not sur-

prisingly, by a withdrawal from all kinds of worldly activities, including those of the churches. His religious affiliation, if he showed one then, was with the sedate and Romanized "Caecilianist" church rather than the majority church of Africa, but he regularly expressed skepticism and criticism about the clerics who populated all the churches.[16]

The death of his son made a real difference, of course. He was actively considering alternate ways of life when he visited Hippo in 391, but it was a genuine surprise, then, when he was made a priest.

Everything about him rebelled at this thought. More than thought rebelled, however: he ran away. Shortly after the ordination, he left Hippo unannounced and returned to Tagaste, to the scandal of his fellow citizens of Hippo. But bad conscience followed him, and shortly thereafter he after wrote to Bishop Valerius, making diplomatic amends, and then, a few weeks later, he skulked back to Hippo and to his future.

Suffice it to say that all three of these narratives can be constructed out of the surviving evidence, but only the first has a place in the biographies we receive. The last seems most persuasive to me for good documentary reasons. The letter in which he asks for his "leave" to study Scripture is an odd document—a written letter to a bishop that most assume was living in the same building complex in Hippo as Augustine at the time. The document is marked by various signs of bad conscience, and not long after, his flock was sharply fearful of the thought of his absence from their city.[17] The mere fact of epistolarity should be our alerting sign, however, for such letters were not, in Augustine's world, intimate and personal communications of information (if ever they are in our world), but public performances, public at the point of writing and at the point of reading. Augustine wrote letters to make an impression and always calculated that impression carefully.

But I believe the *Confessions* themselves point to this episode more clearly than one might expect. Consider this passage at the end of Book X, just at the nodal point where past turns to present and future in his account:

> *conterritus peccatis meis et mole miseriae meae agitaveram corde medita-*
> *tusque fueram fugam in solitudinem, sed prohibuisti me et confirmasti me dicens,*
> *'ideo Christus pro omnibus mortuus est, ut qui vivunt iam non sibi vivant, sed ei*
> *qui pro ipsis mortuus est.' ecce, domine, iacto in te curam meam, ut vivam, et con-*
> *siderabo mirabilia de lege tua.*
>
> Frightened by my sins and the mass of my wretchedness, I had been upset in my heart and was thinking about fleeing into the desert, but you kept me from doing that and you strengthened me, saying, "It is for this reason that Christ died for all men, that those who live do not live any longer for themselves but for those for whom he died." Look, Lord, I put my cares in your care that I may live and meditate on the wonders of your law. (*Conf.* X, 43, 70)

The language of that passage admits, it seems to me, of many readings, but one simple one: that Augustine was considering a monastic retirement from the hubbub of his social and economic life in Tagaste, but the divine hand prevented him and set him instead to the clerical ministry of Hippo. Among other things, the language of this passage matches closely what he says in the next paragraph — the opening of Book XI — about his clerical ministry in Hippo. The prohibiting hand of God was that which seized him and ordained him at Hippo.

We will never know whether Augustine ever ran away from Hippo. But we can say with assurance that the behavior that seems undoubted even on his own avowal will have looked different ways to different people — will have *been* different behaviors, therefore. I will put off for another time the argument about the comparative merits of these narratives and other narratives that can and should be clustered around the evidence that comes to us of Augustine's life.[18] The argument of this paper wants to hew resolutely to the larger question of confession itself: what is it, why do we take it so seriously, and how can we question it effectively?

I take confession in its root form to go to the root of *confessio* — an affirming speech, affirming because it affirms what another would say.[19] It is narrative or avowal that aligns the will of the speaker with the antecedent will or belief of some other and authoritative figure. It is a repudiation of the self in favor of some larger or other truth.

On those terms in classical antiquity, Pseudo-Quintilian could say that anyone who confessed (he was thinking of criminals confessing their crimes) was out of his mind (*demens*).[20] The action was unmitigatedly self-destructive. It is the achievement and the canniness of Augustine to see that confession can be self-constructive instead — that unity of narrative is a pearl of great price and that it can be acquired, in the face of contestations of various kinds, by a rhetorical self-effacement that becomes self-assertion. His *Confessions* are a triumph of that "reverse psychology." For his narratives were widely contested in 397 when he came to write *Confessions*. The members of the majority African Christian church could condemn him as an unreconstructed Manichee who had thrown his lot in with the minority schismatic Caecilianist church[21] and who was thus doubly to be scorned. His claim to valid Christian baptism was suspect — he had left Africa a devout Manichee to all eyes and returned surreptitiously and gone to ground for years after. (That he wrote books against the Manichees was of little value to an audience that had not heard of those books.) His affiliation with the Caecilianists had the look of opportunism about it. When years of collaboration with the Roman government brought his church to the forefront, many would see that opportunism as entirely naked and entirely successful.

In that setting, and at the outset of his war against Donatism, Augustine had every interest in telling the story he did. To make the centerpiece of his life a wholehearted conversion to authentic Christianity in 386 would first repel the claims of continuing Manichaeism, and would second take attention away from the changes he underwent in 391 and the difficulties surrounding them. He converted, not to Caecilianism, his narrative suggested, but to Christianity-degree-zero, Christianity plain and simple, Christianity at the hands of an undoubted saintly and orthodox bishop of imperial distinction.

Perhaps. But what the *Confessions* do not confess here is the extent to which

the changes of 391 were the real turning point in Augustine's life.[22] His social ambitions were staggered when he left Milan for Tagaste, but his economic and social status did not change: he was still emphatically his father's son. It was when
he moved to Hippo and took up a clerical role that he changed into a new legal,
not to say spiritual, person. There in Hippo, he would be a part of a movement to
create a new kind of bishop and a new kind of church, a movement that would
be astonishingly successful over the next quarter-century,[23] and whose success
would make it hard for later centuries, including our own, to see the scope of the
transformation. The religion that Augustine and his Caecilianist/catholic contemporaries were creating was the high-tech religion of late antiquity—Christianity
constituted by texts and by leaders who were masters of textual interpretation and
production—leaders who knew how to confess and in confessing to make a new
past for themselves and thus a new future. But much of the real experience of their
lives was thereby effaced and moved into the shadow world of the things that were
unconfessed.

NOTES

1. On Alypius, see A. Mandouze, *Prosopographie Chrétienne du Bas-Empire* 1.53–65;
and E. Feldmann, A. Schindler, and O. Wermelinger, "Alypius," *Augustinus-Lexikon*
1.246–267.

2. *Conf.* III, 3, 6.

3. The expression reflects the experience of the Philadelphia demimonde of a generation ago, when pay telephone calls cost 10 cents and an individual who chose that
medium to advise the constabulary of the misdeeds of his peers was said thus to "drop a
dime" on them.

4. See, in this sense, the prolegomena to my commentary on the text: *Augustine:
Confessions* (Oxford: Clarendon Press, 1992), I, 1–3.

5. J. J. O'Donnell, "The Next Life of Augustine," in *The Limits of Ancient Christianity*,
ed. M. Vessey and W. Klingshirn (Ann Arbor: University of Michigan Press, 1999), pp.
215–31.

6. His five-million-plus words outrun the four million or so of Chrysostom and the
two million or so of Galen. (I am grateful to Professors Theodore Brunner, Luci Berkowitz,
and Maria Pantelia of the Thesaurus Linguae Graecae project for helping me with these
numbers.)

7. See instructively, Beyle's *Dictionnaire* (E. Beller and M. Lee, *Selections from Beyle's
Dictionary* [Princeton, N.J.: Princeton University Press, 1952]), s.v. Augustine. Beyle makes
a point of asserting the importance of the young and dissolute Augustine for understanding his achievement against a rhetorically pious tradition more inclined to speak of the saint's
intellectual talents. Beyle's account covers the pre-episcopal years in detail, then relegates
the episcopacy to a single dismissive sentence: "The particulars of his Episcopal Life and
Writings would be superfluous here; They may be found in Moréri's *Dictionary*, and in
Mr. du Pin's *Bibliothèque*; and if Those Gentlemen had not too lightly passed over St Augustin's irregular Life, I might wholly have dispensed with this Article: But, for the better
Instruction of the Public, it is proper to discover both the Good, and the Bad, of Great

Men." Thus our own twentieth- (and twenty-first) century pieties take root in the impieties of the eighteenth century: a cautionary observation for anyone who would rebel today against our own pieties, the present writer included.

8. Peter Brown, *Augustine of Hippo* (London and Berkeley: University of California Press, 1967).

9. O'Donnell, "Next Life."

10. Brown, *Augustine of Hippo*, pp. 106–9.

11. Pierre Courcelle's "Les premières confessions de saint Augustin," REL 21–22 (1943–44): 155–74, concentrates on the fragments of narrative that occur in Augustine's earliest works, but I have shown (*Augustine: Confessions*, 1.xlviii) that *de libero arbitrio* I, 11, 22 (not securely datable to before 395, but perhaps as early as 388) is the earliest text in which the form and structure of the *Confessions* narrative can be descried.

12. He has interestingly described the roots of his own experience in Kleinian psychoanalysis in the 1960s more or less contemporaneous with the writing of the biography as part of the explanation of the form and content of his famous "holy man" article of 1971 ("The Rise and Function of the Holy Man in Late Antiquity," *Journal of Roman Studies* 61 [1971]: 80–101): *representations* 1, no. 2 (1983): 1–25.

13. It must be acknowledged in fairness that the visitors were *looking* for a pear tree and would have doubtless re-enacted the theft recounted in *Confessions* if we had found one. For an account of that visit, see http://ccat.sas.upenn.edu/jod/algeria. More seriously, it is sobering that no real archaeological work has been possible in modern Souk Ahras, and doubtless the urbanization of the last fifty years has destroyed at least some of what might be there to be discovered. The Algerian scholars and curators who tend the sites and artifacts of their remarkable country are to be commended for what they have achieved and for their insistence on pointing out how much more could be done.

14. *Conf.* VIII, 12, 28 (and see my commentary ad loc. for the biblical overtones).

15. A special case is his friend, mentor, and benefactor Romanianus, surely the richest man in Tagaste. See my commentary on VI, 14, 24 for the evidence that suggests that the community of religious interests that they shared in the 380s disappeared in after years, with Romanianus subsiding into the predictable life of a country squire, at ease with his wealth and taking sexual comfort from the slave women on his estate. We know that Augustine did not approve of what Romanianus became; it would be a great thing to have Romanianus's views of what Augustine had become.

16. For Augustine's anticlericalism, see *de moribus manicheorum et de moribus ecclesiae catholicae* I, 1, 1; and cf. ibid., I, 32, 69.

17. Ep. XXII, 9, "absentiam enim meam tantum longe Hipponienses vehementer nimisque formidant."

18. See James J. O'Donnell, *Augustine: A New Biography* (New York: Ecco, 2005).

19. See my commentary, *Augustine: Confessions*, 2.3–7.

20. Ps.-Quint., *Declamations* 314.

21. The standard work is W. H. C. Frend, *The Donatist Church* (Oxford: Oxford University Press, 1952; reprinted often with minor corrections). My choice of names for the groups attempts to reflect the lived situation of Africa in the fourth century, when the Donatists were the undisturbed majority church from the 310s to the 340s and again from the 360s to the 390s. Only the forcible intervention of imperial authority in the 340s and again in the 400s would affect that status, and it took Augustine and his collaborators a sustained struggle in concert with imperial force to gain the upper hand, notably at the famous "conference of Carthage" of 411. When Augustine chose sides, he was choosing to belong to a

small minority faction of little consequence. His success is indeed astonishing, the more so for making us forget how great it was.

22. P. Alfaric, *L'évolution intellectuelle de Saint Augustin: I, Du Manichéisme au Néo-platonisme* (Paris: Nourry, 1918), famously, almost notoriously, claimed that Augustine did not truly convert to Christianity until 391, that his intellectual revolution of 386 betook him to Platonism rather than religion. He is wrong as to important facts—the baptism of 387 is real and a real realignment—but right as to seeing that 391 was the truly transformative moment in Augustine's life. The Augustine of 390, had he lived on another forty years in Tagastan obscurity, could have turned into many things, few of them likely to be well known to us, and perhaps he too would have taken up with the slave girls in time.

23. Peter Brown, *Power and Persuasion in Late Antiquity* (Madison: University of Wisconsin Press, 1992), is an important and lucid essay on this transformation of the bishops of the late antique church from charismatic clergy to substantial urban dignitaries.

On Not Retracting
the Unconfessed

Elizabeth A. Clark

We here honor and explore the writings of (as Richard Rorty has put it) "two boys from North Africa who made it big in Europe."[1] From one of them, Jacques Derrida, many of us have learned (however partially and inelegantly) to attend to gaps and absences in texts, to grafts, aporias, and exclusions.[2] From the other, Augustine, we have inherited a precious cache of writings whose gaps, aporias, and exclusions have often been overlooked by scholars in search of "presence." A Derridean reading prompts otherwise.

The particular "gap and absence" on which I shall focus is the mysterious erasure of Donatists (the dominant practitioners of Christianity in late-fourth-century Africa) both from Augustine's *Confessions* and from his reconsideration of that text in the *Retractions*, his late-in-life re-examination of his literary corpus.[3] Here, "erasure" seems to have left no traces of legibility.[4] Yet the erasure from the *Confessions* of Donatists, who flourished in the areas in which Augustine spent his youth, and his failure to rectify this omission in the *Retractions*, prompts questions as to "the absent." Moreover, we can note a second "absence" in Augustine's *Confessions* and other writings from the 390s and early fifth century, namely, the failure of this Derridean "compatriot" to identify himself as a North African.[5] Last, I shall suggest that Geoffrey Bennington's "Derridabase" and Derrida's "Circumfession," the texts on which the third Villanova conference on Religion and Postmodernism centered, could be fruitfully explored in relation to a different set of Augustine's writings, namely, the anti-Pelagian treatises that detail his "mature" views on free will, grace, and predestination. But first, to the *Confessions* and "Circumfession," forgetting and remembering, North Africa, and Augustine's absent Donatists.

Remembering and Forgetting

Remembering and forgetting are notable themes in both the *Confessions* and "Circumfessions." As a testimony, and later a memorial, to Derrida's mother (Circ. 4/25), "Circumfession" also conveys the author's sorrow that his memories of her cannot be matched by her memories of him—for dying as an amnesiac, her memories are gone (Circ. 8, 4/42, 22–23). If, as Augustine asserts, "the power of memory is myself" (*Conf.* 10.16), "the great force of life in a living person" (10.17), do not others' failure or inability to remember us not only reduce them, but also reduce *us*, dis-member *us*?[6] Augustine confesses that his own salvation lay in remembering God; even when he had wandered away (*Conf.* 12.10), God was always present in his memory[7]—and God, he is sure, had never forgotten *him*. As scriptural testimony, Augustine paraphrases Psalm 8:4, "man is nothing unless you [God] remember him" (*Conf.* 12.26).

As one of the great philosophers of memory, Augustine's discussions of the topic in the *Confessions* are especially notable.[8] Although as a teacher of rhetoric, Augustine must have been well acquainted with the memory techniques recommended by orators of classical antiquity (and so his frequent references to memory as a palace, a treasure-house, and a storehouse attest[9]), he does not discuss memory techniques in the *Confessions*. Instead, he explores memory in relation to time and to humans' "innate knowledge" of the principles of language and numbers (*Conf.* 10.12).[10] Like other ancient intellectuals, Augustine holds a "picture-theory" of memory: he claims that scenes of his childhood, for example, are still present as "pictures" in his memory (*Conf.* 11.18).

How, then, to explain "forgetting?" As Mary Carruthers has argued in *The Book of Memory: A Study of Memory in Medieval Culture*, for ancient and medieval (unlike modern) authors, forgetting was not a failure to "reproduce," but rather a failure to have properly imprinted on the mind a "phantasm" of an object or experience in the first place. For them, forgetting might be categorized as a "technical error" of perception in that an insufficient or misaddressed imprinting prevents the "eye of the mind" from later retrieving the phantasm. According to this theory, if images are correctly made and the routes to them in memory properly marked, recollection should be unproblematic.[11]

In the *Confessions*, Augustine is hard-pressed to make sense of forgetting. His memories, he remarks, are there "ready at his summons"—"except for the things which I have forgotten" (10.8–9). But how is it that we forget? Perhaps, he posits, we did not pay sufficient attention at the moment of perception or of learning, so that items "sink back" into the recesses of the mind. Yet Augustine remains largely confident that he can "collect" these lost memories again and "shepherd them again from their old lairs" (10.11).[12] For example, he admits that for a time he had forgotten the discovery of the relics of Gervasius and Protasius in Milan—but later, through God's prompting, he remembered the event (9.7).

Since Augustine was renowned for his ability to recall texts extemporaneously,[13] we might ask how in the *Confessions* he managed to forget so much—for

example, that he had a sister?[14] Pertinent to my present topic, had "Donatists" re-
treated to such deep recesses of Augustine's mind that even years later, when he
wrote the *Retractions*, he could not even recall that he had forgotten them in the
Confessions? Had God not prompted a "remembering" of Donatists, as he had
prompted the memory of the relic discovery in Milan? Or, had "Donatists" been
so nonexistent to the young Augustine that they never had been imprinted on his
mind in the first place and hence offered no retrievable "picture" by which he
might "shepherd [them] from their lairs?" The latter option, I shall argue, is difficult
to countenance.

Derrida's "Circumfession," like Augustine's *Confessions* is a book of remembering: the remembering of a beloved mother, the remembering of lapses,
the "remembering of God."[15] Yet, Derrida acknowledges, what he shares best
with his mother—a mother who never wished to read a single sentence he wrote
(Circ., 44/232–33)—are her capacities for silence and for amnesia (51/272). So
Augustine, Georgette Derrida, and her son "Jackie," Derrida's childhood nickname (16, 35/83, 182), are all "forgetters." But there is a fourth one as well: Derrida accuses "G.," "up there"—Geoffrey Bennington, author of "Derridabase"
printed at the top of the page—of forgetting him (6/33).[16] Are we dealing with
four cases of amnesia?

In *Memoirs of the Blind*, Derrida again speculates on forgetting, this time in
relation to artistic depictions of those deprived of sight.[17] Inspired by an exhibit
that Derrida organized for the Louvre on the theme of blindness, *Memoirs of the
Blind* has been called a "companion piece" to "Circumfession."[18] Derrida notes
in this work that in *Confessions* Book 10, Augustine exhorts himself (and his readers) to turn away from the temptations of sight toward inward "realities." A "pro-
cession of the blind" marches through Augustine's text, Derrida observes: the
biblical characters of Tobit, Isaac, Jacob—blind men who nonetheless were illuminated by God. But the person missing, forgotten, from Augustine's account, is
Paul, who as Saul was struck blind on the road to Damascus: it is he who might
have served as Augustine's closest model for "Christian blindness." Saul's absence,
Derrida claims, is "the blind spot at this point of the *Confessions*."[19] If we agree
with John Caputo that Saul's blinding on the road to Damascus "is arguably the
origin of a distinctly 'Christian' movement after the death of Jesus," then "Christianity itself would originate in a sacrificial act of blindness."[20] Yet even if Augustine forgot Saul's blindness and conversion in the *Confessions*, he nonetheless remembered the episode shortly afterwards in his writing career, not as an exhortation
to inner vision, but as a justification for imperial and ecclesiastical coercion of
Donatists: did not God use strong-arm tactics against Saul to effect his rebirth as
a follower of Jesus?[21] But for the moment, all roads for Augustine seem to lead,
not to Damascus or to Rome, but rather to Carthage.

In a now-classic article, Paula Fredriksen details the ways in which the conversion narratives of Paul and Augustine reveal "only the retrospective moment,
and the retrospective self." Conversion accounts, she argues, are both apologetic
(because the convert must explain himself to his old, his new, and his opposing

audiences), and anachronistic ("because the account rendered in the conversion narrative is so shaped by later concerns"). Never disinterested, "it is a condensed, or disguised description of the convert's *present*, which he legitimates through his retrospective creation of a past and a self." "[R]emade in the image of the present," Fredriksen argues, the "past is too important, in a sense, to be allowed to exist."[22] Yet for Augustine, the "present" in which he wrote the *Confessions* was replete with Donatists, who had occupied his energies for the previous four or five years: might we not have expected this "present" to intrude in Augustine's retrospective creation of his earlier self? Let us turn, then, to these unremembered "pasts" of Augustine, to the *Confessions* and the *Retractions*.

The *Retractions*

Augustine's *Retractions*, a reassessment of ninety-three of his works, has been called "the 'confessions' of his later years."[23] Augustine began the treatise in 426 or 427, at the age of seventy-two, and completed it a year or two later. Apparently his original plan was first to examine systematically his full treatises, and afterwards to scrutinize his letters and sermons—but he never completed the latter task.[24] Relying on the lists of texts provided by the *Retractions* and by Augustine's biographer, Possidius, scholars believe that they have a nearly-complete inventory of Augustine's writings. They also believe that they can with some precision date his treatises, since Augustine presumably catalogued his works in chronological order.[25]

Why did Augustine write the *Retractions*? In the Prologue to the work, he states that he wishes to correct errors in his earlier writings "with judicial severity."[26] But in *Epistle* 224, he claims a broader purpose, one that in fact corresponds more closely with the *Retractions* as we have it: to "defend" what he had written, not just to "correct" mistakes that had come to his attention.[27] Augustine especially needed to "defend" the positions he had advanced in some of his early works, the treatise *On Free Will* in particular, since Pelagian opponents had argued (with considerable justification) that Augustine's views on human freedom expressed in that treatise resonated with their own.[28] Augustine now struggles to rescue his earlier writings from what he calls "misinterpretations"; he claims that he had always held his present notions of grace and predestination, although perhaps he had not expressed them forcefully enough.[29]

To be sure, in the *Retractions* Augustine appears eager to note his earlier errors for readers—yet, strangely, it is often the most trivial of these that he hastens to correct.[30] Thus, when reviewing the defects of the *Confessions*, he offers only two minute and inconsequential changes: first, he inserts a "perhaps" into one sentence; and second, he admits that in explicating the creation story, he overconfidently positioned "the firmament."[31] I want to ask him, "Nothing *else* you want to change or add, Augustine? Nothing about your sister, whom you so completely erased from the tale of your youth? And what about those absent Donatists?"[32] Since modern scholars agree that Donatism was the dominant manifestation of Christianity in North Africa in the years between Augustine's birth and his assumption of the priesthood, we may well be puzzled by their erasure from the *Confessions*. And so to them we turn.

Donatists

A brief review of current approaches to Donatism may here be helpful.[33] By the time that Augustine returned from Italy to his homeland, settled with friends on his family property in Thagaste,[34] and assumed the priesthood, the Donatist Church had flourished for over eight decades. "Short versions" of the Donatist narrative, as told by Augustine and other Catholics,[35] locate the origins of the conflict between Donatists and Catholics in the aftermath of Diocletian's persecution of Christians in the opening years of the fourth century. When Caecilian was chosen as bishop of Carthage, an outcry arose (especially from bishops in the hinterlands of Numidia, which became a stronghold of the Donatist movement[36]) that Caecilian had been consecrated by *traditores*, that is, by those who had handed over copies of Scripture to, and cooperated with, the persecutors. Was his consecration thus not irregular, indeed invalid? Although Catholics claimed that subsequent investigations proved the charge false, the opposition refused to accept their claim—indeed, the matter was still being hotly debated a century later.[37] (Augustine reports that when crossing a field in 396, he was accosted by a Donatist who shouted accusingly at him, *"Traditor!"*[38]) Within a few years, many North African Christians had rallied around Donatus the Great, who gave his name to the movement and reigned as Donatist bishop of Carthage from 313 until his exile in 347.[39] Although Donatists averred that *they* constituted the true Church of Africa, synods in Rome and in Gaul ruled against them; so did the emperor Constantine, but he abandoned his failed attempts at coercion in 321.

In 347, the emperor Constantius proclaimed an edict against the Donatists, but this too proved largely ineffective.[40] And when, in the early 360s, Julian ("the Apostate") granted toleration to various religious sects,[41] exiled Donatists from Africa returned to their homeland and reclaimed their previously confiscated basilicas. Despite a series of edicts from emperors in the 370s and 380s against Donatist "rebaptism,"[42] imperial efforts failed to stem the tide: historian of the Donatist movement William Frend argues that in the period from 388 to 398, Donatists came "almost to achieving complete mastery in Africa."[43] By all accounts, the failure of provincial governors to enforce the anti-Donatist edicts[44]—when coupled with the relative weakness of Catholic bishops in North Africa up till the early 390s,[45] contrasted with the stability of Donatist leadership[46]—left the Donatists largely free to flourish. At the Council of Carthage in 390, Catholic bishops appeared reluctant even to broach the topic of a possible campaign against Donatism.[47] At the Council of Hippo in 393, Catholic bishops conceded that Catholic clerics who had strayed to the Donatists might resume their priestly duties within the Catholic fold, and justified this decision by pleading the shortage of Catholic clergy in North Africa.[48] Only in 404 and thereafter, when Augustine and his vigorous episcopal colleagues, Aurelius of Carthage and Alypius of Thagaste,[49] petitioned the secular authorities for assistance,[50] did Donatist strength begin to wane. An imperial edict of 405 declared Donatism to be a heresy (not just a "schism"); threatened the confiscation of property (including that of owners of landed estates who harbored Donatists); forbade those who practiced rebaptism to make a testament, receive a gift, or enter into contracts; and fined heads of provinces, chief decurions, and defenders of municipalities who failed to carry out the edict's provisions.[51] If, after all these measures, there still were relatively equal numbers of Donatists and Catholics at the Council of Carthage in 411, it is not hard to believe that Donatism flourished freely in North Africa in earlier decades when such harsh repression was absent.[52]

The Donatist account (such as we can decipher it, since Donatists were ultimately "the losers") reads quite differently. The Donatists believed that they, like the ancient Israelites, had been called by God to form a holy community.[53] Over against themselves, the faithful, they saw ranged unholy Catholic *traditores* who, betraying "the people," fawned upon the agents of imperial power. Since these "traitors" had defiled God's Church, faithful Christians—that is, Donatists— should have no association with them. On the Donatist reading of events, much of Christendom (apart from the pure remnant of "the just" in North Africa) had lapsed from the true faith.

Did theological differences divide Catholics and Donatists? The answer is problematic. A few Donatists, it appears, were self-admitted criminals; one notorious Donatist bishop boasted of murder and threatened head-breaking activity against any who "wanted to make something of it."[54] Moreover, Donatists, like Catholics, had taken back schismatics from *their* group without rebaptism, thus voiding the much-touted issue of baptism as a satisfactory explanation for the differences between the groups. No doctrinal differences on such issues as the Trinity or Christology entered the discussion. The most that Augustine could allege against the Donatists (aside from the manifest violence that the controversy occasioned, especially through its terrorist wing, the Circumcellions[55]) was that they did not act "in charity" (*De baptismo* 1.9.12). By this charge, Augustine signals his view that the Donatists had broken away from the true Catholic Church—but since both ancient Donatists and modern historians agree that Donatism probably represented "mainstream" Christianity in North Africa, it is not so evident which group was "breaking away."[56] Thus we can note that by 390, Catholic bishops were "discouraged" by their lack of success in repelling Donatism.[57] According to Jerome, "nearly all of Africa" had gone over to the Donatist party.[58]

Let us next focus more precisely on North African Donatism: were Donatists present in the localities of Augustine's youth?

Donatism in North Africa

Although evidence regarding Donatism and Catholicism from Thagaste and Madauros, towns in which Augustine spent his boyhood from 354 to 371, is not as plentiful as historians might wish, we can note the following data.[59] At the Coun-

cil of Carthage in 411, whose detailed records constitute precious evidence regarding the presence of Donatists and Catholics in North Africa, Alypius of Thagaste claimed that "for a long time" Thagaste had enjoyed "unity," that is, had
been Catholic.[60] Yet in a letter of 407 or 408, Augustine testifies that Thagaste, his
hometown, had formerly been "entirely Donatist" but had been brought around
to Catholicism by fear of the imperial laws. So successful had been the "conversion," he claims, that present residents of Thagaste could not remember when the
town had been "entirely Donatist" (*ep.* 93.5.17)—yet another case of "forgetfulness." Modern scholars speculate on *which* imperial laws had prompted the people
of Thagaste to become Catholic: if the edict is as early as that of Constantius in
347, then the "conversion" may have occurred in the 350s or early 360s.[61] Even
if we accept this early dating for the imperial law that occasioned the change (and
it may well have been issued later), there is a difference to be registered between
a town establishing its first Catholic church and a whole population's being swept
into its fold.

From the *Confessions*, it appears that Augustine knows, or remembers, nothing about Donatists in Thagaste: they are completely absent from his discussion.
Yet an interesting counter-testimony, often overlooked, is given by Augustine himself in a letter dated to 398. In this letter (*Epistle* 44), Augustine, now bishop of
Hippo Regius, suggests that Donatist and Catholic bishops meet for a colloquy in
a small town such as Thagaste because it has both a Catholic and a Donatist presence.[62] Has not Alypius, in testifying to the wholesale "conversion" of the town,
exaggerated the Catholics' hegemony?

Moreover, we know that Augustine had at least one Donatist relative, a certain Severinus, to whom he addresses *Epistle* 52. In this letter, Augustine claims
that he "knows well" Severinus' heart. He has "grieved over" Severinus' Donatist
affiliation "for a long time," and has "long" mourned his relative. What good is
temporal kinship if we overlook our eternal well-being, Augustine asks Severinus?
(*ep.* 52.1–2). How long is "long"? the modern critic wants to know. Was Severinus a relative whom Augustine encountered during his childhood? If so, he must
have known at least *one* Donatist.

Madauros, the town where Augustine received some of his early education,
has been dubbed "the Stratford-on-Avon" of Africa for its literary associations.[63]
In a letter to a pagan grammarian of Madauros dated to about 390, Augustine mentions that Catholics have set up a church in Madauros—one that the grammarian might attend, he hints (*ep.* 17.5). It is hard to believe that the *first* Christian
presence in Madauros would have dated from only the late 380s. In addition, at
the Council of Carthage in 411, both Donatist and Roman Catholic bishops from
Madauros are reported as present.[64] It is thus reasonable to posit that there were
Donatists in Madauros in the late 360s, before Catholic repression of Donatism
intensified.

Furthermore, many Donatist bishops from towns near Thagaste and Madauros are listed on the rolls of the Council of 411, or are said by colleagues to have
died only recently, suggesting that the area was more infused with Donatism than

some have suggested. Donatist bishops are thus listed for Smitthu, Lares, Thibaris, Bulla Regia, Sicca Veneria, Calama, Thubursicu Numidarum.[65] Although some nearby towns appear to have only Catholic bishops (Zattara, Thagura, Celerinae, Thuburnica),[66] others have only Donatist (Drusilana, Tituli).[67] Hippo Regius, the town of Augustine's episcopal see, still had a strong Donatist presence in 411,[68] as did other coastal towns such as Rusicade and Thabraca.[69] In addition to evidence provided by the Acts of the Council of Carthage, Augustine's own correspondence testifies to Donatists in places not so distant from the scenes of his youth: Hasna, Spanna, Milevis, Thubursicu Numidarum, Titia, Calama, Rusicade, Figulina, Fussala.[70]

How can we account for Augustine's complete erasure of Donatism from the *Confessions*? Peter Brown suggests that since by the era of Augustine's youth Thagaste was a "Catholic stronghold" and since Augustine as a Manichean was oblivious to issues of intra-Christian politics, Donatism was simply not in his purview. Augustine had learned his Christianity largely in Italy, Brown argues, and his views of the Church developed in his polemic against Manichees and pagan Platonists.[71] The evidence I have summoned casts doubt on whether we should entirely dismiss a Donatist presence in Thagaste in the 360s and 370s, although Brown surely is correct that Augustine's Christianity was largely formed in response to other currents. Moreover, Brown offers a second reason that may help us account for the Donatist absence from the *Confessions*: that text is a "strictly intellectual biography"[72]—and presumably, Donatist issues were not marked in Augustine's mind as "intellectual." During the time of Augustine's youth, on Brown's account, Donatists are not so much "under erasure" as simply "not there."

But if we turn from the time narrated in the *Confessions* to the time in which that work was actually written—namely, 397[73]—Augustine as priest and bishop had undertaken a vigorous campaign against Donatism. His public debut against Donatism appears to have been at the Council of Hippo in 393. Although still a presbyter, he was invited on that occasion to preach to the assembled bishops.[74] Given the intensity with which Augustine pursued the Donatists in the years directly following, we gather that he must have undertaken a crash course on Donatism. He needed to learn much more, and fast, about this religious movement that he had so neglected. Hippo provided the site for his rapid learning experience.

Writing in about 400, Augustine reports that Catholics had earlier been in the minority in Hippo.[75] To case out the Donatist opposition first-hand, he went to hear sermons that his rival, the Donatist bishop of Hippo, preached to *his* congregation.[76] Yet Augustine did not, it appears, immediately master all the details. In 397, debating with Donatists at Thubursicu Numidarum,[77] he still lacked easy familiarity with documents from the early days of the controversy and postponed the discussion until he could acquire the requisite materials (*ep.* 43.2.5). When Donatists appealed to the fact that they had been recognized by the Council of Sardica, Augustine needed Alypius, at his side, to remind him that Sardica was an Arian council whose actions could not be admitted as evidence for true Christianity (*ep.* 44.3.6). And Augustine kept making mistakes about Donatism in his early writings, such as mixing up the two bishops named "Donatus" and misdating the moment when Caecilian's consecrator was exonerated of *traditio*.[78] He had, nonetheless, joined the fray.

That Augustine considered Donatism intellectually unworthy is suggested by the number of popular works he wrote to combat the movement, and his explanation for why in writing them he adopted the style and genres he did. Around 393, Augustine composed his first anti-Donatist work, the "Psalm Against the Donatist Party." In the *Retractions*, Augustine comments that he wrote this song to instruct the uneducated masses about Donatism, and he explains that he had not composed the poem in meter because he would then have been forced to use a vocabulary above the capacity of his audience (*Retr.* 1.19).[79] One indication that in this poem he was making a conscious appeal to non-elites is his exoneration of the *plebs* from leveling charges of *traditor* against Caecilian and other Catholics: it was, rather, Numidian *bishops* who had been guilty of this lie and who themselves, Augustine claims, were *traditores*.[80]

Likewise in the *Retractions*, he explains why around 407 he composed an "Admonition of the Donatists Concerning the Maximianists":[81] namely, he saw that "many" were hindered from comprehending the truth about Donatism "because of the difficulty of reading"; this short work, he hoped, would be accessible to a wider public (*Retr.* 2.55). In still another populist composition, Augustine penned a set of "proofs" against Donatism that could be posted on the walls of formerly-Donatist basilicas.[82] And yet another piece of evidence is an epitaph Augustine wrote for a certain deacon Nabor (allegedly the victim of Donatist violence for his conversion to Catholicism) in the form of an acrostic poem; the first letters of the eight hexameters spell out "deacon." Here Augustine uses the occasion of a funerary inscription to celebrate in popular form the glories of Catholic martyrdom and to condemn the *furor* of the Donatists.[83]

In these anti-Donatist tracts and in Augustine's later explanations for writing them, a strong sense of class comes to the fore. Peter Brown and Rebecca West both use the word "contempt" to describe Augustine's early relation to the Donatists.[84] Their intuition suggests that Augustine's disdain for the intellectual level of the Donatists may help to account for his early inattention to that movement. As commentators have observed and Augustine himself confessed, he thought that a combination of ignorance and ingrained habit was responsible for Donatist recalcitrance; all they needed was a nudge in order to be brought around to Catholic truth.[85]

Thus, Augustine initiated a flood of anti-Donatist treatises, nineteen in all, of which twelve survive,[86] not counting his numerous letters and sermons pertaining to Donatism. In letters from 392 to the time of the *Confessions'* composition, Augustine addressed issues of Donatist "rebaptism"[87] and Donatist, especially Circumcellion, violence[88]—violence that was also directed against his own person.[89] He launches an attack on the new Donatist bishop of Carthage, Primianus.[90] He pleads with the Donatist bishop of Hippo not to let his party divide families against each other (*ep.* 33.5). He enlists secular authorities to intervene with Donatist bishops (*epp*. 34 and 35). He offers to debate any Donatist who will take him on (with the snide hint that the Donatist bishop of Hippo may fear that he is educationally inadequate to the task; *ep*. 34.6).[91] And in the midst of these interventions, Augustine studies the Donatist Tychonius's *Book of Rules* (for scriptural exegesis) and asks bishop Aurelius of Carthage for his opinion of them (*ep*. 41.2).

Thus, there can be no doubt that when Augustine composed the *Confessions* he was in the midst of controversy with Donatists—although this fact is nowhere evident in this account of his early years. Here, the present seems *not* to have obtruded on the past in any explicit sense—although Book XII of the *Confessions* may be read as an attempt to shore up his reputation as Scripture scholar in the face of Donatist insinuations that they "owned" the Bible.[92]

The case of the *Retractions*, on the other hand, provides a good example of Augustine's "retrospective consciousness," to borrow Paula Fredriksen's phrase. The *Retractions* is colored throughout by Augustine's recent encounters with Pelagian theology; he reads his early writings in light of his present theological interests. Thus it is not, I think, beside the point to imagine that we might have caught a glimmer of his struggles with Donatism in the 390s in the *Confessions*. Perhaps the closest we come in the *Retractions* to deciphering how his struggle against Donatism impinged on his assessment of his earlier writings lies in his reconsideration of the treatise *On True Religion*. In commenting on this earlier treatise, Augustine notes that he had mistakenly claimed that Jesus accomplished everything by persuasion and admonition; he "forgot" that Jesus drove out the money-changers in the Temple by force, as well as forcibly casting out demons.[93] Surely this "correction" stems from his developed view, honed in the Donatist controversy, that force is sometimes necessary to bring the recalcitrant around to the "right" views.

The *Retractions* has been called the "*Confessions* of [Augustine's] later years."[94] We might also ask what a "*Confessions* of his middle years" would have looked like. Would this have been a *Retractions* suffused with his Donatist concerns? Here we are left to speculate. I can, however, suggest one other variable in Augustine's position vis-à-vis the Donatists: the consequences of the Romanization of North Africa in the years previous to Augustine.

The Romanization of North Africa

Scholars of Roman history, literature, and archeology have devoted much attention in recent decades to the topic of the Romanization of the various provinces that came to constitute the empire. Breaking with a diffusionist, "top-down" model, and incorporating postcolonialist perspectives on the subtle ways that resistance and accommodation work together,[95] these scholars have explored the means by which the Roman Empire co-opted the subjugated into the ideology of the conquerors. Historians and archeologists agree that Romanization of the African provinces was far more "successful," from Rome's point of view, than in some other areas.[96]

How and why did Romanization succeed so well in North Africa? How did the colonizers turn memorials of destruction—such as the city of Carthage—into flourishing centers that espoused the values of Rome?[97] One answer, well-accepted by ancient North Africa experts, looks to the role of the native elites.

As early as the first century C.E., "native" Africans had assumed roles as public functionaries in North African towns and cities,[98] and by the second century, a significant number of Roman senators were African-born.[99] In Madauros, for example, it has been calculated that by the second century, around 71 percent of the elites had some African background.[100] Historians agree that Rome itself could not have imposed "Roman" views on provincials simply by the use of force: they had not the means to do so.[101] Rather, after the initial conquest, Rome relied on the cooperation of the local population by wooing the local elites to share in the "rewards and charms" of Roman power.[102] Now, as the Roman historian Tacitus put it in another context, "a competition for honor could take the place of compulsion."[103]

The means by which Roman imperial authorities won local leaders to their side is complex; although there were clear economic advantages, especially as concerned agricultural development,[104] Romanization was also achieved through more "symbolic" means.[105] The role of a Romanizing education was an important part of the process. Such an education could be gained in at least some provincial schools, but journeying to Rome itself for higher education was also popular for those with sufficient means. By 370 C.E., so many African students had flooded into Rome that special laws were passed to control them.[106] Those who had the opportunity for such an education would learn "from their Latin classics that it was by divine providence that Rome ruled the civilized world"—as Virgil wrote, "*imperium sine fine.*"[107]

Clifford Ando's recent book, *Imperial Ideology and Provincial Loyalty in the Roman Empire*, details the "symbolic" ways by which Rome won over the North African provinces, through "a complex conversation between center and periphery."[108] Despite Ando's endorsement of optimistically Habermasian theories of consensus-building and communicative action,[109] his thesis conforms to the findings of other Roman historians: that the creation of stable government in the African provinces did not rest on warfare, but on the cooperation of the local elites.[110] (*Why* these local populations cooperated in their own subjugation remains somewhat of a mystery, yet the paucity of revolts suggests that they must have.) Ando exhaustively documents the symbolic *means* by which Rome communicated its values and swept provincials into them.[111] Central to the original process was "the charismatic power of the imperial office" (pp. 410, xii). The precise means by which the emperor bound those who otherwise might have resisted included the dissemination of imperial portraits; the widespread publication of information of all sorts, especially that which broadcast the emperor's benefactions to his people; the sharing of holidays; the taking of loyalty oaths; and much more (e.g., pp. 41, 175–76, 359). As in other provinces, the local population was able to transform images that might have signaled "the iconography of defeat into one celebrating unification" (p. 313). Noting the fact that almost all imperial Latin literature was written by provincials, Ando, like other ancient historians, stresses the important role played by the educational process for local elites, who through it "came to view the history of their conquerors as their own" (p. 311).

This, I posit, is Augustine's story. Today it seems unbalanced either to style Augustine an "African" at heart because he wept over Dido,[112] or, conversely, to cast him as an urban, educated, Romanized Catholic against uneducated Donatist "natives" of the Numidian hinterlands, Berber- or Punic-speaking agricultural workers.[113] His relationship to Africa seems more complex. In one early letter dating from around 390 to a pagan grammarian of Madauros, Augustine chastises his correspondent for making fun of Punic names: isn't he ashamed to mock the land of his birth, in which, "until very recently, Punic was still the language of the people?" (ep. 17.2). But such an intervention by Augustine on the side of "African-ness" is rare. Rather, he is quick to laud the benefits that Roman rule brought to her captive peoples, including the Latin language (De civ. 5.17, 19.7). Later, he bristles sharply when, in his literary debates with Julian of Eclanum, he himself is mocked as a "Punic debater" and the "Aristotle of the Carthaginians."[114] Although Augustine turns a senatorial view of Rome's glorious past against itself in the City of God, he surely does not self-identify as an African native. As Robert Markus notes, although Augustine's theology was a critique of "establishment theology," he was no critic of the "establishment."[115] The son of a local decurion, Augustine had earlier aimed, as a "seller of words,"[116] to raise his social status in Italy, but now lived as a servant of Christ in a lackluster North African town.[117] Augustine as bishop still believes in the universalism of Rome—although now a universalism manifest in the Catholic Church.

In his contests with Donatists, Augustine repeatedly contrasts the universalism of Catholic Christianity with the provincialism of the Donatists, who (he claims) argue as if Christianity survived in Africa alone. Thus Augustine mocks the Donatist identification of "North Africa" with the "midday" (meridies) at which the hero of the Song of Songs (interpreted as Jesus) will pasture his flock (Song of Songs 1:7): they even have their geography wrong, Augustine argues, since the meridian falls, not in Africa, but in Egypt, the home of Catholic monks.[118] Psalm 72:8, in Augustine's interpretation, prophesies that the Church will stretch from "sea to sea," not be sequestered in the highlands of Numidia.[119] Since "Carthage" is not mentioned in the Bible, the closest that the Donatists could come to identifying "Africa" in Scripture is to associate it with "Tyre." But, Augustine rejoins, have they forgotten that in Ezekiel 28 the Prince of Tyre meets an evil end? Here at last, he caustically remarks, is one biblical text appropriate to Africa, but far from giving comfort to Donatists, it announces a terrible scourge.[120]

A recently discovered inscription from Roman Arabia reads: "The Romans always win."[121] In the case of Augustine and others, the "winning" was not through the type of conquest that had demolished Carthage centuries earlier, but through engaging the hearts, minds, and aspirations of young intellectuals and those eager to assume positions of authority at home or abroad: "conquest by book" seems an appropriate description.[122]

"Circumfession" and the Pelagian Controversy

Last, I would like to suggest another group of Augustine's writings that might be considered an appropriate matrix for consideration of "Derridabase" and "Circumfession," namely, his literary debate with Pelagians that occupied him from 412 to the end of his life in 430. In this controversy pertaining to grace, free will, and predestination, Augustine argued that since the "Fall" in the Garden of Eden, no human can win salvation except through a sheer gift of God,[123] who has predetermined those who will be among the blessed elect and who has left others in the *massa perditionis*. Free will, if that term signals humans' independent ability to choose and do the good, has been forfeited with Adam and Eve.[124]

By embedding Geoffrey Bennington's "Derridabase" and Jacques Derrida's "Circumfession" in this different Augustinian context pertaining to freedom and predestination, an unexpected displacement occurs: Derrida can no longer be identified with SA, Augustine, but with Pelagius (so we'll call him "P." from now on); and Geoff, "G. up there" (Circ., 7, 19/37, 97), now assumes the role, not just of God, but also of Augustine, opponent of Pelagius. Assuming a friskier presence than the "historical" Pelagius ("weighed down with Scottish porridge," Jerome sneered),[125] the Pelagius who championed human free will to protect the justice of God,[126] Derrida-as-Pelagius protests mightily against G.'s attempts to control him. Derrida-as-P. wants to "gain his name against G.," not let G. take it from him (Circ., 8/43–44). And although "Circumfession" is written as a present "for him [i.e., "G."] alone" (Circ., 58/305), it is a gift that will be given on P.'s terms. Derrida-as-Pelagius complains: G. wants to have predicted everything; he will even take away P.'s right to his own corpus; he has dismembered it, has "circumcised" the body of P.'s writings ("*Hoc est corpus meum*," P. in effect protests) (Circ., 5/26–28).

Derrida-as-Pelagius's game is to outwit G., to prevent G. from depriving him of a future, of future writings (Circ., 5/30). G. thinks that he knows not just P.'s past and present, but P.'s future as well; so Derrida-as-P. will keep G. in the dark as to his future plans, whether, for example, he will abandon this memoir of his mother's death (28/142). The trick will be, by writing "Circumfession," to use even the present to derail G.'s control of him and his corpus (6, 59/32, 311). If G. expects an "idiomatic, unbroachable, unreadable, uncircumcised piece of writing" from P., isn't he going to be surprised! (37/194). But is there anything left with which Derrida-as-Pelagius can surprise G., since G. seems to know everything already? (3/18). P. will fight him down, not let him deprive P. of his life's events; P.'s own salvation will come through unpredictability (6/31–32). If Derrida-as-Pelagius can win, his "success" will lie in surprising G., in putting an end to his "owner's tour" of P.'s corpus (6/32–33).

For the "singularity of the event" to stay "unanticipatable" (Circ. 6/33–34), Derrida-as-Pelagius must be able to "dismantle G.'s theologic program" (28, 58/141, 305). P. may even found another religion, just to keep the surprise going (42/222). But in the end, G. "up there" is not the all-knowing, all-predestining God; he is the "floating toy at high tide and under the moon," with "no lighthouse and no book" (59/315). But neither is P. "Saint Augustine," but a celebrated heretic . . . or perhaps unbeknownst to himself, the deviser of some novel form of process theology that celebrates God's freedom and unpredictability . . . about which theological readers may speculate better than I. I suspect that we will not know the end of this struggle between freedom and determinism until the Last Judgment . . . unless Jack Caputo decides to stage another conference.

NOTES

1. Richard Rorty, "Derrida and the Philosophical Tradition," in *Truth and Progress: Philosophical Papers*, vol. 3 (Cambridge: Cambridge University Press, 1998), p. 347.

2. For some older but still useful discussions of deconstructive reading, see, among others, Barbara Johnson, "Introduction," in Jacques Derrida, *Dissemination* (Chicago: University of Chicago Press, 1982), p. xv; Jonathan Culler, *On Deconstruction: Theory and Criticism after Structuralism* (Ithaca, N.Y.: Cornell University Press, 1982), pp. 85, 135, 155; Gayatri Chakravorty Spivak, "Introduction," in Jacques Derrida, *Of Grammatology* (Baltimore and London: Johns Hopkins University Press, 1976; French original, 1967), esp. pp. lxxiv–v, lxxvii.

3. Rebecca West, *St. Augustine* (Edinburgh: Peter Davies, 1933), p. 25, notes the gaps, absences, understatements, and misstatements of the *Confessions* that should prompt the reader to be wary of taking the work as " faithful to reality."

4. On erasure, see Spivak, "Introduction," p. xxii.

5. Jacques Derrida, "Circumfession," 3, 9, in Geoffrey Bennington and Jacques Derrida, *Jacques Derrida*, trans. Geoffrey Bennington (Chicago/London: University of Chicago Press, 1993; French original, 1991), pp. 18, 46. Page references in the text are given with the page number of the English text preceding that of the French original.

6. For Augustine's "dis-memberment" in the world, see *Conf.* 12.16.

7. *Conf.*, 10.25—although not in the form of a "picture." Augustine's exploration of how "memory" might be seen as one mark of the Trinity's creative activity, its formation of us "in the image of God," in *De Trinitate* 14.3.4–5, 12.15–16.

8. Mary J. Carruthers, *The Book of Memory: A Study of Memory in Medieval Culture* (Cambridge: Cambridge University Press, 1990), p. 146. Also see Brian Stock, *Augustine the Reader: Meditation, Self-Knowledge, and the Ethics of Interpretation* (Cambridge and London: Belknap Press of Harvard University Press, 1996), pp. 13, 211, 224, 226–27, for comments on the topic.

9. See, for example, Cicero, *De oratore* 2.350– 60; Quintilian, *Institutio oratoria* 11; and *Rhetorica ad Herrenium* 3; Augustine, *Conf.* 10.8.

10. Whether Augustine still here toys with a notion of reminiscence, which in turn rests on a notion of the soul's pre-existence, has been much debated. He is aware of this issue in his early writings: see *Soliloquies* 2.20.35; *De quantitate animae* 20.34. For a brief

discussion, see A. Solignac in BA 14, pp. 562–63. At some point, Augustine abandoned a theory of reminiscence and never, to the end of his life, pronounced definitively on the question of the origin of the soul. (See Elizabeth A. Clark, *The Origenist Controversy: The Cultural Construction of an Early Christian Debate* [Princeton, N.J.: Princeton University Press, 1992], pp. 196, 197, 219, 229, 231–36, 238–44, for a summary of this point.) By the time Augustine concluded *De Trinitate*, he had in hand an alternative explanation, namely that memory is something that has been "imprinted" on humans at creation and that serves as one of the inner signs of the Trinity in a human being (*De Trinitate* 14.3.4–5, 12.15–16).

11. Carruthers, *Book of Memory*, pp. 61–62.

12. But a further puzzle: how do we remember forgetfulness, remember that we have forgotten something? Does not the thing have to be in some sense present in order for us to say that we remember that we forgot? Augustine here recalls the parable of the lost coin (Luke 15:8–10): how could the woman have found the coin unless she knew that she had lost it? If she—and we—had completely forgotten something, we would not be able to look for what was lost (*Conf.* 10.16, 18, 19).

13. For the powers of memory involved in Augustine's technique of sermon composition and delivery, see Roy J. Deferrari, "St. Augustine's Method of Composing and Delivering Sermons," *American Journal of Philology* 43 (1922): 97–123, 193–219.

14. We know he had a sister both from Possidius's *Vita Augustini* 26 and from Augustine's reference to her in *ep.* 211.4.

15. Circ. 23, 7, 17, 28, 32, 36, 44 / 117, 36–37, 86–87, 142–43, 165, 187, 232–33. Derrida's approach to "re-membering" himself lies not so much in "confession" as in his meditations on circumcision and uncircumcision (Circ. 11/ 59–60). Here, with the foreskin, lies some approach to truth, unlike "confession," which can deceive: Circ. 26, cf. 21/132, 135, 107.

16. And, as G. "up there" himself notes in another context, the search for certain foundations "is threatened at any moment by forgetting" ("Derridabase," p. 115).

17. Jacques Derrida, *Memoirs of the Blind: The Self-Portrait and Other Ruins*, trans. Pascale-Anne Brault and Michael Naas (Chicago and London: University of Chicago Press, 1993).

18. So John D. Caputo, *The Prayers and Tears of Jacques Derrida: Religion Without Religion* (Bloomington and Indianapolis: Indiana University Press, 1997), p. 309.

19. Derrida, *Memoirs of the Blind*, pp. 117–18, discussing *Confessions* 10.34.

20. Caputo, *Prayers and Tears*, p. 323; sight as the archetypal Western paradigm (p. 311). It is notable that it is three "Jews" who "see" although blind; contrast this with images Derrida discusses of the blindfolded synagogue (*Memoirs of the Blind*, p. 18).

21. Augustine, *ep.* 185.6.22.

22. Paula Fredriksen, "Paul and Augustine: Conversion Narratives, Orthodox Traditions, and the Retrospective Self," *Journal of Theological Studies*, n.s. 37 (1986): 33–34.

23. Stock, *Augustine the Reader*, p. 11. Goulven Madec, *Introduction aux "Revisions" et à la lecture des oeuvres de Saint Augustin* (Paris: Institut d'Etudes Augustiniennes, 1996), p. 12, attributes the sentiment to Gustav Bardy (BA 12, p. 217). The 93 works were divided into 252 books, not the "232" he mistakenly reports in *ep.* 224.2. The *Retractions* is divided into two books: the first book considers 26 treatises he wrote before he became a bishop; and the second, 67 writings composed during his episcopate.

24. Madec, *Introduction*, pp. 17–22: some of the works counted as treatises started out as letters and grew; moreover, Augustine's treatise *On Heresies* is missing from his account. After he wrote the *Retractions*, he composed three more works: *On the Predestination of*

the Saints, On the Gift of Perseverance, and the *Unfinished Work against Julian of Eclanum,* none of which made it into the *Retractions.*

25. This assumption has recently been questioned by Pierre-Marie Hombert, *Nouvelles Recherches de chronologie Augustinienne* (Paris: Institut d'Etudes Augustiniennes, 2000), summaries on pp. 2–5, 201. Hombert dates several of Augustine's works later than they were traditionally assigned, both because of new evidence provided by study of the Mayence sermons and because of what he deems to be anti-Pelagian references in them.

26. Augustine, *Retr.,* prologus 1: *"cum quadam iudiciaria severitate."*

27. Augustine, *ep.* 224.2: *"partim reprehendendo, partim defendendo."* See discussion in John Burnaby, "The 'Retractiones' of Saint Augustine: Self-criticism or Apologia?" *Augustinus Magister: Congrès International Augustinien, Paris, 21–24 Septembre, 1954: Communications* (Paris: Etudes Augustiniennes, 1954–55), p. 87.

28. Burnaby, "The 'Retractiones,'" pp. 88–89.

29. See, for example, Augustine's comments in *Retr.* 1.1.3, 6.5, 8.3–6, 9.2–3, 14.2, 4–6, 8. Augustine is also eager to correct any misimpressions that some expressions in his early treatises about his views on the origin of the soul and a theory of reminiscence: see, for example, *Retr.* 1.1.3, 4.4, 6.6, 7.2.

30. For example, he now has been informed that Jesus ben Sirach did not write the Wisdom of Solomon, as he had previously assumed; in his treatise *Against Julian* he failed to identify his source as Soranus or to give the correct details of the story (*Retr.* 2.30.2, commenting on *De doctrina Christiana* 2.8.13; and 2.88, commenting on *Contra Iulianum* 5.14.51).

31. *Retr.* 2.32, commenting on *Conf.* 4.6.11 and 13.32.47.

32. So engrossed in the dispute with Pelagians is Augustine that he even discusses the prime biblical text of the *Donatist* controversy—Ephesians 5:2, that the church should be "without spot or wrinkle"—in the context of the *Pelagian* debate (*Retr.* 1.6.5).

33. The standard work in English remains W. H. C. Frend, *The Donatist Church: A Movement of Protest in Roman North Africa* (Oxford: Clarendon Press, 1952).

34. Possidius, *Vita Augustini* 3.1–2.

35. Brown, *Augustine,* p. 228: "a use of propaganda unparalleled in the history of the African church." As Augustine scholar Emilien Lamirande remarked, it takes considerable effort to imagine that the "author of the anti-Donatist treatises is also the philosopher who wrote *De libero arbitrio* and the *Confessions* (*La Situation ecclésiastique des Donatistes d'après saint Augustin* [Ottawa: Editions de l'Université d'Ottawa, 1972], p. 187).

36. Around 390, it was believed that Donatists outnumbered Catholics in Numidia: see *Gesta Collatio Carthaginensis* 1.165; Augustine, *epp.* 129.6, 209.2; *Enarrationes in Psalmos* 21.26. Note the comment of Serge Lancel, *Actes de la Conference de Carthage en 411. Tome 1: Introduction générale.* Sources Chrétiennes 194 (Paris: Les Editions du Cerf, 1972), p. 155: It is not modern critics who have invented a "Donatist Numidia"; contemporaries admit that Numidia was overwhelmingly Donatist. Donatists had "massive superiority" there; on this point, Lancel proclaims Frend's argument regarding the strength of Donatism to be correct.

37. The fight remained one over "origins." As Rebecca West noticed even in 1933, Augustine cannot resist telling the story of the Donatist baker who refused to make bread for Catholics—an incident that happened probably in the early 360s, forty years earlier—as if it happened yesterday (*St. Augustine,* p. 139). See Augustine, *Contra Petilianum* 2.83.184 for the story.

38. Augustine, *ep.* 35.4. In the discussion following the presentation of this paper, Mark

Vessey hypothesized that one reason for Augustine's "turn" to the exegesis of Scripture at the end of the *Confessions* stemmed from his desire to display his reverence for, and scholarly interest in, the sacred books—against the charge that he was aligned with *traditores*. It is also worth registering that Augustine's election to the bishopric of Hippo while the current bishop was still alive and functioning was "irregular," much as Donatists considered Caecilian's.

39. Frend, *Donatist Church*, pp. 148, 180–81 (Donatus died in exile, presumably around 355). For a sharp critique of ancient and modern "labeling techniques" in regard to the Donatists, see Brent D. Shaw, "African Christianity: Disputes, Definitions, and 'Donatists,'" in *Orthodoxy and Heresy in Religious Movements: Discipline and Dissent*, ed. Malcolm R. Greenshields and Thomas A. Robinson (Lewiston, N.Y.: Edwin Mellen Press, 1992), pp. 5–34.

40. Some investigators sent to North Africa by all accounts acted overzealously against Donatists. On the heavy-handed operations of the imperial agents Paul and Macarius, see Frend, *Donatist Church*, pp. 177–79. Also see Optatus of Milevis, *De schismate Donatistarum* 3.3. Even Augustine admits that they may have gone too far: *Psalmus contra partem Donati* 151–53, 165.

41. Although Julian's edict is not preserved, it is referred to in Ammianus Marcellinus 22.5 and Optatus of Milevis, *De schismate Donatistarum* 2.16. See Paul Monceaux, *Histoire littéraire de l'Afrique Chrétienne depuis les origines jusqu'à l'invasion Arabe*, Tome 4, *Le Donatisme* (Paris, 1912; reprint ed., Bruxelles: Culture et Civilisation, 1963), pp. 40–41, for discussion of Julian's edict and the Donatist response.

42. See Monceaux, *Histoire* t. 4, pp. 46–51, 55–57, and *Codex Theodosianus* 16.6.1, 5.5, 6.2–3; already in 373, Valentinian had sent an edict to the *proconsul Africae* forbidding second baptism (*CT* 16.6.1). In 377, an edict directed to the *vicarius Africae* (*CT* 16.6.2), again forbidding second baptism, gave to Catholics the churches of clerics who had rebaptized and ordered the confiscation of houses and *fundi* where heretics met.

43. Frend, *Donatist Church*, p. 210. Some Donatists in 372 may have sided with a rebellious African chieftain, Firmus, but it remains unclear to what extent populist feeling here aligned with religious sentiment. Count Theodosius, the father of the future emperor Theodosius I, who had put down Firmus's rebellion, was decapitated at Carthage for "aspiring to empire" (Jerome, *Chronicon ad ann.* 376; discussed in Monceaux, *Histoire*, t. 4, p. 47). By the late 370s, if not earlier, there was a Donatist contingent in Rome (See Optatus of Milevis, *De schismate Donatistarum* 2.4; Augustine, *ep.* 53.1.2; *Epistula ad Catholicos* [=*De unitate ecclesiae*] 3.6; *Contra litteras Petiliani* 2.109.247; Monceaux, *Histoire* t. 4, pp. 47, 268; see also the evidence assembled in Gerald Bonner, *St. Augustine of Hippo: Life and Controversies* [London: SCM Press, 1963], pp. 247–51). For summaries of the movement, see Frend, *Donatist Church* chaps. 1, 4, 5, 11–13; Bonner, *St. Augustine of Hippo*, chap. 6; Peter Brown, *Augustine of Hippo: A Biography* (Berkeley/Los Angeles: University of California Press, 1969), chaps. 18–21. For an old but richly detailed study of Donatism, see Monceaux, *Histoire littéraire, t. 4, Le Donatisme*; t. 6 of the same work contains an analysis of all known Donatist literature.

44. See suggestive evidence in Monceaux, *Histoire* t. 4, pp. 50, 51, 55–57 (the edicts of 395, 399, and 399 seem not to have applied). In another example, Optatus of Milevis, *De schismate Donatistarum* 2.18, reports an instance of the city magistrate of Tipasa standing by as Donatists attacked Catholics and Catholic property.

45. Lancel, *Actes* t. 1, p. 164.

46. For a brief review of that stability, see Maureen A. Tilley, *The Bible in Christian*

North Africa: The Donatist World (Minneapolis: Fortress Press, 1997), p. 131; Monceaux, *Histoire* t. 4, p. 323, stresses the fact that the Donatist Church was strongly centralized in organization. Frend (*Donatist Church*, p. 193) notes the long tenure (363–91) of the strong Donatist bishop, Parmenian of Carthage.

47. J. D. Mansi, *Sacrorum conciliorum collectio nova et amplissima* (Florence, 1759), III, 691, 867; discussion in Monceaux, *Histoire* t. 4, pp. 51–52, 351, who notes the bishops' "discouragement" and "despair." Augustine (*ep.* 44.5.12) hints that bishop Genethlius of Carthage actually prevented the application of imperial edicts attacking schismatics.

48. Mansi, *Sacrorum conciliorum collectio* III, 924; discussion in Monceaux, *Histoire* t. 4, pp. 367–70. Another Council of Carthage in 397 decided to send to Rome and Milan to ask their respective bishops about this move; although both rejected the idea, no repercussions seem to have resulted from their dissent.

49. Aurelius assumed the bishopric of Carthage in 392 (Monceaux, *Histoire* t. 4, p. 55); Augustine's close friend, Alypius, that of Thagaste, probably in 394 (see Lancel, *Actes* t. 1, p. 287, n.14, and Paulinus and Therasia, in Augustine, *ep.* 24.1).

50. See Monceaux, *Histoire* t. 4, pp. 56–57, 257, 376, and Tilley, *Bible*, p. 135, for a brief review of events. The Catholics hoped, up till 404, that they could win simply by propaganda and persuasion: Monceaux, *Histoire* t. 4, p. 67.

51. *Codex Theodosianus* 16.6.4, dated February 12, 405. Of course, one might argue that the edict was not well enforced, encouraging Donatists to carry on with their activities.

52. The leading modern investigator of the Council of Carthage in 411, Serge Lancel, posits that there was only a slight decline in Donatist power between 390 and 411 (*Actes*, p. 119). Donatists had lost around a dozen sees since 393 (p. 130).

53. For a strong statement of Donatist sympathies focusing on this principle, see Tilley, *Bible*, pp. 177–80. This community constituted the original Church of North Africa, which claimed the mid-third-century martyr-bishop of Carthage, Cyprian, as its ancestor and hero.

54. Purpurius of Limata: see Optatus of Milevis, *De schismate Donatistarum* 1.13, 1.19; also reported in the Acts of the Council of Cirta (305), Appendix 11 to Optatus's work. For Purpurius's penchant for theft, see Appendix 2 to Optatus's work, the *Gesta apud Zenophilum*.

55. For a few of the numerous reports in Augustine's writings on Circumcellion violence, see *Contra Cresconium* 3.42.46–43.47; *Breviculus collationis cum Donatistis* 11.22; *Ad Donatistas post collationem* 17.22; *Contra Gaudentium* 1.22.25, 36.46; *ep.* 185.3.13, 14.15, 7.25, 7.27, 7.30. Augustine is still railing against Donatist terrorism in the *Contra Iulianum* 3.2.5. Also see Optatus of Milevis, *De schismate Donatistarum* 3.4, 6.1–2, 4.

56. R. A. Markus, "Christianity and Dissent in Roman North Africa: Changing Perspectives in Recent Work," in *Schism, Heresy and Religious Protest*, ed. Derek Baker, Studies in Church History 9 (Cambridge: Cambridge University Press, 1972), p. 28: "It would be less misleading to speak of a 'catholic' than of a 'Donatist' schism" (discussing J. P. Brisson's *Autonomisme et Christianisme dans l'Afrique romaine* [Paris, 1958]).

57. "Discouraged": see Monceaux, *Histoire* t. 4., p. 51. Sources: The Catholic bishop, Optatus of Milevis, writing a generation before Augustine, around 366–67, gives some details in his *De schismate Donatistarum* of the earlier history of the controversy and appends to his account several documents concerning investigations of the Donatists; some limited accounts of church councils supplement this information, as well as various sermons and Donatist martyr stories. We also have some imperial edicts preserved in the *Codex Theodosianus*—of interest, but they seem largely to have been unenforceable.

58. Jerome, *De viris illustribus* 93.

59. For a discussion of evidence regarding the Romanization of towns such as Madauros and Thagaste, see Jean-Marie Lassère, *Ubique Populus: Peuplement et mouvements de population dans l'Afrique romaine de la chute de Carthage à la fin de la dynastie des Sévères (146 a.C.–235 p.C.)* (Paris: Editions du Centre National de la Recherche Scientifique, 1977).

60. *Gesta collatio Carthinagensis* 1.136.

61. Monceaux, *Histoire* t. 4, p. 77; Frend, *Donatist Church*, p. 184.

62. Augustine, *ep.* 44.6.14. Or, alternatively, they could pick a village that had no church of either persuasion, Augustine suggests.

63. West, *St. Augustine*, p. 140. Most notably, it was Apuleius's hometown. Augustine acknowledges this in *ep.* 138.4.19 and in *De civ. Dei* 8.14.2. On the "ancient Romanization" of Madauros, see Lassère, *Ubique Populus*, pp. 252–54.

64. *Gesta collatio Carthinagensis* 1.126.

65. Ibid., 1.126, 131, 133, 135 and 207, 139 and 217, 139, 143.

66. Ibid., 1.128, 143, 180, 217.

67. Ibid., 1.187, 202.

68. Ibid., 1.138, 201.

69. Ibid., 1.198, 215, 187.

70. Augustine, *epp.* 29.12; 35.2; 34.5; 43.8.24; 44.1.1; 44.6.14; 51; 66; 105.2.4; 87.10; 105.2.4; 209.2, respectively.

71. Brown, *Augustine*, p. 216.

72. Ibid., p. 167.

73. James J. O'Donnell, *Augustine: Confessions*, Vol. I, *Introduction and Text* (Oxford: Clarendon Press, 1992), p. xli (either all in 397, as O'Donnell believes; or between 397 and 401, as others have argued).

74. *Retr.* 1.16. Augustine's first possible reference to Donatism occurs in *Epistle* 20, in which he mentions "schism," although he does not specify it as "Donatist" (*ep.* 20.3).

75. Augustine, *Contra litteras Petiliani* 2.83.184. Indeed, they retained a strong presence at the time of the Council of Carthage in 411 (*Gesta collatio Carthinagensis* 1.138, 1.201; Macrobius, then the Donatist bishop of Hippo, reports in). Donatists still flourished in Hippo after the 405 edict: see Augustine, *epp.* 89.8; 111.1; 105; 106; 108.

76. Augustine, *Epistula ad Catholicos* (=*De unitate ecclesiae*) 5.9.

77. On this town, see Stéphane Gsell and Charles Albert Joly, *Khamissa, Mdaourouch, Announa: Fouilles exécutées par le Service des Monuments Historiques de l'Algerie. T. I: Khamissa* (Alger: Adolphe Jourdan; Paris: Fontemoing, 1914). Khamissa is ancient Thubursicu Numidarum.

78. Augustine, *Retr.* 1.20.3, commenting on a treatise no longer extant, *Contra epistulam Donati; Retr.* 2.54; cf. 2.60.

79. Editors comment that the *Psalmus contra partem Donati* is one of the earliest extant examples of Latin rhythmic poetry.

80. Augustine, *Psalmus contra partem Donati* 49–50, 57, 77. It is interesting to speculate whether Augustine borrowed the idea for composing propaganda via a rhyming song from Parmenian, Donatist bishop of Carthage, who had composed such songs for Donatists. See Frend, *Donatist Church*, pp. 193–94, citing Augustine, *ep.* 55.18.34 and Praedestinatus, *De haeresibus* 43. In commenting on Psalm 118 (an acrostic psalm), Augustine remarks that acrostic psalms have been devised in Latin and in Punic (*Enarrationes in Psalmos* 118.32.8); one wonders if the "Punic" ones were associated with the Donatists. See Fergus

Millar, "Local Cultures in the Roman Empire: Libyan, Punic and Latin in Roman Africa," *Journal of Roman Studies* 58 (1968): 133.

81. So dated by Mary Inez Bogan, *Saint Augustine, The Retractions* (Washington, D.C.: Catholic University of America Press, 1968), p. 180. The work is not extant.

82. *Retr.* 2.55, describing the *Probationum et testimonium contra Donatistas*.

83. See Yvette Duval, *Loca Sanctorum Africae: Le Culte des martyrs en Afrique du IVᵉ au VIIᵉ siècle. T. I* (Rome: Ecole française de Rome, 1982), pp. 182–83 (from a manuscript in the Bibliothèque Vittorio Emmanuele at Rome, ms. 2099 fol. 168).

84. Brown, *Augustine*, p. 221; West, *St. Augustine*, p. 140.

85. Monceaux, *Histoire*, t. 4, p. 67; Frend, *Donatist Church*, p. 234; Brown, *Augustine*, pp. 235–37. Thus in *ep.* 43.1.1, he is willing to give the Donatists of Thubursicu Numidarum the benefit of the doubt: they simply inherited the wrong teaching from their parents; he is convinced that they are eager for the truth and are prepared to be set aright. Augustine, *Retr.* 2.31, commenting on *Contra partem Donati* admits that in his earlier encounters with Donatism he did not understand how much evil they would attempt and how the strong hand of "discipline" might be necessary to bring them over.

86. Thus the editor of the Fathers of the Church translation of the *Retractions* (Sister Mary Inez Bogan), p. 87.

87. Augustine, *epp.* 23.2–4, 35.2.

88. Augustine, *epp.* 23.6, 29.12, 34.2–3, 35.1, 43.8.24; *Psalmus contra partem Donati* 25, 90, 156; *Enarrationes in Psalmos* 10.5.

89. Possidius, *Vita Augustini* 12.

90. Augustine, *Enarrationes in Psalmos* 36.2.20.

91. Understandably, some Donatists were reluctant to take him on (*ep.* 35.4). Also, see *ep.* 44 for an account of his discussion/debate at Thubursicu.

92. See the comments of Mark Vessey, above, n. 38.

93. *Retr.* 1.12.6; the story of Jesus' casting out the moneychangers is found in Mark 11:15–17 and parallels. For other "corrections" to his earlier reluctance concerning his use of force in the Donatist controversy, see *Retr.* 2.31; now, he bluntly classifies the Donatists as heretics, not just as schismatics (2.52). For two essays by Peter Brown detailing Augustine's growing willingness to countenance "coercion" of Donatists, see "St. Augustine's Attitude to Religion Coercion," *Journal of Roman Studies* 54 (1964): 107–16, and "Religious Coercion in the Later Roman Empire: The Case of North Africa," *History* 47 (1963): 283–305; both essays are reprinted in Brown, *Religion and Society in the Age of Saint Augustine* (New York: Harper & Row, 1972), pp. 260–78, 301–31.

94. See above, n. 23.

95. D. J. Mattingly, "Africa: A Landscape of Opportunity?" in *Dialogues in Roman Imperialism: Power, Discourse, and Discrepant Experience in the Roman Empire*, ed. D. J. Mattingly (Portsmouth, R.I.: Journal of Roman Archaeology Supplementary Series 23, 1997), p. 135; Greg Woolf, *Becoming Roman: The Origins of Provincial Civilization in Gaul* (Cambridge: Cambridge University Press, 1998), pp. 19–20.

96. Mattingly, "Africa," p. 134. For Greece, see S. E. Alcock, "Greece: A Landscape of Resistance?" in *Dialogues in Roman Imperialism*, pp. 103–15, and her monograph, *Graecia Capta: The Landscapes of Roman Greece* (Cambridge: Cambridge University Press, 1993).

97. J. B. Rives, *Religion and Authority in Roman Carthage from Augustus to Constantine* (Oxford: Clarendon Press, 1995), p. 41.

98. L. A. Thompson, "Settler and Native in the Urban Centres of Roman Africa," in

Africa in Classical Antiquity: Nine Studies, ed. L. A. Thompson and J. Ferguson (Ibadan: Ibadan University Press, 1969), p. 170.

99. Mattingly, "Africa," p. 123.

100. Rives, *Religion*, p. 161, n.106, extracting data from the tables provided by Thompson, "Settler and Native," pp. 170–81. Rives comments that elites were now happy to be identified with Africa (pp. 149, 250).

101. P. A. Brunt, *Roman Imperial Themes* (Oxford: Clarendon Press, 1990), p. 268 (the chapter from which these references are taken, "The Romanization of the Local Ruling Classes in the Roman Empire," originally appeared in *Assimilation et résistance à la culture gréco-romaine dans le monde ancien* [Paris: Les Belles Lettres, 1976]); also see W. S. Hanson, "Forces of Change and Methods of Control," in *Dialogues in Roman Imperialism*, p. 78.

102. Brunt, *Roman Imperial Themes*, pp. 268, 269, 271, 276; C. R. Whittaker, "Imperialism and Culture: the Roman Initiative," in *Dialogues in Roman Imperialism*, p. 159; C. D. B. Jones, "Concluding Remarks," in *Dialogues in Roman Imperialism*, pp. 195–96; Rives, *Religion*, p. 169; Woolf, *Becoming Roman*, pp. 18, 30ff.

103. Tacitus, *Agricola* 21, cited in Woolf, *Becoming Roman*, p. 69. In Peter Brunt's phrase, "Provincials Romanized themselves" (*Roman Imperial Themes*, p. 268).

104. Mattingly, "Africa," pp. 17ff., 130.

105. Woolf, *Becoming Roman*, pp. 15, 18, 74–75; Rives, *Religion*, p. 169.

106. *Codex Theodosianus* 14.9.1. For Africans in Rome, see the epigraphical study of Cecilia Ricci, "Africani a Roma: Testimonianze epigrafiche de età imperiale provenienti dal Nordafrica," *Antiquités africaines* 30 (1994): 189–207 (the social level of Africans settling in Rome rises, she concludes, starting from the middle second century C.E.). For relics of an African martyr in Rome, see Damasus, *Epigrammata* 46 ("the birth which creates saints made him a Roman citizen"); I thank Maura Lafferty for pointing out this epigram to me.

107. Brunt, *Roman Imperial Themes*, p. 273, citing *Aeneid* 1.278–79. Brunt pointedly remarks that, unlike the later colonial powers of France and Britain, the Romans brought no notions of liberty and equality that would eventually subvert their own rule. For a discussion of the inscription from Thubursicu Numidarum celebrating the "Greek and Latin" culture of two young men, sent by their father to Carthage for education but who died at ages 18 and 21, see Tadeusz Kotula, "*Utraque lingua eruditi*: Une page relative à l'histoire de l'éducation dans l'Afrique romaine," in *Hommages à Marcel Renard*, ed. Jacqueline Bibauw. Collection Latomus 102 (Bruxelles: Latomus/Revues d'Etudes Latines, 1969), pp. 386–92.

108. Clifford Ando, *Imperial Ideology and Provincial Loyalty in the Roman Empire* (Berkeley, Los Angeles, and London: University of California Press, 2000), p. xiii.

109. Ibid., explicit at pp. 75–79.

110. Ibid., e.g., pp. 277, 59, 66, 68.

111. Ibid., pp. 374, cf. 338. An African uprising of 238 is discussed on pp. 243–44.

112. So John Ferguson, "Aspects of Early Christianity in North Africa," in *Africa in Classical Antiquity*, p. 184.

113. A central thesis of Frend's *Donatist Church*; see esp. chaps. 2 and 3. Among other points that have been raised against Frend's thesis is that the language division does not fall out so neatly: several of Augustine's Donatist sparring partners were well-educated, even to the degree of arguing with him about Graecizing word constructions (see Augustine's retorts to the Donatist grammarian Cresconius in his *Contra Cresconium*). For an early cri-

tique of Frend's thesis, see Peter Brown, "Christianity and Local Culture in Late Roman Africa," *Journal of Roman Studies* 58 (1968): 85–95 (= *Religion and Society*, pp. 279–300).
114. Julian in Augustine, *Contra Iulianum* 3.17.32; *Opus imperfectum* 3.199.
115. Robert A. Markus, *Saeculum: History and Society in the Theology of St. Augustine*, rev. ed. (Cambridge: Cambridge University Press, 1988), p. 155.
116. *Conf.* 1.13.22; 9.5; cf. *Ep.* 118.2.9.
117. See, e.g., *Conf.* 6.6.9; 8.12.30; Possidius, *Vita Augustini* 1, and discussions of Augustine's social situation in Brown, *Augustine*, pp. 21–27; Claude Lepelley, "Un Aspect de la Conversion d La Rupture avec ses ambitions sociales et politiques," *Bulletin de littérature ecclésiastique* 88 (1987): 229–46; idem, "Saint Augustin et la Cité Romano—Africaine," in *Jean Chrysostome et Augustin: Actes du Colloque de Chantilly 22–24 septembre 1974*, ed. Charles Kannengiesser. Théologie Historique 35 (Paris: Editions Beauschesne, 1975), pp. 13–39; and idem, "*Spes Saeculi*: Le Milieu social d'Augustin et ses ambitions séculières avant sa conversion," *Atti: Congresso Internazionale su S. Agostino nel XVI centenario della conversione, Roma, 15–20 septembre 1986.* Studia Ephemeridis "Augustinianum" 24 (Roma: Institutum Patristicum "Augustinianum," 1987), pp. 99–231, for the social and geographical background of Augustine.
118. Augustine, *Epistula ad Catholicos* (=*De unitate ecclesiae*) 16.40–41, 24.69; *Sermo* 46.15.37.
119. Augustine, *Contra litteras Petiliani* 1.13.14; cf. 2.8.20, 2.13.30, 2.14.33, 2.109.247, 3.6.7, 3.50.62. Similar themes in *Epistula ad Catholicos* (=*De unitate ecclesia*) 3.6, 7.16, 8.20; *Contra Cresconium* 1.33.39, 4.60.73; *Enarrationes in Psalmos* 85.1; 119.7; 54.20; *Sermo* 46.37; *ep.* 185.1.3, 1.5. Likewise, they imagine that the word *catholic* means "having the fullness of the sacraments," not, as Augustine claims is correct, "being in communion with all nations" (*Breviculus collationis cum Donatistis* 3.3.3).
120. *Epistula ad Catholicos* (=*De unitate ecclesiae*) 16.42. Elsewhere, Augustine interprets "Tyre" to signal "*angustia sive tribulatio*" (*Enarrationes in Psalmos* 82.7). The Donatist equation of Tyre with Carthage (its colony, according to ancient mythology) comes through in the chronicle known as the *Liber genealogicus* 196, with some assistance from *Aeneid* 1.12: *Tyrii tennere coloni Karthago "urbs antiqua fuit utique Tyrorum"* (*Monumenta Germaniae Historica, Auctorum Antiquissimorum IX: Chronica Minora Saec. IV.V. VI. VII*, ed. Theodor Mommsen [Berlin: Weidmann, 1891], p. 169).
121. Bill Jobling, "The 'Aqaba-Ma'an Archaeological and Epigraphic Survey 1988–1990," *Syria* 70 (1993): 244.
122. I borrow the title of Keith Hopkins' essay, "Conquest by Book," in *Literacy in the Roman World*, ed. Mary Beard et al., Journal of Roman Archaeology Supplement Series 3 (Ann Arbor: University of Michigan Press, 1991), pp. 133–58.
123. "Gratitude" for the gift does not, in Augustine's scheme, make the gift any less a gift; Augustine might disagree with Bennington's description of Derrida's writings on this point ("Derridabase," p. 188).
124. For a discussion of Augustine's anti-Pelagian writings and activities, see the overview in Brown, *Augustine*, chaps. 29–33.
125. Jerome, *In Hieremiam*, prologus 4: *stolidissimus et Scottorum pultibus praegravatus.*
126. See, for example, Pelagius, *Ad Demetriadem* 16.2.

Why Augustine? Why Now?

Jean Bethke Elshtain

The fate of St. Augustine in the world of academic political theory has been, at best, mixed. He is, first of all, enveloped in that blanket of suspicion cast over all "religious" or "theological" thinkers: do they *really* belong with the likes of Plato and Aristotle, Machiavelli and Hobbes, Marx and Mill? Weren't their eyes cast heavenward rather than fixed resolutely on human political and social affairs? There are, as well, particular features to St. Augustine's work that make him a tough nut to crack. He is an ambitiously discursive and narrative thinker. From the time of his conversion to Catholic Christianity in 386 to his death as Bishop of Hippo in 430, Augustine wrote some 117 books. He touches on all the central themes of Christian theology and Christian life: the nature of God and human persons, the problem of evil, free will and determinism, war and human aggression, the bases of social life and political order, church doctrine, Christian vocations—the list is nigh endless.

Although a number of his works follow an argumentative line in the manner most often favored by political theorists, especially so given the distinctly juridical or legalistic cast of so much modern political theory, most often he paints bold strokes on an expansive canvas. His enterprise is at once theological, philosophical, historical, cultural, and rhetorical. His works are characterized by an extraordinarily rich surface as well as vast depth, making it difficult to get a handle on them if one's own purposes are not so ambitious. He traffics in what we generally call "universals," but he is also a nuanced "particularist" and historicist.

Given this towering enterprise, it is perhaps unsurprising that attempts have been made to reduce Augustine to manageable size. To that end he got tagged a political realist and canonized, if you will, as the theological grandfather of a tradition that includes Machiavelli and Hobbes. Then too, Augustine, if he is read at all, is read primarily in and through excerpts from his great works that most favorably comport with this "political realism." To this end, his *Confessions* are ignored and Book XIX of his 1,091-page masterwork *The City of God* (in the Penguin Classics unabridged version) is reproduced with certain bits highlighted, along with, perhaps, a chunk from Book I, chapter 1, on "the city of this world, a city which aims at dominion, which holds nations in enslavement, but is itself dominated by that very lust of domination."[1] Book II, chapter 21, is helpful on Augustine's alternative to Cicero's judgment (according to Scipio) on the Roman commonwealth. Book XV, chapter 1, traces lines of descent of the "two cities, speaking allegorically"; Book XIX, chapter 14, as already noted, is mined for a few precepts about the interests government should serve; chapter 15 makes an argument against slavery "by nature"; and chapter 21, in which Scipio's definition of a commonwealth as advanced by Cicero makes a second appearance, also seems pertinent. Chapter 7 of Book XIX is culled as the justification of war argument. Perhaps—just perhaps—excerpts are drawn from chapters 14, 15, and 16, in order to demonstrate Augustine's insistence that there is a connection between the peace and good of the household in relation to the city. That, plus his scathing comment that what pirates do with one boat, Romans do with a navy, but the one is called brigandage while the other is named Empire, and the student has her quick intake of what I have called "Augustine Lite." The upshot is a shriven Augustine, numbered among the pessimists and charged with being among those who stress human cruelty and violence with a concomitant need for order, coercion, punishment, and occasional war.

Recognizing the inadequacy of this "normalized" Augustine doesn't mean one has an easy task if one's purpose is to be fair to Augustine's complexity with the enterprise of political theory in mind, in part for the reasons noted above concerning Augustine's way of writing and arguing. But even more pertinent is the theorist's sense of the task of political theory. If one construes that task as a way of putting together anthropological presuppositions (what we used to call "theories of human nature"), claims about the political and social order in light of those presuppositions, the role of political theory in relation to these interrelated tasks, and the perils and possibilities inherent to any political activity or order, then Augustine's expansiveness is a welcome thing indeed. If one's aims are narrower or more modest, Augustine's expansiveness is a frustration. I begin from the point of view that his expansiveness is welcome. What follows is a way of highlighting key points of theoretical demarcation in Augustine's work that are rich with implications for political theory.

Augustine on the Self

In his wonderful biography of St. Augustine, noted historian of the late antique world Peter Brown claims that Augustine has "come as near to us . . . as the vast gulf that separates a modern man from the culture and religion of the later empire can allow."[2] How so? One reason, surely, lies in Augustine's complex ruminations on the nature of selfhood. This is a theme close to our own preoccupations. Augustine, in fact, anticipates postmodern strategies in dethroning the Cartesian subject even before that subject got erected. For Augustine, the mind can never be transparent to itself; we are never wholly in control of our thoughts; our bodies are essential, not contingent, to who we are and how we think; and we know that we exist, not because "I think, therefore I am," but rather, "I doubt, therefore I know I exist." Only a subject who is a self that can reflect on itself can doubt. His *Confessions* is a story of a human being who has become a question to himself.

The story begins with an infant—here too, Augustine is radical within the context of political theory, which often seems to assume that human beings spring full-blown from the head of John Locke! Augustine starts with natality and intimates a developmental account featuring a fragile, dependent creature who is by no means a *tabula rasa*, but rather, a being at once social and "quarrelsome." The human being is driven by hunger, desire, and frustration at his or her inability to express himself or herself and to get others to respond. Growing up is not about getting rid of these childish emotions—these are key ingredients of our natures and our ability to understand—but rather, it is about forming and shaping our passions in light of certain presuppositions about human beings, human willing, and our faltering attempts to will and to act rightly. Augustine's awareness of the sheer messiness of human existence lies at the heart of his withering fire directed at Stoic *apatheia*. For the mind to be in a state "in which the mind cannot be touched by any emotion whatsoever, who would not judge this insensitivity to be the worst of all moral defects?"(DCD XIV, 9, 565).[3] We begin as, and we remain, beings who love, who yearn, who grieve, who experience frustration. The most important point here is Augustine's insistence that thought can never be purged of the emotions and that the thinking self expresses complex emotion through thought and in a language that is, it is hoped, up to the task.

Epistemologically, thinking, including that mode of thinking called philosophic, should not pretend to a clean separation between emotion and reason; rather, these are interlaced and mutually constitute one another. Augustine argues that certain philosophies abstract from, or offer unreal assessments of, our human condition by taking insufficient account of embodiment and should be rejected for that reason. The body is epistemologically significant, a source of delight, of travail, of knowledge of good and evil. The body is the mode through which we connect to the world and through which the world discloses itself. Mind is embodied; body is thought. The heart of Augustine's case against the Pelagians also lies here, given their over-estimation of human control of the will, of *voluntas*. In the words of philosopher James Wetzel, "Pelagius seemed in the end to deny that there were ever significant obstacles to living the good life, once reason had illuminated its nature, [thus] he stood in more obvious continuity with the philosophical tradition than Augustine, who came to disparage the worldly wisdom of pagan philosophy for its overconfidence."[4] Augustine is an epistemological skeptic who believes, nonetheless, that we can come to know certain truths. There are warranted beliefs, but we can approach these only through complex indirection and through love (*caritas*), a formed desire and the name given to a "good" of a sort that spills over the boundaries of the self and reaches out to others and to the source of love, God. We may not be able to verify most of what we believe—for we cannot be everywhere, see everything, experience everything—but our believing isn't a flying leap into the darkness.

Given the fact that all human beings are creatures attempting to express desire (whether disordered or ordered), and that they must do so though language, our words are open to misunderstanding and to multiple, ambiguous interpretation by other similarly desiring creatures. This suggests a theory of language, and Augustine offers one that influenced the work of Ludwig Wittgenstein, among others. (I will say more on this below.) What captures the interest of such desiring creatures? Our selves, for one thing. Because we are driven by *delectio*, by desire and yearning, we search for enjoyment, including pleasures of the intellect. Indeed, we acquire self-knowledge by trying our "strength in answering, not in word but in deed, what may be called the interrogation of temptation" (*DCD* XVI, 32, 693–94). We come to self-knowledge through our interaction with the world. We make mistakes—proving that we exist—and we carry on, having learned something from the very clumsiness of our deed-doing.

But it is never easy for the mind to unlock things. As beings circumscribed by the boundaries of time and space, we require certain fundamental categories in order to *see* the world at all. Otherwise, all would be flux. In addition to time and space, we require a form that incorporates reason and the will—that is, so to speak, up to our complexity. Augustine finds this form in the Trinity, a principle that works through complex relational analogies involving similarities and dissimilarities, things seen and unseen, at one and the same time.[5] We are capable of forming concepts about things we have seen and things we have not seen. We imagine many things to be, in part because we know what it means to have, or to bear, the "trace" of an image. We believe many things exist—rightly so—that are not personally known to us. Augustine writes:

> And in fact when I wish to speak of Carthage, I seek for what to say within myself, and find an image of Carthage within myself; but I received this through the body, that is, through the sense of the body, since I was present there in the body, and have seen and perceived it with my senses, and have retained it in my memory, that I might find the word about it within myself whenever I might wish to utter it. For its image in my mind is its word, not the sound of the three syllables when Carthage [Car-tha-go in Latin] is named, or even when that name is silently thought of during some period of time, but the word that I see in my mind when I utter this word of three syllables with my voice, or even before I utter it. . . . So too, when I wish to speak of Alexandria which I have never seen, an image of it is also present within me.[6]

Augustine uses the metaphor of fabrication—of making things—in order to drive home this point. "A worker makes a chest. At first he has the chest in his skill-knowledge: For if he did not have it in his skill-knowledge, how could it be brought forth by making? But the chest as it is in his skill-knowledge is not the chest as it appears to our eyes. In skill-knowledge it exists invisibly, in the work it will exist visibly."[7] When we gaze upon things in the mind, through a complex word-name-image nexus, we are not untrammeled in this imagining. There is an available repertoire. It is linguistic, historic, contingent, time-bound. It is caught within the confines and limits of our embodiment. So although naming and imagining is "wonderful," it is also constrained. We cannot imagine just anything. If, as Wittgenstein says, a lion could speak and we could not understand him, so we can say that if a giraffe could imagine, we could not recognize the imagining. We are not nibbling off treetops and gazing across the savannah from a great height! (This and more, but I assume the point is taken.)

This leads directly to Augustine on language and the constraints imposed on us by language. As *par excellence* the language users among God's creatures, we bump up all the time against opacity and constraint. In Book XIX, chapter 7, Augustine muses about the ways in which all humans are divided by linguistic differences. These differences make it very hard for us to understand one another:

> The diversity of languages separates man from man. For if two men meet and are forced by some compelling reason not to pass on but to stay in company, then if neither knows the other's language, it is easier for dumb animals, even of different kinds, to associate together than these men, although both are human beings. For when men cannot communicate their thoughts to each other, simply because of difference of language, all the similarity of their common human nature is of no avail to unite them in fellowship. So true is this that a man would be more cheerful with his dog for company than with a foreigner. I shall be told that the Imperial City has been at pains to impose on conquered peoples not only her yoke but her language also, as a bond of peace and fellowship, so that there should be no lack of interpreters but even a profusion of them. True; but think of the cost of this achievement! Consider the scale of those wars, with all the slaughter of human beings, all the human blood that was shed! (*DCD* XIX, 7, 861)

Here Augustine moves from the murkiness of language, how it divides us despite our common human nature, to the imposition of a language on diverse peoples but at a truly terrible price. We find, then, a drawing together of notions of human nature; language and its centrality in constituting us as living creatures; the complexity of a search for fellowship; and a pithy critique of the enforced homogeneity of empire.

The upshot of the force of linguistic convention, finally, is that human beings can only achieve what Augustine calls "creature's knowledge." Full knowledge is not available to human knowers, no matter how brilliant and learned that knower. We are both limited and enabled by the conventions of language. No one can jump out of his or her linguistic skin. We are obliged to bow to "normal usage" if we hope to communicate at all, and we are driven to communicate by our sociality, a sociality that goes all the way down. This sociality lies at the basis of Augustine on the nature of human societies.

Augustine on Social Life

Human beings are, I noted above, social all the way down. Created in the image of God, human relationality defines us. The self is not and cannot be freestanding. Social life is full of ills and yet to be cherished. Thus, civic life, among those social forms, is not simply what sin has brought into the world but what emerges, in part, given our capacity for love, our use of reason, as well (alas) as a pervasive lust for domination attendant upon human affairs. "The philosophers hold the view that the life of the wise man should be social, and in this we support them heartily." Indeed the city of God—Augustine's way of characterizing that pilgrim band of Christians during their earthly sojourn in and through a community of reconciliation and fellowship that presages the heavenly kingdom—could never have had "its first start . . . if the life of the saints were not social" (DCD XIX, 6, 860). All human beings, without exception, are citizens of the earthly kingdom—the city of Man—and even in this fallen condition there is a kind of "natural likeness" that forges bonds between us. These "bonds of peace" do not suffice to prevent wars, dissensions, cruelty, and misery of all kinds, but we are nonetheless called to membership based on a naturalistic sociality and basic morality available to all rational creatures. A kind of unity in plurality pushes toward harmony; but the sin of division—with its origins in pride and willfulness—drives us apart.

Yet it is love of friendship that lies at the root of what might be called Augustine's "practical philosophy," his history, ethics, social and political philosophy.[8] Pinioned between alienation and affection, human beings—those "cracked pots"—are caught in the tragedy of alienation but glued by love. Our sociality is a given, so for Augustine the question is not should we be social or should we trust enough to love, but rather: "What shall I love and how shall I love it?"[9] His complex ethical theory follows and can only be touched on here, but it must be noted that political life is one form that human social and ethical life assumes. We are always in society, and we always seek the consolation of others. Society, for Augustine, is a species of friendship, and friendship is a moral union in and through which human beings strive for a shared good. All of Augustine's central categories, including war and peace, are in the form of a relationship of one sort or another. And the more we are united at all levels in a bond of peace, the closer we come to achieving that good at which we aim and which God intends.

For Augustine, neighborliness and reciprocity emerge from ties that bind, beginning with familial bonds and extending from these particular relations outward: the filaments of affection must not stop at the portal to the *domus*. Augustine writes: "The aim was that one man should not combine many relationships in his one self, but that those connections should be separated and spread among individuals, and that in this way they should help to bind social life more effectively by involving in their plurality a plurality of persons" (DCD XV, 16, 623). The social tie is "not confined to a small group" but extends "more widely to a large number with the multiplying links of kinship" (624). The importance of plurality, of the many emerging from a unique one—for God began with the singular—cannot be underestimated in Augustine's work. It is his way of putting into a single frame human uniqueness and individuality with sociality and plurality. Bonds of affection tied human beings from the start. Bonds of kinship and affection bound them further. These relationships got dispersed, finally encompassing the entire globe.

In light of the confusion and confounding of human languages, it is sometimes difficult to repair this fundamental sociality, but we yearn for it and seek it in and through the social forms we create: thus civic order, a primary requisite for human existence. This civic order is a normative good although, *pace* Aristotle, civic order, or what we routinely call "the state," does not fulfill or complete our natures; rather, it expresses them and may do so in ways deadly or ways less cruel. Here it is important to note that for Augustine no human being has natural dominion over any other. There is no slavery by nature. We are by nature social, but that doesn't dictate any particular form of social order. Nor does Augustine analogize from the authority of fathers in households to political rule. Classical patriarchal theory holds that rule by fathers is at once natural and political, that a natural right translates into political authority and legitimation. But for Augustine, political authority is different from familial authority. To the extent that one is subject to a ruler, one is subject in status only and not by nature.

There are temporal goods that are worthy—first and foremost, peace. So human civic life is not simply a remedy for sin—with order and coercion needed to constrain our wickedness—but an expression of our sociality, our desire for fellowship, our capacity for a diffuse *caritas*. It follows that Cicero's definition of a *Res publica*, as refracted through the writings of Scipio, is wanting. For Cicero, civic order is an association based on common agreement concerning right and on shared interests. Insufficient, argues Augustine. Rather, a people gathered together in a civic order is a gathering or multitude of rational beings united in fellowship by sharing a common love of the same things. Using this definition, we not only define what a society is, but we can also assess what it is people hold dear— what *sort* of society is *this*?

It is worth noting at this juncture that a debate in current Augustinian scholarship concerns precisely how one should rank the good of political society for Augustine. The traditional (and overly simple) claim that for Augustine civic order is simply a remedy for sin has been effectively challenged. Now the question seems to be just how important to Augustine's thought overall is the good at which civic life tends and how much this derives from, and can be achieved through, the exercise of human voluntary activity. The dangers inherent within earthly political life are manifest, the fruits of pride that seeks domination over others and glories only in the self or the "empire." The goods to be attained through civic life are sketchier, but they begin with Augustine's basic rule for human earthly life, namely, that we should do no harm and should help whenever we can (a requisite of neighbor love).

It is the interplay of *caritas* and *cupiditas* that is critical, and whether one or the other prevails at a given point in time, whether within the very being of a single person or within the life of a civic order. Augustine would tame the occasions for the reign of *cupiditas* and the activation of the *libido dominandi*, or lust to dominate, and maximize the space within which *caritas* operates. For a lust to dominate taints and perverts all human relations, from family to city. Similarly, a decent love, a concern for the well-being of all in the household or in the city, strengthens the delicate filaments of peace. The sin that mars the earthly city is the story of arbitrary power or the ever-present possibility of such. By contrast, the basis for a more just order is fueled by love. The theme of the two cities is the metaphor that enables Augustine to trace the choreography of human relations. Every human community is plagued by a "poverty stricken kind of power . . . a kind of scramble . . . for lost dominions and . . . honors," but there is simultaneously present the life-forgiving and gentler aspects of loving concern, mutuality, domestic and civic peace (*DCD* XI, 1, 429).

There are two fundamentally different attitudes evinced within human social life and enacted by human beings. One attitude is a powerful feeling of the fullness of life. A human being will not be denuded if he or she gives, or makes a gift of, the self to others. One's dependence on others is not a diminution but an enrichment of the self. The other attitude springs from cramped and cribbed selfishness, resentment, a penury of spirit. The way one reaches out or down to others from these different attitudes is strikingly distinct. From a spirit of resentment and contempt, one condescends toward the other; one is hostile to life itself. But from that fellow feeling in our hearts for the misery of others, we come to their help by coming together with them. Authentic compassion (the working-out of *caritas*) eradicates contempt and distance. But this working out can never achieve anything like perfection in the realm of earthly time and history (the *saeculum*).

In Robert Markus's book *Saeculum*, widely acknowledged as one of the most important attempts to unpack and to situate Augustine as a civic and political theorist, he argues that Augustine aimed for a number of complex things with his characterization of the two cities. One was to sort out the story of all earthly cities. Augustine, he argues, provides an account of the earthly city (*civitas terrena*) from Assyria through Rome and shows the ways in which even the cherished goal of peace all too often ends in conquest and domination, hence no real peace at all. The fullness of peace is reserved for the heavenly city (*civitas dei*) and its eternal peace. In this way Augustine creates barriers to the absolutizing of any political arrangement.[10] Markus suggests that Augustine's repudiation of the theology underwriting the notion of an *imperium Christianum* lies in part in his worry that any identification of the city of God with an earthly order invites sacralization of human arrangements and a dangerous idolatry. At the same time, as I point out, earthly institutions have a real claim on us, and our membership in a polity is not reducible to misery and punishment for Augustine. He begins with a presumption of the priority of peace over war, and he repudiates all stories of mythical human beginnings that presume disorder and war as our primordial condition. The earthly city derives from our turning away from love and its source (God) toward willfulness and a "poverty stricken kind of power." The upshot is division—within the self, between self and other, between nations and cultures: this is a destructive division by contrast to the plurality and contrast Augustine cherished.

So temporal peace is a good. Amidst the shadows that hover over and among us, there are, as I already noted, two rules that are within our reach and that we should follow: "first, to do no harm to anyone, and, secondly, to help everyone whenever possible" (DCD XIX, 14, 873). The most just human civic arrangements are those that afford the widest scope to non-harm-doing and to fellowship and mutuality. If mutuality, even of the earthly imperfect sort, is to be attained, there must be a compromise between human wills, and the earthly city must find a way to forge bonds of peace. This human beings find very difficult by definition, given the distortions of the *libido dominandi,* the lust to dominate.

By contrast, the heavenly city on earthly pilgrimage is better able to forge peace by calling out "citizens from all nations and so collect[ing] a society of aliens, speaking all languages." She—the *civitas dei*—does this, not by annulling or abolishing earthly differences, but even through maintaining them so "long as God can be worshipped" (DCD XIX, 18, 878). Here it is important to note that whatever Augustine's acquiescence in the received social arrangements of his time, he left as a permanent legacy a condemnation of that lust for dominion that distorts the human personality, marriage, the family, and all other human social relations, including civic life and membership. Augustine is scathing in his denunciation of arrogant pridefulness; unstinting in his praise of the works of service, neighborliness, and a love that simultaneously judges and succors. (Judges because we must distinguish good from evil, selfishness from kindness, and so on.) Love and justice are intertwined both on earth and in heaven. Yet the world is filled with horrors, including war. How does Augustine square his regretful justification of a certain sort of war with his call to love and peace? It is to this theme that I now turn.

Augustine on War and Peace

A full treatment of this theme—indeed of all the issues taken up to this point—would require an assessment of Augustine's complex theodicy. That is beyond the scope of this essay. But a brief discussion is needed in order to grasp Augustine's theology of war and peace. Augustine acknowledges the seductive allure of evil. He famously tells the story of a youthful prank—stealing pears—that was done, not from hunger but from pleasure in the deed itself and in the fellowship with others who took part in the deed. It took Augustine many years, including a sustained detour through Manicheanism, before he rejected metaphysical dualism decisively and repudiated any claim that evil is a self-sustaining, generative principle of opposition to good. The Manicheans had located evil in creation itself as the work of a demonic demiurge; thus, the body was tainted by definition. But for Augustine, creation is good. The body is good, not polluted. It is what we do with the body, what we do to creation, that marks our bodies with the stain of sin, wickedness, and cruelty at any given point in time. Augustine's famous articulation of human free will enters at this juncture—a concept Hannah Arendt credits with being an original contribution by Augustine. We can choose to do wrong and we often do, for we are marked from the beginning with the trace of originary disobedience. The choice of evil is in and of itself "an impressive proof that the *nature* is good" (*DCD* XI, 17, 448).

Evil is a falling away from the good, and we are the agents of this falling away, not because the body is corrupt, but because we can defile it. There is no such thing as evil "by nature." Evil is the turning of a limited creature from God to himself, and hence to an absolutizing of his own flawed will. This turning may become habitual, a kind of second nature. In this way, Augustine gives evil its due without giving it the day. Evil is the name we give to a class of acts and putative motives. The fruits of this turning away include a hatred of finitude and a fateful thirst for what might be called a kind of anti-creation: a lust to destroy. War is a species of that destruction; hence, war is always a tragedy even "when just." But if war is *primus inter pares* an example of human sinfulness and a turning from the good, how can it possibly be justified under any circumstances?

It works like this. Augustine begins by deconstructing the Roman peace as a false claim to peace. Instead, Rome conquered and was herself conquered by her own lust to dominate over others. "Think of all the battles fought, all the blood that was poured out, so that almost all the nations of Italy, by whose help the Roman Empire wielded that overwhelming power, should be subjugated as if they were barbarous savages."[11] Rome was driven by a lust for vengeance and cruelty, and these triumphed under the cherished name of peace. The Empire became a kingdom without justice, and this is little more than a criminal gang on a grand scale. Here Augustine famously repeats the story of the rejoinder given by a captured pirate to Alexander the Great when Alexander queried him about his idea in infesting the sea. "And the pirate answered, with uninhibited insolence, 'The same as yours, in infesting the earth! But because I do it with a tiny craft, I'm called a pirate: because you have a mighty navy, you're called an emperor.'" Augustine even suggests that the Romans should have erected a monument to the foreign "other" and called her "Aliena" because they made such good use of her by proclaiming that all their wars were defensive; it was therefore necessary to conjure up an implacable foreign foe in order to justify these ravages. For Rome, peace became just another name for *dominium*. If war's ravages are in part a punishment for sin, human beings sin, often savagely, in enacting that punishment. Primarily, however, Augustine emphasizes the freely chosen nature of war and assigns responsibility to those who engage in it.

If you reflect on the terrible slaughter of war carried out for wicked motives and to unworthy ends, you will determine to wage only limited, justifiable wars, even as you lament the fact that they must sometimes be waged, given injustice: so Augustine argues. There are occasional real wars of defense. The wise ruler and polity takes up arms only with great reluctance and penitence. Given Augustine's account of limited justifiability for wars fought only for certain motives, he is frequently lodged as the grandfather of just-war thinking. (Others, of course, rank him as a forebear of political realism. There is no reason he cannot be both, depending on what one understands by realism and just war respectively.) Augustine appreciates what modern international relations theorists call the "security dilemma." People never possess a kingdom "so securely as not to fear subjugation by their enemies; in fact, such is the instability of human affairs that no people has ever been allowed such a degree of tranquility as to remove all dread of hostile attacks on their life in this world. That place which is promised as a dwelling of such peace and security is eternal, and is reserved for eternal beings, in 'the mother, the Jerusalem which is free'" (DCD XVII, 13, 743– 44). One must simply live with this shadow, a penumbra of fear and worry on this earth. But one must not give oneself over to it, not without overweening justification. When one capitulates to this fear, one gets horrible wars of destruction, including social and civic wars. And each war invites another, given the mimetic quality of instantiations of destruction. Each war breeds discontents and resentments that invite a tendency to even the score.

By contrast, the just ruler wages a justifiable war of necessity, whether against unwarranted aggression and attack or to rescue the innocent from certain destruction. The motivation must be neighbor love and a desire for a more authentic peace. This is a grudging endorsement of a lesser evil, and war is never named as a normative good, but only as a tragic necessity. It must be noted that rescuing the self alone is not a justification for violence: better to suffer wrong than to commit it. But our sociality imbeds certain requirements of neighbor love, most powerfully and poignantly so in the case of the ruler who bears the responsibility for the well-being of a people. It is, then, because of our intrinsic sociality and under the requirement to do no harm and to help whenever one can, that war is occasionally justifiable. Augustine's reasoning here falls within the domain of accounts of comparative justice and his argument, which is not a fully fleshed- out systematic theory of war so much as a theological account of war, involves the occasional violation of a fundamental principle—do not kill unjustly, or murder—in the name of an overriding good. It is important to observe that a close reading of Augustine's account shows that one must lament even justifiable wars and reflect on them, not with vainglory, but with great sorrow. Not to look back with grief marks one as pitiable and contemptible. There are no victory parades in Augustine's world, for however just the cause, war stirs up temptations to ravish and to devour, often in order to ensure peace. Just war, for Augustine, is a cautionary tale, not an incautious and reckless call to arms. For peace is a great good, so good that "no word ever falls more gratefully upon the ear, nothing is desired with greater longing, in fact, nothing better can be found." Peace is "delightful" and "dear to the heart of all mankind" (DCD XX, 11, 866).

Augustine Concluded

The vast mountain of Augustinian scholarship keeps growing. It long ago surpassed a book version of Mt. Everest, so much so that no single scholar or group of scholars could master it all. This is true of Augustine's work alone. Peter Brown claims that Isidore of Seville once wrote that "if anyone told you he had read all the works of Augustine, he was a liar."[12] One always has the sense with Augustine that one has but scratched the surface. Indeed, his works have not yet been translated entirely into English. That project is now underway, and some seventeen volumes of his homilies alone have made their way into translation. Much of the new scholarship on Augustine remarks, often with a sense of critical wonderment, on just how "contemporary" he is, given the collapse of political utopianism, by which I mean attempts to order political and social life under an overarching *Weltanschauung* that begins, as any such attempt must, with a flawed anthropology about human malleability and even perfectibility. We recognize, looking back, the mounds of bodies on which so many political projects rest, including the creation of the nation-state system we took for granted for over three centuries and now observe to be fraying around the edges.

The teleology of historic progress is no longer believable although a version of it is still touted by voluptuaries of techno-progress or genetic engineering that may yet "perfect" the human race. The presumably solid underpinnings of the self gave way in the twentieth century under the onslaught of Nietzsche and Freud. Cultural anthropology taught lessons of cultural contingencies. Contemporary students of rhetoric have rediscovered the importance and vitality of rhetoric and the ways in which all of our political and social life and thought must be cast in available rhetorical forms.

None of this would have surprised Augustine. What would sadden him is the human propensity to substitute one extreme for another, for example, a too thorough-going account of disembodied reason gives way to a too thorough-going account of reason's demise. Importantly, one must rescue Augustine from those who would appropriate him to a version of political limits or "realism" that downplays his insistence on the great virtue of hope and the call to enact projects of *caritas*. That does not mean he should be called to service in behalf of "markets and democracy." It does mean he can never be enlisted in behalf of the depredators of humankind.

NOTES

1. St. Augustine, *The City of God*, trans. Henry Bettenson (Baltimore: Penguin Books, 1972), p. 5. Hereafter references in the text will be abbreviated *DCD*. I borrow prose for this characterization from my *Augustine and the Limits of Politics* (Notre Dame, Ind.: Notre Dame University Press, 1995).

2. Peter Brown, *Augustine of Hippo* (Berkeley: University of California Press, 1967), p. 181.

3. Whether Augustine offers an adequate account of Stoic philosophy is, of course, a separate question. Whatever one's position on that issue, the most important point here is Augustine's insistence that thought can never be purged of the emotions.

4. James Wetzel, *Augustine and the Limits of Virtue* (Cambridge: Cambridge University Press, 1992), p. 15.

5. I cannot unpack the complexities of Augustine's analogical reasoning here. The interested reader is advised to turn to the key text itself, *The Trinity* (Washington, D.C.: Catholic University of America Press, 1992).

6. *Trinity* VIII, 6, 257.

7. Augustine, *Select Writings (from Homilies on the Gospel of St. John: First Homily)* (New York: Paulist Press, 1984), p. 278.

8. A recent interesting entry on the nigh infinite secondary works on Augustine on this theme is Donald X. Burt, *Friendship and Society. An Introduction to Augustine's Practical Philosophy* (Grand Rapids, Mich.: Eerdmans, 1999).

9. Ibid., p. 5.

10. See Robert Markus, *Saeculum: History and Society in the Theology of St. Augustine* (Cambridge: Cambridge University Press, 1970).

11. The key Augustinian discussion of war is, of course, *DCD*, Book XIX. But his deconstruction of the Roman *Pax* takes place throughout all of Part I, Books I–X. See, for example, *DCD*, Book IV, chapter 15. Citations in this section are internal to my discussion of Augustine in *Women and War* (New York: Basic Books, 1987), here p. 130.

12. P. R. L. Brown, "Political Society," in Richard Markus, ed., *Augustine: A Collection of Critical Essays* (Garden City, N.J.: Doubleday Anchor Books, 1972), p. 311.

CONTRIBUTORS

Geoffrey Bennington is Asa G. Candler Professor of Modern French Thought at Emory University. He has published extensively on French literature and philosophy. His most recent books are *Interrupting Derrida* and *Frontières kantiennes*. He is currently completing two volumes on the question of literary and philosophical reading, and working on the philosophy of democracy.

Philippe Capelle is Dean of the faculty of philosophy at the Institut Catholique de Paris. He is the author of *Subjectivité et transcendance: Hommage à Pierre Colin; Philosophie et apologétique: Maurice Blondel cent ans après; Philosophie et théologie dans la pensée de Martin Heidegger; Jean Nabert et la question du divin;* and *Phénoménologie et christianisme chez Michel Henry.*

John D. Caputo is the Thomas J. Watson Professor of Religion and Humanities at Syracuse University. He is also David R. Cook Professor Emeritus of Philosophy at Villanova University, where he taught from 1968 until 2004. His most recent publications include *On Religion; More Radical Hermeneutics: On Not Knowing Who We Are; The Prayers and Tears of Jacques Derrida: Religion Without Religion;* and *Deconstruction in a Nutshell: A Conversation with Jacques Derrida.* He serves as chairman of the board of editors of *Journal of Cultural and Religious Theory.*

Elizabeth A. Clark is the John Carlisle Kilgo Professor of Religion at Duke University. Among her books are *Women in the Early Church; Ascetic Piety and Women's Faith: Essays on Late Ancient Christianity;* and *The Origenist Controversy: The Cultural Construction of an Early Christian Debate.* She is co-editor of *The Journal of Early Christian Studies* and of *Church History,* and has served as president of the American Academy of Religion.

Jacques Derrida, École des Hautes Études en Sciences Sociales (Paris) and the University of California, Irvine, is one of the most important philosophers of our time. Among his more recent works are *Genèses, généalogies, genres et le génie: Les secrets de l'archive* and *Voyous.* His most recent work to be translated into English is *Negotiations: Interventions and Interviews 1971–2001; The Problem of Genesis in Husserl's Phenomenology; Who's Afraid of Philosophy: Right to Philosophy I;* and *The Work of Mourning.*

Jean Bethke Elshtain is the Laura Spelman Rockefeller Professor of Social and Political Ethics at the University of Chicago. Her books include *Public Man, Pri-*

vate Woman: Women in Social and Political Thought; Meditations on Modern Po-
litical Thought; Women and War; Power Trips and Other Journeys; Democracy on
Trial; Augustine and the Limits of Politics; and Real Politics: Political Theory and
Everyday Life.

Richard Kearney is Charles B. Seelig Chair of Philosophy at Boston College and
visiting professor at University College Dublin. His most recent books include The
Wake of Imagination; On Stories; The God Who May Be; and Strangers, Gods and
Monsters. He is also the author of Poetics of Imagining; Postnationalist Ireland;
and Poetics of Modernity. He is also a novelist, poet, and cultural critic.

Catherine Malabou is "maître de conferences" at the Université Paris-X Nanterre.

James J. O'Donnell is Provost of Georgetown University. He was formerly Professor of Classical Studies and Vice Provost for Information Systems and Com-
puting at the University of Pennsylvania. In 2003, he served as president of the
American Philological Association. He has published a commentary on Augustine's Confessions, which is now available at http://ccat.sas.upenn.edu/jod/conf.
His book Augustine: A New Biography is forthcoming.

Michael J. Scanlon, O.S.A., holds the Josephine C. Connelly Endowed Chair
in Theology at Villanova University. He is a past president of the Catholic Theological Society of America. His area of specialization is systematic theology. He
has published and taught in the areas of Christian anthropology and eschatology,
the doctrine of the Trinity, religious language, and the thought of St. Augustine.

Mark Vessey is Associate Professor of English at the University of British Columbia
and Canada Research Chair in Literature, Christianity and Culture. He is the editor (with Hilmar Pabel) of Holy Scripture Speaks: The Production and Reception
of Erasmus' Paraphrases on the New Testament and (with Karla Pollmann) of Augustine and the Disciplines: Cassiciacum to "Confessions," the latter based on a
symposium held at Villanova University in November 2000.

Hent de Vries holds the Chair of Metaphysics in the Department of Philosophy
at the University of Amsterdam and is director of the Amsterdam School for Cultural Analysis. He is also a professor in the Humanities Center at John Hopkins
University. He is the author of Theologie im pianissimo (forthcoming in English
translation); Philosophy and the Turn to Religion; and Religion and Violence: Philosophical Perspectives from Kant to Derrida.

INDEX

Italicized page numbers indicate illustrations.

JOHN D. CAPUTO is the Thomas J. Watson Professor of Religion and Humanities at Syracuse University. He is also David R. Cook Professor Emeritus of Philosophy at Villanova University, where he taught from 1968 until 2004. His most recent publications include *More Radical Hermeneutics* and *The Prayers and Tears of Jacques Derrida*. He is co-editor of *God, the Gift, and Postmodernism* and *Questioning God*.

MICHAEL J. SCANLON, O.S.A., is Josephine C. Connelly Chair of Christian Theology at Villanova University. He is co-editor of *God, the Gift, and Postmodernism* and *Questioning God*.

6. That brings us to Richard Kearney's question about why he says he "rightly passes"... for an atheist instead of just saying "I am" an atheist.

... He does not say "I am" an atheist for the simple reason that he does not know. There is within each of us a believer and non-believer, and the one does not give the other any rest.